Christie's Collectors Guides

ANTIQUE MAPS

Carl Moreland and David Bannister

Third Edition

Phaidon · Christie's   *Oxford*

Phaidon · Christie's Limited
Musterlin House
Jordan Hill Road
Oxford OX2 8DP

Third edition 1989
First published by Phaidon·Christie's 1986
Originally published 1983 by the Longman Group
Limited
©Carl Moreland and David Bannister 1983, 1989

A CIP catalogue record for this book is available from the
British Library.

Set in 10pt Lasercomp Garamond
Printed and bound in Great Britain by William Clowes
Limited, Beccles and London.

Frontispiece: Lucas Janszoon Waghenaer *Chart of Europe*
Leyden 1586. Chart from the first engraved sea atlas, the
Spiegel der Zeevaerdt. Originally published in 1584 in
Dutch, there were many editions of the atlas in different
languages until 1615.

CONTENTS

'The Work I have undertaken, is so difficult and obnoxious to Doubt and Error, so slippery and obscure, that it must be confest, by any man of solid judgment, that I must have been bold, to make an Adventure upon such a Subject . . .'

WILLIAM TURNER: *The compleat History of the most Remarkable Providences . . .* 1697.

FOREWORD TO THE THIRD EDITION

In the foreword to the second edition of this book the authors noted the suggestions by reviewers that the expansion of a number of chapters would give a more complete history of the subject. Many of the ideas put forward then have been adopted in producing this enlarged edition, although the need to keep printing costs at a reasonable level has imposed some limitations on the method of presentation.

Briefly, about 70 biographies have been added in a Supplement at the end of the book: an asterisk in the original text indicates such an entry. Most of these biographies cover new material – with emphasis on cartographers of North America, Scandinavia and Switzerland – but some are revisions or expansions of existing entries and, occasionally, this has led to repetition of detail for which we must be forgiven. Where dates and/or spellings differ from the original text, the amendments are intentional and can be accepted as correct.

Special attention is drawn to the amended – and expanded – biographical note in the Supplement on Martin Waldseemüller which includes detail provided by recent German researchers not readily available – as far as the authors are aware – in the English language.

Apart from the Supplement, other additions have been made where space allowed within the old text. Notably, Chapter 8, which originally gave a short history of the Ordnance Survey in the British Isles, has been expanded to cover topographical maps generally as well as brief details of national surveys in European countries. The opportunity has been taken to give a more detailed account of the history of the British Ordnance Survey.

It is hoped that these considerable additions to the book will widen still further its appeal not only to map collectors but also to all those interested in the history of cartography.

ACKNOWLEDGEMENTS

The Authors are grateful for assistance received from many quarters in the preparation of this Handbook; in particular they wish to express special thanks to the following: Peter Baxter, Clive Burden, Edinburgh University, Robert Evans, Dr J. V. Garrett, Lord Herstmonceux, Mr and Mrs G. Hill, Mr and Mrs R. Linter, Louis Loeb-Larocque, Magna Gallery (Oxford), Dr Tony Morris, the Revd S. Salter, Rodney Shirley, Mr and Mrs P. M. Walshaw, Jack Watson and Simon and Clair Bannister. They are also grateful to the Dean and Chapter of Hereford Cathedral for their permission to quote from the booklet, *The World Map in Hereford Cathedral* (8th edn), published by Friends of the Cathedral, and to reproduce an illustration of a portion of the map. Also to William Heinemann Ltd for permission to use a quotation from *Summer of the Red Wolf* by Morris West.

And, finally, their especial thanks are due to Audrey Greenwell and Jenni Wilson for typing, re-typing and, dare we say, typing yet again those drafts, lists of cartographers and map titles in half a dozen different languages, with their seemingly endless amendments and additions – all absorbed with equal facility.

PREFACE

Nobody would argue that the ideal collectors' handbook should contain every imaginable detail on its subject and yet be small enough to fit neatly into a pocket to be readily available at a moment's notice. An ideal it might be, but, at least where our subject is concerned, unattainable, for to be useful at all a book about maps must provide some historical background, however brief, and include information on an immensely wide range of individual cartographers, engravers and publishers as well as illustrations of reasonable size. Having said that and made our excuses for producing a book of conventional size we have to confess that, even within its present bounds, we cannot pretend that we have been able to treat the subject exhaustively, but we hope that, especially in Part II, we have included in readily accessible form a great deal of information from many sources which collectors, or anyone interested in antique maps, may wish to find at short notice. Indeed, we emphasize 'short notice', for over many years our experience of dealing and cataloguing has shown that in seeking information about a particular cartographer one often has to browse through maybe half a dozen different works; our constant aim, therefore, has been to set out such detail so that it can be found in a few moments. We have included notes on cartographers, publishers and engravers of many countries but fuller biographies, for obvious reasons of space, have been limited to names prominent in the history of map making. Generally speaking, in listing their works, we have restricted our detail to complete atlases with occasional reference to individual maps where these are of special importance, always bearing in mind that this book is addressed to the general collector rather than to the specialist. Some may say that we have been too brief; to that our answer must be that a definite limit has to be set to the size and scope of a book of this nature otherwise it may well become as voluminous as the works it attempts to condense. To emphasize our declared purpose of providing a guide for the general collector it may be of interest to note that all the maps illustrated, with about half a dozen exceptions, are, or have been at one time or another, in the possession of the authors.

For those who wish to pursue the subject in greater detail we include an extensive bibliography, although it must be noted that many of the works quoted are now out of print and copies may be available only in specialist libraries to which few of us have access.

The authors make no claim to any original research beyond that needed to develop the theme of the book; indeed, they can do no better than to recall yet another of John Speed's apt comments to his 'Gentle, well favoured reader' wherein he says 'It may be objected that I have laid my building on other men's foundations, as indeed, who can do otherwise in a subject of this nature.'

Part I
MAP MAKING

CORNELIS DE JODE   *Novae Guineae*. From the *Speculum Orbis Terrarum* published
in Antwerp in 1593. This is one of the first printed maps to hint at a possible
coastline of an Australian continent; the first landfall was not made until 1605–6.

Chapter 1

A BRIEF HISTORICAL SURVEY

In a general work of this kind it would be tedious and out of place to embark on a long and detailed history of cartography; newcomers to the subject might well be bored, the knowledgeable could not be blamed for regarding it as trivial. In any case, the subject has been splendidly covered by many writers and all we attempt to do is to provide some background which we regard as an essential part of a fascinating study, and which we hope will have some interest for all our readers.

When the first maps, in whatever form, were used it is impossible to say but, as soon as writing and the use of symbols evolved, man undoubtedly felt the need to illustrate a route by land or sea, to show a river crossing, to warn of a mountain barrier or simply to draw the locality in which he lived. The oldest recorded representation of this sort is a 9-ft (275 cm)-long wall-painting found in 1963 in Çatal Höyük, a prehistoric site in Anatolia, which is dated between about 6100 and 6300 BC. The painting outlines a town 'plan' showing very clearly some eighty 'buildings' with a volcano, possibly erupting, in the background. Later plans sketched on papyrus by the Egyptians and on moulded clay tablets by the Assyrians and Babylonians have survived and it is recorded that about 600 BC. Greek thought was turning to geographical problems. Strabo, writing in Alexandria in the period 20–10 BC, tells us that the first map of the world was compiled by Anaximander of the School of Philosophy at Miletus in the early part of the sixth century BC, followed soon afterwards by a treatise on geography, including a map showing the earth as a plane or disc by Hecataeus. They and others of that school believed in the Homeric theory of a disc-shaped world surrounded by the great river Okeanus with Delphi and the Aegean at the centre of the habitable world. Others, however, leaned to the Pythagorean theory of a spherical world, a theme taken up by Plato, Herodotus and Aristotle, which gradually came to be accepted throughout the Hellenic world.

Over the centuries, answers to the practical problems of calculating the size of the earth and its habitable areas, the partitioning into climatic zones and the relative positions of different countries and places were sought by mathematicians and astronomers, especially in Alexandria. There, Strabo in his 17-volume *Geographica* summarized the long story for posterity, fortunately as it happened, for few of his original sources survived the destruction of the great library. Not that his record was always critical or accurate; his misinterpretation of the rival calculations of the circumference of the world made by Eratosthenes and Posidonius was accepted a century later by Claudius Ptolemy who consequently presented a distorted view of the world which influenced geographical thought until the fifteenth and sixteenth centuries. Ptolemy, a Greek mathematician, astronomer and geographer, living in Alexandria, assembled and codified his predecessors' cartographic theories including those of Marinus of Tyre (*c.* AD 120) to whom he was especially indebted. In about AD 150 he published his *Geographia*, a work in 8 volumes, supposedly illustrated with a world map, 26 regional maps and a profusion of smaller maps. Although, as we shall see later, the text of the *Geographia* survived, no maps older than about the twelfth century have come down to us and, in consequence, we have no means of knowing whether the 'Ptolemy' maps on which we set so much store were, in fact, drawn by him or were the interpretations of later map makers using his text as a basis.

Although Ptolemy's work was compiled at the time of Rome's greatest power it seems to have had little influence on Roman ideas of mapping which were practical rather than scientific. A map, known only from literary sources, entitled *Orbis Terrarum* (Survey of the World), was made in the years round 10 BC for the Emperor Augustus by his son-in-law Vipsanius Agrippa, but apart from this and our knowledge of a

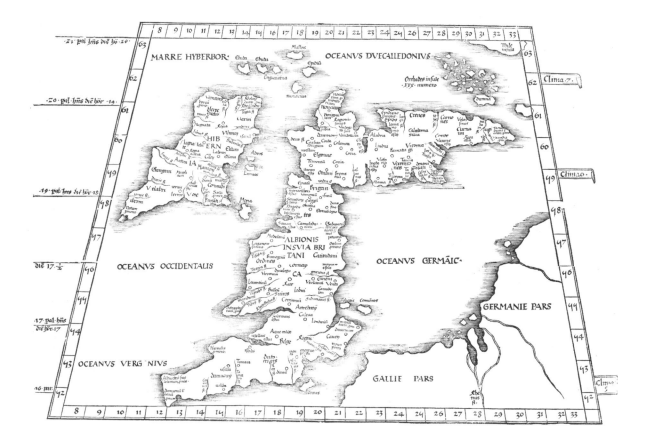

MARTIN WALDSEEMÜLLER   *British Isles* Strassburg 1522. This very early woodcut map of the British Isles, with Scotland on an East–West axis and Ireland somewhat misplaced, was derived from the Ptolemaic map published in Rome in 1478.

stylized road map, known from a thirteenth-century copy as the Peutinger Table, there is little direct evidence of their interest in cartography. All the same, considering their highly developed administrative abilities, it is hard to believe that maps were not in common use even though so few have survived.

With the fall of the Roman Empire the accumulated wisdom of earlier civilizations was dissipated, the great libraries destroyed or dispersed, scientific thought and speculation rejected in favour of religious fanaticism and, eventually, a return to belief in a flat or disc-shaped world, now with Jerusalem at the centre. Maps of these times in their simplest diagrammatic form are known as T–O maps, showing the world with East at the top surrounded by a circular ocean (the letter O), the three continents, Europe, Asia and Africa, being separated by the arms of the T representing the

Mediterranean, the river Nile to the South and the river Don flowing into the Black Sea to the North.

From the seventh to the fourteenth century there is little evidence of any real development in map making in Western Europe, although a dozen or so maps do survive, but in that period Ptolemy's work had a powerful influence on Islamic thought and translations of the *Geographia* were certainly available to the Arabs from about the year 800 onwards. In turn, Arab knowledge of astronomy and mathematics influenced cartographers in Italy and Majorca and from the thirteenth, fourteenth and fifteenth centuries there are surviving manuscript sea charts known to the Italians as portulan charts (from the Italian *portolano*), which formed the basis of many later maps. Of particular fame is the Catalan Atlas of 1375, a masterpiece of its time, produced in Majorca, consisting of an 8-sheet

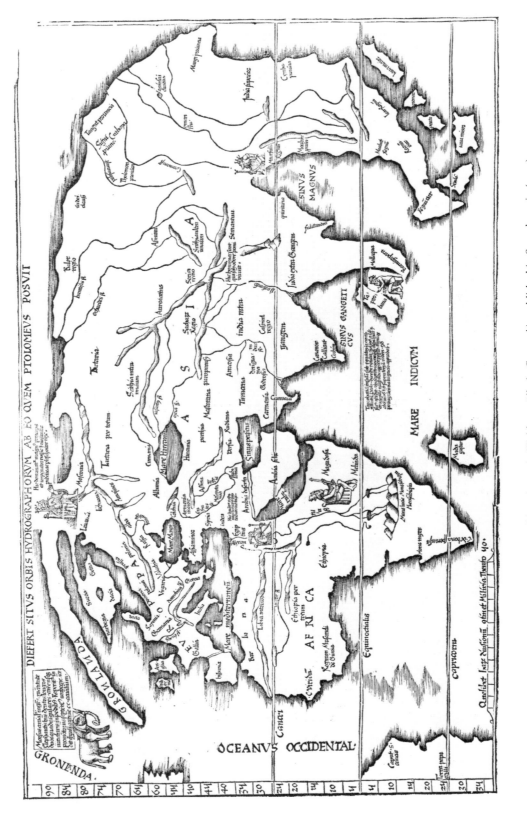

MARTIN WALDSEEMÜLLER *World Map.* The Modern World as shown in Waldseemüller's *Geographia* published in Strassburg in (1522) 1525.

map of the world on which Asia, for the first time, has acquired recognizable form.

In the Middle Ages some of the finest manuscript maps were produced in England, reflecting the strong monastic and religious influences then dominant. They were probably intended for the guidance of pilgrims and crusaders travelling to Dover and the Continent and, although crude in execution, give a recognizable diagrammatic picture of the country. The best-known surviving maps are those of Matthew Paris, a monk of St Albans, drawn about the year 1250, the 'Gough' map of about 1360, and the Hereford *Mappa Mundi* of about 1300, preserved in Hereford Cathedral. This richly decorated circular map on vellum illustrates the medieval idea of the Biblical world with Jerusalem at its centre.

In Europe the initial awakening of interest in geography arose from the revival of knowledge of Ptolemy's *Geographia* soon after the year 1400. Greek manuscript copies made in the twelfth to fourteenth centuries were brought by scholars to Italy from Constantinople and were subsequently translated into Latin and widely studied. This work coincided with, and was much influenced by, the development of printing techniques, particularly, of course, by the invention of movable-type printing by Gutenberg about 1450, which made possible for the first time the production of printed books in quantity. Apart from this factor, other more far-reaching influences were compelling the peoples of Western Europe to look beyond the horizon they had known for so many centuries. With the conquest of Constantinople in 1453 the Turks effectively closed Europe's trade routes to the East and shut off access to traditional sources of luxuries and precious metals from Asia and, above all, denied the supply of the spices which had become so important in the lives of ordinary people. Other factors often based on long-believed myths and legends added to the urge to break out into the unknown world.

It would be tempting at this stage to launch into a chapter on the 'Age of Discovery' but we must content ourselves with only a passing reference to the influence of Henry the Navigator and the voyages of the Portuguese southwards down the coast of Africa and subsequently to India, to those of Columbus to the West Indies, of Cabral to Brazil, Cabot to Labrador and to Magellan's circumnavigation of the world, and to the long controversies over the merits and possibilities of the North-West and North-East passages to the Orient. Suffice it to say that in rather less than a century

knowledge of the geography of the world changed profoundly, a change which was reflected in the gradual abandonment of the Ptolemaic ideas which appeared in the early printed editions of the *Geographia* from 1477 onwards. Furthermore, from about the year 1500, the development of improved geometrical methods of survey and the invention of more precise instruments by geographers in Germany and the Netherlands enabled relatively large land areas to be surveyed more rapidly and accurately and, on a wider scale, Gerard Mercator, regarded as the greatest name in cartography since Ptolemy, produced the first map on his new projection in 1569. Publication of Ptolemy's maps continued during the century under many names including Waldseemüller, Münster and Gastaldi; successive editions contained an increasing number of 'modern' maps until, in 1570, the Ortelius *Theatrum Orbis Terrarum*, composed entirely of contemporary maps, was published in Antwerp. This Atlas, containing at first about 70 maps, was an immediate success and publication continued through 40 or more editions until 1612, but it was not the only success story of the time. There was extraordinary activity in every facet of map making: Mercator's Atlas in three parts was printed in Amsterdam between 1585 and 1595; also printed there in 1584 was the first Atlas of engraved sea charts *De Spiegel der Zeevaerdt* by Waghenaer with an English edition in London in 1588 and many editions in other languages; in the Rhineland, there was the superb collection of over 500 town plans in 6 volumes compiled by Braun and Hogenberg, published between 1572 and 1618; and, not least, Christopher Saxton's survey of England and Wales was being carried out soon after 1570 followed by publication of his Atlas in 1579 which set a standard unsurpassed for the best part of two centuries.

Considering the all-important rôle played by the Spanish and Portuguese in the events of the time it is remarkable that only a handful of early charts made by them have survived. Understandably, fear of trading competition imposed secrecy on their pilots and chart makers until new discoveries had been exploited, and to this end the preparation and distribution of charts in both countries was kept under official control. But the trading monopoly to the Americas and the Far East held by Spain and Portugal for so long was broken abruptly by two events in the years 1579 and 1581. First, the Northern Provinces in the Netherlands finally achieved independence from Spain and, second, Philip II annexed Portugal to the Spanish crown and in

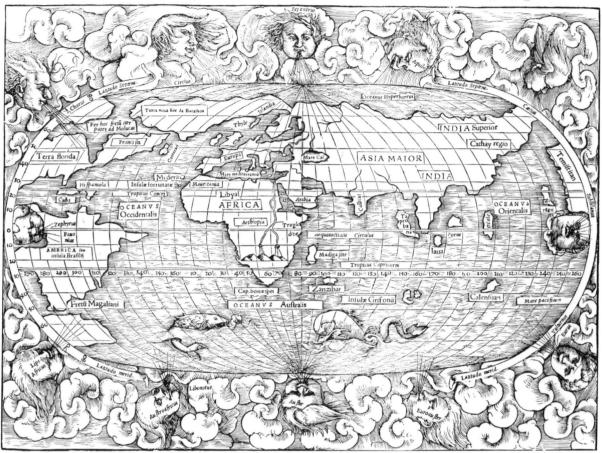

SEBASTIAN MÜNSTER   *Typus Orbis Universalis*. Published in the *Geographia* in Basle in 1540, this famous map was the standard world map until the publication of the Ortelius Atlas in 1570.

the process granted the Portuguese exclusive rights to European coastal trade, hitherto the preserve of the Dutch. So far from achieving his aim of bringing the Dutch to heel, Philip's action had the opposite effect; in the twenty years to the end of the century Dutch navigators, after false starts to find a North-East Passage, sailed in strength round the Cape to what soon became a new preserve, the Dutch East Indies. In 1602, to bring their numerous trading companies under control, the Dutch East India Company was formed. Soon afterwards, in 1605, they discovered Australia and for much of the century Dutch shipping dominated the world's trade routes; as a consequence it was hardly surprising that Amsterdam supplanted Antwerp as the great cartographic centre. Their map makers kept pace with the growth of geographical knowledge and from the workshops of Hondius, Blaeu, Jansson, de Wit and others the European market was supplied with atlases, sea charts, town plans and every kind of map reflecting the expansionism of the age. The maps produced in this period have always been highly esteemed as superb examples of engraving and design, never equalled in any other age.

In England the seventeenth century opened with Saxton's atlases still in publication, but expanding trade and the stimulation of the discovery of new lands created an eager interest in local and national geography which was met by Camden's *Britannia* (a history of England,) republished in 1607 containing Saxton's maps in reduced form, soon followed by John

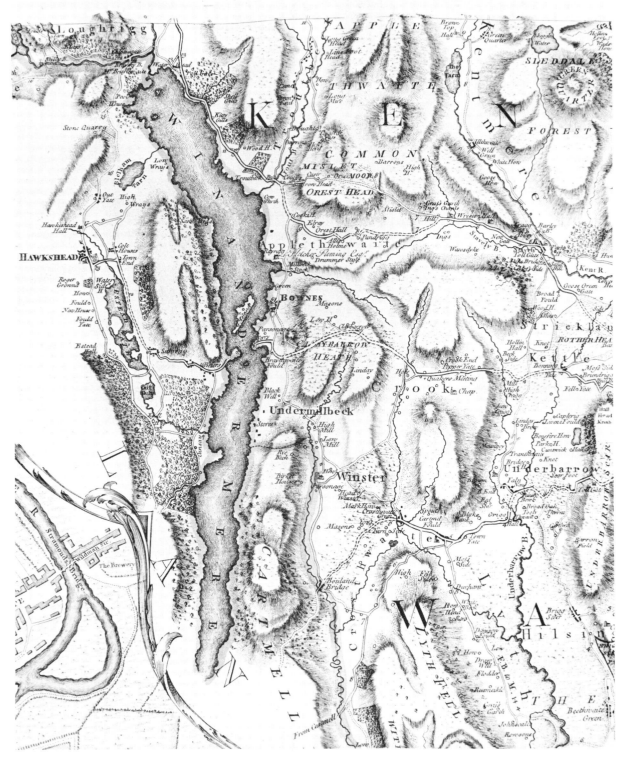

THOMAS JEFFERYS   *County of Westmorland* London 1770. Detail from the 1 in. to 1 mile map of Westmorland, one of a number of notable large-scale maps of English counties compiled by Jefferys.

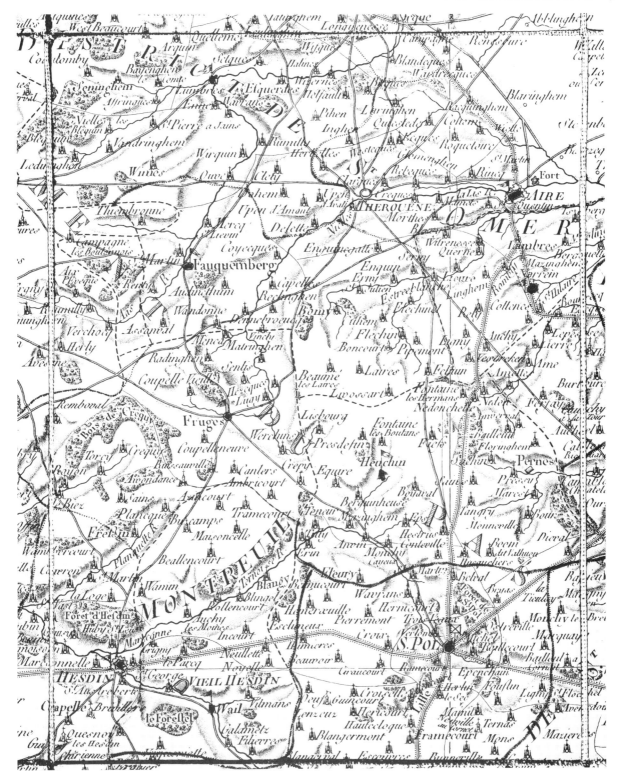

CÉSAR FRANÇOIS CASSINI *Department de Calais*. Detail from map in the Cassini style published in accordance with a decree of the National Assembly dated 20 January 1790. As the map bears scale bars in metres it was probably issued after the year 1800.

Speed's famous Atlas in 1610–11 which also was part of a *History of Great Britain*. Speed's maps, with their detailed town plans, boundaries of hundreds and descriptive texts, were immensely popular and continued in use through many editions until almost the end of the eighteenth century. About the same time Michael Drayton's *Poly-Olbion* appeared, containing a series of allegorical maps based on country legends and myths.

For the next forty or fifty years no notable English names appear. Apart from a small number of pocket atlases produced to meet the needs of the opposing armies in the Civil Wars of the 1640s and the continuing editions of Speed's maps, the market in England, as elsewhere in Europe, was dominated by the Dutch publishing houses of Blaeu and Jansson, although some editions of Dutch publications were issued in London with English texts. Surprisingly, through all this period, roads, with few exceptions, were not shown on any county maps, but in 1675 John Ogilby's *Britannia* broke new ground, showing the post roads of the country in strip form, and from then onwards roads were incorporated in practically all maps of this country. Ogilby was followed by John Seller, Richard Blome, Robert Morden and Herman Moll, amongst others, all of whom produced attractive, if not very original, county maps. Seller was better known for his sea charts and about the same time Captain Greenvile Collins, commissioned by Trinity House, carried out the first complete survey of the coasts of Britain in the years 1681 to 1688, publishing the *Great Britain's Coasting Pilot* in 1693.

Despite the declining influence of Holland late in the century, London publishers were still dependent to some extent on Dutch map makers, but the levy of a duty on imported maps in the early 1700s led to a great expansion of publishing business in London, which continued throughout the century. Notable names in this period were John Senex, Robert Sayer, Emanuel Bowen, Thomas Kitchin, John Rocque, Thomas Jefferys and John Cary, to whose work we refer elsewhere. Notwithstanding this expansion in London's trade, it was to France that the initiative and leadership in map producing passed from the Dutch at the end of the seventeenth century. Secure in royal patronage and support, especially during the long reign of Louis XIV, French cartographers took the lead in scientific mapping by astronomical observ-

ations and by triangulation and the names of the Sanson and Cassini families, Delisle, d'Anville and others, dominated the map world. A major task was the completion of a survey of France, initiated by one of the Cassini family, César François, which resulted in the publication of the *Atlas National* in 1789, the finest work of its kind up to that time.

The English were slow to follow the French lead but after the year 1759, when the Society for the encouragement of Arts, Manufactures and Commerce (now Royal Society of Arts) offered rewards for the best accurate surveys of the English counties, many splendid maps on the scale of 1 in. to 1 mile and even larger were produced. The influence of César François Cassini in France and General William Roy in England led to a joint operation to link the Greenwich and Paris observatories by the new methods of survey by triangulation and, as a result of the experience gained then, the Ordnance Survey Office was set up in England in 1791, followed soon afterwards by the establishment of a Hydrographic Office.

In later chapters we shall see that in most European countries surveying and mapping had been carried on with varying degrees of accuracy from the sixteenth century onwards. The maps produced then satisfied the needs of the time, but towards the end of the eighteenth century the Governments of Austria, Switzerland, the Low Countries, the German and Italian states and the Scandinavian countries, realizing the need for up-to-date surveys, were quick to profit from the methods evolved by the Cassinis in France and General William Roy and the Ordnance Survey Office in the British Isles. Inevitably, progress on such widespread projects covering much of the Continent was slow and very uneven, frequently dogged by lack of funds, by political upheavals and war, and, not least, by obsessive secrecy which, in some countries, bedevilled the whole concept of mapping on a national scale. However, in course of time problems were solved; indeed, there was often unexpected co-operation between nations in the preparation of base lines and the use of common triangulation points, so that, by mid century, the re-mapping of most of Europe was well advanced. The new style of maps, as demanded by the modern world, was severely practical and utilitarian, and finally brought to an end the long history of decorative map making which provides the main theme of this book.

Chapter 2

THE PRINTING OF OLD MAPS

In a later chapter we pose – and attempt to answer – a number of questions which come to mind when considering the purchase of old maps. To forestall at least some of these questions it is necessary to consider various aspects of map making, not, we hope, too technically, but in sufficient detail to enable a prospective buyer to have some idea of what to look for.

The main methods of printing which concern us are:
(a) Relief processes (woodcuts and wood engravings) in which the design to be printed is cut in relief on a woodblock base.
(b) Intaglio processes (line engraving, dry-point, etching, stipple engraving, aquatint, mezzotint) in which the required design is cut on a metal plate by an engraving tool or is bitten into the plate by acid.
(c) Surface processes (lithography) in which the design is drawn on a specially prepared surface.

WOODCUTS

The earliest technique for making prints and maps involved transferring a design cut in relief on woodblocks to paper, known as block prints. In this method of printing the design was drawn on the smooth flat surface of a plank of wood such as sycamore or beech, the unwanted background being cut away with a knife or gouge. The 'relief' portions of the block were then inked and paper applied under pressure against the block, leaving the impression of the design. In China it was the classical form of printing used at least as far back as the eighth century AD and possibly much earlier, reaching its peak at the time of the Sung dynasty between the years 960 and 1280. In Europe, however, the earliest dated block prints which have survived were executed soon after the year 1400 in the Central German states where there was a strong tradition of wood carving.

Woodcut prints were made on a comparatively simple type of press using minimum pressure, and since the impression was taken from the relief surface of a block which could be the same thickness as the standard height of type, the method was particularly suitable for book printing, enabling the printer to produce text and illustrations in one operation. In the case of maps, lettering was often cut separately in metal and fitted as necessary to holes in the wooden block. In general, printing from woodblocks gave a bold, simple, black and white finish which, however, could show little subtlety, shading or gradation of tone except perhaps in the hands of a master, such as Dürer or Holbein. Blocks were used for many years, though with use the design gradually lost its first clarity and crispness, a fact which, in itself, can be a valuable clue to dating. Maps were often brought up to date by 'infilling' parts of the woodblock and re-cutting, and if necessary type could easily be removed and re-set.

In the case of wood engravings the design was cut into the hard end-grain of the wood instead of the softer edge surfaces of a plank and this gave a finer and more lasting base.

In the century from about 1450 to 1550 it was to be expected that printers in such centres of geographical knowledge as Nuremberg, Augsburg, Basle and Strassburg, where the technique had a long and flourishing history, should turn to the use of woodcuts rather than to the newly introduced Italian method of copper engraving, and it followed that most of the maps in this period were included in books as part of the text and were not printed as separate sheets. Round about 1550, however, the centre of map production moved away from Germany to Italy where, especially in Rome, Venice and Florence, copper engraving had long been in use in the print-sellers' trade and its general adoption for printing maps was a natural step. In consequence, from the middle of the century, fewer and fewer woodcut maps appeared and engraving on copper became general with emphasis on the produc-

PRINTING STUDIO Engraving from *Nova Reperta & Alia* by Jan van der Straet called Stradanus. An interesting print dated about 1550–60 showing the processes involved in printing from copper plates. On the extreme right the master engraver can be seen teaching apprentices and (lower left) an apprentice at work. On the bench in the centre, a copper plate is being heated before inking and, behind, on the same bench, ink being applied. In the centre is the large flat-bed press and, behind that, completed prints are being hung up to dry.

tion of sheet maps. There was a revival of woodblock printing in the mid nineteenth century when it proved an effective method of producing illustrations of news items for weekly magazines and maps for encyclopaedias.

LINE ENGRAVING

Engraving is a method of printing which was first used in the fifteenth century and is still used today, notably for printing banknotes and some postage stamps. Starting with a metal plate – usually copper, but latterly (around 1830) steel – the engraver cuts into the metal, in mirror image, the design which is to be printed. The inked plate is passed through two rollers rather like a mangle with a piece of dampened paper on top of it; the

paper bearing the printed impression derived from the ink-filled recesses of the plate is then removed. One of the characteristics of prints produced in this way is that the printed lines stand proud on the surface of the paper; this can be felt quite plainly by lightly running a finger over the surface of a banknote. Another distinctive feature of old engravings is the 'plate mark' normally present on the unprinted border, caused by the pressure of the edges of the metal plate during printing.

Metal plates were often kept in use for a very long time and, in fact, some of the original plates for sporting prints by Henry Alken (*fl.* 1816–31) and others are still being printed today. A few of the plates for John Speed's maps were in use 150 years after they first appeared, later engravers having updated them by beating out the comparatively soft copper base and re-

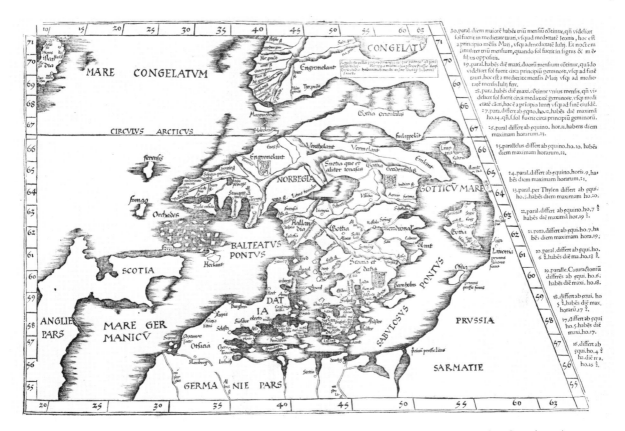

MARTIN WALDSEEMÜLLER *Tabula Nova Norbegiae & Gottiae* (Scandinavia). Woodcut map published in Strassburg in 1522 (1525 edition) based on the earlier map of Scandinavia by Claudius Clavus (*c.* 1425).

cutting with new detail. Alterations made in this manner are a way of dating maps and they can make a fascinating study for the collector.

LITHOGRAPHY

Lithography is a 'planographic' process of printing from a surface which is neither raised nor recessed – as opposed to woodcuts where the design appears in 'relief', or line engravings where the design is cut into the surface ('intaglio'). The process, based on the antipathy of water and grease, was discovered in 1796 and therefore has only been used for comparatively 'modern' maps. It was found that by using greasy chalk or tallow to draw an image on the surface of a suitably treated piece of limestone, the greasy image would repel moisture, whereas the other parts of the stone's surface would accept it. When inked with a roller the wet surface repelled the ink but the greasy image accepted it. Paper applied with equal pressure to the

inked surface produced a printed image – in reverse. In practice the image was drawn in reverse or transferred onto the stone's surface. By the use of separate stones for different colours, multi-coloured prints could be obtained provided that great care was taken over the precise colour registration of each colourstone. The lithographic process was not used to any great extent for quantity production until 1820, and not mechanized until 1860. Present-day methods of lithography do, of course, use different materials and methods, although the principle – antipathy of oil and water – remains the same.

COLOURING AND CONVENTIONAL SIGNS

Setting aside manuscript maps, all early maps were printed in black and white, although there are examples of maps dated 1511 on which place names were printed in red. Map makers soon discovered that colouring

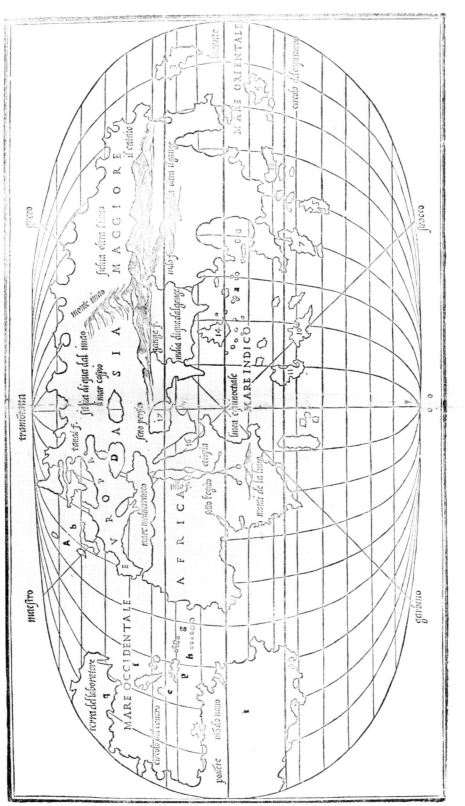

Queste linee che sono per il longo di questo vniuersale da gli sapienti furono appellate linee parallele, & quelle che tengono forma curua in modo di arco sono nominate meridiani, & il clima tiene da leuante fino in ponente, si come sanno la linea, de lo equinottio, & quella del tropico del cancro, & del capricorno.

BENEDETTO BORDONE *World Map* Venice 1528. This World Map (woodcut) on an oval projection was included in Bordone's *Isolario* or *Island Book*, one of the most important publications in the early part of the sixteenth century.

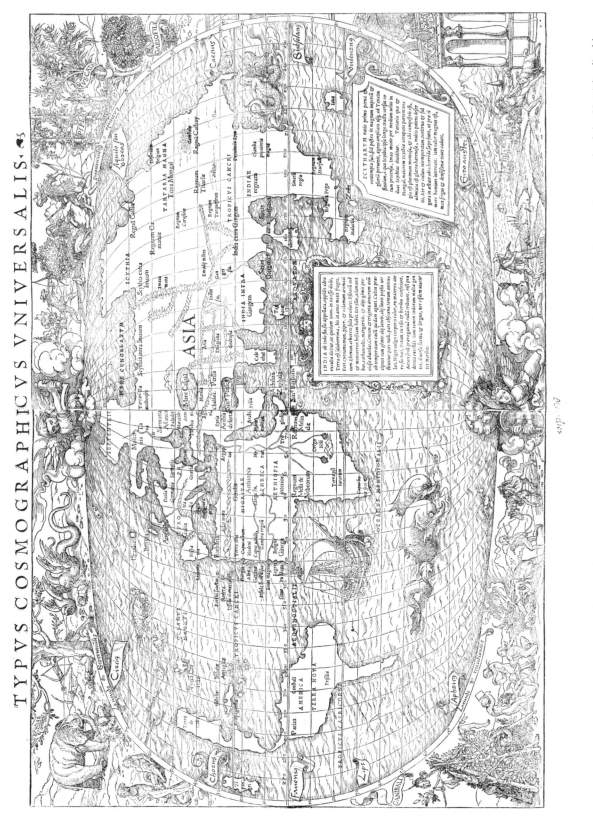

SIMON GRYNAEUS   *Typus Cosmographicus Universalis.* Woodcut. An elegant world map first published in 1532 in a collection of voyages by John Huttich edited by Grynaeus. This map is attributed by some authorities to Hans Holbein the Younger.

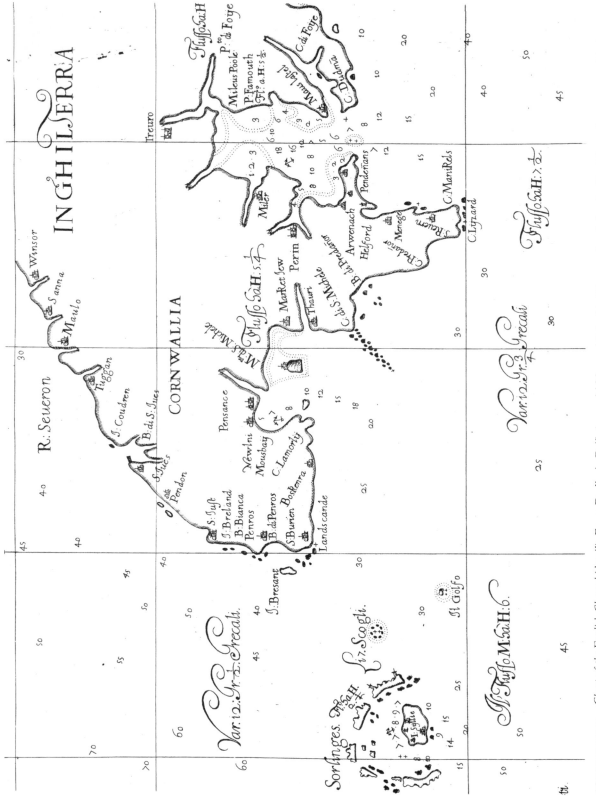

ROBERT DUDLEY *Chart of the English Channel* (detail). From Dudley's *Dell'Arcano del Mare* published in Florence in 1646 and 1661. These charts are notable for the beautiful engraving by Antonio Lucini.

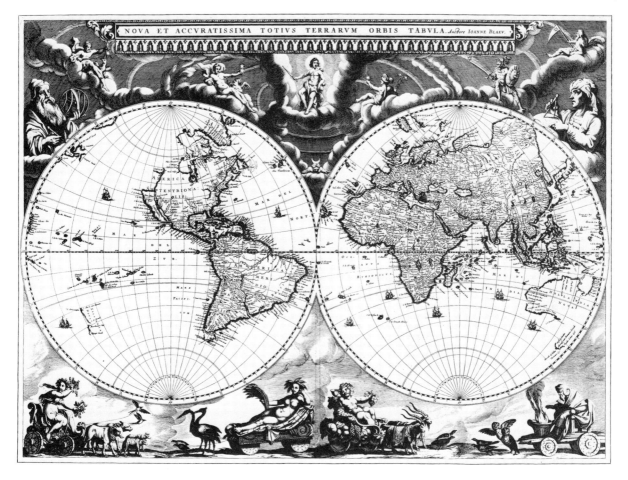

JOAN BLAEU   *Nova et Accuratissima totius Terrarum Orbis Tabula.* This elegantly engraved twin hemisphere world map was published in Amsterdam in the *Atlas Maior* from 1662 to 1672, when the plate was lost in the fire which destroyed the Blaeu printing establishment.

helped to sell their products and maps were advertised for sale as 'coloured or plain'. In consequence engraved maps were frequently coloured by hand immediately before issue, but to colour large numbers was a slow and expensive process and many were sold uncoloured.

Traditional methods used on earlier manuscript maps governed the way colourists worked and the basic colours used changed very little over the centuries – forests, woods and estates in green, hills in brown or black, towns in red, the sea, lakes and rivers in indigo and so on. Armorial bearings were usually carefully painted, the colourist using a recognized heraldic code. Cartouches, compass roses, ships, sea monsters and human figures gave the map painter ample scope to use his imagination, although to some extent the colours of these, too, were governed by the fashions of the period. Nevertheless, although the

colours used over the years did not change greatly, obviously style and fashion did, reflecting the ages in which the maps were printed. Before about 1550 the sea was usually represented by swirling lines, then stippling became the vogue and later still a wash of plain colour was used. In very early maps, towns were shown disproportionately large and were indicated by towered castles and house roofs but after the first quarter of the sixteenth century the castle symbols were replaced by church spires or towers. In most woodcut maps hills were shown by using caterpillar-like lines which in the later 1500s gave way to picturesque, gently rising mounds – then towards the end of the seventeenth century the first attempts were made to give a true indication of height and slope by means of appropriate shading.

Maps were often dominated by elaborate cartouches

giving the title, the cartographer, the dedication and perhaps details of scale. Those on woodcuts were quite plain and simple but on engraved maps they became more and more elaborate through the sixteenth and seventeenth centuries; in later years they were less formal, passing through baroque and rococo phases but often incorporating many aspects of the life of the times, especially scenes in tropical lands.

PAPER USED FOR OLD MAPS

When the fragility of maps is considered, it is remarkable that so many have survived over three or four hundred years, and we must admire the quality of the hand-made paper on which they were produced and the splendid bindings of the early 'Atlases'. Apart from those manuscript maps and charts produced on vellum or parchment, most early maps which collectors are likely to find were printed on strong, thick hand-made paper from France, Germany and Switzerland and the finest of all from the Ancona area of Northern Italy. In England paper was made on a limited scale during the sixteenth century and, in general, French paper was imported until about 1610 when good home-produced handmade paper became available in quantity. Practically all early paper bore a watermark which can be a useful guide in dating a map although the evidence of such marks should be treated with caution. A batch of paper might have been used for a limited number of prints over perhaps as long as twenty or thirty years but, considered in conjunction with other clues, a date of printing can be sometimes closely determined. The absence of a watermark does not necessarily imply that a map is a fake nor does it have any effect on value.

The size of paper on which maps were produced was almost standard and was conditioned by the size of the trays used for making paper by hand – 28 × 24 in. – and by the size of the presses available. In the early days of paper-making, handmade paper was produced almost entirely from linen and rags pulped in water. After thorough mixing a close-meshed wire tray was dipped into the pulp and sufficient lifted out to give the required thickness of paper – the water was drained off, the sheet subsequently dried between layers of felt and then hung to dry. The wire mesh of the tray, into which the watermark motif was also worked, produced the vertical and horizontal lines apparent on holding the paper up to the light.

TECHNICAL TERMS

It may be useful to note here some of the technical terms used in the map trade which, incidentally, differ in some degree from those common in the book trade. Let it be said at once that there is no general agreement among carto-bibliographers on some of these definitions but the authors of the present work suggest those given below which they have found to be generally acceptable.

- A PROOF, which is a print taken before engraving is completed.
- An IMPRESSION, which is a single print: impressions showing differences in the engraving on a plate are said to be in different 'states'.
- An EDITION, which is the term likely to concern most of us, consists of the impressions made from a distinct state of a plate.
- A RE-ISSUE. In an endeavour to simplify matters this term has been used in the biographical notes in Part II of this work to cover any edition, issue, state or whatever, printed after the first edition.

Book terms:

- INCUNABULUM/A: Latin: 'things in the cradle' – a term applied arbitrarily to books printed up to the year 1500.
- COLOPHON, a note, often in the form of, or accompanied by, a device or mark, giving particulars of the printer and perhaps the date and place of printing, found on the end page of early printed books.

The following Latin terms are often used on maps themselves to indicate

(a) *the cartographer or draughtsman*: auctore, composuit, delineavit (del., delin.), descripsit, invenit.

(b) *the engraver*: caelavit, engr., fecit. (fec.), incidit, incidente, sculpsit (sec., sculp.).

(c) *the printer or publishers*: apud., excudit (excud., exc.), ex officina, formis, lith., sumptibus.

(d) *the points of the compass*
Oriens = the rising sun, the East;
Occidens = the setting sun, the West;
Meridio = the midday sun, the South;
Septentrio = the seven stars of the Great Bear, the North.

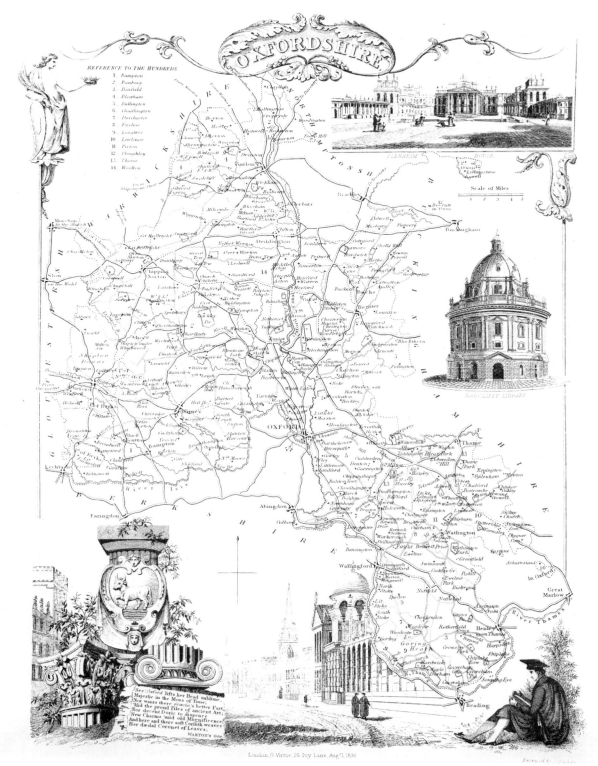

THOMAS MOULE   Map of Oxfordshire (steel engraving) from *The English Counties Delineated*, first published separately in 1830 and subsequently in Atlas form.

Chapter 3

HEREFORD WORLD MAP c. 1300

Maps may be regarded either as a guide to help the traveller on his way from one point to another or as a source of information about the varied countries of the world. The world map preserved in Hereford Cathedral since about the year 1300 was certainly of very limited use for the first purpose but, as to the second, no 'map' ever produced has crowded into a space 52 in. (1,320 mm) in diameter on a piece of vellum such an encyclopaedic amount of geographical, historical, biblical and mythical information. All the more extraordinary that such a masterpiece should have been created by a churchman, by name Richard of Haldingham (in Lincolnshire) of whom little is known but the bare facts of his movements between various livings and cathedral appointments. It seems safe to assume that the map was his personal work and, although it bears no signature as such, it is inscribed with a note in Norman French which reads:

Let all who have this estoire [history], or shall hear or see or read it, pray to Jesus in God for pity on Richard of Haldingham and Lafford who has made and drawn it, that joy in heaven be granted to him.

Where it was compiled can only be conjectured; the author was treasurer of Lincoln Cathedral in the years between 1250 and 1260 and subsequently held an appointment at Salisbury Cathedral, apart from other livings, including Haldingham, before moving to Hereford in 1305.

The creation of such a map in the late thirteenth century must have called for a quite remarkable and exceptional depth of study of classical manuscripts and it is probable that most of it was completed during his appointment at Lincoln Cathedral. But if we look beyond the scholarship involved and visualize the task of assembling the information required, the actual drawing of the map itself and the hazards of travel on medieval roads over thirty or forty years it is little short of a miracle that the map survived the long period of preparation, let alone the 700 years since its completion.

The map itself, roughly based on the T-O design so commonly used in medieval times, is considered to be derived, albeit by a very devious route and with many variants, from the Agrippa map of the Roman world prepared in the first century AD by the order of the Emperor Caesar Augustus who is here shown enthroned in a lower corner of the map. Surrounding the map are two concentric circles subdivided into twelve sections containing descriptive details of the winds of the earth illustrated so frequently in the borders of Ptolemaic maps. As a map of the medieval world it is naturally based on the three known continents, Asia, Africa and Europe, the whole encircling Jerusalem at the hub of the 'wheel', whereas on the Agrippa map Rome was placed at the centre of the known world. Of the countries and oceans represented little is recognizable by shape; even England, Scotland and Ireland are crudely shown, much out of scale, by three oval-shaped outlines, Scotland being drawn separately as an island. Numerous cities and towns appear within turrets and castellated walls and rivers are given undue prominence with little regard to geographical position; but more important than the manuscript's geographical purpose is its pictorial message. It provides us with an account of ancient legends: the Golden Fleece, the Minoan Labyrinth and St Brendan's 'blessed isles'; the campaigns of Alexander the Great and his containment of Gog and Magog within the confines of Asia; biblical scenes from Adam and Eve and the Garden of Eden and the Ark to the Crucifixion. Apart from the representation of Caesar Augustus instructing his officials to survey the world there are few references to Rome, but to make up for that the geographical and historical detail is overlaid by fantasies culled from the literature of the times; monsters of every sort, human and animal, recognizable or imagined, abound — imagined as far as the twentieth century is concerned

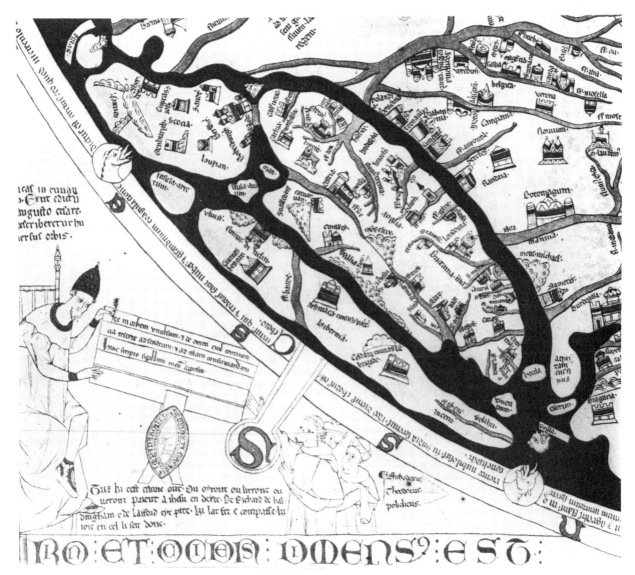

HEREFORD WORLD MAP   *The British Isles and Parts of France and Spain.* Britannia Insula (centre) includes Anglia, Cornubia, Scotia and Wallia. Hibernia is adjacent. The Rhine flows from right to left (top) and the turreted city of Paris is on the Seine (centre right). Spain is at the bottom right. In the left corner the Emperor Caesar Augustus delivers a mandate to three officials appointed to survey the world. Below this mandate, in Norman French, is the plea for prayers for the map maker, Richard of Haldingham. (Portion of the *Hereford World Map* reproduced by courtesy of the Dean and Chapter of Hereford Cathedral.)

but no doubt then accepted as facts of life.

We can only guess at the reasons behind the creation of such a map; one purpose at least must have been to provide in a simple and compact form, especially for the illiterate, a pictorial encyclopaedia of knowledge available at the time, but, as it was compiled by a churchman within cathedral precincts, it does seem more likely that its primary purpose was to teach biblical history in the context of the thirteenth-century world, an objective Richard of Haldingham achieved in a unique manner.

Chapter 4

NUREMBERG CHRONICLE 1493

The invention of printing from movable type about the year 1450 was, without doubt, one of the major cultural milestones in the history of Europe. At last laborious transcription of manuscripts by hand could be dispensed with, and the new processes, combined with the spread of paper manufacture, made possible the reproduction of books in almost any quantity on any subject. It was an invention which represented a revolution in the intellectual opportunities available to ordinary people; apart from the Bible and sacred literature, scholars of the day compiled editions of the Greek and Latin classics, histories, dictionaries and textbooks of every kind, hitherto available only in church or monastic libraries. Although for a time there was considerable opposition from churchmen (who saw their grip on education being set aside) and from the old craft guilds (who feared the threat to their livelihood) it has been calculated that, by the end of the century, not far short of 10 million books, including over a hundred editions of the Bible had been printed.

In the story of printing Nuremberg plays a major part and soon became one of the most important and influential publishing centres. Although not founded until soon after the year 1000, the city's position at the meeting point of North–South and East–West trade routes in Central Europe, and its designation in the middle of the thirteenth century as an Imperial Free City, led to rapid growth in wealth and status.

By the fifteenth century it had become one of the great cultural centres of Europe, its scholars and craftsmen exercising powerful influence throughout the Continent, not only on the development of cartography but on scientific thought in general. Many famous scholars worked or lived there including Regiomontanus (Johann Müller), the astronomer; Johann Schöner, astronomer and globe maker; Hartmann Schedel, cosmographer and entrepreneur; Anton Koberger, master printer; Martin Behaim, cosmographer and globe maker; and Ehrhard Etzlaub,

an instrument maker who produced a road map of Central Europe, the earliest printed map of its type. And, most important of all, Albrecht Dürer who was born there in 1471.

Amongst all the magnificent books printed in the fifteenth century – which are known as incunables – one stands out as being the finest illustrated topographical work of the period: the *Liber Chronicarum* or Nuremberg Chronicle. Published by Hartmann Schedel and printed by Anton Koberger in July 1493 it contained a total of 1,809 woodcuts which include a Ptolemaic world map, a 'birds-eye' map of Europe and the first known printed view of an English town. These woodcuts were made by Michael Wohlgemut (Wolgemut) (1434–1519), and his son-in-law, Wilhelm Pleydenwurff. Wohlgemut was Dürer's tutor between 1486 and 1490.

The print of 'Anglie Provincia' opposite was once thought to be a representation of Dover or even London but is now considered to be an illustration of a typically European city of the day and actually has a striking resemblance to the architecture of Nuremberg in 1493. The description accompanying the view (see translation below) is written in medieval Latin and includes the following: '. . . many say that the Kings and Princes of England and the Parliament of the people meet to this day with the merchants there'. This seems a clear implication that the authors were not sure of these facts and illustrates how remote London was from Nuremberg in medieval times.

Apart from its general interest as a very early descriptive topographical work, the Nuremberg Chronicle is also, by virtue of its date of publication, an historical document of the greatest importance. Issued seven months after Columbus landed in the New World, the Chronicle presents us with a 'last' view of the known medieval world as seen by the peoples of Western Europe. Within a few years new editions were being issued incorporating news of the successful

ANGLIE PROVINCIA

Nglia ínfula quã veteres Albion a qbufdã albis mõtib⁹ q ad eã nauigãtib⁹ pꝛi⁹ apparét vocauere
ꝉtum Bꝛittãnía a bꝛuto Siluíj poftumí latínoꝛ regí filío albíonã ínfulã quã gígátes incolebãt fupatã
ab ípo bꝛittãníã appellauít. Et ꝉ bꝛittãnía maíoꝛ ad míoꝛis bꝛittãníe differétías gallías ꝑtíngẽs
dicebaꝉ. Núc a qdã anglo potẽtíffímo rege anglía ín hodíernũ díẽ appellata eft. Hec eí tríãgꝉarís é inter
feptẽtríonẽ τ occídẽtẽ fíta. q ab oí ꝑtínẽte habet díuífa. Naꝫ a germanía q fb feptẽríóe eft íncípít. Et íurta
gallíã τ byfpaníã verfus occídẽtẽ ꝑtendíf. Et íõ folín⁹ díxít. Fínís erat oꝛbís oꝛa gallící líttoꝛís. nífí bꝛíttã-
nía ínfula nomẽ pene oꝛbís alterí⁹ mereret. Vñ vírgíl⁹. Et penít⁹ toto díuífos oꝛbe bꝛíttãnos. Bꝛut⁹ aũt
cũ ín bꝛíttãníá feu anglía mãfíoné fíbí telegíffet e veftígío feꝯ Rameffís fluuíj rípas Trímoatem ꝯdídít vꝛ-
bem muníttíffímã. Et qꝫ oíbus copíjs feracíffímã ad veterí Troye memoꝛíã recẽfendã. Beutũ hũc tres ge-
nuíffe fílíos ferũt. f. Locrínũ Albanetũ τ Cambꝛẽ. Quí pꝛío ínfulã ínter fe díuídẽtes. Locríno natu maíoꝛí
medía ínfula ꝑs obuenít. Que ab ípo lochꝛía poftea fuít cognoíata. Et í ea adhuc lundínũ cíuítas extare dí
Vꝛbs mercatoꝛíb⁹ τ negocíatoꝛíb⁹ maríe celebꝛata. In q adhuc anglíe reges pꝛíncípefꝫ ac fenat⁹ ꝑpꝉí cum
mercatoꝛíb⁹ cõueníre vt plꝛímũ tradũt. Albaneto vo eí⁹ fílío qꝛta ínfula ꝑs obuenít. q ab eo albanía fuít dí
cta. Et ꝉ fcocía núc núcupaf. Eft eí eí⁹ ínfula ín q eft anglía fcocía fupꝛía ps ín aqlones verfa fluuíb⁹ haud
magnís τ mõte qdaꝫ ab anglía dífcreta. Cambꝛí vero tercío fílío cambꝛía q núc Thyle de ínfula ínter feptẽ-
tríonalé plagã τ occídẽtalé. q vltíma fuerat ex cognít a romanís. ín q eftíuo folftícío fole de cancrí fídere fací-
ente trãfítũ noꝛ nulla. bꝛumalí folftícío. ꝓínde díes nullⁱ. Huⁱ ínfule maría ꝑs fructífera é. Abũdat pecoꝛe
Auro τ argẽto ferroꝗ. Efferútur ꝗ ex ea pelles τ mãcípía. Et caues ad venãdũ aptíffímí. Multⁱ ínfulís nec
ígnobílíb⁹ círcũdaꝉ. qꝫ bíbernía eí pꝛímat magnítudíe: paruo a bꝛíttãnís díſíũcta freto. Et ífule pue Oꝛ-
chades appellate. Gregoꝛⁱ⁹ bꝛíffím⁹ põtífer hⁱ noís fcós eo míffís Auguftíno míleto τ íohãe mõchís cuꝫ
alíjs ꝑbatíffíme víte vírís. Pꝛímũ anglíã ad fídẽ ꝯuertít. Et ín ea deín mltí reges claruere míraclís. Círcuí-
tu bꝛíttãníã patere trígínta octo mílía paffus feptuagíta quíqꝫ mílías pythíaꝫ τ yfídoꝛus tradũt. ín q fpacío
magna τ multa flumína. pꝛeterea metalloꝛ larga varíaꝗ copía. Eoꝛum byftoꝛías Beda optíme defcríbít.

Atlantic voyages and the discoveries on the American continent; discoveries which proved to be key factors in the complex problems of mapping the modern world as we know it.

The following is a translation of the Latin text accompanying the illustration of 'England' in early editions of the Chronicle:

Anglie Provincia

The island of England was originally called Albion after certain white mountains which were seen by those steering towards it; but was then named Britain perpetuating the name of a fierce son (Brutus) of Silvius, the last king of the Latins, who overcame the giants inhabiting the island. It was called 'Greater' (Great) Britain to distinguish it from the lesser Britain (Brittany) of France which adjoins it. Its present-day name of England is taken from a certain 'Anglus' who was a powerful king. England forms a triangle between North and West and is separated from the continent at all points, beginning near Germany in the North and extending alongside France and Spain towards the West. Solinus regarded the French shore as the limit of this world and the island of Britain almost as belonging to another. And Virgil thought of it as separated from the rest of the globe. But Brutus having decided to settle in England, immediately founded on the banks of the River Thames a city so well fortified that it recalled in all its forces the memory of ancient Troy. This Brutus is said to have had three sons; Locrinus, Albanetus and Camber and they divided the island amongst themselves. To Locrinus, the first born, fell all of the centre of the kingdom, which later became known as Lochria after him, and his city of London is still greatly celebrated for its merchants and traders. And many say that the Kings and Princes of England and the Parliament of the people meet to this day with the merchants there. To the second son Albanetus fell another part of the island and this was called 'Albania', but nowadays Scocia (Scotland). This Scotland occupies the higher part of the island, which lies towards the North winds and is separated from England by some smallish rivers and a certain mountain range. The third son inherited Cambria, now called Thule, the districts to the North and West which were the last to be explored by the Romans and where, during the summer solstice, the sun passes only from the star of Cancer and there is thus no night; while during the winter there is no day. The greater part of the Island is fertile. It is surrounded by many other islands of some dimensions, the largest of them Hibernia (Ireland) which is divided from Britain by a narrow channel, and some smaller ones called the Orchades (Orkneys). The blessed Pope Gregory, second of this name, sent to Britain the monks Augustine of Miletus and John with other men of outstanding character and they first converted the English. Since then many of their kings have shone forth for their miracles. The dimensions of Britain are given by Pythies and Ysidore as 38,075 [square] miles, and in it are many fine rivers, besides large and varied supplies of metals. Its history is to be found best described in Bede.

Chapter 5
ROAD MAPS, ATLASES & ROAD BOOKS

To the modern eye roads are as vital a part of a map as rivers, place names or mountain ranges and yet maps had been produced for centuries before roads were considered an essential feature of cartography. At sea, as we have described elsewhere, portulan charts were in common use in the thirteenth and fourteenth centuries and had reached a high degree of sophistication, but with one or two important exceptions, there was no counterpart for land maps.

In a sense, mobility on land in early times was not the essential factor it has become in the last century or so, but when one thinks of the hazards and dangers of travelling, guidance was far more necessary than in our own day. In fact, in spite of primitive roads and restrictions imposed by lack of transport, movement must have involved great numbers of people: for centuries emissaries and armies moved across the face of Europe and Asia, wool traders came even from Turkey to the Cotswolds, pilgrims and crusaders covered enormous distances. In the British Isles there were the drovers' or drift roads along which cattle were driven from the North and West to the fairs and markets near the centres of population as well as the Salt Ways used throughout the Middle Ages for the distribution of salt from Cheshire to all parts of England.

As might be expected, it was the Romans who produced a remarkably practical and accurate map of the 50,000 or more miles of roads in the Empire, probably in the third century AD. Known as the Peutinger Table, from the name of a sixteenth-century German antiquarian who possessed a thirteenth-century copy, now in Vienna, it was in the form of a roll about 22 feet long and a foot wide, showing roads in straight lines with distances between stages. By its nature, the shapes of most countries and land masses were much distorted, but no doubt it served its purpose as an efficient guide.

In Britain, as elsewhere, the Roman roads fell into decay over the centuries and by the Middle Ages were reputedly among the worst in Europe. Indeed, more often than not, they were narrow winding lanes or bridle tracks between cultivated fields and, in the absence of hedges and fences, frequently changed course as weather conditions or changes in land ownership dictated. Perhaps these factors impelled the English chronicler, Matthew Paris, and the monks of the Benedictine Abbey of St Albans to draw, about the year 1250, a crude but picturesque map of the country included in their *History of the English*. Although not a road map as such, it was clearly intended as a guide rather than a true geographical representation of England and part of Scotland. Rivers and river crossings are shown prominently and the positions of towns are distorted so that they appear almost in a straight line from the North to Dover, the intention being to show travellers, whether pilgrims, crusaders or traders, the shortest route to Dover and the Continent.

A century later appeared the 'Gough' map of Great Britain (so named after its eighteenth-century discoverer) which can be said to be a real map, numerous roads being shown diagrammatically in red, leading from town to town with staging distances. There is evidence that the 'Gough' map and copies of it were in use 200 years later and yet, even so, roads were still ignored by Saxton and Speed in spite of their dependence on them for carrying out countrywide surveys.

Although road maps were so neglected in England and elsewhere, there was a notable exception in Germany where, in 1492, Ehrhard Etzlaub, an instrument maker, compiled decorative woodblock road maps of the surroundings of Nuremberg and other German cities, as well as a much larger map of Central Europe known as 'The Rome Way'. This is thought to have been prepared in time for the Holy Year celebrations held in Rome in the year 1500, its obvious purpose being to indicate routes from as far away as Denmark in the North, Paris in the West and Poland in the East, to Rome – which, incidentally, was placed towards the top of the map with North at the bottom. Etzlaub's ideas, like those of the anonymous compiler of the 'Gough' map in England, were exceptional innovations, far ahead of their time, and were not followed up for a century or more.

In the absence of any indication of roads on their maps, we must assume that English travellers had *some* means of guidance in their travels and we do indeed find that in this period there were in existence 'road books' which usually consisted of brief descriptions of the countryside through which roads passed and, of more importance, details of the main 'high Wais' with distances between stopping-places. Of these books the earliest was the *Itinerary* of John Leland written about 1535–45, followed by a number of others published in the last quarter of the century, notably Holinshed's *Chronicles of England, Scotland and Ireland*, first printed in 1577, containing tables of roads and stage distances, which were frequently copied by other publishers.

In France, road books in similar style were published from about 1522 onwards, one of them by Jean Bernard, printed in Paris in 1579, being of particular interest. A short history of England and Scotland, it contained a volume giving details of many main roads in England and Wales with occasional warnings of the dangers of thieves and brigands. The earliest sheet map produced in France showing the post roads of that country was published in 1632 by Melchior Tavernier, copies of which are extremely rare. It was also printed in later atlases by Nicolas Sanson from 1654 onwards. In Central Europe, if we ignore the very early maps by Ehrhard Etzlaub (*c.* 1500) already mentioned, the first road map covering the German States, Switzerland, the Low Countries and bordering lands was published by Johann and Conrad Jung (1641) followed by others by Johann Ulrich Müller (1692) and Johann Peter Nell (1709–11).

In England it was left to John Norden (1593–98) and Philip Symonson (1596), contemporaries of Saxton, to be the first to show roads on half a dozen county maps but few examples have survived, and their work was not following up by either Kip or Hole in preparing the maps for Camden's Britannia or by Speed in his atlases. In fact, the only works of any note in this field were Norden's *An Intended Guyde for English Travailers* (1625), in which he demonstrated for the first

time the use of triangular distance tables much as we use them today, and Matthew Simmons' *A Direction for the English Travailer* (engraved by Jacob van Langeren), a series of very small maps published in 1635. An edition with enlarged maps was issued in 1643 by Thomas Jenner who is also known for the Quartermaster's Map of England and Wales, so called because of its use in the Civil War. The Quartermaster's Map continued in use until late in the century but by that time much more detailed and up-to-date guidance was required to meet travellers' demands.

From about 1668 sheet maps showing post roads and 'cross-roads' in England and Wales appeared, of which the most important were by Robert Walton/Thomas Porter (*c.* 1668), William Berry/ Wenceslaus Hollar (*c.* 1669–76, 4 sheets), John Adams (*c.* 1677–79, 12 sheets, and 1685, 2 sheets) and Robert Walton (1680). John Adams also published an *Index Villaris*, a gazetteer of cities and market towns with distance tables. For practical purposes, however, there were obvious limitations to the amount of detail which could be included on sheet maps and it was not long before these defects were remedied by the invention of the 'strip map' by John Ogilby.

In 1675 Ogilby published, to 'Great Applause', the *Britannia – a Geographical and Historical Description of the Principal Roads thereof*, consisting of 100 maps of the principal roads of England and Wales, engraved in strip form, giving details of the roads themselves and descriptive notes of the country on either side, each strip having a compass rose to indicate changes of direction. According to advertisement his survey was said to have measured over 25,000 miles of road (in fact, the maps covered 7,500 miles), all surveyed on foot, of course, with a 'perambulator' or measuring wheel to log the distances from place to place. He used throughout the standard mile of 1,760 yards, which had been introduced by statute in 1593 but which had never supplanted the old long, middle and short miles, an endless source of confusion to travellers. There were four issues of the *Britannia* in 1675–76 and a reprint in 1698.

As Ogilby's maps primarily indicated the post roads of England and Wales it is, perhaps, an opportune moment to note that, contrary to the generally accepted idea that our posts started in 1840 with Hill's 'Penny Post', there had, in fact, been a system of Royal Posts ever since the time of Edward I, and in the early part of the sixteenth century a Master of the Posts was

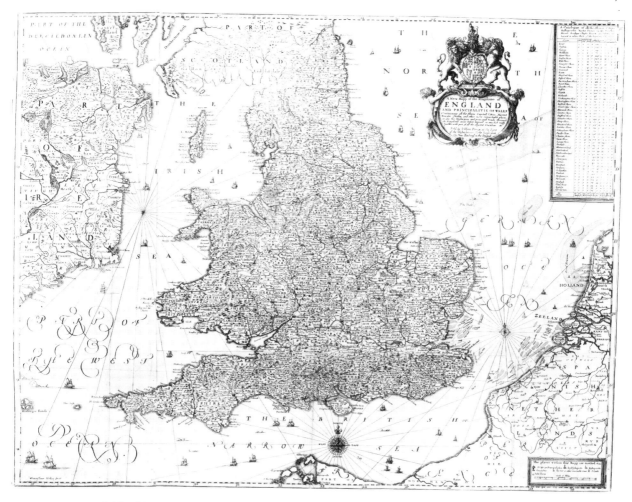

WILLIAM BERRY *A New Mapp of the Kingdome of England and Principalitie of Wales.* A recently discovered large road map of England and Wales engraved by Wenceslaus Hollar and dated *c.* 1669–76. This map may have pre-dated John Ogilby's *Britannia.*

appointed by Henry VIII. This postal system was exclusively for royal use but in 1660 a 'Letter Office of England and Scotland' was established for public mail and a distribution network using the post roads soon became widely used. Clearly Ogilby's maps, and those which soon followed, met a great and growing need. In 1676 Robert Morden, inspired by Ogilby's strip maps, issued packs of playing cards giving a very fair indication of the main roads in each county and from then onwards practically all county maps included roads even though the roads themselves were still hardly recognizable as such. Only when Turnpike Trusts were set up with the express purpose of levelling charges to offset the costs of road improvements was there any real change. As a result people

began to travel for pleasure rather than of necessity with a consequent demand for road books and atlases which were issued in ever increasing quantity and variety, usually in quarto, octavo or pocket size volumes; Ogilby's *Britannia*, splendid though it was in its original form, was far too cumbersome as a travelling companion. Among the most popular works in the early part of the eighteenth century were those by John Senex, and John Owen and Emanuel Bowen, followed by Daniel Paterson, William Faden and, at the end of the century, by John Cary, the most popular of all. Not only were their guides constantly enlarged and re-issued in numerous editions but there is evidence that some individual editions ran to as many as 5/10,000 copies.

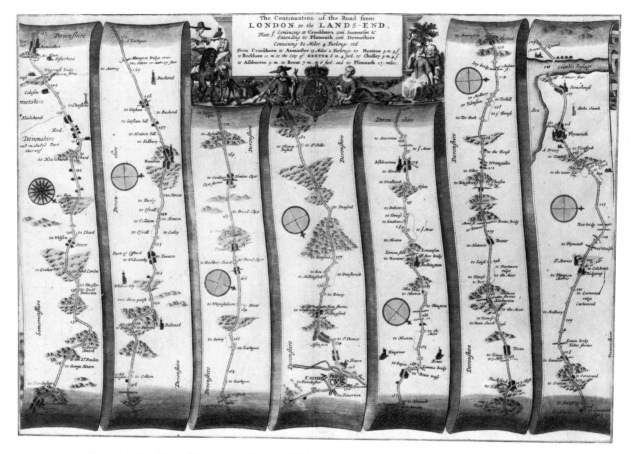

JOHN OGILBY *Map of the Road from Crewkerne to Exeter and Plymouth.* From the famous *Britannia – a Geographical and Historical Description of the Principal Roads thereof,* first published in 1675.

In the same period, in France, Germany and Italy, cartographers developed their own methods of compiling road maps, generally following the style of Tavernier's Post Road Map of France (1632), already mentioned, rather than Ogilby's strip maps, although some examples in that form were published in France and Italy. Notable examples of Continental maps, often in many editions, were published by N. de Fer (1700), A. H. Jaillot (1711), L. Denis (1768, 1774), L. C. Desnos (1761 France and 1766 England), J. B. Homann (1714), C. Weigel (1745) and C. G. Rossi (*c.* 1703).

The following list includes brief details of the better known road books and atlases of England and Wales published from 1676 onwards.

JOHN OGILBY and WM MORGAN

1676   *The Traveller's Pocket Book* (no Maps)

WILLIAM BERRY

c. 1669–76   *A New Mapp of the Kingdome of England and Principlaitie of Wales*
Large road map (620 × 790 mm) engraved by Wenceslaus Hollar

1679   *Grand Roads of England*

ROBERT WALTON

c. 1680   *A New Mapp of England and Wales to which the roads or highways are playnly layd forth*

PHILIP LEA

c. 1687   *The Traveller's Guide – A New Map of England and Wales with the direct and cross roads*

1690–92   *Angliae Totius Tabula* (John Adams)

1695   *A Travelling Mapp of England containing the Principall Roads*

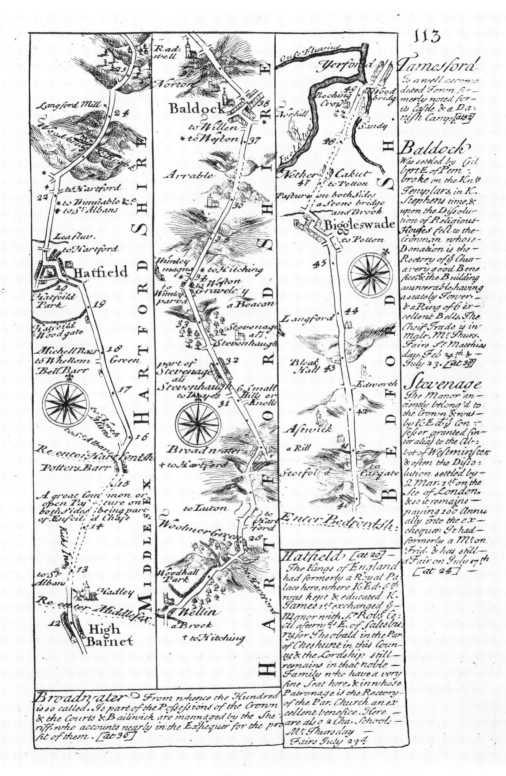

JOHN OWEN and EMANUEL BOWEN *High Barnet to Biggleswade.* Road map from *Britannia Depicta or Ogilby Improved*, published in many editions from 1720 to about 1764.

THOMAS GARDNER

1719   *A Pocket Guide for the English Traveller*

JOHN SENEX

1719–75   *An actual survey of all the Principal Roads of England and Wales* – Ogilby's maps reduced in size.

JOHN OWEN and EMANUEL BOWEN

1720–64   *Britannia Depicta or Ogilby Improved*

I. V. KIRCHER

1730   *The Traveller's Guide or Ogilby's Roads Epitomized*

JOHN ROCQUE

1746   *The English Traveller*
1763   *The Traveller's Assistant*

JOHN BOWLES

1757   *Roads through England Delineated*

THOMAS KITCHIN

1767   *Post Chaise Companion*
1783   *Traveller's Guide through England & Wales*

DANIEL PATERSON

1771–1832 *A New and Accurate Description of all the Direct and Principal Cross Roads in Great Britain*
1772–79   *Paterson's Travelling Dictionary*
1785–1807 *Paterson's British Itinerary*

CARRINGTON BOWLES

1772   *Atlas of Road Maps*
1782   *Bowles Post Chaise Companion*

THOMAS JEFFERYS

1775   *Itinerary or Traveller's Companion*

MOSTYN JOHN ARMSTRONG

1776   *An actual survey of the Great Post Roads between London and Edinburgh*

TAYLOR and SKINNER

1776   *A Survey of the Great Post Roads between London, Bath and Bristol*

WILLIAM FADEN

1781–1833 *The Roads of Great Britain*

GEORGE WALPOOLE

1784   *New British Traveller*

JOHN CARY

1790–1828 *Traveller's Companion*
           The maps in this work, prepared at the request of the Postmaster General, were based on a completely new survey of the turnpike roads of England and Wales, carried out by John Cary from 1780 onwards with the assistance of Aaron Arrowsmith. The *Traveller's Companion* became immensely popular and had a considerable influence on the formative work of the Ordnance Survey Office, which was established in 1791.
1798–1828 *Cary's New Itinerary*

LAURIE and WHITTLE

1806   *New Travellers' Companion*

EDWARD MOGG

1817–22   *A Survey of the High Roads of England and Wales*

JAMES DUGDALE

1819   *New British Traveller*

GEORGE GRAY

1824   *New Book of Roads*

CHARLES SMITH

1826   *New Pocket Companion to the Roads of England and Wales*

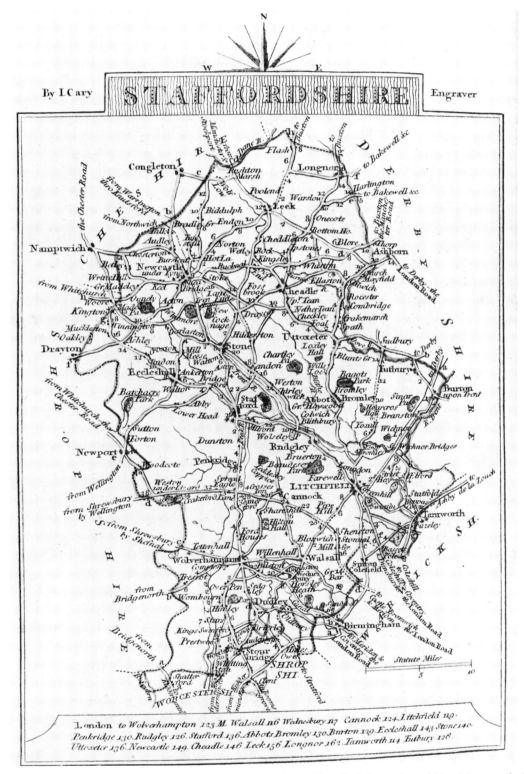

JOHN CARY   *Staffordshire* London 1792. The pocket road maps in Cary's *Travellers' Companion* and *New Itinerary*, of which the above is an example, were issued in numerous and quite large editions from about 1790 to 1828.

Chapter 6

SEA CHARTS & ATLASES

It requires no great effort to imagine that sea charts of some kind must have been in use in the Mediterranean from the earliest times and Ptolemy wrote in AD 150 that, half a century before that date, Marinus of Tyre was drawing charts based on Rhodes, then the focal point of the Eastern Mediterranean. Beyond that, we really have only the scantiest knowledge of methods of navigation, until the invention in Italy in the early years of the thirteenth century of the compass, at first consisting of an elementary iron needle and compass stone from which the magnetic compass soon evolved. The discovery was decisive in the development of sea charts, then known as portulan charts, a term based on the word 'portolano', which was an Italian pilot book or seaman's guide containing written sailing directions between ports and indicating prominent coastal landmarks and navigational hazards. These were also known to English seamen in the Middle Ages as 'rutter' from the French 'routier'. Essentially, the charts showed only the detail of coastlines with placenames written on the landward side at right angles, prominent ports and safe harbours usually being shown in red and other names in black. In the sea areas there were compass roses from which direction or rhumb lines extended over the chart enabling a navigator to plot his route, whilst other open spaces were embellished with flags and coats of arms of the coastal states and vignettes of cities and ports. By their very nature and usage comparatively few have survived and the earliest, thought to originate in Genoa, date from the beginning of the fourteenth century. The finest collection, drawn on skin, known as the Catalan Atlas, was prepared for Charles V of France in 1375 by Majorcan pilots, the leading navigators of their day, whose voyaging ranged from the Baltic to the Black Sea. Their navigational skills and practical application of the use of sea charts were major influences on the development of Italian cartography and, in particular, on the projects of Henry the Navigator in Portugal where, in the early years of the fifteenth century, the first tentative voyages down the west coast of Africa were being made.

In Venice, about 1485, the first printed book of sea charts of islands in the Mediterranean compiled by Bartolommeo dalli Sonetti was published. In this Isolario, or island book, and in others of a similar type which appeared in later years, islands were shown in stylised outline, embellished only with compass points. Otherwise they were left plain, sometimes even without place names. It is thought they were printed in this manner so that names and navigational detail could be inserted by hand. Surviving copies are frequently annotated in this way. No doubt these books were useful in their day but by the middle of the sixteenth century the development of commerce, especially in North West Europe, called for better aids to navigation in the seas beyond the Mediterranean. Not surprisingly the Dutch provided the answer. Their seamen had acquired a virtual monopoly of the coastal trade of Western Europe, trans-shipping the wealth of the East and the New World from Lisbon and Spanish ports to Holland, the Baltic and the British Isles. To meet the demands of this trade a pilot in Enkhuizen on the Zuider Zee, Lucas Janszoon Waghenaer, compiled and had published in Leyden, in 1584, a collection of charts entitled *Spiegel der Zeevaerdt*, which was greeted with immediate acclaim and many editions in Dutch, English, French and German were issued in the following thirty years. The English edition translated by Sir Anthony Ashley, with entirely re-engraved charts, was published in London in 1588, the year of the Armada. So great was its popularity that the name, anglicized to 'Waggoner', came into use in English as a generic term for sea charts of all kinds.

Also in 1588 there appeared a series of charts drawn by Robert Adams showing the engagements, almost day by day, between the English and Spanish fleets and the subsequent destruction of the Armada. Reproduc-

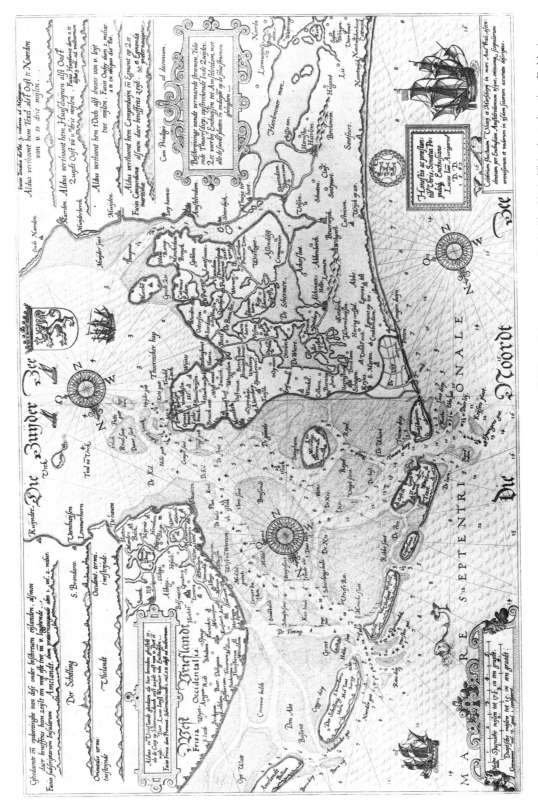

LUCAS JANSZOON WAGHENAER *Celebrium Fluctuum Vlietij et Marsdiepij in mari australi* (Chart of the entrance to the Zuider Zee). This chart showing Enkhuizen, Waghenaer's home town, was first published in Leyden in 1584.

tions of these charts were made about 150 years later in a book entitled *The Tapestry Hangings of the House of Lords representing the several Engagements between the English and Spanish Fleets in the ever memorable year 1588*. Issued in 1739 by John Pine, this was possibly the finest English book of eighteenth-century engravings.

In 1569, a few years before the issue of Waghenaer's charts, Gerard Mercator published in Germany a world map using for the first time his new method of projection, which was to mark the greatest advance in map making since Ptolemy. In fact, for ordinary seamen of the time, Mercator's new ideas were too advanced and difficult to apply in practice and it was not until Edward Wright, an Englishman, provided the necessary mathematical formulae in a book entitled *Certaine Errors of Navigation*, followed by a world chart in 1600, that the merits of the new system were generally recognized and appreciated by navigators.

In the early years of the seventeenth century the Blaeu family in Amsterdam published a number of marine atlases, now extremely rare, based largely on Waghenaer, but the first such atlas wholly based on Mercator's projection was the *Dell' Arcano del Mare* (Secrets of the Sea) by Sir Robert Dudley. A skilled mathematician and navigator, Dudley, after exile from England, had settled in Florence where the atlas was published in 1646. The charts, beautifully engraved by an Italian, Antonio Lucini, are now greatly valued. With this single exception, however, Dutch domination of the seas for the greater part of the seventeenth century enabled them to maintain their position as the leading and most prolific cartographers of the time; in particular Anthonie Jacobsz (Lootsman), Pieter Goos, de Wit, Hendrick Doncker and, above all, the van Keulen family, are famous names in this sphere.

Although there were few printed sea charts from English sources to rival the Dutch there was no scarcity of manuscript charts by Englishmen. From about 1590 onwards the demand for such charts, arising out of the seafaring developments of the late Elizabethan period, was met by a group of draughtsmen who have become known as the Thames School, named from their obvious association with London and the river. This group, active over a long period until the early years of the eighteenth century, embraced about thirty to forty names including Gabriel Tatton (*c.* 1600), John Daniell (1614–42), Nicolas Comberford (1626–70), John Burston (1638–65), John Thornton (1667–1701) and William Hack (*c.* 1680–1700). Of these, the most active were William

Hack, who is credited with about 1,600 charts, Nicholas Comberford and John Thornton: the last named, of course, also published printed maps and charts.

The charts of the Thames School covered practically every part of the known world and although most of them were not noted for originality, usually being based on Dutch prototypes, in total they probably exercised an important influence on the later charts printed by Thornton himself and on those by John Seller and others associated with the preparation of the later volumes of the *English Pilot*. Before that appeared, however, the English suddenly awakened to the dangers of the Dutch monopoly in map and chart making. In 1667 the Dutch sailed up the Thames and destroyed a great part of the British Navy in the Medway and bombarded Chatham. Already occupied with the rebuilding of London after the Great Fire and with an outbreak of plague, the Government was shaken still further by the realization that the Dutch knew more about the coastline of England than the English themselves, and their confidence was not increased when it was found that John Seller, in producing the first volume of his marine atlas, the *English Pilot*, in 1671, was still using Dutch plates and often very old ones at that. As now, government was tardy in action and it was not until 1681 that Samuel Pepys, as Secretary of the Navy, instructed Captain Greenvile Collins to carry out a survey of British coasts and harbours. In due course, after a seven-year survey, Captain Collins issued in 1693 the *Great Britain's Coasting Pilot*, an outstanding work consisting of 48 charts, the first complete Pilot Book in English of all the coasts of Great Britain and the surrounding islands with special attention, of course, to the ports. At about the same time as the publication of the *Coasting Pilot*, Edmund Halley was preparing his thematic charts of the Oceans which were issued in the years 1700–02. Although it has to be agreed that England's contribution to marine cartography in the eighteenth century and much of the nineteenth was short in quantity and often quality, there can be no doubt that Halley's charts, linked with Edward Wright's *Certaine Errors of Navigation*, published just a century earlier, and John Harrison's perfection of the chronometer in 1772 were the most important scientific contributions to the art of navigation in the whole period.

In France during the later years of the seventeenth century the ambitions of Louis XIV had awakened his countrymen's interest in the sciences. After the establishment of the Paris Observatory in 1667 a survey

ROBERT DUDLEY *Chart of the East Coast of England.* From the *Dell' Arcano del Mare*, first published in Florence in 1646.

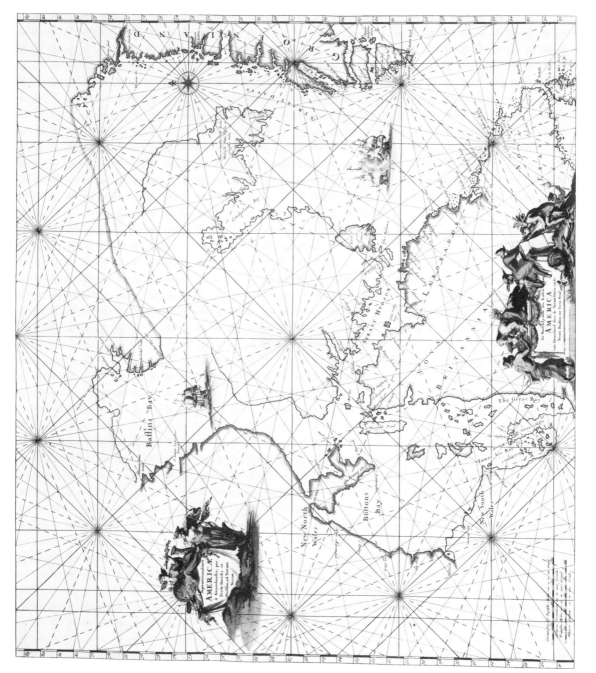

FREDERICK DE WIT *Septemtrionaliora Americae* . . . Amsterdam 1675. This splendid example of de Wit's beautifully engraved marine charts shows the discoveries (and some assumptions!) in the North-Eastern parts of Canada at the time.

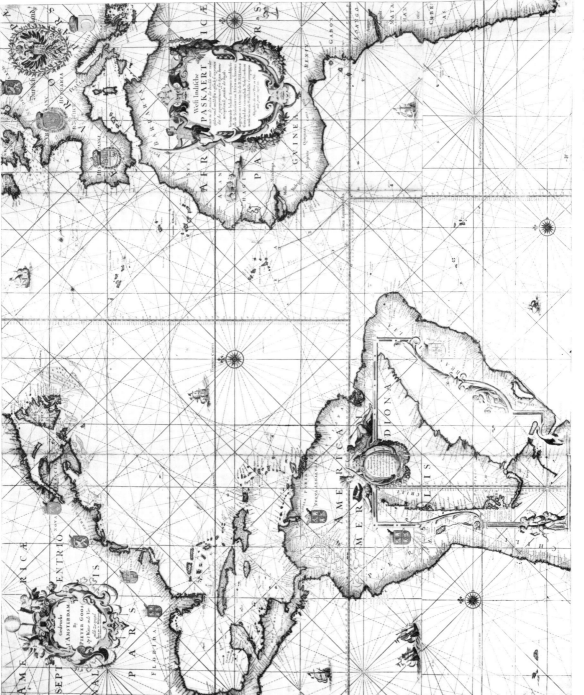

PIETER GOOS/JOHANNES VAN KEULEN *West Indische Paskaert* Amsterdam (1680) *c.* 1720. Portion of a rare chart of the North and South Atlantic based on work by Pieter Goos.

by triangulation of the coasts of France was put in hand and the resultant charts appeared in *Le Neptune François* in 1693, published by Hubert Jaillot and the elder Cassini. These were beautifully produced maps, much superior to those of Captain Collins, and the French maintained their lead in this field, following the foundation of a National Hydrographic Service in 1720, until well into the eighteenth century. A revision of *Le Neptune François* was completed in 1753 by J. N. Bellin and many charts of other parts of the world were published during this time.

Towards the end of the century Britain began to play a leading role in chart making, influenced by the invention of Harrison's timepiece, which solved the problem of calculating longitude at sea, and by the voyages of Captain Cook and the growing supremacy of the Navy as a world force. Sea charts issued in this period are too numerous to mention individually but of particular note were the charts of Cook's voyages published between 1773 and 1784, the *North American Pilot* and *West Indian Atlas* by Thomas Jefferys (1775); the *North American Atlas* (1777) and *General Atlas* (1778) by William Faden, successor to Jefferys; the *Atlantic Neptune* (1784) by J. F. W. des Barres, a Swiss serving with the British Army in North America; and charts of all parts of the world by Sayer and Bennett, Laurie and Whittle and Aaron Arrowsmith over the turn of the century.

In 1795, no doubt influenced by the establishment of the Ordnance Survey Office four years earlier, the British Admiralty set up a Hydrographic Office to co-ordinate the production and issue of sea charts for the Royal Navy, appointing as Hydrographer, Alexander Dalrymple who had held the same post with the East India Company since 1779. As in the case of ordnance maps, the charts produced under the authority of the Office gradually superseded those printed by private enterprise and by 1850 vast areas of the oceans of the world had been officially surveyed and charted.

COMPILERS & PUBLISHERS

The following list includes, in chronological order, names of the best-known compilers or publishers of sea charts (ms = manuscript).

Italian
B. dalli Sonetti
B. Bordone

G. A. di Vavassore
T. Porcacchi
G. Rosaccio
V. M. Coronelli

Spanish & Portuguese
Diogo Homen
Vincente Torfiño de San Miguel
José de Espinosa

Dutch
L. J. Waghenaer
W. Barentsz (Barentzoon)
J. H. Linschoten
B. Langenes
Blaeu family
H. Gerritsz
J. Jansson
J. A. Colom & A. Colom
Anthonie, Jacob & Caspar Jacobsz (Lootsman)
P. Goos
F. de Wit
H. Doncker
P. van Alphen
J. van Loon
A. Roggeveen
Van Keulen family
J. Robijn
Covens & Mortier
Joh. Loots
R. & J. Ottens

French
N. de Nicolay
A. H. Jaillot
L. Renard
L Bremond & Michelot
G. L. le Rouge
J. B. d'Après de Mannevillette
J. N. Bellin
J. Roux
R. Bonne
C. F. Beautemps-Beaupré
J. S. C. Dumont d'Urville

British
Edward Wright
Gabriel Tatton (ms)
John Daniell (ms)
Nicholas Comberford (ms)

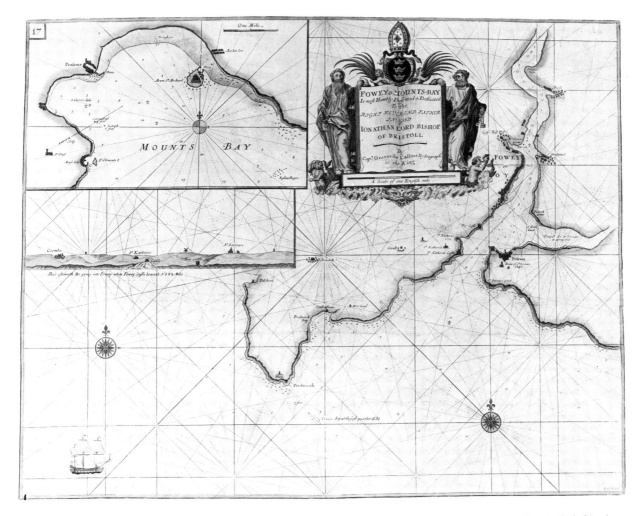

CAPTAIN GREENVILE COLLINS   *Fowey to Mount's Bay* London *c.* 1781. Chart of a stretch of the Cornish coastline included in the
Great Britain's Coasting Pilot, first published in 1693.

John Burston (ms)	Sayer and Bennett
Robert Dudley	Joseph Speer
John Seller	Alexander Dalrymple
Greenvile Collins	Wm. Faden
John Thornton	J. F. W. des Barres
William Hack (ms)	Robert Laurie & James Whittle
Mount and Page	A. Arrowsmith (& Sons)
Edmund Halley	William Heather
John Adair	Capt. George Vancouver
Murdoch Mackenzie	Matthew Flinders
James Cook	J. W. Norie
Thos. Jefferys	James Wyld (& Son)
William Herbert	

Chapter 7
TOWN PLANS

For a variety of reasons town plans were comparatively late comers in the long history of cartography. In the Middle Ages populations of the most notable cities were surprisingly small and it is likely that Amsterdam, Antwerp and Nuremberg – to take a few names at random – had no more than about 20,000 inhabitants in the thirteenth and fourteenth centuries and it has been estimated that even late Elizabethan London embraced only some 100–150,000 people which was probably about ten times as many as any other English city at that time. Travellers were few and such major buildings as existed were built over many decades, so that the layout of even the larger cities scarcely changed from generation to generation. In consequence there was little need for planned guidance in the form expected today.

Before printed plans became available, the compilers of early manuscript maps of the countryside made use of pictorial symbols in elevation, based on the outline of well-known buildings, to distinguish town from town. Those on Matthew Paris's maps of about the year 1250 are particularly attractive and left the traveller in no doubt of the landmarks on his route. The 'Gough' map, too, by the use of different symbols and colours, distinguished between cathedral cities, monastic foundations and ordinary towns and villages. Very often on manuscript maps and portulan charts there were picturesque vignettes of capital cities and places of note inset in any space available.

Not until the late fifteenth century, as a result of the wider dissemination of books and documents made possible by movable-type printing, do we find printed topographical works containing town views in any number. The first, a very rare volume called *Sanctarum Peregrinationum* by Bernhard von Breydenbach, printed in Mainz in 1486, covering a pilgrimage to the Holy Land, contained woodcut views of Jerusalem, Venice and other places on the route. Still rare, but more commonly seen, is the Nuremberg Chronicle (1493)

about which we have written at greater length in Chapter 4. The illustration shown there is of a town view in the style typical of the time. Thereafter, for most of the sixteenth century, German cartographers led the way in producing town plans in a more modern sense. In 1544 Sebastian Münster issued in Basle his *Cosmographia* containing about sixty plans and views, some in plan form, but many still using the old type of outline in elevation, and still others in bird's-eye view. Very soon afterwards Frans Hogenberg, who engraved maps for Ortelius, together with another noted engraver of the time, Georg Hoefnagel, compiled and issued in Cologne a City Atlas intended as a companion work to the *Theatrum Orbis Terrarum*. Entitled *Civitates Orbis Terrarum* and edited by Georg Braun, the six volumes of this famous work were issued between the years 1572 and 1618 and contained in all more than 500 plans including the following in the British Isles:

1572	London
1575	Cambridge, Oxford/Windsor Castle
1581	Norwich, Bristol, Chester, Edinburgh
1588	Canterbury
1598	Palace of Nonsuch
1618	Exeter
	York/Shrewsbury/Lancaster/Richmond
	Dublin/Galway/Limerick/Cork

The Atlas provides a fascinating sixteenth-century picture of the principal cities and towns in Europe, Asia, Africa and even America and records details of public buildings, heraldic devices and rural and domestic scenes, besides many street names. Towns are usually shown in bird's-eye view, set in picturesque and romantic backgrounds with figures of inhabitants in local dress placed boldly in the foreground. Although some of them had been included in the earlier works already mentioned, in a great many instances these were the first views to appear in print. The Braun and Hogenberg plates eventually passed to

LUXEMBOURG

BRAUN and HOGENBERG   Town plan of Luxembourg first published in the *Civitates Orbis Terrarum* in 1581 in Cologne.

Jan Jansson who reissued the plans in Amsterdam in 1657, having removed the costumed figures which, of course, by this time were no longer of contemporary interest. Further issue details are given in Chapter 12.

Meanwhile, in England, a plan of Norwich had been drawn in 1559 by Wm Cunningham; of London, about the same time, probably by a Flemish artist; and of Cambridge in 1574 by Richard Lyne, this being the earliest engraved town plan by an Englishman. Towards the end of the century the pace of development was quickening and plans of London by Valegio (*c.* 1580), Norden (1593) and Münster (1598) exist. It is, however, to John Speed that we owe our knowledge of

the layout of over seventy towns shown as insets on the maps in his Atlas published in 1610–11. Some of these were based on manuscript plans in William Smith's *Description of England* prepared in 1588, and others by Norden, but many were the result of his own travels and surveys throughout the country.

For the next 150 years or so, the work of Braun and Hogenberg and Speed formed the basis of practically all town plans in this country. Many of the maps issued by Kitchin, Bowen, Jefferys and others in the 1700s contained inset plans and vignettes of county towns and other places of importance but until the latter half of that century towns, excluding London, of course,

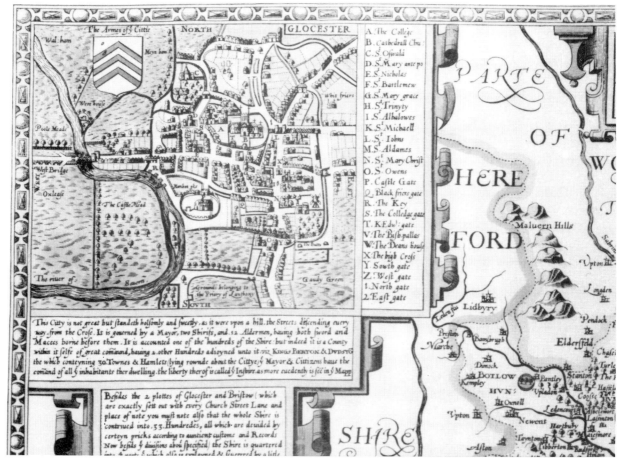

JOHN SPEED   Town plan of the City of Gloucester shown on Speed's map of Gloucestershire first published in 1611.

were still comparatively small and plans tended to be decorative rather than useful. Not until well into the nineteenth century were comprehensive series of town plans on a good scale published. For maps of London, which are too numerous to note here, reference should be made to *Printed Maps of London, Circa 1553–1850* by Darlington and Howgego, who have covered the subject exhaustively. The sheer size and rate of growth of London called for more frequent resurveying and mapping than elsewhere, especially after the Great Fire. Maps of particular interest are those by Wenceslaus Hollar (1655, 1664, 1666, *c.* 1675) before and after the Fire, by John Ogilby and William Morgan (1676), William Morgan (1681–82) and John Rocque (1746 and other editions).

We note below some of the more important works relating to British towns published up to about 1850.

FRANÇOIS DE BELLEFOREST
1575   *La Ville de Londres*: Paris

FRANCESCO VALEGIO (VALESO)
1595–1600 London, Bristol, Cambridge, Canterbury, Chester, Norwich, Edinburgh: Venice

D. MEISSNER
1623   Bristol, Norwich
1637   *Nuremberg in Sciographia Cosmica*
          Bristol, Carlisle, Chester, Exeter, Hull, Norwich, Oxford, Windsor, Cork, Edinburgh

MATTHEW MERIAN
1642–72   *Topographia*: Frankfurt-am-Main
          London*, Dover, Oxford, Edinburgh*, Londonderry   (*panoramic views)

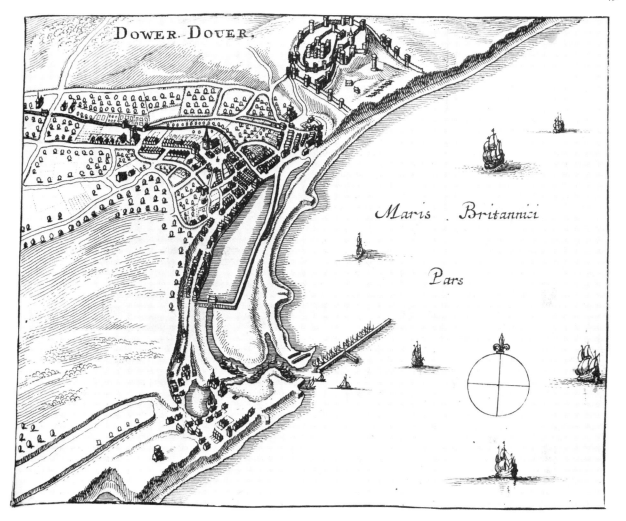

RUTGER HERMANNIDES   *Dover* Amsterdam 1661. Town plan included in *Britannia Magna*, the first book devoted entirely to plans of British towns and cities. Most of the thirty-one plans in the book were based on Speed but *Dover* was probably derived from a Merian plan.

WENCESLAUS HOLLAR

1640   Hull, Oxford

SAXTON (WEB)

1645   Inset plans of Berwick, Hull and York on revised Saxton County Maps

RUTGER HERMANNIDES

1661   *Britannia Magna*: Amsterdam
          31 plans mostly based on Speed. This was the first book devoted entirely to plans of British cities

MANESSON MALLET

1683   *Description de L'Univers, Paris*
1685   *Description de L'Univers, Frankfurt*
          London, Edinburgh, Dublin

SAXTON/PHILIP LEA

1689–93   Revised editions of Saxton's maps incorporating Speed's plans: London

VINCENZO CORONELLI

1706   *Teatro della Guerra*, Vol. III *Inghilterra*: Venice. Maps based on Braun and Hogenberg and Speed

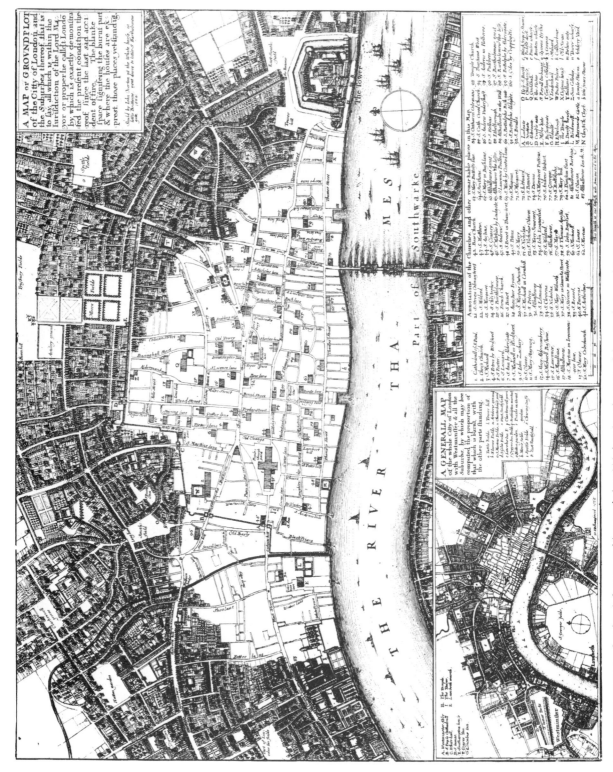

WENCESLAUS HOLLAR   *London*. A famous etching made in 1666 showing the area of the city destroyed in the Great Fire.

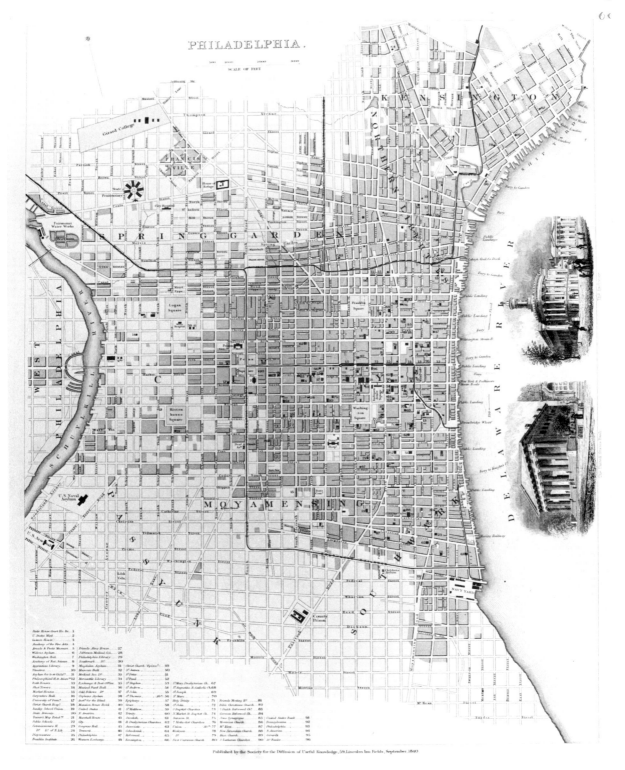

PHILADELPHIA.

SCALE OF FEET

Published by the Society for the Diffusion of Useful Knowledge, 59, Lincolns Inn Fields, September, 1840.

SOCIETY FOR DIFFUSION OF USEFUL KNOWLEDGE (SDUK)   *Plan of Philadelphia* London 1840. This is one of a number of plans of American towns included in the very popular collections of maps published by the SDUK between 1829 and about 1876.

JOHN KIP

1720   *Britannia Illustrata*
         London, Edinburgh and many other cities

PIETER VAN DER AA

1729   *Galérie Agréable du Monde*: Leyden
         Plans based on Braun and Hogenberg and
         Speed

PIERRE CHASSEREAU

1750–66   Plans of York

JOHN ROCQUE

1746   *An exact survey of the Cities of London and*
         Westminster (scale 26 in. to 1 mile)
1746   *Environs of London*
         1748, 1751 Re-issued
1750   Large-scale plan of Bristol
1756   Large-scale plan of Dublin
1764   *A Collection of Plans of the Principal Cities of*
         Great Britain and Ireland

G. L. LE ROUGE

1759   *Recueil des villes, ports d' Angleterre*: Paris
         Plans of 17 towns

JOHN ANDREWS

1792   *Plans of the principal cities of the world*

G. COLE and J. ROPER

1804–10   *Beauties of England and Wales*
         Includes plans of many towns and cities

R. K. DAWSON

1832   *Plans of the cities and boroughs of England and*
         Wales
1833–50   *Collection of the Plans of the most Capital*
         Cities in every Empire

THOMAS MOULE

1836   *The English Counties delineated*
         Includes many plans

JOHN TALLIS

1851   *Illustrated Atlas*
         Includes vignette views and about 26 town
         plans

Chapter 8

TOPOGRAPHICAL MAPS & SURVEYS

Before looking at the development of surveying on a national scale it may be of interest to go back over the centuries to consider some of the topographical (i.e. large-scale) maps which were the forerunners of those produced today. Generally speaking, the earlier maps mentioned in this chapter are known only from unique or very rare copies and they are, therefore, outside the range of our collectors' maps, but it is felt that they represent another aspect of map history which most collectors will find worthy of note.

It is appropriate to consider first events in Italy, where more than anywhere else in Europe, a tradition of map making had taken root, especially in the northern cities. Portulan charts, of which we have already written, were in use by Italian seamen throughout the fourteenth and fifteenth centuries and probably earlier; the first translations of the Ptolemy manuscripts into Latin were made about the year 1406 in Florence and, above all, the intellectual and artistic atmosphere of the time provided the skills needed for drawing what may be best described as picture maps. For the most part those that survive depict the chief cities of Northern Italy – Venice, Padua, Verona, Mantua – and the districts around them, often distinguishing between defended and undefended positions, no doubt intended for use in the wars between Venice and Milan.

It seems likely that the Italian enthusiasm for map drawing in this manner influenced ideas in neighbouring states. In Germany, for example, in 1492 Ehrhard Etzlaub, noted for his later 'Rome Way' road map, produced large-scale maps of the surroundings of Nuremberg and other German cities. In the following year the Nuremberg Chronicle with its very large number of woodcut illustrations – both bird's eye views and prospects – of European towns was published. The Kingdom of Wurttemberg was mapped in some detail round the year 1500 and Saxony soon afterwards, but Philipp Apian's map of Bavaria on 40 sheets was the first really large-scale map of a wide area: the original

is lost but a reproduction on 24 sheets was published in 1568. A later picture map of the Black Forest published in 1578 (reissued in 1603) by Johann Georg Tibianus (1541–1611) is a particularly pleasing example of its kind, so clear and self-explanatory that the use of a key to symbols is hardly necessary.

Elsewhere we have written of large-scale maps of Switzerland by Aegidius Tschudi, Jos Murer and Thomas Schoepf, of Austria and Hungary by Wolfgang Lazius, of the Netherlands by Jacobus van Deventer, of Denmark by Mark Jorden and of Scandinavia by Olaus Magnus.

In the rather less sophisticated atmosphere of England, there seems to have been no tradition of map drawing such as had existed in Central Europe. Although surveys of estate and monastic lands were made in the fourteenth and fifteenth centuries very few were accompanied by 'maps' in any useful sense and only a few dated prior to the year 1500 are known. Soon after that year, however, Continental influences awakened interest in the technicalities of map making. A book by Gemma Frisius, A *Method of Delineating Places*, published in Louvain in 1533 was followed in England by the work of William Cunningham, *The Cosmographicall Glasse*, in 1559 and by Leonard Digges, *Pantometria*, in 1571 on the subject of surveying, land measurement, the use of theodolites and the principles of triangulation. About the same time, subsequent to the dissolution of the monasteries in the 1540s, an increasing need arose for estate mapping on a wide scale and there were other projects such as maps of the coastline and fortresses made for Henry VIII and later for Lord Burghley in the face of threats of Spanish invasion. These, and no doubt many others of which we have no knowledge, must have been used by Laurence Nowell in compiling his 19 sheet map of England and Wales in 1563 and by Christopher Saxton in his survey for the *Atlas of England and Wales* published in 1579.

These English maps cannot really be called large-scale and indeed, in the years ahead, perhaps only the inset town plans on maps by John Speed and others merit that description: they, of course, covered only very small areas. Later in the century between the years 1675 and 1685 the publication of the strip road maps in Ogilby's *Britannia*, the work of John Adams who contemplated a survey by triangulation of England and Wales, and the general survey of Ireland by William Petty all pointed the way to larger-scale mapping, but inspiration for greater projects was lacking and these advances were overshadowed by events in France.

In Chapter 14 we describe briefly the fundamental work in France of the Cassini family and Jean Picard, but the turbulent years of the 18th century were not conducive in any sense to international co-operation, certainly not in the field of cartography, and most nations were slow to adopt the new surveying techniques developed by the French. The Russians were an exception: as early as 1720 Tsar Peter the Great embraced French ideas wholeheartedly (as we have described in Chapter 19), setting up an Academy of Sciences and beginning, with the help of French cartographers Joseph Nicolas and Louis Delisle, the enormous task of mapping Russia. Even with every encouragement, a real survey by triangulation was not started until 1816 and took many years to complete. This time scale was not unusual and the following dates give some idea of the long periods involved before complete sets of maps were published: Denmark 1762–1834, Sweden 1758–1857, Norway 1773–c1850, the Austro–Hungarian Empire *c.* 1762–1860 and Switzerland 1832–1864.

In the British Isles map makers were just as complaisant and only the lack of accurate maps to meet military requirements in Scotland following the 1745 Jacobite rising stimulated official action. In the following years (1747–1755) practically the whole of Scotland was mapped on a scale of 1000 yards to one inch, but the maps were never printed. The actual survey was carried out at the instigation of Colonel David Watson by William Roy, later to become Deputy Quartermaster General and Surveyor of Coastal Defence. As a result of his practical experience in Scotland Roy became a determined advocate of mapping the rest of the British Isles in the same manner, but for various political and military reasons his advocacy met with no success until 1783. In that year the French Government suggested that the Observatories of Paris and Greenwich should be linked by Cassini's method of triangulation, the

French claiming that the latitude of Greenwich, as previously calculated, was incorrect.

The challenge was too great to be ignored and Roy was charged with the work on this side of the Channel, his first task being to measure a base-line on Hounslow Heath, from which the triangulation was to be extended to Greenwich and Dover for the purpose of linking up with the French. This was completed in 1784, but Roy was far more interested in regarding the Hounslow Heath base as the start of a general survey of the British Isles, and so it was to prove. Unfortunately, Roy died in 1790 but detailed work was continued under the direction of the Duke of Richmond, the Master General of Ordnance who, in 1791, formally set up a Survey Office in the Tower of London, then the Headquarters of the Board of Ordnance, to administer the whole task of surveying Britain. At that time and in the following years under threat of Napoleonic invasion accurate mapping was regarded as a military requirement – hence the assignment of the task to the Board of Ordnance and our use of the term today.

The first objective was to produce a map on a scale of one inch to one mile, the scale which had been used for so many of the county maps in the previous thirty or forty years. Work on the Trigonometrical Survey, as it was originally called, started in Kent and Essex using the data prepared by General William Roy, and by 1801 a map of Kent on four sheets was ready for publication: this was printed by William Faden.

The early surveying carried out by officers of the Royal Artillery and Royal Engineers under the command of Major (later General) William Mudge (1762–1820) and his successor Major (General) Thomas Colby (*c.* 1784–1852) was never an easy or speedy process: the requirements of the British armies fighting Napoleon in Europe claimed priority until 1815 and frequently opposition from big landowners made life very difficult for the surveyors. No doubt these reasons and the time required to train staff to a sufficiently high standard resulted in indifferent work, and there were many inaccuracies in the earliest maps produced up to about 1820–30. These difficulties were emphasized by the high-quality maps which were being published at private expense in direct competition with the national survey.

As the accuracy and presentation of Ordnance maps improved, however, output from private sources declined and the official maps became the accepted standard. Their overall accuracy was quite remarkable and base lines 350 miles apart were found to differ by only 5 inches! Of course, at this stage the survey was by no means complete and in 1825, at short notice, most of the Army teams involved in field work were moved to Ireland to undertake a complete new survey there for fiscal purposes to replace the old "townland" system on which Irish taxation had long been based. For this purpose maps were required in great detail and they were drawn therefore to a scale of six inches to one mile: the resulting maps were so successful that, in 1840, it was decided to use that scale for the rest of the survey of England, Wales and Scotland and, in spite of much controversy, to extend it still further to 25 inches to one mile. Soon afterwards, in 1853, it was agreed internationally that the overall scale of 25 inches to one mile (and its metric equivalent) was necessary for a really adequate survey, and that remains the standard today.

To meet the growing demand for maps the Ordnance Office developed new methods of printing and, from about 1853 onwards, maps in the one inch series appeared with the words 'Printed from an Electrotype' in the bottom margin. This was a method of duplicating the original engraved copper plates to enable printers to produce more copies without any significant loss of quality, besides reducing the price from around three shillings (15p) per quarter sheet in 1831 to about sixpence (slightly less than 3p) in 1862.

The complete First Edition (or Old Series as it has become known) of one inch to one mile maps was finished by 1873: the New Series on the six and 25 inch scales, after much revision and resurveying, was finally completed in 1893. Printing was only in black and white but individual examples were sold hand-coloured, often in bound volumes, by many of the official agents. Then, late in the 1890s, printed partially coloured copies became available, followed in 1912 by full colour printing.

The period of seventy years to complete the one inch survey seems a long time, and one cannot but reflect on the extraordinary achievement of Christopher Saxton in completing his 'perambulations', surveying the length and breadth of England and Wales in the years 1573–1579.

By contrast with the flamboyance of the engravings made for Saxton, the first Ordnance maps, although still engraved on copper plates, were plain, even austere; they bore no list of symbols, but the delineation of geographical features was beautifully clear. The methods of shading and hachuring to show the heights of hills was not considered satisfactory and, starting in 1843, they were eventually replaced by the use of contour lines as we know them. Basically, apart from constant revision and refinement, the maps remain the same today and few countries anywhere can boast of so complete and meticulous a system of mapping.

Specialist Reference

CLOSE, Col. Sir CHARLES, *The Early Years of the Ordnance Survey*. Institution of Royal Engineers 1926; New Edition with Introduction by J. B. Harley, Whitstable 1969, Latimer Trend & Co. Ltd.

Chapter 9
PLAYING CARDS

It seems very likely that playing cards were in use in China and India centuries before they appeared in Europe, where the first reference to them is said to have been in the year 1299. In Italy the earliest packs were 'Tarot' cards consisting of twenty-two cards of allegorical designs used for fortune telling which later were combined with Oriental cards to make a set of seventy-eight, on which the game of 'Tarrochi' was based. In England it is known that the use of cards was well established in 1463, when an Act of Parliament banned their importation from the Continent.

As might be expected, engravers and printers found great scope for their skills in the production of playing cards. One of the most noted, an anonymous German artist known as the 'Master of the Playing Cards', produced splendid sets, line engraved, in the years 1430 to 1450 and, in Italy, some of the earliest copperplate engravings were used for sets of Tarrochi cards; it is quite likely that the engravers of these sets also prepared the plates for the Ptolemaic maps issued in Rome in 1478.

In the sixteenth century the pack of fifty-two cards, introduced in France, became the accepted standard and in times when there was little or no organized schooling they were widely used for educational purposes and were illustrated with texts on a great variety of subjects. It was natural, therefore, to find among the beautifully illustrated cards produced in the days of the first Queen Elizabeth sets of cards showing a map of the British Isles and the counties of England and Wales. The earliest surviving packs of this type were published in 1590 and although their authorship is not known for certain they are attributed to a William Bowes. The maps depicted on them were evidently copies from Saxton's famous Atlas of 1579 and possibly were engraved by William Kip or Pieter van den Keere, noted map engravers of the period. By a fortunate coincidence there are fifty-two counties in England and Wales and the maps were so arranged in

w. REDMAYNE Example of playing card showing the County of Gloucestershire issued in 1676.

the 1590 pack that in any suit the smallest county is No. I and the largest XIII. Each card is divided into three parts showing the county name, the map and brief details. In spite of their small size each map shows the principal places in the county, identified by initial letters. There are only three packs of the 1590 cards known, with a further one dated 1605. It is thought that the maps drawn for these cards formed the basis for one of the first pocket atlases, producing in 1635 by

ROBERT MORDEN   Examples of playing cards issued in 1676. Published by Robert Morden and William Berry.

Matthew Simmons, a London bookseller and printer who published many of Milton's works.

Later, in 1676, Robert Morden, who subsequently published notable atlases, produced a pack of cards in very similar form, the upper portion showing the suit, stencilled by hand, the title of the map and the designation of the card; the centre portion consisted of a sketch map and the lower panel, the dimensions of the county. Each 'King' is indicated by a portrait of King Charles II in a circle and the 'Queen' by the head of his Queen, Catherine of Braganza. The Northern counties are represented by Clubs, the Eastern by Hearts, the Southern by Diamonds and the Welsh counties by Spades. In spite of limitations of size these maps were among the first to give an indication of the main roads in each county, no doubt being inspired by John Ogilby's 'strip' road maps published in the previous year. There was a second issue in 1676 and further issues in 1680 and 1770 showing additional towns and roads. Also in 1676 another pack of cards was compiled by W. Redmayne, presumably in competition with Morden, and they are now equally scarce. In the next century a set in similar style, probably based on Redmayne's, was printed *c.* 1711 by John Lenthall who, as a publisher and stationer, rather than an original engraver, produced packs of cards of all types based on the work of many other designers.

All English sets and those published on the Continent, of which one by Pierre Duval, *Les Tables de Géographie c.* 1667, is a good example, are now very scarce indeed and will be found only by the most dedicated collector.

Chapter 10

'Here be Dragons . . .'
MYTHS & LEGENDS ON OLD MAPS

Definitions:

MYTH: A purely fictitious narrative, magnified by tradition, usually involving supernatural persons or events and expressive of primitive beliefs.

LEGEND: An unauthentic story handed down by tradition and popularly regarded as historical.

A study of cartography may well seem to many to be a weighty subject, so let us digress in lighter vein for a moment to look at some of the myths and legends which over the ages have intrigued our ancestors and which, to a surprising extent, may be claimed to have affected the course of historical discoveries.

Writing in 1665 John Bunyan could have conjured up the most unlikely dragons in the awareness that his readers would accept them, however fearsome, as nothing more than allegorical. Chaucer, writing three hundred years earlier, would not have been so confident of readers' acceptance of his dragons as mythical beasts and, indeed, in the setting of the time, why should he have done so. In the fourteenth century anyone looking, shall we say, at the Hereford World Map would not doubt the existence of the most extraordinary creatures and, more important, could not be blamed for contemplating with wonder, and perhaps fear, the outside world beyond the encircling ocean, the 'Sea of Darkness'.

When we consider, then, the myths and legends of medieval times we should not be deceived into thinking that stories which we may now regard simply as folklore were always accepted as such. On the contrary, in the thirteenth, fourteenth and fifteenth centuries they represented very live issues and European thought was strongly influenced by, for example, the belief in the Kingdom of Prester John, in Marco Polo's 7,448 Spice Islands in the Far East and in the possibility of a second great river, a Western Nile, in Africa. Today, with any part of the world only hours away, it is perhaps hard to imagine the intense excitement and the intellectual ferment created among scholars in general, and geographers in particular, by the knowledge that it was possible to sail 'around the world' and not be lost 'over the edge'. It was surely the conquest of the fear of the unknown world, rather than the physical prowess involved in its exploration, however great that may have been, which was the true measure of achievement in the Age of Discovery and in the long period of European renaissance.

Where better to start than by looking at the mythical island of Hy Brazil which appeared out in the Atlantic to the west of Ireland in charts as early as 1325, in the famous Catalan Atlas dated 1375 and, subsequently, on numerous maps for the next 200 years, including Waldseemüller's map of the British Isles issued at Strassburg in 1513 and its later editions. It was also shown on Toscanelli's chart dated about 1457 which was said to have been used by Columbus on his first voyage. Early Celtic legends say that the island only appeared at sunset in the mists of the Atlantic and they called it 'the blessed stormless isle, where all men are good and all the women pure and where God retreats for a recreation from the rest of us'.* To add to our confusion these early charts depicted not only Brazil off the coast of Ireland but also St Brendan's Island far out in the ocean half way to Zipangu (Japan). We can imagine the Irish monk, St Brendan, setting sail sometime in the sixth century on a seven-year voyage in search of this paradise and arriving, according to one version, in the Fortunate Isles (the Canaries), then the limit of the known world. According to other interpretations he reached not only the Hebrides and the Faroes but even America. It is hard to believe that as late as the eighteenth century seamen were still seeking these islands, and so often had Brazil been 'sighted' that geographers were reluctant to abandon the possibility

*From *Summer of the Red Wolf* by Morris West, William Heinemann Ltd (1971).

MARTIN WALDSEEMÜLLER *British Isles.* Map originally published in Strassburg in 1522. This extract, showing the island of Brazil set in the Atlantic to the west of Ireland, is from an edition issued at Vienne (Dauphiné) in 1541.

of its existence; in fact it was not finally removed from British Admiralty charts until the 1870s. The Celts were not alone in their belief in the existence of an earthly paradise in the Western Ocean; the Greeks too, among others, imagined these 'Isles of the Blest' beyond the Pillars of Hercules which legend claimed were 'peopled not by the dead but by mortals on whom the Gods had conferred immortality' and where there was perpetual summer and abundance.

In the medieval mind Brazil and St Brendan's Island were by no means the only islands in the Atlantic; Martin Behaim's famous globe constructed about 1492 in Nuremberg shows the ocean abounding in islands stretching as far as Zipangu, without the American continent, of course. Among these, in the region of the West Indies, was Antillia, the island of the Seven Cities,

recorded on Genoese charts about 1450. According to Portuguese tradition, following the conquest of Spain and Portugal by the Moors in the year 734, the island was colonized by Christian refugees led by an Archbishop of Oporto and six Bishops, each of whom founded and ruled a utopian city far from the turmoil of the Old World. In later years the Portuguese dispatched expeditions to search for the island and so absolute was the belief in its existence that Columbus was advised that the island was a principal landmark for measuring distances between Lisbon and Zipangu. The name itself has been perpetuated as The Antilles, the island group in the West Indies. Although the island with its Seven Cities failed to materialize, the legend lived on in new guise as The Seven Cities of Cibola, the site of gold and silver mines in the

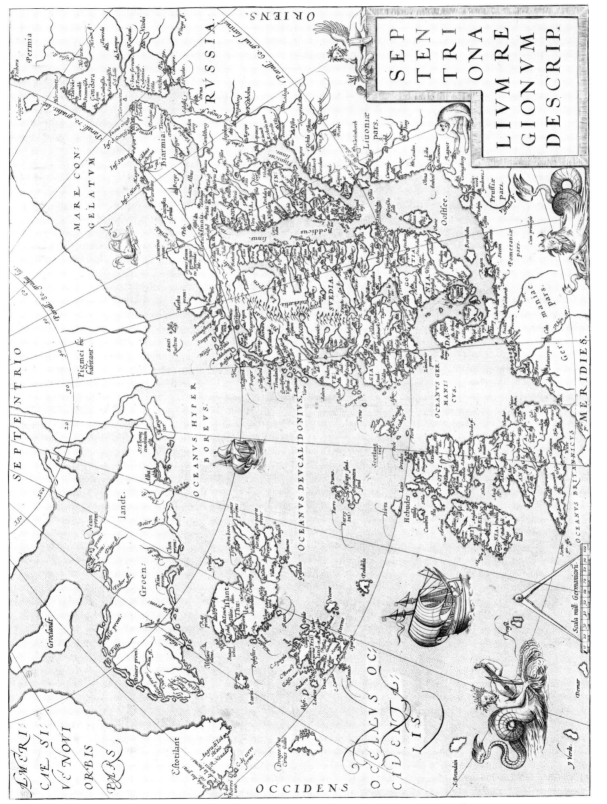

ABRAHAM ORTELIUS *Septentrionalium Regionum Descrip* Amsterdam (1570) 1573. An interesting map of the Northern Regions showing many non-existent islands including Brazil and St Brendan's Island and a note in the Arctic stating that 'Pigmys live here'!

continental interior north of the Gulf of Mexico, confidently said to have been visited in the year 1536 by Spanish explorers. The claim was soon dashed by later expeditions but the search nevertheless revealed great areas of Colorado and the prairie lands.

In the vastness of South America there was ample scope for such legends. The El Dorado, somewhere in Guiana, was long sought by the Spanish and twice by Raleigh who was executed for his failure to find the promised land. Even in Patagonia there is the story of Sebastian Cabot's pilot, Francisco César, who in 1528 travelled up country from the River Plate and saw yet another city of gold. Expeditions to find it were mounted as late as the end of the eighteenth century.

On the same map in the Catalan Atlas mentioned above, and on the tenth-century Anglo-Saxon world 'map', there appear in the furthermost part of Siberia the names of Gog and Magog. It was widely believed in medieval times that those mythical giants existed somewhere in Asia, penned in by Alexander the Great behind the great mountain walls shown so prominently on early world maps. The source of the belief lay in the Bible story that they represented the forces of evil who would appear immediately before the end of the world. In England, Gog and Magog were supposed to be the survivors of a race of giants destroyed by Brutus, the legendary founder of Britain who brought them to London and condemned them to act as porters at the gates of the royal palace; hence their place over the entrance to the Guildhall.

Many stories as early as the year 1122 centred on Prester John, who was thought to have been a Tartar chief converted to Christianity, ruling somewhere in the East beyond Armenia and Persia. As a great warrior, all-powerful in Asia, his help was sought as an ally by the Crusaders in their attempts to free Jerusalem from the Saracens. Stories of his existence were taken so literally that emissaries and letters were despatched to him on a number of occasions by the Popes; the travels of Marco Polo and others, in their search for his Kingdom, led directly to the re-establishment of links with China and other Eastern lands. Later legends placed Prester John in Abyssinia or Central Africa, an idea which influenced not a little the Kings of Portugal in their efforts to penetrate the Indian Ocean, and by linking up with the mythical Kingdom, to outflank the power of Islam. Ortelius's map of 1573 entitled *A Representation of the Empire of Prester John, or of the Abyssinians*, showing Africa from the Mediterranean to the Mountains of the Moon, placed well below the Equator, is a splendid illustration of the ideas current even in the sixteenth century.

The whereabouts of the Kingdom of Prester John was only one of the many legends associated with Africa. The source of the river Nile, one of the few rivers known to the ancient world which flowed from south to north, was an unsolved mystery and Ptolemy wrote that he was told that the river rose in the Mountains of the Moon, an idea which persisted until the beginning of the last century. Seamen had long believed that a western flowing Nile (or Niger) also existed, running across or round Africa to the Atlantic, which would provide a short route to the Indies and to those 7,448 Spice Islands spoken of so confidently by Marco Polo. Indeed, the first Portuguese voyages planned by Henry the Navigator in the early part of the fifteenth century were intended to find just such a route. They failed to find a river, of course, except the mouths of the Niger and the Congo, but the lure of the Indies proved strong enough to take Bartholomeu Dias round the Cape in 1486 and, a few years later, Vasco da Gama into the Indian Ocean and to India.

In the other direction, the idea of reaching India and the Spice Islands by a 'short voyage' across the Atlantic was strongly influenced by the fanciful facts and figures quoted by Marco Polo, added to which Ptolemy's exaggeration of the size of the land mass of Europe and Asia led Columbus and other explorers to believe that their landfall in America was, in fact, in the Indies. It is said that Columbus, even after four Atlantic crossings, never reconciled himself to the fact that he had not really landed in Asia or its islands, and in 1523 a Florentine captain, Giovanni da Verazzano, sailing along the coast of North America seeking a North West Passage, claimed that he had seen across a comparatively narrow isthmus, probably near Chesapeake Bay or Pamlico Sound, a great stretch of water which, he believed, was an arm of the Indian Ocean. This became known to navigators as the Mare de Verazzano and for sixty years or more was regarded as a possible route to Asia. Verazzano's claims must always have been treated with a degree of scepticism for we do not hear of any further exploration of his 'sea', but even so it is still shown on a map by Sir Humphrey Gilbert drawn about 1583 and on a number of others of about the same time. As late as 1651 Farrer's map of Virginia indicated that it was only 'ten days' march' from the Atlantic to the far coast and throughout that century a shorter route to the Pacific was still hoped for, if not to the south, then to the

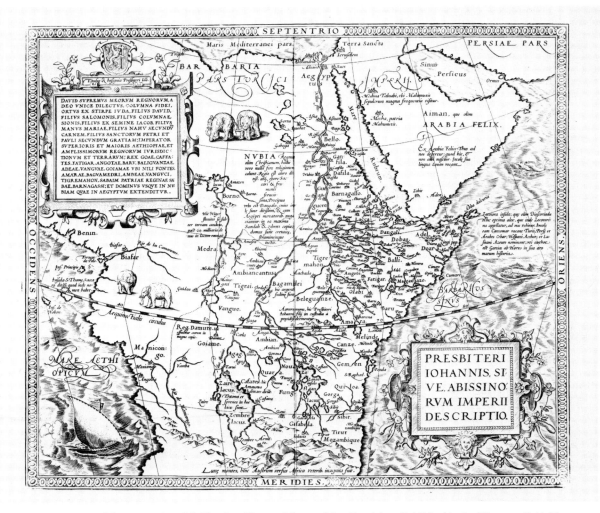

ABRAHAM ORTELIUS *A Representation of the Empire of Prester John, or of the Abyssinians.* Published in the *Theatrum Orbis Terrarum* in Antwerp in 1573, this is one of the most famous maps by Ortelius.

north, through a North West Passage. To some extent we have once again to blame Marco Polo for the suggestion of the existence of such a route. He mentions the Kingdom of Anian in the far north off the coast of Asia and the idea grew that adjacent to this land was open water, the Strait of Anian, through which a way could at last be found to the Pacific Ocean and the Orient. The idea was taken up by Giacomo Gastaldi in *A Description of the World* written in 1562 and the name subsequently appeared on maps of the New World for a century or more.

The remoteness and vast extent of the Pacific Ocean itself inevitably led to confusion among explorers and cartographers and in particular there was argument for more than a century over the outline of California. Although originally believed to be an island somewhere near the Garden of Eden, Spanish charts and the maps of Mercator, Ortelius and others showed it correctly, but in about 1602 a Carmelite friar, following further voyages up the West Coast, prepared and dispatched to Spain a chart showing it again as an island. The chart fell into Dutch hands and it was not long before Speed and others were showing the new island in their atlases, a practice almost universally followed until early in the eighteenth century when exploration by Father Kino disproved the 'island'

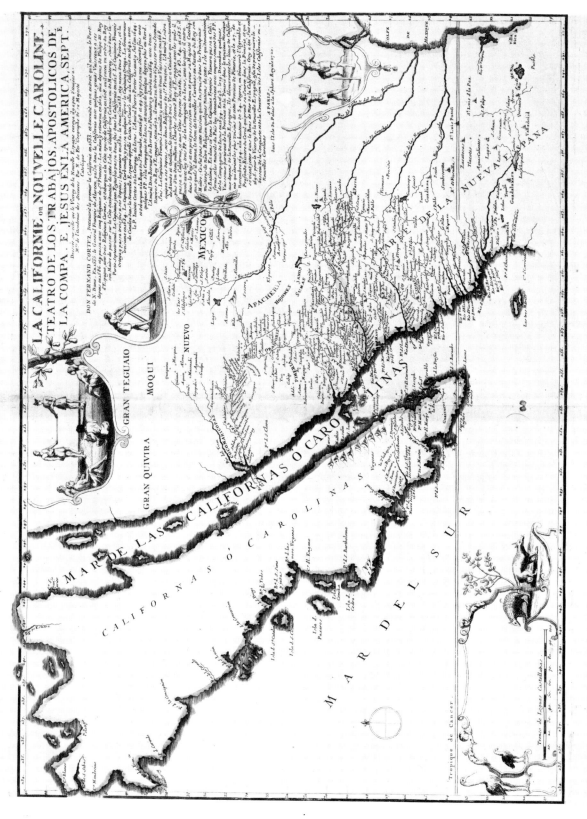

NICOLAS DE FER   *La Californie ou Nouvelle Caroline*. Published in Paris in 1720, based on an earlier map of 1705, still showing California as an island.

theory and a new generation of cartographers, especially Guillaume Delisle, reverted to the peninsula outline.

In the sixteenth century the enormous distances across the Pacific proved to be far greater than the early explorers had suspected. The Spaniards particularly were intrigued by the story of Lochac, yet another of Marco Polo's 'lands of gold and spices' (probably Malaysia) and in 1567 an expedition sailing from Peru eventually made landfall in a large group of islands near the Equator. These so enchanted the explorers that they were identified in their minds as the biblical land of Ophir, and hence were named King Solomon's Islands.

As to the lands to the south of the Pacific, speculation about a hypothetical southern continent – *terra incognita* – had intrigued geographers from the earliest times. To those who believed the world was disc-shaped, it was logical to suppose that there must be a great land mass somewhere to the south to counter-balance Europe and Asia in the north. Indeed, how else, they argued, could the disc of the earth maintain its equilibrium? In the first century AD Pomponius Mela, a Spaniard, postulated the theory of a wide ocean stretching across the world to the south of Egypt, thus dividing the 'disc' neatly into two halves, the southern portion containing the undiscovered continent. In AD 150 Ptolemy, although believing the world to be spherical, visualized land across the base of the world stretching from the lower parts of Africa to somewhere beyond India and embracing a landlocked Indian Ocean. Ptolemy's ideas persisted well into the sixteenth century and as late as 1570 Ortelius's world map showed land spanning the globe, and his 1589 map of the Pacific Ocean marks it as 'Terra Australis, sive Magellanica, nondum detecta'. Even after the discovery of Australia by the Dutch in 1605 there seemed to be a marked reluctance in Europe to accept the discovery and the idea of a continent still further south lingered on. Only after Cook's return from his second voyage to the South Seas in 1775, during which he had annexed, in the name of the Crown, the bleak and uninhabited land of South Georgia, was the almost fanatical belief in a vast southern continent abandoned, at least temporarily, only to be revived again when modern exploration proved that the conjectures of the ancient geographers were right after all and that their *Terra Incognita* could now be renamed *Antarctica*.

THE STORY OF THE WINDROSE

Collectors new to our subject may wonder about the significance of those figureheads symbolizing the winds which frequently border fifteenth- and sixteenth-century maps. In seeking their origins it soon becomes apparent that here, myth, legend and historical fact intermingle and, as so often happens in studies of cartography, we have to start by going back to the earliest days of the Greek world.

In classical lore the names of the four principal winds – Boreas (north), Notos (south), Eurus (east) and Zephyrus (west) – are ascribed to Homer who told of Aeolus, the son of Hippotes, the father of the winds. Aeolos, it was said, jealously guarded the winds in a remote cave in Thrace, but was prevailed upon to release them as a gift to Odysseus who had long awaited a favourable wind to take him on the next stage of his Aegean adventures. The adverse winds were to be restrained in a leather bag but the story in the *Odyssey* relates how they were unwittingly released with dire consequences for Odysseus and his crew. The compilers of the early medieval maps followed the Homeric legend, the winds being represented by 'wind-heads', sometimes using their 'Aeolus' bags or, more often, simply by figures blowing benignly or ferociously depending on the nature of the wind they represent. Apart, however, from the genesis of the wind names in Greek mythology, what do we know of the more practical aspects of the subject?

Life for the peoples of the Mediterranean was inseparable from the sea; Minoans, Phoenicians, Greeks and Romans all left their mark and all were dependent for survival at sea on their knowledge of the winds. The Greeks – who deified the winds – developed and refined the basic idea of the four principal winds by adding others adjusted to the summer and winter sunrise and sunset, roughly equivalent to the north-west, north-east, south-west and south-east. From the earliest times the 'winds' became synonymous with 'direction' and chart makers must have soon found that it was convenient to combine indications of direction with the names of the winds: in consequence, the windrose took shape. One of the earliest, consisting of twelve winds, was set out by Timosthenes of Rhodes, a Greek admiral of the third century BC on whose work Marinus of Tyre is said to have relied for calculations of distances in the eastern Mediterranean. These in turn were accepted by Ptolemy in compiling his *Geographia*. It would be too much, however, to expect to find in those early times a 'standard' windrose acceptable to all seamen throughout the Mediterranean. Long after Timosthenes, the Tower of the Winds, erected in Athens about the year 100 BC had only eight sides bearing emblematic figures representing Boreas (north), Cecias (Kaikias) (north-east), Eurus (east), Apeliotes (south-east), Notos (south), Lips (south-west), Zephyrus (west) and Skiron or Corus (north-west).

Following the Greeks, the Romans were no less mindful of the need to propitiate the gods, or rather goddesses, before any major undertaking at sea; white animals were sacrificed to the beneficent winds, black animals to those regarded as malevolent. Later generations of seafarers in north-west Europe and the Mediterranean may not have deified the winds as their ancestors did but they were equally dependent on them. Charlemagne is said to have introduced new Frankish names for the 12 point windrose and, centuries later, traders from the Low Countries started to use their equivalent of the modern English terms North, South, East and West for the four principal winds.

About the end of the 13th century the discovery of the magnetic compass finally enabled sailors to plot a more accurate course even if they were still reliant on wind power. In the new era the windrose was combined with a compass card with as many as 32 directional points but it seems that its use was not always welcome. Traditional knowledge of the winds gained over many centuries was not to be discarded lightly and there was always suspicion of the accuracy of the compass itself due, no doubt, to magnetic variation, then, of course, not understood. In fact, the use of the wind names

persisted for centuries and appeared on most of the first printed world maps. These show a confusing array of wind heads bearing what seem sometimes to be almost a random choice of names, Greek, Latin and medieval. During the century which spanned the printing of the first maps down to Mercator's elegant drawing of Ptolemy's maps in 1578, engravers conjured up every style of wind head ranging from those on the Ulm Ptolemy (1482/6) – where they look like benign citizens of Ulm rather than Greek Gods – to those on the Ortelius world map of 1564 where they seem to have become contemporary figures of the Low Countries. A particularly fascinating example is the Gregor Reisch (c. 1470–1525) map of the world (1503) embellished with twelve windheads bearing a variety of Greek, Latin and medieval names – in the case of 'South' using all three, while in another, 'Vulturnus' is looking through a pair of spectacles, perhaps not surprisingly, as he has been placed in the north-east quadrant of the map instead of the south-east where he properly belongs! 'Vulturnus' is similarly misplaced in a number of other maps of the time. On occasion, as in the Laurent Fries World Map (1522), the wind names are incorporated in a decorative border without the benefit of windheads.

By the fourth quarter of the 16th century the classical 'wind-blowers' had outlived their time and were giving way to other more abstract forms of decoration. About the same time the compass rose, which of course had long appeared on portulan and manuscript sea charts, finally displaced the windrose and for centuries became an essential and highly decorative feature of printed charts and of many other maps which included an area of sea.

Part II
MAP MAKERS

INTRODUCTION

In the following chapters, a short account is given of the development of map making in the major countries, followed by notes on the work of prominent cartographers, engravers and publishers in each country. In our preface we have already stressed that map listings in this section have generally been restricted to complete atlases although details of individual maps are included where these are of special importance. Manuscript maps are frequently mentioned but as far as our 'average collector' is concerned, unless he is extraordinarily lucky, they must remain a matter of historical interest and are only included for that reason.

The following notes read in conjunction with these listings may be helpful to readers unfamiliar with the subject.

METHODS OF PRINTING

Maps printed from woodblocks are shown as woodcuts, otherwise it may be accepted that all maps were printed from engraved copper plates with the exception of a few in the nineteenth century printed by lithography which are specially noted. Further details on the printing of maps have been given in Chapter 2.

MAP SIZES

We have only to consider for a moment the vast numbers of maps printed over the centuries to realize the difficulty of giving more than a very general idea of map sizes. In any work dealing with individual maps there is no problem but here, short of providing a collation of every atlas – obviously impossible in a single volume – an acceptable solution is less easy to find. Certain terms, e.g. folio, quarto, octavo and so on, which originally referred to specific book sizes, are still widely used but so many variations within these

main sizes occur that the terms have lost their precise meaning. Even so, they still remain a convenient method of differentiating between sizes of books and hence of maps also, and in the absence of more satisfactory terminology they are used here. Some examples will serve to illustrate their use:

FOLIO	Speed Atlases
	Blaeu Atlases
	Jansson Atlases
SMALL FOLIO	Camden – *Britannia*
	Drayton – *Poly-Olbion*
	Morden – *Britannia*
LARGE FOLIO	Bellin *et al.* – *Neptune François*
	Bowen/Kitchin – *Large English Atlas*
QUARTO (4to)	Mercator/Hondius – *Atlas Minor*
	Kitchin – *English Atlas*
	Cary – *New and Correct English Atlas* (1787)
OCTAVO (8vo)	Van den Keere – 'Miniature Speeds'
	Moll – *Atlas Manuale*
	Kitchin – *Pocket Atlas*
	Cary – *Travellers' Companion*

DUODECIMO (12mo)
SEXTODECIMO (16mo)
VICESIMO-QUARTO (24mo)

These small sizes are less easy to define and tend to be used indiscriminately for very small atlases or maps, e.g. Bowen – *Atlas Minimus* (16mo/24mo); Badeslade – *Chorographia Britannica* (12mo/16mo)

It has to be remembered, of course, that maps in any atlas, large or small, frequently varied considerably in size; two maps (or more) were often printed on one sheet and large individual maps were folded to fit the overall atlas size. It follows, therefore, that any size quoted should be accepted only as a guide.

DATING OF MAPS

When referring to dates of issue of atlases and maps (especially loose maps) it is not unusual to find different dates quoted by different authorities. This is not to say that one writer is necessarily 'correct' and others 'wrong' for in so wide a field covering a great number of items it would indeed be surprising if differences of opinion or interpretation were not to occur. Apart from differences of opinion, one has only to think of the unrecorded editions which are discovered, of the research which brings to light unsuspected information about existing editions, to realize that no record, however meticulous, can remain completely accurate for very long.

Where reference is made to a particular map it is conventional to quote the date of its first publication in brackets followed by the date of its actual issue, viz. 'Map of the World (1615) 1623'. If a single unbracketed date is given it may be assumed that the map is from the first edition or was issued only in that year.

CROSS-REFERENCES

Throughout this work every effort has been made to avoid the need to cross refer, which can be time wasting and is often confusing, but in some cases the complexities of the different issues of atlases have defeated attempts at complete simplification. The authors have in mind particularly the Mercator/ Hondius/Jansson series of atlases, full details of which are given under the Mercator heading with shorter references in the appropriate biographies of the Hondius family and Jan Jansson. The Dutch chart makers in the second half of the seventeenth century also posed problems in this respect and there are occasionally others which it is hoped will not be too distracting.

MERIDIANS

Dictionaries define a meridian as a 'circle of constant longitude passing through the terrestrial poles and a given place on the earth's surface intersecting the equator at right angles: the prime, or base meridian, dividing the hemispheres into eastern and western portions.' The word 'meridian' itself is derived from meridies = midday.

Some time in the third century BC Eratosthenes of Alexandria, philosopher, mathematician and astronomer, set out to calculate the circumference of the world basing his theories on the relationship between the estimated distance from Alexandria to Syenë (Aswan) in Lower Egypt and the differences in the angle of the sun at the summer solstice at the two places. His final figure, in spite of many false assumptions, was remarkably accurate, but more important was his imaginary north/south line – or meridian – joining Alexandria and Syenë which he extended to the north to link Rhodes, Byzantium and the estuary of the River Dnieper on the Black Sea, and to the south to Meroë in the Sudan. He placed other meridians at irregular intervals joining the positions of well-known places as they were perceived in his day.

In the following centuries Eratosthenes' ideas and calculations were much criticized, but the use of meridians was accepted and refined, especially by Ptolemy who devised a grid system covering the habitable world based on 36 meridians converging on the North Pole: his zero meridian ran through the area of the Fortunate Isles – the Canaries, then the limit of the known world.

As in so many other matters Ptolemy's concepts were accepted without question in the fifteenth century and for many years ahead the prime meridian continued to be placed through the Canaries, but as other islands further west became known so the zero meridian was adjusted. The islands of St. Mary and St. Michael in the Azores and Isla del Fuego in the Cape Verde group were favourites although the French chose the Isle de Fer (Ferro or Hierro) in the Canaries to be used on all French maps until about the year 1800. Later cartographers, in a spirit of patriotism, placed their prime meridians through their own principal cities, state observatories or even through special landmarks. In the British Isles London was first used (by John Seller) in 1676 and for the first Ordnance Survey maps it was narrowed down to St. Paul's Cathedral although by then the zero meridian through Greenwich Observatory had become widely accepted, especially for marine charts. In the next century the almost universal use of British Admiralty charts was the main factor in the international acceptance in 1884 of Greenwich as the world's prime meridian, finally ending centuries of confusion.

Chapter 11

ITALY

Since classical times the countries bordering the enclosed waters of the Mediterranean had been well versed in the use of maps and sea charts and in Italy, more than anywhere else, the traditional knowledge was kept alive during the many hundreds of years following the collapse of the Roman Empire. By the thirteenth and fourteenth centuries the seamen of Venice, Genoa and Amalfi traded to far countries, from the Black Sea ports and the coasts of Palestine and Egypt in the East to Flanders and the southern coasts of England and Ireland in the West, their voyages guided by portulan charts and the use of the newly invented compass. For a time Italian supremacy in cartography passed to Aragon and the Catalan map makers based on Majorca, but by the year 1400 the power and wealth of the city states of Venice, Genoa, Florence and Milan surpassed any in Europe. Florence, especially, under the rule of the Medici family, became not only a great trading and financial centre but also the focal point of the rediscovery of the arts and learning of the ancient world. In this milieu a number of manuscript world maps were produced, of which one by Fra Mauro (c. 1459) is the most notable, but the event of the greatest importance in the history of cartography occurred in the year 1400 when a Florentine, Palla Strozzi, brought from Constantinople a Greek manuscript copy of Claudius Ptolemy's *Geographia*, which, 1,250 years after its compilation, came as a revelation to scholars in Western Europe. In the following fifty years or so manuscript copies, translated into Latin and other languages, became available in limited numbers but the invention of movable-type printing transformed the scene: the first copy without maps being printed in 1475 followed by many with copper-engraved maps, at Bologna in 1477, Rome 1478, 1490, 1507 and 1508, and Florence 1482.

About the year 1485 the first book of sea charts, compiled by Bartolommeo dalli Sonetti, was printed in Venice and in the first part of the sixteenth century a number of world maps were published, among them one compiled in 1506 by Giovanni Contarini, engraved by Francesco Rosselli, which was the first printed map to show the discoveries in the New World. In the following years there were many attractive and unusual maps of Islands (Isolario) by Bordone, Camocio and Porcacchi, but more important was the work of Giacomo (Jacopo) Gastaldi, a native of Piedmont who started life as an engineer in the service of the Venetian Republic before turning to cartography as a profession. His maps, produced in great variety and quantity, were beautifully drawn copperplate engravings and his style and techniques were widely copied by his contemporaries. From about 1550 to 1580 many of Gastaldi's maps appeared in the collections of maps known as Lafreri 'atlases', a term applied to groups of maps by different cartographers brought together in one binding. As the contents of such collections varied considerably they were no doubt assembled at the special request of wealthy patrons and are now very rare indeed.

About this time, for a variety of historical and commercial reasons, Italy's position as the leading trading and financial nation rapidly declined and with it her superiority in cartography was lost to the vigorous new states in the Low Countries. That is not to say, of course, that Italian skills as map makers were lost entirely for it was not until 1620 that the first printed maps of Italy by an Italian, Giovanni Magini, appeared, and much later in the century there were fine maps by Giacomo de Rossi and Vincenzo Coronelli, the latter leading a revival of interest in cartography at the end of the century. Coronelli was also famous for the construction of magnificent large-size globes and for the foundation in Venice in 1680 of the first geographical society.

In the eighteenth century the best-known names are Antonio Zatta, Rizzi-Zannoni and Giovanni Cassini, examples of whose work are noted in the following pages.

Before leaving this chapter we ought to mention the work of Baptista Boazio who drew a series of maps in *A Summarie and True Discourse of Sir Francis Drake's West Indian Voyage*, published in 1588–89, and who is especially noted for a very fine map of Ireland printed in 1599 which was incorporated in the later editions of the Ortelius atlases. It is perhaps appropriate also to refer to two English map makers who spent many years in exile in Italy: the first, George Lily, famous for the splendid map of the British Isles issued in Rome in 1546, and the second, Robert Dudley, who exactly one hundred years later was responsible for the finest sea atlas of the day, *Dell' Arcano del Mare*, published in Florence. Both of these are described in greater detail elsewhere in this handbook.

Biographies

CLAUDIUS PTOLEMY AD *c.* 87–*c.* 150
The early Italian editions of Ptolemy's *Geographia* up to 1511 are set out below: later editions are shown under the name of the appropriate cartographer or publisher. See also Appendix A for complete list of Ptolemy editions.

c. 1477	Bologna: Latin text: 26 copperplate maps
1478	Rome: do : 27 do 1490, 1507 (plus 6 modern maps), 1508 (plus world map)
c. 1480–82	Florence: Italian text: 31 copperplate maps
1511	Venice : Latin text: 27 woodcut maps plus world map on heart-shaped projection

BARTOLOMMEO DALLI SONETTI (ZAMBERTI) *fl.* 1477–85
Sonetti, whose real name was Zamberti, was a Venetian sea captain who compiled and had published about 1485 an 'island-book'. These were the very first printed sea charts and were the forerunners of a number of similar works which appeared during the following century. The descriptive text was in verse or sonnet form, hence the name by which Zamberti became known.

c. 1485	*Isolario* (island- book) (4to) 49 woodcut charts of the Greek islands 1532 Re-issued with the addition of a world map by Francesco Rosselli

GIOVANNI MATTEO CONTARINI *d.* 1507
FRANCESCO ROSSELLI 1445–*c.* 1513
The world map compiled by Contarini and engraved by Rosselli is the oldest surviving printed map showing any part of the American continent, the only known copy of which is in the British Library. Little is known of Contarini but Rosselli was established in Florence as an engraver, publisher and map seller, the earliest business of that kind of which we have record. He probably engraved some of the 'new' maps in the editions of Ptolemy's *Geographia* published in Florence in 1480–82.

c. 1506	World Map

PIETRO COPPO *c.* 1470–1555
Venetian geographer, of interest for a small woodcut map of the British Isles printed in Venice and a map of Istria.

c. 1520–25	British Isles: woodcut
c. 1524	World Map
1525	Istria: woodcut 1540 Re-issued

BENEDETTO BORDONE 1460–1539
Born in Padua, Bordone trained as an 'illuminator' and wood-engraver, working in Venice where, in 1508, he was given permission by the Senate to print maps of Italy and the world. No copies of these maps seem to have survived and he is known, therefore, only for his *Isolario*, printed in Venice in 1528. Although issued as an 'Island Book' it gave prominence to discoveries in the New World and contained three full-size woodcut maps: the World, on an oval projection probably devised by the Florentine engraver, Francesco Rosselli, a map of Europe as a whole, and one of Greece and the North-Eastern Mediterranean. The remainder, about 80 woodcuts, are small maps or 'charts' set in the text of the book.

1528	*Isolario* (small folio) 1534, 1547, *c.* 1565 Re-issued

GIOVANNI ANDREA DI VAVASSORE *fl. c.* 1520–72
A Venetian engraver and book printer notable for having produced in 1539 what is claimed to be the first printed chart intended for use at sea rather than as a decorative map. Although it was no doubt based on manuscript portulan charts, the distortion of coastlines and lack of scale and landmarks would have made its

BENEDETTO BORDONE   *Island of Kalóyeros/Caloiero*. Published in Bordone's *Isolario*, 1547. A rocky islet in the Aegean, possibly in the neighbourhood of Kos, surmounted by a chapel to which two Christian monks devoted their lives. In spite of their presence it was a place of ill repute to seafarers. According to one account, their unusual method of safeguarding themselves against pirates was circumvented by stratagem and they were carried off to bondage in nearby Turkey.

practical use hazardous in the extreme. Vavassore also issued a 4-sheet map of Italy which was eventually used by Magini in compiling his Atlas of Italy. Throughout his life Vavassore continued to use woodcut engraving for producing maps although most of his contemporaries followed Gastaldi in the use of copper.

c. 1532–59   Maps of Spain, France and other European
              countries
1539   Chart of the Adriatic, Aegean and Eastern
              Mediterranean
              1541, 1558 Re-issued
c. 1550–60   Map of Italy: 4 sheets

GEORGE LILY *fl.* 1528–59
See Chapter 15 for a biographical note and details of his map of the British Isles.

GIACOMO (JACOPO) GASTALDI *c.* 1500–*c.* 65
Praised as 'that most excellent of cartographers',

Gastaldi was a native of Piedmont and worked in early life as an engineer in the service of the Venetian Republic before turning in the early 1540s to cartography as a profession. Eventually he was appointed Cosmographer to the Republic. From 1544 onwards he produced a large number of maps beautifully engraved on copper, using a style which was widely copied by his contemporaries; indeed, his technique marked the final transition away from woodblock printing which had been predominant for so long. Apart from compiling maps of the world and the continents he was responsible for the maps in an edition of Ptolemy issued in 1548 and in a noted collection of voyages and travels called *Delle Navigazioni e Viaggi* by Giovanni Battista Ramusio (1485–1557). Many of his maps were included in the Lafreri collections of maps in the 1560–80 period.

Gastaldi is credited with popularizing the idea that a route round the north of the American continent led to a passage which he called the Strait of Anian, named

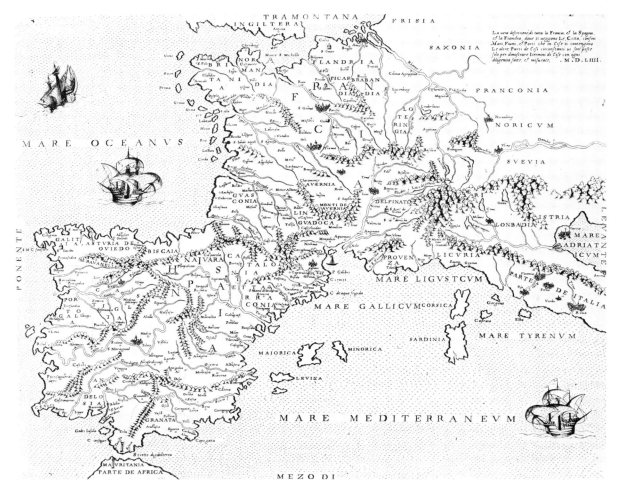

ANTONIO LAFRERI   *La Francia & la Spagna & la Fiandra*. This map of South-Western Europe published in Rome *c.* 1554 was the first map of the area issued by Lafreri.

after Marco Polo's Kingdom of Anian. The name appeared on many maps until well into the seventeenth century.

1546   *Universale*: the World on oval projection. Widely copied by other cartographers of the period.

1548–99   Ptolemy's *Geographia*: Venice. The first edition in Italian, translation by Pietro Mattioli of Siena and the first printed 'pocket atlas': 170 × 115 mm
            (See Appendix A for issue details.)

c. 1554–65 Maps in Ramusio's *Delle Navigazioni e Viaggi*
            Numerous re-issues

1559–64   Maps of Africa, Asia and Europe

1561   Map of Italy: 3 sheets

ANTONIO LAFRERI (Rome) 1512–77
MICHELE TRAMEZINI (Rome) *fl.* 1539–82
ANTONIO SALAMANCA (Rome) *fl.* 1553–62
CLAUDIO DUCHETTI (Rome) *fl.* 1554–97
GIOVANNI FRANCESCO CAMOCIO (Venice) *fl.* 1558–75
DONATO and FERANDO BERTELLI (Venice) *fl.* 1559–84
PAOLO FORLANI (Venice) *fl.* 1560–74

For a short time round the middle of the sixteenth century, in the period between the publication of Münster's *Geographia* (1540) and *Cosmographia* (1544) in Basle and the Ortelius *Theatrum Orbis Terrarum* in Antwerp (1570), the increasing demand for sheet maps was met by engravers and publishers in Rome and Venice, of whom the above-named were the most active. It became the practice in those cities to issue in one volume maps by various cartographers, the maps varying in shape and size but being bound in uniform style and usually arranged in standard 'Ptolemaic' order. The collections, of which no two are quite alike, were probably made up to individual requirements and are now exceedingly rare. They have become known generically as Lafreri Atlases from Lafreri's imprint in a number of them but similar collections were issued by other publishers.

c. 1550–75　Map collections with varying contents and without title until c. 1570–72 when a frontispiece showing the title 'Tavole Moderne di Geografia' and a figure of Atlas was included in some issues

NICOLO ZENO fl. 1558

In 1558 Nicolo Zeno published in Venice a book of travels, accompanied by a map, based on manuscripts which he claimed gave an account of a voyage to the Arctic regions by his ancestors, Nicolo and Antonio Zeno, in the year 1380. Imaginary or not, the map gave a remarkably accurate picture of the lands of the far north and was accepted as authentic by Frobisher, Davis and other explorers and, not least, by Mercator.

1558　*Carta da Navegar de Nicolo et Antonio Zeni*:
woodcut: 275 × 375 mm
1561–74 Re-engraved on copper plate by G. Ruscelli and published in Venice: 180 × 240 mm

GIROLAMO RUSCELLI c. 1504–66

Ruscelli was editor of a revised and expanded edition of Ptolemy's *Geographia* which was issued in Venice several times between 1561 and the end of the century. The newly engraved maps were based, generally, on those compiled by Giacomo Gastaldi for the Venice edition of 1548.

1561　*Geographia*
1562, 1564, 1574, 1598–99 Re-issued
(See Appendix A for further detail.)

BOLOGNINO ZALTIERI fl. 1566

Noted for the publication in Venice of a map of North America which was the first printed map to show the Strait of Anian as propounded a few years earlier by Giacomo Gastaldi.

c. 1566　*Il Disegno del discoperto della nova Franza*

GIOVANNI FRANCESCO CAMOCIO fl. 1558–75

Apart from contributing many individual maps to the Lafreri Atlases (q.v.), Camocio also issued in Venice an *Island Book* and an important 4-sheet map of the world copied from a work, now lost, by Gastaldi.

1569　*Cosmographia Universalis* (after Giacomo Gastaldi)
1581 Re-issued

1572–74　*Isole famose*

TOMASO PORCACCHI DA CASTILIONE 1530–85

Following Bordone and Camocio, Porcacchi issued in Venice another 'Island Book' incorporating later discoveries and including maps of the world and the continents. It continued to appear in new editions for over a century.

1572　*L'Isole piu Famose del Mondo* (4to)
Miniature maps engraved by Girolamo Porro
1576, 1590, 1604, 1605, 1620, 1713 Re-issued
1586 Re-engraved: many reissues

GIROLAMO PORRO fl. 1567–96

A Venetian engraver and book illustrator who engraved maps in the following works:

1572　*L'Isole piu Famose del Mondo* (4to) by Tomaso Porcacchi
1596　Ptolemy's *Geographia* (4to) edited by Giovanni Magini
(See Appendix A for further detail.)

MATTEO RICCI 1552–1610

A Jesuit priest who spent much of his life in the Far East and became known as 'the Apostle of China'. Ricci compiled a map of the world which was printed in China in 1584 followed by two later versions also printed there.

1584　World map: Shao-King
1599 Re-issued in Nanking
1602 Re-issued in Peking

LIVIO SANUTO c. 1530–c. 86　★

1588　*Geografia dell'Africa* (large folio): Venice
The first 'atlas' of Africa containing 12 maps engraved by Giulio Sanuto

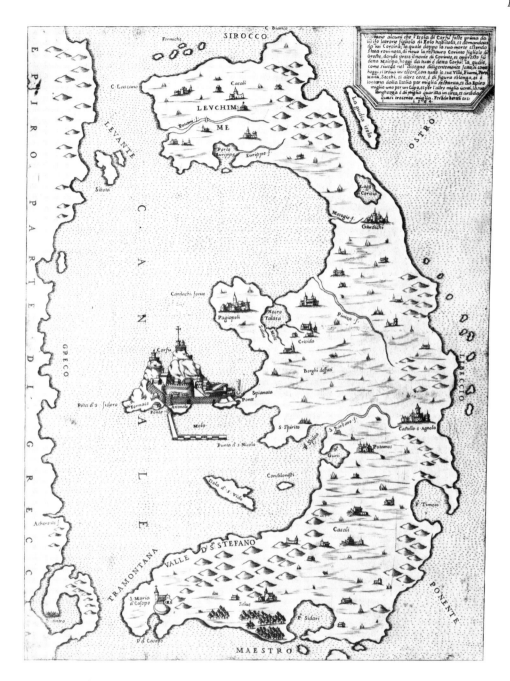

FERANDO BERTELLI   *L'Isola di Corfu.* Map of Corfu published in a Lafreri Atlas, Rome 1564.

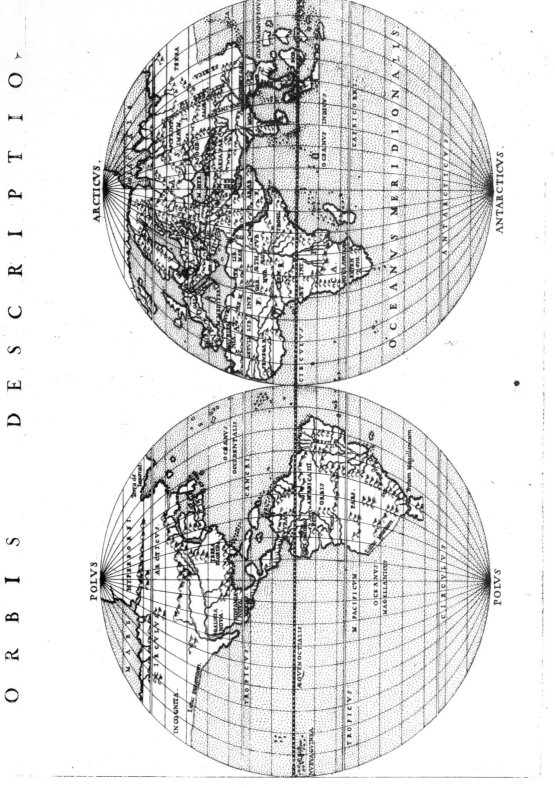

ORBIS DESCRIPTIO

GIROLAMO RUSCELLI *Orbis Descriptio.* This map, the first in an Atlas to show the Old and New Worlds in separate hemispheres, was used by Ruscelli to illustrate his edition of Ptolemy's *Geographia*, first issued in 1561. This example is dated 1574.

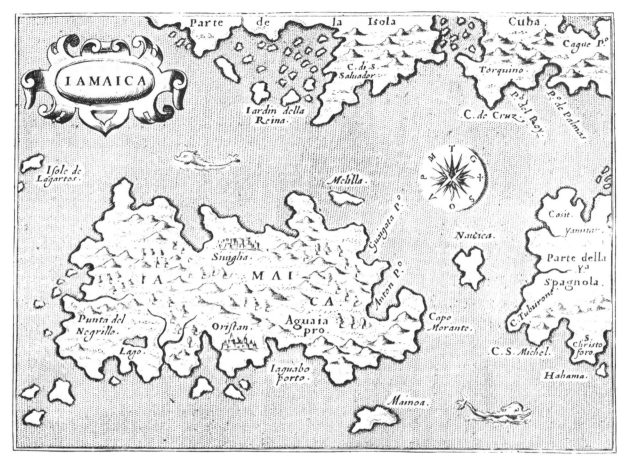

TOMASO PORCACCHI DA CASTILIONE   *Jamaica*. One of the many island maps included in Porcacchi's *L'Isole piu Famose del Mondo*, first published in 1572.

BAPTISTA BOAZIO *fl.* 1588–1606

An Italian cartographer who spent many years working in England and is particularly noted for his map of Ireland which was widely copied and was used in later editions of the Ortelius *Theatrum Orbis Terrarum*.

1588–89	A chart and four maps in *A Summarie and True Discourse of Sir Francis Drake's West Indian Voyage* by Walter Bigges, published in Leyden (1588) and London (1589)
1599	Ireland Engraved by Renold Elstracke: published by John Sudbury

FILIPPO PIGAFETTA 1533–1603

1590–91	Map of Eastern and Southern Africa: Rome 1597 English edition

GIOVANNI BOTERO 1540–1617

1591	World Map: Rome (195 × 295 mm)
1596	Maps including the Continents and the British Isles Issued in many editions in Cologne and other cities until *c.* 1662

GIUSEPPE ROSACCIO *c.* 1550–1620

1594–95	*Il Mondo*: Florence Re-issued a number of times with different titles until *c.* 1724
1598	Ptolemy's *Geografia* Revision of edition by Girolamo Ruscelli, first published in 1561
1606	*Viaggio da Venetia a Constantinopli*: Venice (4to) 72 charts, maps and town plans
1615	*Teatro del Cielo e della Terra* (12mo): woodcut maps *c.* 1640 Re-issued

GIOVANNI ANTONIO MAGINI 1555–1617

A native of Padua, Magini was the first Italian to prepare a printed atlas of his native country although it was only completed and published three years after his death by his son, Fabio. The maps were based on those of Gastaldi, Vavassore and others and many were engraved by Benjamin Wright, the noted English engraver who was specially commissioned to carry out the task.

Magini also edited a new edition of Ptolemy's *Geographia* with maps engraved by Girolamo Porro.

1596–1621	Ptolemy's *Geographia* (See Appendix A for issue details.)
1620	*Italia* Atlas of Italy containing about 55–60 maps

ARNOLDO DI ARNOLDI *fl. c.* 1595–1602

Arnoldi, an engraver employed in Bologna by Magini, the noted Italian cartographer, compiled a reduced version of the famous wall map by Petrus Plancius (1592). All the issues of these maps are extremely rare.

1600	World Map: Siena (10 sheets). (Published by Matteo Florini) *c.* 1640, 1669 Re-issued in Siena by Pietro Petrucci

SIR ROBERT DUDLEY 1573–1649

See Chapter 15 for a biographical note and details of his sea charts.

1646	*Dell' Arcano del Mare* 1661 Re-issued

MARTINO MARTINI 1614–61

A Jesuit priest who compiled remarkably accurate maps of China and a map of Japan which were published in Amsterdam in 1655 and were also incorporated in Blaeu's *Theatrum Orbis Terrarum* in that year. The maps were used in later years by other publishers including Jansson and Schenk.

1655	*Novus Atlas Sinensis*

FRANCESCO MARIA LEVANTO *fl. c.* 1664

c. 1664	*Prima parte dello Specchio del Mare*: atlas consisting of 25 maps and charts of the Mediterranean published in Genoa

GIACOMO GIOVANNI DE ROSSI *fl.* 1674–90

1674	World map based on Sanson
1677	Maps of Asia and North America
c. 1690	*Mercurio Geografico* Further editions to 1714

VINCENZO MARIA CORONELLI 1650–1718

Ordained as a Franciscan priest, Coronelli spent most of his life in Venice, becoming a noted theologian and being appointed, in 1699, Father General of his order. By that time he was already famous as a mathematician, cartographer and globe maker and his influence led to a revival of interest in these subjects in Italy at the end of the seventeenth century. He was certainly the greatest cartographer of his time there and became Cosmographer to the Venetian Republic, taught geography in the University and, in 1680, founded the first geographical society, the 'Academia Cosmografica degli Argonauti'.

In his lifetime he compiled and engraved over 500 maps including a large 2-volume work, the *Atlante Veneto*, somewhat reminiscent of Robert Dudley's *Dell' Arcano del Mare*; he is equally well known for his construction of very large terrestrial and celestial globes even finer than those of Blaeu, including one, 15 feet in diameter, made for Louis XIV of France.

1690–91	*Atlante Veneto*
1696–97	*Isolario dell' Atlante Veneto*
1692	*Corso geografico universale* 1695 Re-issued
1693	*Epitome Cosmografica*
1693	*Libro dei Globi* 1701 Re-issued
1695	World Map
1696	Pacific Ocean

GIOVANNI-BATTISTA CANALI *fl.* 1701

1701	The World and the Continents: Padua

RAFFAELO SAVONAROLA *fl.* 1713

1713	*Universus terrarum orbis*

GIOVANNI ANTONIO RIZZI-ZANNONI 1736–1814

Rizzi-Zannoni was a noted astronomer, surveyor and mathematician of great versatility. His achievements included a large scale map of Poland, appointments as Geographer to the Venetian Republic and as Hydrographer to the Dépôt de Marine in Paris. The maps in his various atlases were beautifully engraved, showing minute detail and embellished with elaborate cartouches. His earlier atlases were published in Paris but

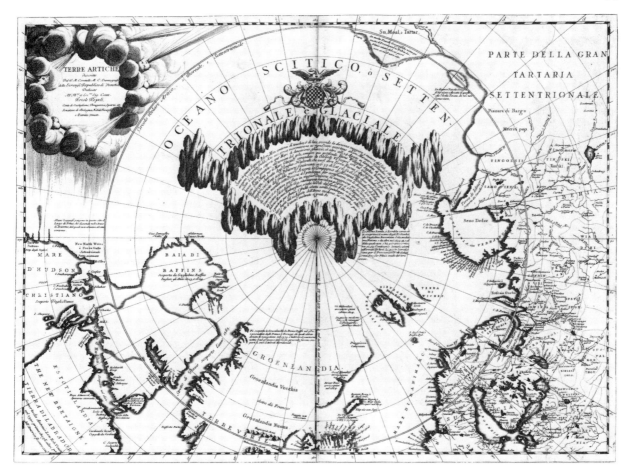

VINCENZO CORONELLI *Terre Artiche*. Map of the Arctic Regions, published in the first part of Coronelli's marine atlas, *Atlante Veneto*, Venice, 1690–91.

his later works first appeared in Naples.

1760	*Etrennes géographiques*: Paris	
	Maps compiled in association with L. A. du Caille	
1762	*Atlas géographique*: Paris	
1763	*Atlas géographique et militaire*: Paris	
1765	*Atlas historique de la France*: Paris	
1765	*Le Petit Neptune François*: Paris	
1772	*Carte Générale de la Pologne* (24 sheets): Paris	
1792	*Atlante Maritimo delle due Sicilie*: Naples	
1795	*Nuova carta della Lombardia*: Naples	

ANTONIO ZATTA *fl. c.* 1775–97

A Venetian cartographer and publisher whose atlases include maps of groups of English, Scottish and Irish counties.

c. 1775–85	*Atlante novissimo*: 218 maps in 4 volumes	
c. 1799	*Nuovo atlante*	

P. SANTINI *fl.* 1776–84

An Italian publisher working in Venice whose major work, an *Atlas Universel*, included a large number of maps by French cartographers.

1776–84	*Atlas Universel*: 2 volumes
1783	*Atlas portatif d'Italie*

GIOVANNI MARIA CASSINI *fl.* 1792–1805

1792	*Nuovo atlante geografico universale*	Vol. I
1797	*do*	Vol. II
1801	*do*	Vol. III
1793	*General Map of Italy: 15 sheets*	

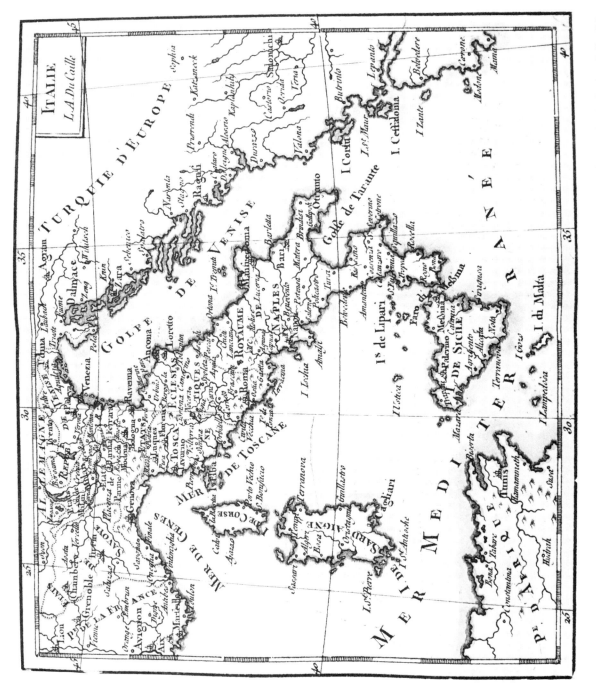

GIOVANNI ANTONIO RIZZI-ZANNONI *Italy.* This map appeared in a very small atlas entitled *Etrennes Géographiques* published 'Chez Ballard' in Paris in 1760, containing maps based on those by Rizzi-Zannoni.

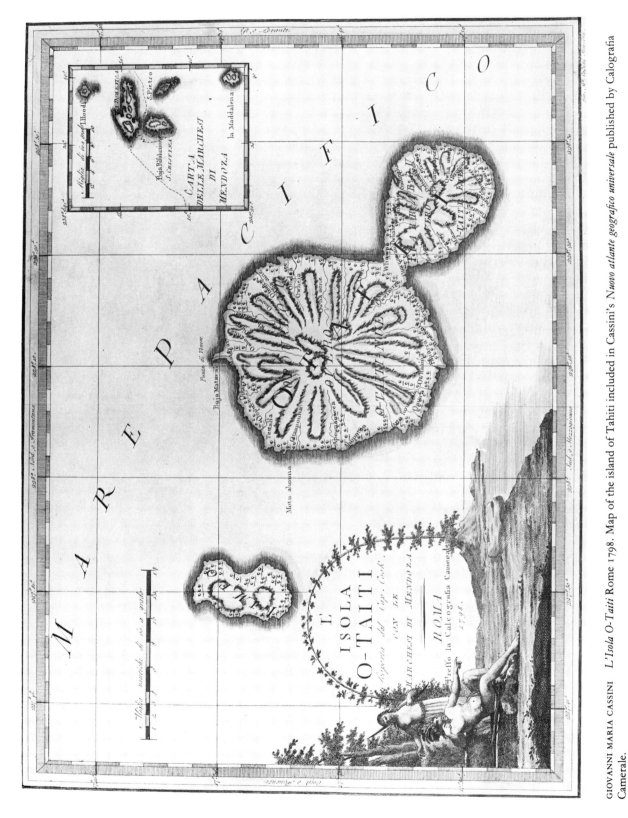

GIOVANNI MARIA CASSINI   *L'Isola O-Taiti* Rome 1798. Map of the island of Tahiti included in Cassini's *Nuovo atlante geografico universale* published by Calografia Camerale.

Specialist References

BAGROW, L., *History of Cartography*

HOWSE, D. and SANDERSON, M., *The Sea Chart*
Gives a number of examples of early Italian sea charts

NORDENSKIÖLD, A. E., *Facsimile Atlas to the Early History of Cartography*
Reproductions of Ptolemaic and other early maps

SHIRLEY, R. W., *The Mapping of the World*
Numerous examples of early Italian maps with descriptive detail

THEATRUM ORBIS TERRARUM NV
Bartolommeo (Sonetti): *Isolario*
Bordone: *Isolario*
Ptolemy: *Geographia/Cosmographia* 1477, 1478, 1513, 1540
Sanuto: *Geografia dell' Africa*
Magini: *Italia*
Coronelli: *Libro dei Globi*
Reproductions of complete atlases

TOOLEY, R. V. *Maps in Italian Atlases of the 16th Century*
Detailed analysis of early Italian maps

Chapter 12
GERMANY & AUSTRIA

In the latter half of the fifteenth century Germany, though nominally still part of the Holy Roman Empire, was a fragmented land, split into a score of principalities and Imperial Cities, fiercely jealous of each other but having in common an extraordinary creative urge which produced builders of great churches and cathedrals, workers in stone and wood, metal engravers, painters and makers of scientific instruments, who were the envy of the world. Of all their achievements, the invention of movable-type printing was to have the most profound effect on human relationships. Printing industries soon grew up in many cities, including Nuremberg and Augsburg where wood engraving already flourished and which, with Basle and Strassburg, were also the centres of geographical knowledge. Not only were local and regional maps produced in considerable variety and quantity, but more particularly the geographers and mathematicians of Nuremberg are famous for their globes of the world, some of which are still preserved.

The most important map of the whole of Germany produced in this period was a manuscript dated *c.* 1464 by Nicholas Cusanus (Khryfts), Cardinal, humanist and scholar, friend of Toscanelli, the Italian geographer, and one of the most brilliant men of his day. The map covering Germany, Southern Scandinavia and the Baltic was printed in 1491, long after the author's death, and it served as a model for a similar map in the Nuremberg Chronicle. We have written in some detail in Chapter 4 of this famous book, first published in 1493, which contained a great number of woodcut views and maps, but as far as cartography is concerned the printing of Ptolemy's *Geographia* at Ulm in 1482 (and 1486) – the first edition with woodcut maps – was an event of the greatest importance. The most ambitious editions of the Ptolemy maps appeared in 1513 in Strassburg, containing not only maps of the ancient world but also twenty new ones, including one of the 'New World', based on the latest contemporary knowledge. This was produced under the guidance of Martin Waldseemüller, a German cartographer, at St Dié in Lorraine, at that time a noted centre of learning. Other editions followed in the years up to 1541, overlapping with the newer work of Sebastian Münster, an eminent mathematician and linguist, who settled in Basle and whose prolific output of atlases and maps contained also many plans and views of the great cities of the time. These in turn were superseded by Braun and Hogenberg's *Civitates Orbis Terrarum* issued in Cologne between the years 1572 and 1618, which was one of the most famous publications of the period.

In the seventeenth century Dutch supremacy in map making and publishing overshadowed Germany no less than England and France and there was to be no revival until the foundation in Nuremberg about the year 1700 of the printing firm of J. B. Homann, whose business acumen started a resurgence of map publishing. He became a member of the Berlin Academy of Sciences and was appointed Geographer to the Emperor in 1715. The business was continued by his son, Johann Christoph, and was eventually bequeathed to the founder's son-in-law on condition that he continued the business under the name of Homann Heirs. Other notable publishing houses active during the century were run by Matthäus Seutter and Tobias Lotter in the rival city of Augsburg.

At the end of the century, between 1799 and 1804, the German naturalist and traveller, Alexander von Humboldt, made epic journeys in South America and, although not primarily a cartographer, he added immensely to knowledge of the northern areas of the continent. His travels and studies there led him to formulate new theories in the spheres of meteorology, geology and oceanography which had world-wide application. Indeed, after Napoleon and Wellington, he was the most famous man of his time in Europe and his ideas made a major contribution to German and European cartography in the nineteenth century. In particular, his assertion that maps should embrace far more than a simple topographical view induced German cartographers to publish 'physical' atlases in the modern sense which were unsurpassed until our own times.

Biographies

CLAUDIUS PTOLEMY AD *c.* 87–*c.* 150
The edition of Ptolemy's *Geographia* printed at Ulm in 1482 was the first published outside Italy and the first with woodcut maps; it contained 26 maps based on Ptolemy and 6 'modern' maps. Later German issues are shown under the name of the appropriate cartographer. See also Appendix A for a complete list of Ptolemy editions.

1482   *Geographia*
        1486 Re-issued

★
★

MARTIN WALDSEEMÜLLER *c.* 1470–1518
Waldseemüller, born in Radolfzell, a village on what is now the Swiss shore of Lake Constance, studied for the church at Freiburg and eventually settled in St Dié at the Court of the Duke of Lorraine, at that time a noted patron of the arts. There, in the company of likeminded savants, he devoted himself to a study of cartography and cosmography, the outcome of which was a world map on 12 sheets, now famous as the map on which the name 'America' appears for the first time. Suggested by Waldseemüller in honour of Amerigo Vespucci (latinised: Americus Vesputius) whom he regarded, quite inexplicably, as the discoverer of the New World, the new name became generally accepted by geographers before the error could be rectified, and its use was endorsed by Mercator on his world map printed in 1538. Although only one copy is now known of Waldseemüller's map and of the later *Carta Marina* (1516) they were extensively copied in various forms by other cartographers of the day. Waldseemüller is best known for his preparation from about 1507 onwards of the maps for an issue of Ptolemy's *Geographia*, now regarded as the most important edition of that work. Published by other hands in Strassburg in 1513, it included 20 'modern' maps and passed through a number of editions which are noted below. It remained the most authoritative work of its time until the issue of Münster's *Geographia* in 1540 and *Cosmographia* in 1544.

1507   World Map (12 sheets)
1513   Ptolemy's *Geographia*
        Strassburg: 47 woodcut maps published by Jacobus Eszler and Georgius Ubelin (large folio)
        1520 Strassburg: re-issued
        1522 Strassburg: 50 woodcut maps, reduced in size, revised by Laurent Fries (Laurentius Frisius) and included the earliest map showing the name 'America' which is likely to be available to collectors
        1525 Strassburg: re-issue of 1522 maps
        1535 Lyon: re-issue of 1522 maps, edited by Michael Servetus who was subsequently tried for heresy and burned at the stake in 1553, ostensibly because of derogatory comments in the atlas about the Holy Land – the fact that the notes in question had not even been written by Servetus, but were copied from earlier editions, left his Calvinist persecutors unmoved
        1541 Vienne (Dauphiné): re-issue of the Lyon edition – the offensive comments about the Holy Land have been deleted
1516   *Carta Marina*: World Map on 12 sheets

PETER APIAN (PETRUS APIANUS) 1495–1552
1520   *Tipus Orbis Universalis* (World Map): woodcut on heart-shaped projection
1524   *Cosmographia*: woodcut maps (4to)
        1533, 1534, 1545 (including World Map on heart-shaped projection by Gemma Frisius) and numerous other editions to *c.* 1650
1530   World Map: woodcut on heart-shaped projection
1534   Europe: woodcut

SEBASTIAN MÜNSTER 1489–1552
Following the various editions of Waldseemüller's maps, the names of three cartographers dominate the sixteenth century: Mercator, Ortelius and Münster, and of these three Münster probably had the widest influence in spreading geographical knowledge throughout Europe in the middle years of the century. His *Cosmographia*, issued in 1544, contained not only the latest maps and views of many well-known cities, but included an encyclopaedic amount of detail about the known – and unknown – world and undoubtedly must have been one of the most widely read books of

MARTIN WALDSEEMÜLLER *Tabula Moderna Germanie* Strassburg 1522 (woodcut). An interesting map embracing most of Central Europe.

Lesnordeste.   Orient, o Leste.   Lessueste.

Charte Cosmographique, auec les Noms, Proprietez, Nature & Operations des Vents.

Nordnordeste.   Septentrion, o Nord.   Nordnordeste.

Vestnordueste.   Occident, o Weste.   WestSudueste.

Sudueste.   Midy, ou Sud.   Susueste.

K.

PETER APIAN   *World Map.* Map on heart-shaped projection by Gemma Frisius first published in Apian's *Cosmographia* in 1545.

SEBASTIAN MÜNSTER *Regiones Septentrionales–Scandinavia* Basle 1588–1628. This woodcut map engraved 'in the copperplate manner' from Münster's *Cosmosgraphia* replaced that used in the early editions from 1540 to 1544.

its time, going through nearly forty editions in six languages.

An eminent German mathematician and linguist, Münster became Professor of Hebrew at Heidelberg and later at Basle, where he settled in 1529. In 1528, following his first mapping of Germany, he appealed to German scholars to send him 'descriptions, so that all Germany with its villages, towns, trades etc. may be seen as in a mirror', even going so far as to give instructions on how they should 'map' their own localities. The response was far greater than expected and much information was sent by foreigners as well as Germans so that, eventually, he was able to include

many up-to-date, if not very accurate, maps in his atlases. He was the first to provide a separate map of each of the four known Continents and the first separately printed map of England. His maps, printed from woodblocks, are now greatly valued by collectors. His two major works, the *Geographia* and *Cosmographia* were published in Basle by his step-son, Henri Petri, who continued to issue many editions after Münster's death of the plague in 1552.

1525	Map of Germany
1532	*Typus Cosmographia Universalis*
	1537, 1555 Re-issued

1538	Maps in Münster's editions of the *Polyhistor* by Solinus and *De Situ Orbis* of Pomponius Mela (8vo) 1543 Re-issued
1540	Ptolemy's *Geographia*: Basle, Henri Petri: 48 maps (4to) 1541, 1542 Re-issued 1545 Re-issued with some amendments and 6 new maps 1551, 1552 Re-issue of 1545 maps
1544	*Cosmographia Universalis*: Basle, Henri Petri (4to) 1545, 1546, 1548, 1550 (enlarged) and further editions, about 30 in all, to 1578: text in German, Latin, French and Italian (Italian editions printed in Venice 1571, 1575) 1588 Re-issued by Sebastian Petri, followed by four further editions: 1592, 1598, 1614, 1628. In some cases detail from earlier editions is omitted and it may well be that the maps were hastily re-engraved to prolong the life of the Cosmography in the face of competition from Ortelius and others. These were woodcut maps but engraved in the 'copperplate' manner.
1571	Münster's maps issued in an edition of Strabo's *Geographia – Strabonis noblissimi et doctissimi philosophi acque geographi rerum geographicarum*: Greek and Latin text: 27 separate maps and 6 in text

SIMON GRYNAEUS *fl.* 1532

The world map detailed below was published in a collection of voyages by John Huttich edited by Grynaeus. Apart from the elegance of its design it is important as the first printed map to indicate the rotation of the globe on its own axis.

1532	*Typus Cosmographicus Universalis* (World Map): woodcut map: design attributed (doubtfully) to Hans Holbein the Younger 1537, 1555 and other re-issues

JACOB ZIEGLER 1470–1549

1532	*Quae intus continentur etc*: Strassburg, containing 8 woodcut maps, 1 map of Scandinavia (the first printed map to show Finland) and 7 maps of the Biblical lands 1536 Re-issued

JOHANNES HONTER 1498–1549

c. 1542	*Rudimentorum Cosmographicorum*: 13 woodcut maps 1546, 1549, 1564, 1570 Re-issued

WOLFGANG LAZIUS 1514–65

Hungarian historian and cartographer whose work was published in Vienna. His early maps of Central Europe were used by Mercator and Ortelius, among others, in the preparation of their atlases. It can be claimed that his Austrian atlas of 1561 was one of the first three national atlases, the others being by Johann Stumpf (Switzerland, 1548–52) and Christopher Saxton (1579).

1545	Austria: large-scale map 1565 Reduced version: Venice
1556	Hungary: large-scale map 1559 Reduced version: Rome
1561	*Typi Chorographici Prouin-Austriae* (Atlas of the Austrian Provinces): Vienna (published by Michael Zimmerman) First printed atlas of Austria covering the hereditary lands of the Austrian crown

PHILIPP APIAN 1531–89

1554–61	Large-scale map of Bavaria 1568 Reduced edition on 24 sheets

CASPAR VOPELL 1511–64

1556	*Typo de la Carta Cosmographica* (World Map): woodcut

★

GEORG BRAUN 1541–1622 and FRANS HOGENBERG *c.* 1536–88

In Chapter 7 on Town Plans we include a description of the *Civitates Orbis Terrarum* and note there the dates of issue of plans of various British towns; here we confine ourselves to the general issue details of the first and subsequent editions.

1572	*Civitates Orbis Terrarum*	Vol. I
1575	do	Vol. II
1581	do	Vol. III
c. 1588	do	Vol. IV
c. 1598	do	Vol. V
1618	do	Vol. VI

These volumes were published originally with Latin text followed by re-issues with German and French translations. Volume VI comprised an issue of 'Supplementary' plans. Sometime after 1618 the plates passed into possession of Abraham Hogenberg who was responsible for a number of further re-issues and after his death the plates were acquired by Jan Jansson. Using them as a basis Jansson published an 8-volume edition and this in turn was followed by further re-issues.

1652–57	*Illustriorum Germania Superior (etc) urbium tabulae* (town plans): 8 volumes: Latin text: Jan Jansson
	1682 Re-issued by Jansson's heirs in abridged form – no text
c. 1694–1700	*Theatrum praecipuarum totius Europae urbium* by Frederick de Wit
1729	*La Galerie Agréable du Monde*, by Pieter van der Aa, reproduced many plans from plates formerly in F. de Wit's possession
c. 1750	Re-issued for the last time by Cornelis Mortier and Johannes Covens

HEINRICH BÜNTING 1545–1606

c. 1581–85	*Itinerarium – Sacrae Scripturae*, including World Map in clover-leaf form
	Several re-issues in various languages as late as 1650

JOHANNES MAURITIUS (MYRITIUS) *fl.* 1590

1590	*Universalis orbis descriptio*: World Map: woodcut (4to)

THEODORE DE BRY c. 1527–98

De Bry was an engraver, bookseller and publisher, active in Frankfurt-am-Main, who is known to have engraved a number of charts in Waghenaer's *The Mariners Mirrour* published in London in 1588. In that same year, also in London, an account was published by Thomas Hariot, illustrated by the artist John White, describing Raleigh's abortive attempt to found a colony in Virginia, and this was to be the inspiration for de Bry's major work, the series of *Grands Voyages* and *Petits Voyages*. In all, 54 parts of these two works were issued containing very fine illustrations and beautiful, and now very rare, maps, much sought after by collectors.

Grands Voyages: Accounts of voyages to North and South America: Frankfurt-am-Main

1590	Part 1 by Theodore de Bry, published in English, French, German, Latin
1592–97	Parts 2–6 by Theodore de Bry, published in German and Latin
1598–1602	Parts 7–9 published by de Bry's widow and his sons in German and Latin
1619–30	Parts 10–14 published by Matthäus Merian in German and Latin

Petits Voyages: Accounts of voyages to India and the Far East: Frankfurt-am-Main

c. 1598–1628	Parts 1–13 started by Theodore de Bry, continued by his widow and sons and completed by Matthäus Merian, in German and Latin (Part 13 in German only)

MATTHEW QUAD 1557–1613

A German cartographer active in Cologne at the end of the sixteenth century: his maps were printed by Johannes Bussemacher.

1592	*Europae totius orbis terrarum* (small folio)
	1594 and 1596 Re-issued
c. 1600	*Geographisch Handtbuch*
	1608 Maps re-issued in *Fasciculus geographicus* (small folio)

PHILIPP CLÜVER 1580–1622

Clüver was born in Danzig and after studying at Leyden and Oxford, he became interested in historical geography; his subsequent publications made a wide and influential contribution to knowledge of the subject.

1616–31	*Germania Antiqua*
1619	*Sicilia Antiqua*
	1659, c. 1724 Re-issued
1624	*Italia Antiqua*
	1659, 1674, 1724 Re-issued
1624	*Introductionis in Universam Geographicam* (4to)
	1667, 1676, 1683, 1711, 1729 and later issues

PHILIPP ECKEBRECHT *fl.* 1627–30

1630	*Nova Orbis Terrarum*
	World Map to accompany the Rudolphine Tables (Star Catalogue) by Johannes Kepler – the first printed map to show parts of the North and West coasts of Australia

MATTHÄUS MERIAN 1593–1650
MATTHÄUS MERIAN (son) 1621–87
Merian was a notable Swiss engraver, born in Basle, subsequently studying in Zurich and then moving to Frankfurt where he met Theodore de Bry, whose daughter he married. In Frankfurt he spent most of his working life, and with Martin Zeiller (1589–1661), a German geographer, and later with his own son, he produced a series of *Topographia* consisting of 21 volumes including a very large number of town plans as well as maps of most countries and a World Map – a very popular work issued in many editions. He also took over and completed the later parts and editions of the *Grand Voyages* and *Petits Voyages* originally started by de Bry in 1590.

c. 1640–   *Topographia* (21 volumes)
1730

JOHANN GEORG JUNG 1583–1641
GEORG KONRAD JUNG 1612–91
1641   *Deutsche Reisekarte* or *Totius Germaniae Novum Itinerarium*
           The first comprehensive road map of Central Europe covering Germany, the Netherlands, Switzerland, Bohemia and neighbouring parts of France, Italy and Poland

★ ATHANASIUS KIRCHER c. 1601–80
A scientific scholar, Kircher published a number of works including one on compass variations, but he is best remembered as the inventor of the magic lantern! Maps in his book *Mundus Subterraneus* were the first to describe tides and ocean currents besides showing the sites of all the volcanoes known at that time. Also included was a map of the island of 'Atlantis'.

c. 1665   *Tabula Geographica-Hydrographica motus oceani*

HANS GEORG BODENEHR 1631–1704
1677–82   Atlas of Germany

HIOB LUDOLF 1624–1704
A German scholar who wrote a History of Ethiopia published in 1681. His map, based on details in a notable book of the time, *A Voyage to Abyssinia*, was engraved and published by his son Christian Ludolf.

1683   *Habessinia seu Abassia Presbyteri Johannis Regio*

JACOB VON SANDRART 1630–1708
Active as a portrait painter in Nuremberg, Sandrart also produced a decorative map of Africa.

1700   *Accuratissima totius Africae Tabulae* (engraved by J. B. Homann)

JERIMIAS WOLFF 1663–1720
c. 1700–02   The World and the Continents: Augsburg

HEINRICH SCHERER 1628–1704
A professor of mathematics and cartographer in Munich, Scherer issued one of the first series of thematic atlases (1703).

1702   *Atlas Marinus*
1703   *Geographia politica/naturalis/hierarchia*
1710   *Atlas Novus*

JOHANN BAPTIST HOMANN c. 1663–1724
JOHANN CHRISTOPH HOMANN c. 1703–30
Following the long period of Dutch domination, the Homann family became the most important map publishers in Germany in the eighteenth century, the business being founded by J. B. Homann in Nuremberg about the year 1702. Soon after publishing his first atlas in 1707 he became a member of the Berlin Academy of Sciences and, in 1715, he was appointed Geographer to the Emperor. After the founder's death in 1724, the firm was continued under the direction of his son until 1730 and was then bequeathed to his heirs on condition that it traded under the name of Homann Heirs. In fact, the firm remained in being until the next century and had a wide influence on map publishing in Germany. Apart from the atlases noted below, the firm published a very large number of individual maps.

1702–07   *Atlas novus terrarum*
           1712 Enlarged edition with re-issues to c. 1753
c. 1714   *Neuer atlas*
           Re-issues to c. 1730
1719   *Atlas Methodicus*
1730   *America Septentrionali Britannorum*
1737   *Grosser atlas*
           Re-issues to c. 1770

MATTHEW QUAD *World Map.* First published in Cologne in 1596 in Quad's *Europae totius orbis terrarum.*

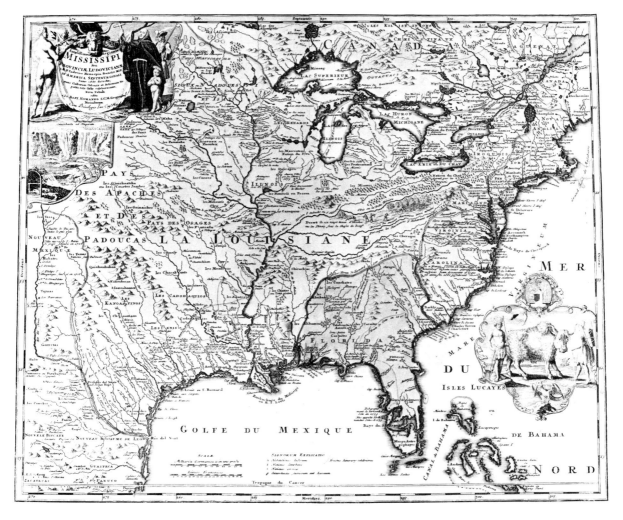

JOHANN BAPTIST HOMANN   *Mississipi seu Provinciae Ludovicianae* Nuremberg 1719. Map of the Mississippi and Louisiana, based on earlier maps by G. Delisle and Louis de Hennepin.

★ *Homann Heirs (Homannische Erben)*
JOHANN MICHAEL FRANZ 1700–61
JOHANN MATTHIAS HASE (HASIUS) 1684–*c.* 1742
JOHANN GEORG EBERSPERGER 1695–1760
and others

c. 1747	*Homannischer atlas*
	Re-issues to *c.* 1780
c. 1750	Atlas of Germany
1750	Atlas of Silesia
c. 1752	*Atlas compendiarus*
	Re-issues to 1790
1754	*Bequemer Hand-atlas*

1759	*Atlas Geographicus*
	Re-issues to *c.* 1784
1769	*Atlas novus republicae Helveticae*
1780	*Atlas maior*

GABRIEL BODENEHR *c.* 1664–*c.* 1750
1704   *Atlas curieux* (4to)

★

ADAM FREIDRICH ZÜRNER *c.* 1680–1742
c. 1710   *Mappa Geographica Delineatio* (Maps of the Continents)

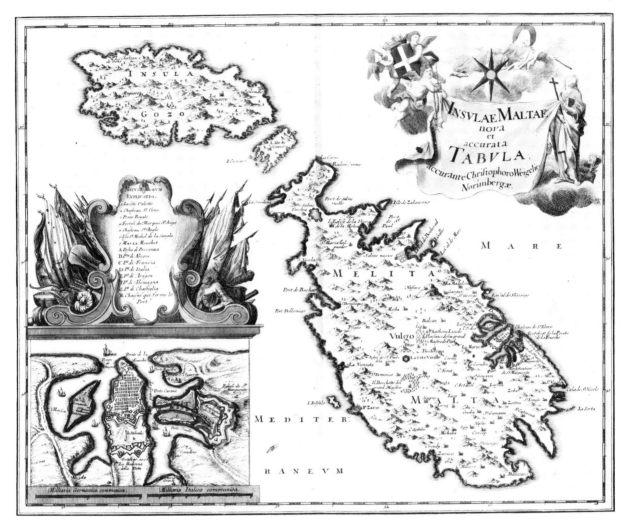

CHRISTOPH WEIGEL *Insulae Malta* Nuremberg *c.* 1720. Very decorative map with a plan of Valletta.

CHRISTOPH WEIGEL *c.* 1654–1725

JOHANN WEIGEL –1746

Engravers and publishers in Nuremberg: their business was carried on in later years under the name Schneider and Weigel.

1712	*Atlas Scholasticus*
	1740 Re-issued
1720	*Descriptio orbis antiqui* (with J. D. Koehler)
1724	*Atlas Manualis*
1745	*Neuer Post-Reise Atlas von Deutschland*

JOHANN DAVID KOEHLER 1684–1755

| 1720 | *Descriptio orbis antiqui* (with J. and C. Weigel) |

| 1724 | *Atlas Manualis* |

GEORG MATTHÄUS SEUTTER (the Older) 1678–1756

GEORG MATTHÄUS SEUTTER (the Younger) 1729–60

ALBRECHT CARL SEUTTER *fl.* 1741

After serving an apprenticeship to J. B. Homann, the Nuremberg map publisher, Seutter set up his own very successful business in Augsburg and was appointed Geographer to the Imperial Court. With his son, Albrecht, and son-in-law, Conrad Lotter, he issued in about 1741 a large series of town plans. For much of his life he worked in competition with his old employer and, not surprisingly, his maps are often very similar to those of Homann.

c. 1720	*Atlas Germanicus*
1725	*Atlas Geographicus*
1728	*Atlas Novus*: Vienna and Augsburg
	1730, 1736 Re-issued
c. 1735	*Grosser Atlas*
c. 1741	*Atlas novus sive tabulae geographicae totius*
	orbis (town plans)
1744	*Atlas minor* (4to with folded maps)

JOHANN MATTHIAS HASE (HASIUS) 1684–*c.* 1742
Also published maps as a member of the firm of 'Homann Heirs'.

1737	*Africa secundum*
	Re-issues to 1745
1746	*Atlantis historici Hasiani*
1746	*Americae mappa generalis*

JOHANN GEORG SCHREIBER 1676–1745

| *c.* 1740 | *Atlas Selectus* |
| | 1749 Re-issued |

TOBIAS CONRAD LOTTER 1717–77
GEORG FRIEDRICH LOTTER *fl.* 1762–87
MATHIAS ALBRECHT LOTTER 1741–1810
Tobias Lotter was a German publisher and engraver who married the daughter of the elder Matthäus Seutter. He engraved many of Seutter's maps and eventually succeeded to the business in 1756, becoming one of the better-known cartographers in the eighteenth-century German School. After his death the business was carried on by his son, M. A. Lotter.

c. 1744	*Atlas Minor*
c. 1760–62	*Atlas Geographicus portabilis*
c. 1770	*Atlas Novus*
1776	*A Map of the most inhabited part of New England*
1778	*Atlas Géographique*
1778	(M. A. Lotter) World Map showing Cook's voyages

GERHARD FRIEDRICH MÜLLER *fl.* 1754

| 1754 | *Nouvelle Carte des Decouvertes faites par des Vaisseaux Russiens* |
| | 1758, 1773, 1784 Re-issued |

PETER ANICH 1723–66

| 1774 | *Atlas Tyrolensis* (Blasius Hueber) |

FRANZ ANTON SCHRÄMBL 1751–1803
In the last decades of the eighteenth century Anton Schrämbl and Joseph von Reilly led a successful revival of map making in Vienna. Completion of Schrämbl's ambitious World Atlas, started in 1786, based on the best available sources of the time, was much delayed and the maps were issued piecemeal year by year until the whole atlas appeared in 1800.

| 1786–1800 | *Allgemeiner Grosser Atlas* |

FRANZ JOHANN JOSEPH VON REILLY 1766–1820
Joseph von Reilly was a Viennese art dealer who in his early twenties turned to map publishing, and between the years 1789 and 1806 produced a total of no less than 830 maps. His *Schauplatz . . . der Welt* (World Atlas) in fact covered only maps of Europe, whilst the *Grosser Deutscher Atlas* also included maps of other continents and was, therefore, the first World Atlas produced by an Austrian.

| 1789–1806 | *Schauplatz der fünf Theile der Welt* |
| 1794–96 | *Grosser Deutscher Atlas* |

JOHANN G. A. JAEGER 1718–90

| 1789 | *Grand Atlas d' Allemagne* |

ALEXANDER VON HUMBOLDT 1769–1859
Traveller, naturalist, geologist, famous for his exploration in Venezuela (1799–1800) and his subsequent publications.

1805–14	Maps in *Voyage de Humboldt et Bonpland*
	Numerous re-issues
1811–12	*Atlas Géographique et Physique de Royaume de la Nouvelle Espagne*
1814–34	*Atlas du Nouveau Continent*

ADAM CHRISTIAN GASPARI 1752–1830

| 1804–11 | *Allgemeiner hand-atlas* |
| | 1821 Re-issued |

CARL FERDINAND WEILAND 1782–1847

| 1824–28 | *Atlas von Amerika* |
| 1828–48 | *Allgemeiner hand-atlas* |

ADOLF STIELER 1775–1836

| 1826–28 | *Hand Atlas* |
| | Numerous re-issues throughout the century |

WILHELM ERNST AUGUST VON SCHLIEBEN 1781–1839

| 1829 | Atlas of Europe |
| 1830 | Atlas of America |

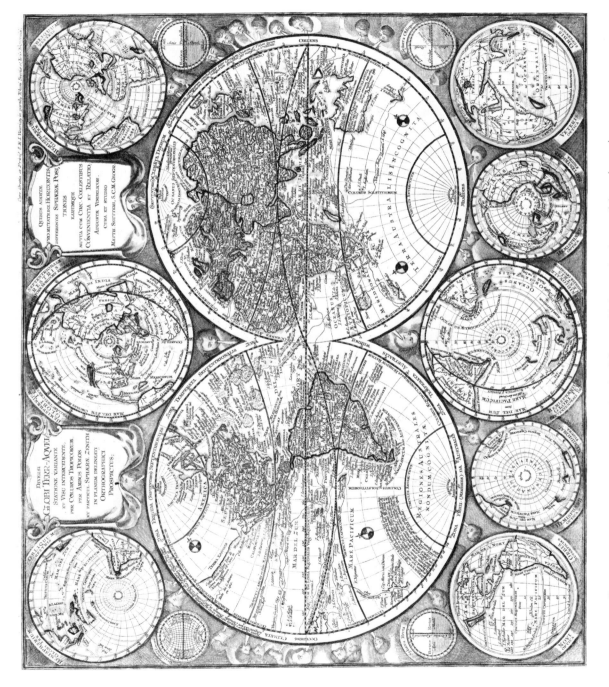

GEORG MATTHÄUS SEUTTER   *World* Augsburg *c.* 1730. A splendid map with interesting insets of the polar regions.

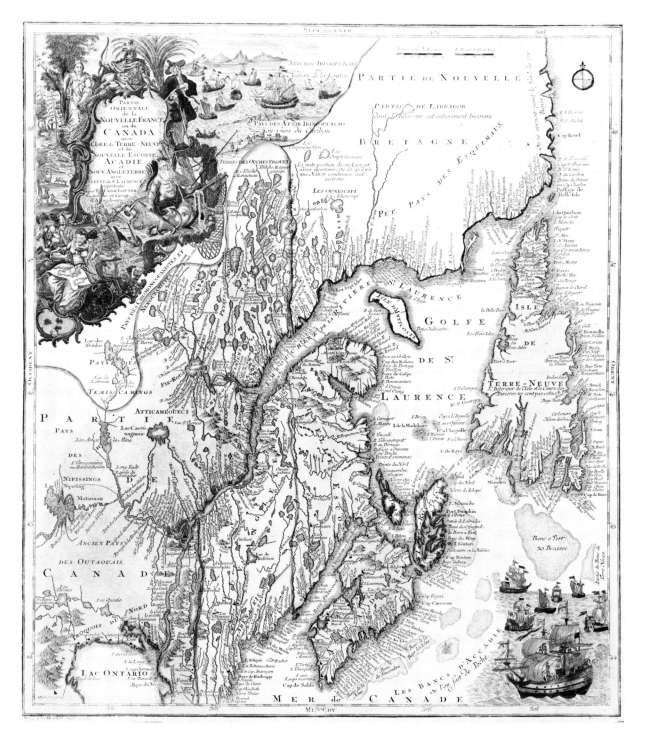

TOBIAS CONRAD LOTTER   *Nouvelle France ou du Canada* Augsburg *c.* 1755. Although Newfoundland is somewhat misshapen this is a highly decorative and attractive map, typical of the period.

HEINRICH BERGHAUS 1797–1884

Berghaus founded a School of Geography at Potsdam where he came into contact with, and was much influenced by, Alexander von Humboldt, whose ideas of physical geography he incorporated in a *Physikalischer Atlas* issued in sections over the years 1837–48. This was an important and influential work on the subject with a very wide international circulation.

1832–43   *Atlas von Asia*
1837–48   *Physikalischer Atlas*: Gotha (published by J. Perthes)

Specialist References

BAGROW, L., *History of Cartography*

GROSJEAN, G. and KINAUER, R., *Kartenkunst und Kartentechnik*

KOEMAN, C., *Atlantes Neerlandici*
Although this work covers Dutch Atlases it also includes a detailed account of Braun and Hogenberg's *Civitates Orbis Terrarum*

NORDENSKIÖLD, A. E., *Facsimile Atlas to the Early History of Cartography*
History and reproductions of Ptolemaic and other early maps

SHIRLEY, R. W., *The Mapping of the World*
Numerous examples of early German maps with descriptive detail

THEATRUM ORBIS TERRARUM NV
Braun and Hogenberg: *Civitates Orbis Terrarum*
Lazius: *Austria*
Ptolemy: *Geographia/Cosmographia* 1482, 1513, 1540
Quad: *Geographisch Handtbuch*
Reproductions of complete atlases

TOOLEY, R. V., *Maps and Map Makers*

The authors are indebted to the Service Documentation of the Mairie de Saint-Dié-des-Vosges and the Stadtarchiv of the Grosse Kreisstadt Radolfzell am Bodensee for information (on pages 286–7) on the life (and death) of Waldseemüller, for details of the printing of the *Cosmographiae Introductio* and for extracts of the work of former Stadtarchivdirektor Dr Franz Laubenberger (1976), Kreisarchivar Dr Franz Götz (1964) and Albert Ronsin in *Découverte et Baptême de l'Amérique*, Montreal, 1976, G. le Pape.

Chapter 13

HOLLAND & BELGIUM

It would be hard to imagine a more inauspicious period for a nation's cultural development than the years between 1520 and 1600 in the Low Countries. Under the harsh domination of the Spanish Emperors, facing fanatical religious persecution and the threat of the Inquisition, the constant presence of foreign troops and even the destruction of some of their cities, the Dutch, nevertheless, in 1581 contrived to break their subservience to Spain and form their own federation. Belgium, being mainly Catholic, remained within the orbit of the Empire though henceforward was recognized as a separate state. In such circumstances there would seem to have been little chance for growth of a national entity in the small Northern Provinces but, on the contrary, under the leadership of Amsterdam, their banking and commercial enterprise soon dominated Europe. The attempt by Philip II to eliminate their control of European coastal trade by the use of Portuguese craft inspired the Dutch, first, to seek a North East passage to India and Asia and then, failing that, to challenge Spanish and Portuguese power directly, not only in European waters but also in the East, and eventually to eclipse it. English attempts to gain a foothold in the Indies were bitterly opposed and the English turned their attention to India where only a handful of Dutch settlements existed.

In spite of the turmoil arising out of these events, first Antwerp and then Amsterdam became centres of the arts and their cartographers, engravers and printers produced magnificent maps and charts of every kind which many claim have never been surpassed. Later in this chapter an account is given of Gerard Mercator, who studied at Louvain under Gemma Frisius, the Dutch astronomer and mathematician, and later moved to Duisburg in the Rhineland where most of his major work was carried out. There he produced globes, maps of Europe, the British Isles and the famous World Map using his newly invented method of projection, all of which were widely copied by most

of the cartographers of the day. The first part of his Atlas – the word chosen by Mercator to describe a collection of maps – was published in 1585, the second in 1589, and the third in 1595, a year after his death.

Other great names of the time were Abraham Ortelius, native of Antwerp, famous for his world atlas, *Theatrum Orbis Terrarum*, issued in 1570; Waghenaer, noted for his sea atlases of 1584 and 1592, Gerard de Jode and Jodocus and Henricus Hondius, followed in the next century by W. J. Blaeu and his sons and Jan Jansson. The Blaeu and Jansson establishments were noted mainly for land atlases but their sea atlases and pilot books were also published in numerous editions which went some way to meeting the rising demand for aids to navigation in European and Mediterranean waters. Their productions were challenged by other, smaller publishers specializing in such works, Jacob Colom, Anthonie Jacobsz, Pieter Goos, Hendrick Doncker, to mention a few, and, later, the charts issued by the van Keulen family and their descendants covered practically all the seas of the known world. As we reach the second half of the seventeenth century the details of publication of these sea atlases and pilot books become more and more interwoven and complicated. Not infrequently the same charts were issued under the imprint of different publishers; at death the engraved plates were sold or passed to their successors and were re-issued, with minor alterations and often without acknowledgement to the originator, all of which adds to problems of identification. Although, in this period, charts of every kind must have been issued in great quantity, good copies are now hard to find.

By about the year 1700 Dutch sea power and influence was waning and although their pilot books and charts remained much in demand for many years to come, leadership in the production of land atlases passed into the hands of the more scientific French cartographers who, in their turn, dominated the map

ABRAHAM ORTELIUS   *Islandia* Antwerp 1585. A famous map of Iceland compiled from original work by Gudbrandur Thorlaksson.

trade for most of the following century.

LEO BELGICUS

Before leaving this chapter it is worth noting a famous series of maps known as Leo Belgicus, or the Lion of Belgium, which was started in 1583 by Michael Aitzinger, an Austrian nobleman who had studied at the universities of Vienna and Louvain. He travelled extensively in Europe for about thirty years before settling in Cologne where he published a book describing the Low Countries which contained the first 'Leo Belgicus' and a further 112 plates engraved by Frans Hogenberg. The area covered was extensive, including the whole of today's Netherlands and Belgium.

The idea of a map in the shape of a lion was very appealing and was copied by many other cartographers, including Jan van Doetecum, C. J. Visscher, P. van den Keere and Rombout van den Hoeye. Variants on the original were issued as late as 1807 and three distinct types are found: the Aitsinger form with the lion standing facing right with the right paw raised; the Cornelius Jansson form of 1611 with the lion sitting facing left, and the 'Leo Hollandicus', showing only the area of Holland, which was first published between 1608 and 1625.

All of these maps are rare and generally expensive; the 'commonest' is probably the one which was first issued by Famiano Strada, a Jesuit, at Rome in 1632 This appeared as the title page to a history of the Low Countries which proved very popular, many editions (in various formats) being published at Antwerp, Rome, Amsterdam and Lyon amongst other places.

The authors have seen a number of fakes of these maps produced mainly by photo-lithography using old paper, which are very deceptive. Some are not of the correct size and may quickly be dismissed as not genuine by reference to the excellent illustrated paper by R. V. Tooley in the Map Collector's Circle Series No. 7 of 1964. Collectors should beware of buying rare maps of this type other than from recognized dealers.

Biographies

GEMMA FRISIUS (REINER/REGNERUS) 1508–55
Of German extraction, Gemma Frisius became the foremost astronomer, mathematician and surveyor of

his time. He was an influential figure, not only for his teaching of Mercator at his School of Geography at Louvain but for his scientific contributions to practical aspects of cartography. He invented an improved form of cross-staff for astronomical use and in his book *A Method of delineating places* he set out the principle of triangulation in map making. Later, he was the first to suggest the use of portable clocks to determine longitude.

1533	Published *A Method of delineating places*
1545	World Map on heart-shaped projection, included in an enlarged edition of Peter Apian's *Cosmographicus liber* (1524) edited by Frisius

JACOBUS VAN DEVENTER 1500–75
Geographer to Charles V and Philip II.

1540–60	Map of Holland and large-scale maps of the Dutch provinces

CORNELIS ANTHONISZ(OON) *c.* 1499–1556

1543	*Caerte van Oostlandt* Woodcut map of Scandinavia on 9 sheets known only from re-issues in Antwerp, Rome (1558) and Venice (1562): subsequently used by Mercator and Ortelius
1544	Plan of Amsterdam: 12 sheets

GERARD MERCATOR (KREMER) 1512–94
  ARNOLD MERCATOR (SON) 1537–87
  RUMOLD MERCATOR (SON) *c.* 1645–*c.* 99
  BARTHOLOMEUS MERCATOR (SON) *fl.* 1540–63
  GERARD MERCATOR (GRANDSON) *c.* 1565–1656
  JOANNES MERCATOR (GRANDSON) *c.* 1562–95
  MICHAEL MERCATOR (GRANDSON) *c.* 1567–1600

For nearly sixty years, during the most important and exciting period in the story of modern map making, Gerard Mercator was the supreme cartographer, his name, second only to Ptolemy, synonymous with the form of map projection still in use today. Although not the inventor of this type of projection he was the first to apply it to navigational charts in such a form that compass bearings could be plotted on charts in straight lines, thereby providing seamen with a solution to an age-old problem of navigation at sea. His influence transformed land surveying and his researches and calculations led him to break away from Ptolemy's conception of the size and outline of the Continents, drastically reducing the longitudinal length of Europe

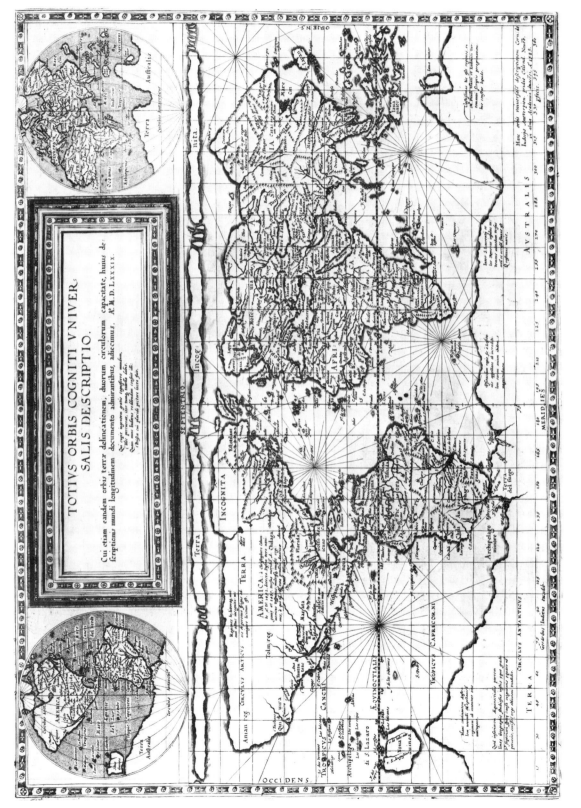

CORNELIS DE JODE *Totius Orbis Cogniti Universalis Descriptio*. This rare World Map dated 1589 was engraved and signed by Gerard de Jode prior to his death in 1591. It was included in his son's Atlas published in 1593.

GERARD MERCATOR *Septentrionalium Terrarum Descriptio.* Map of the North Pole which is shown as a rocky 'island' with four rivers around it. This was the first map to be devoted specifically to the Arctic, published in Amsterdam in 1595 (this being a later issue).

and Asia and altering the shape of the Old World as visualized in the early sixteenth century.

Mercator was born in Rupelmonde in Flanders and studied in Louvain under Gemma Frisius, Dutch writer, astronomer and mathematician. He established himself there as a cartographer and instrument and globe maker, and when he was twenty-five drew and engraved his first map (of Palestine) and went on to produce a map of Flanders (1540) supervising the surveying and completing the drafting and engraving

himself. The excellence of his work brought him the patronage of Charles V for whom he constructed a globe, but in spite of his favour with the Emperor he was caught up in the persecution of Lutheran protestants and charged with heresy, fortunately without serious consequences. No doubt the fear of further persecution influenced his move in 1552 to Duisburg, where he continued the production of maps, globes and instruments culminating in large-scale maps of Europe (1554), the British Isles (1564) and the famous

World Map on 18 sheets drawn to his new projection (1569). All these early maps are exceedingly rare, some being known by only one copy.

In later life he devoted himself to his edition of the maps in Ptolemy's *Geographia*, reproduced in his own engraving as nearly as possible in their original form, and to the preparation of his 3-volume collection of maps to which, for the first time, the word 'Atlas' was applied. The word was chosen, he wrote, 'to honour the Titan, Atlas, King of Mauritania, a learned philosopher, mathematician and astronomer'. The first two parts of the Atlas were published in 1585 and 1589 and the third, with the first two making a complete edition, in 1595, the year after Mercator's death.

Mercator's sons and grandsons, named above, were all cartographers and made their contributions in various ways to the great atlas. Rumold, in particular, was responsible for the complete edition in 1595. After a second complete edition in 1602, the map plates were bought in 1604 by Jodocus Hondius who, with his sons, Jodocus II and Henricus, published enlarged editions which dominated the map market for the following twenty to thirty years.

1578	Ptolemy's *Geographia*: 27 maps
	1584, 1605, 1618–19, 1695, 1698, 1704, 1730 Re-issued (details of these issues are shown in Appendix A)
1585	Atlas Part I: Duisburg: Latin text
	51 maps: Holland, Belgium, Germany
1589	Atlas Part II: Duisburg: Latin text
	23 maps: Italy, Greece and Central Europe
1595	Atlas Part III: Duisburg: Latin text
	36 maps: The World, the Continents, British Isles, Northern Europe, Russia
	1595 Re-issued as a complete Atlas with 111 maps
	1602 Re-issued

Mercator/Hondius/Jansson Atlas

Below is a very brief summary of the various editions of Mercator's Atlas by Jodocus and Henricus Hondius and Jan Jansson, issued with text in Latin, Dutch, French, German and Spanish. Apart from the main editions quoted, there were many variants too numerous to show here.

1606–19	Jodocus Hondius
	Hondius died in 1612 but editions bearing his name were published by his widow and sons, Jocodus II and Henricus, until 1619

1607, 1609, 1611, 1613, 1619 Re-issued

1623–33	Henricus Hondius
	1628, 1630, 1631, 1633 Re-issued by Henricus alone
1630–41	Henricus Hondius and Jan Jansson
	In 1629–30, after the death of Jodocus II, the plates of about 40 maps were sold to W. J. Blaeu who used them in his *Atlantis Appendix* (1630). To meet this competition, replacement plates were engraved from which maps were issued by Jansson, also in 1630, in an *Atlantis Maioris Appendix*. By 1633 new editions of the Mercator Atlas were in production and continued until 1641, some in the joint names of Hondius and Jansson, some in separate names.
1636–38	English editions – title *Atlas or Geographicke Description of the Regions, Countries and Kingdoms of the World*
1638–66	*Atlas Novus* (Jan Jansson)
	At this stage the Mercator Atlas was developed by Jansson under the title *Atlas Novus*, starting with 2 volumes in 1638 and passing through many editions and enlargements until its later editions formed the basis of the *Atlas Major* published during the 1650s to rival Blaeu's *Atlas Maior*.
	1638, 1639, 1641, 1642, 1644, 1645, 1646, 1647, 1649, 1650, 1652, 1656, 1657, 1658, 1659, 1666 – editions in Latin, Dutch, French, German and Spanish

Atlas Minor

The editions of the *Atlas Minor*, summarized below, were issued in the main European languages, including English. There were many variants to these editions which are not included here.

1607	Jodocus Hondius and Jan Jansson the Elder (average size 170–190 × 210–230 mm)
	Maps engraved by Jodocus Hondius and published in co-operation with Jan Jansson the Elder, bookseller and publisher, the father of the better-known cartographer of the same name, whose work on the *Atlas Minor* began with the 1628 edition.
	1608, 1609, 1610 Re-issued

1612	Jodocus Hondius II and Jan Jansson the Elder (average size 170–190 × 210–230 mm)
	1613, 1614, 1620, 1621 Re-issued
1625	William Stansby: London
	Maps included in *Purchas His Pilgrimes* by Samuel Purchas. Maps printed from the 1607 plates
1628	Jan Jansson
	Maps newly engraved by Pieter van den Keere and Abraham Goos (average size 180–190 × 230–245 mm)
	1628, 1630(2), 1631, 1634(2), 1648, 1651 Re-issued
1630	Johannis Cloppenburgh
	Maps re-engraved in slightly larger format (average size 210–220 × 270–280 mm)
	1632, 1636 Re-issued
1635	Thomas Cotes/W. Saltonstall: London
	Issued as *Historia Mundi* with English text: maps printed from the 1607 plates
	1637, 1639 Re-issued
1673	Jansson's Heirs: Janssonius van Waesbergen: no text
	1676 Re-issued
1734	Henri du Sauzet
	1738 Re-issued

GERARD DE JODE *c.* 1509–91

CORNELIS DE JODE (son) 1568–1600

Gerard de Jode, born in Nijmegen, was a cartographer, engraver, printer and publisher in Antwerp, issuing maps from 1555 more or less in the same period as Ortelius. He was never able to offer very serious competition to his more businesslike rival although, ironically, he published Ortelius's famous 8-sheet World Map in 1564. His major atlas, now extremely rare, could not be published until 1578, eight years after the *Theatrum*, Ortelius having obtained a mono-poly for that period. The enlarged re-issue by his son in 1593 is more frequently found. On the death of Cornelis, the copper plates passed to J. B. Vrients (who bought the Ortelius plates about the same time) and apparently no further issue of the atlas was published: however, at least one further issue of the Polar Map, *c.* 1618, is known.

Gerard de Jode

1555	World Map by Gastaldi
1564	World Map by Ortelius (8 sheets)

1578	*Speculum Orbis Terrarum*
	1593 Re-issued by Cornelis de Jode as *Speculum Orbis Terrae* (112 maps)

Cornelis de Jode

1589	World Map
1592	*Gallia Occidentalis*
c. 1595	The 4 Continents
c. 1598	Belgium

ABRAHAM ORTELIUS 1528–98

Abraham Ortel, better known as Ortelius, was born in Antwerp and after studying Greek, Latin and math-ematics set up business there with his sister, as a book dealer and 'painter of maps'. Travelling widely, especi-ally to the great book fairs, his business prospered and he established contacts with the literati in many lands. On one such visit to England, possibly seeking temporary refuge from religious persecution, he met William Camden whom he is said to have encouraged in the production of the *Britannia*.

A turning-point in his career was reached in 1564 with the publication of a World Map in eight sheets of which only one copy is known: other individual maps followed and then – at the suggestion of a friend – he gathered together a collection of maps from contacts among European cartographers and had them en-graved in uniform size and issued in 1570 as the *Theatrum Orbis Terrarum* (Atlas of the Whole World). Although Lafreri and others in Italy had published collections of 'modern' maps in book form in earlier years, the *Theatrum* was the first uniformly sized, systematic collection of maps and hence can be called the first atlas, although that term itself was not used until twenty years later by Mercator.

The *Theatrum*, with most of its maps elegantly engraved by Frans Hogenberg, was an instant success and appeared in numerous editions in different lan-guages including addenda issued from time to time incorporating the latest contemporary knowledge and discoveries. The final edition appeared in 1612. Unlike many of his contemporaries Ortelius noted his sources of information and in the first edition acknowledge-ment was made to eighty-seven different cartographers.

Apart from the modern maps in his major atlas, Ortelius himself compiled a series of historical maps known as the *Parergon Theatri* which appeared from 1579 onwards, sometimes as a separate publication and sometimes incorporated in the *Theatrum*.

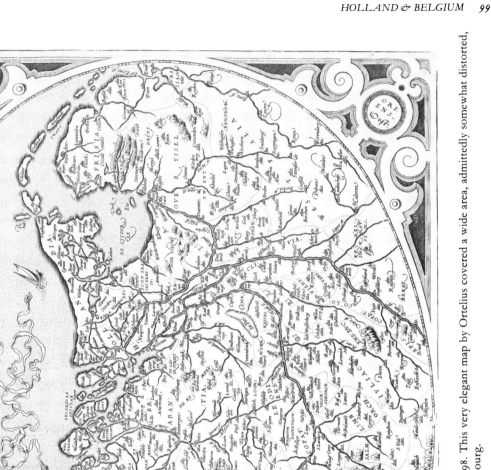

ABRAHAM ORTELIUS *Descriptio Germaniae Inferioris* Antwerp (1570) *c.* 1598. This very elegant map by Ortelius covered a wide area, admittedly somewhat distorted, including Holland, Belgium and parts of France, Germany and Luxembourg.

1570   *Theatrum Orbis Terrarum*
1570–1612 Between these years the Theatrum was re-issued in 42 editions with 5 supplements with text in Latin, Dutch, German, French, Spanish, Italian and English. The English edition was published in 1606 by John Norton, the maps being printed in Antwerp and the text added in London.

Three years after Ortelius died in 1598, his heirs transferred publication rights to Jan Baptiste Vrients who produced the later editions until he died in 1612

1577–85   *Spiegel der Werelt* (8vo)
Maps from the *Theatrum*, reduced in size, engraved by Philip Galle: text by Pieter Heyns. 6 editions with Dutch, French and Latin text.

1588–1603 *Epitome theatri orbis terrarum* (12mo/8vo)
11 further editions of the smaller maps with an increasing number of maps with text also in Italian and English (1603).

1601–12 7 further editions with improved engravings by Arsenius Brothers: text by Michel Coignet in Latin, French, German, Italian and English (1603).

1598–1724 *Theatro del Mondo* (4to/12mo/24mo)
8 editions with Italian text; plates engraved in Italy.

1579–1606   *Parergon Theatri*
The number of maps included in the *Parergon* increased from 4 in 1579 to 43 in 1606 with text in Latin, French, Italian, German and English (1606)

1624 Re-issued in Antwerp as a separate publication by Balthasar Moretus. This edition included a reproduction of the Peutinger table.

CHRISTIAAN VAN ADRICHOM 1533–90
1584   *Theatrum terrae sanctae*: 12 maps
Maps of the Holy Land much copied by later cartographers.

c. 1590–
1680   Numerous re-issues

LUCAS JANSZOON WAGHENAER 1534–98
By the third quarter of the sixteenth century an ever

increasing volume of the wealth of the New World and the Indies was reaching Lisbon and the Spanish ports, there to be trans-shipped to Northern and Western Europe. This trade was almost entirely in the hands of the Dutch so it was logical that one of their pilots should produce the first set of effective navigational charts. These were compiled under the title *Spiegel der Zeevaerdt*, by Lucas Janszoon Waghenaer, a native of Enkhuizen on the Zuider Zee, an experienced seaman and pilot. His magnificently produced charts embodying all the latest contemporary knowledge of navigation and position-finding set a standard which was followed by others for the next century or more – indeed, some of the symbols employed are still in use today. The charts in the first edition, covering the coast lines from Holland to Spain and the North Sea and Baltic, were engraved by the van Doetecum brothers and printed by Plantin: those in the English edition, which was translated by Sir Anthony Ashley and issued in 1588 – the year of the Armada – were engraved by de Bry, Hondius, Rutlinger and Ryther, who also engraved some of Saxton's maps. The charts are extremely picturesque with elaborate cartouches, ships in full sail and the sea monsters so commonly used as decoration in maps of the period. Place names are given on the coasts but comparatively few are shown inland; cliffs on the coastline are drawn in elevation; navigational landmarks and hazards, anchorages, soundings and tidal details are indicated and the scale is shown in English, Spanish and Dutch leagues. Altogether some of the most handsome maps ever produced.

The charts became so universally popular that their name, anglicized to 'Waggoner', came into use in English as a generic term for sea charts of all kinds.

Spiegel der Zeevaerdt
Charts engraved by Baptist and Jan van Doetecum

DATE	PUBLISHED BY	NO. OF CHARTS	TEXT
1584	Plantin, Leyden	23	Dutch
1585	Plantin, Leyden	44	Dutch
1585	Plantin, Leyden	44	Dutch
1586	Plantin, Leyden	45	Latin
1588	Plantin, Leyden	47	Dutch
1588	A. Ashley, London[a]	45	English
1589	Cornelis Claesz, Amsterdam	47	German
1589–90	Cornelis Claesz, Amsterdam	47	Dutch

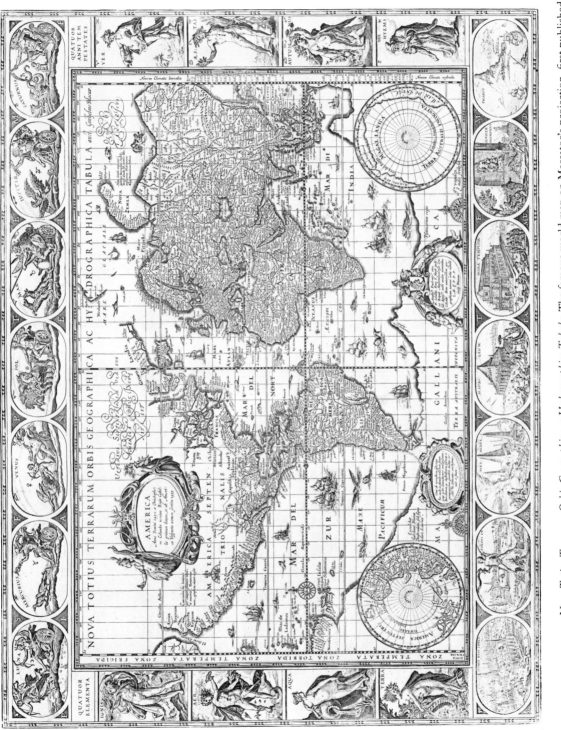

WILLEM JANSZOON BLAEU *Nova Totius Terrarum Orbis Geographica ac Hydrographica Tabula.* The famous world map on Mercator's projection, first published in Amsterdam in 1666 and in the Blaeu atlases from 1630 onwards. This map is one of the masterpieces of Dutch cartographic engraving and was eventually superseded by the hemispherical map of 1662.

Spiegel der Zeevaerdt (contd.)

DATE	PUBLISHED BY	NO. OF CHARTS	TEXT
1590	Cornelis Claesz, Amsterdam	47	French
1591	Cornelis Claesz, Amsterdam	47	Latin
1590	Jean Bellère Antwerp	47	French
1591	Jean Bellère, Antwerp	47	Latin
1615	Johann Walschaert, Amsterdam[b]	47	German

[a] Issued in London as *The Mariner's Mirrour*: charts engraved by Theodore de Bry, Jodocus Hondius, Joh. Rutlinger and Augustine Ryther.

[b] Based on 1589 German edition.

Thresoor der Zeevaerdt

DATE	PUBLISHED BY	NO. OF CHARTS	TEXT
1592	Plantin, Leyden[a]	22	Dutch
1596	Cornelis Claesz, Amsterdam	24	Dutch
1601	Cornelis Claesz, Amsterdam	27	French
1602	Cornelis Claesz, Amsterdam[b]	28	Dutch
1606	Cornelis Claesz, Amsterdam	28	French
1608	Cornelis Claesz, Amsterdam	28	Dutch
1609	Cornelis Claesz, Amsterdam[c]	31	Dutch

[a] Plates in the first 3 editions engraved by Jan van Doetecum.

[b] Plates re-engraved by Benjamin Wright and Joshua van den Ende.

[c] Re-issued as *Nieuwe Thresoor der Zeevaerdt*.

Den nieuwen spiegel der Zeevaerdt

DATE	PUBLISHED BY	NO. OF CHARTS	TEXT
1596	Cornelis Claesz, Amsterdam	49	Dutch
1597	Cornelis Claesz, Amsterdam	49	Dutch

Den nieuwen spiegel der Zeevaerdt (contd.)

DATE	PUBLISHED BY	NO. OF CHARTS	TEXT
1600	Cornelis Claesz and Jean Bellère, Amsterdam/Antwerp	49	French
1605	Cornelis Claesz and Jean Bellère, Amsterdam/Antwerp	49	French
1605	Jodocus Hondius, Amsterdam[a]	47	Dutch/ English

[a] Reprint of 44 plates used in *The Mariner's Mirrour* (1588) plus 3 new charts.

JODOCUS HONDIUS 1563–1612
JODOCUS HONDIUS (son) 1594–1629
HENRICUS HONDIUS (son) 1587–1638

Jodocus Hondius, one of the most notable engravers of his time, is known for his work in association with many of the cartographers and publishers prominent at the end of the sixteenth and the beginning of the seventeenth century.

A native of Flanders, he grew up in Ghent, apprenticed as an instrument and globe maker and map engraver. In 1584, to escape the religious troubles sweeping the Low Countries at that time, he fled to London where he spent some years before finally settling in Amsterdam about 1593. In the London period he came into contact with the leading scientists and geographers of the day and engraved maps in *The Mariner's Mirrour*, the English edition of Waghenaer's Sea Atlas, as well as others with Pieter van den Keere, his brother-in-law. No doubt his temporary exile in London stood him in good stead, earning him an international reputation, for it could have been no accident that Speed chose Hondius to engrave the plates for the maps in *The Theatre of the Empire of Great Britaine* in the years between 1605 and 1610.

In 1604 Hondius bought the plates of Mercator's Atlas which, in spite of its excellence, had not competed successfully with the continuing demand for the Ortelius *Theatrum Orbis Terrarum*. To meet this competition Hondius added about 40 maps to Mercator's original number and from 1606 published enlarged editions in many languages, still under

Mercator's name but with his own name as publisher. These atlases have become known as the Mercator/ Hondius series. The following year the maps were re-engraved in miniature form and issued as a pocket *Atlas Minor*. After the death of Jodocus Hondius the Elder in 1612, work on the two atlases, folio and miniature, was carried on by his widow and sons, Jodocus II and Henricus, and eventually in conjunction with Jan Jansson in Amsterdam. In all, from 1606 onwards, nearly 50 editions with increasing numbers of maps with texts in the main European languages were printed. Summaries of these issues are given under the entry for Gerard Mercator.

Jodocus Hondius the Elder

1588	Maps in *The Mariner's Mirrour* (Waghenaer/Ashley)
1590	World Map in two hemispheres illustrating Drake's circumnavigation
c. 1591–92	*Hiberniae novissima descriptio*: Boazio's map of Ireland: Engraved by Pieter van den keere
1595	Europe (wall map): with Pieter van den Keere
1598	World and the Continents
1599	Maps for *Caert Thresoor* (Langenes/ Cornelis Claesz), with Pieter van den Keere
1602–03	12 English County maps for William Smith ('anonymous maps')
1605	Ptolemy's *Geographia* (Mercator) 1618–19 Re-issued
1605–10	Maps for *The Theatre of the Empire of Great Britaine* (Speed)
1606	World Atlas (Mercator/Hondius series) (see under 'Gerard Mercator' for further detail)
1607	*Atlas Minor* (Mercator/Hondius series) (see under 'Gerard Mercator' for further detail)
1608	World Map on Mercator's projection

Jodocus Hondius II

1612–21	(Mercator) *Atlas Minor* 5 editions published in co-operation with Jan Jansson the Elder (see under Gerard Mercator (*Atlas Minor*) for further detail)
1613	Map of Scandinavia
1616	*View of London* (Cl. J. Visscher)
1616	*Tabularum geographicarum* (Petrus Bertius)

	Miniature world atlas (8vo): edition (with new maps) of the *Caert Thresoor* published in 1598–99 1618 Re-issued in Latin and French
1617–18	World Map: double hemisphere The first map to show Tierra del Fuego as an island as a result of the discoveries made on the Schouten/Le Maire voyage of 1615–17.
c. 1624	World Map on Mercator's projection
1629	Atlas (without title or text) 42 maps, mostly by Hondius, not included in the Mercator/Hondius editions

Henricus Hondius

(1606)	*Mercator's Atlas* (Mercator/Hondius/ Jansson) 1613, 1619 Editions published by the widow of Jodocus Hondius the Elder, and Jodocus II and Henricus. 1623–33 5 editions published by Henricus alone. 1633–41 5 editions in conjunction with Jan Jansson (for further detail see entry under Gerard Mercator)

PETRUS PLANCIUS 1552–1622

Plancius was a theologian and minister of the Dutch Reformed Church who fled with many of his compatriots from religious persecution in Flanders to settle in Amsterdam in 1585. There he became interested in navigation and cartography and, being fortunate enough to have access to nautical charts recently brought from Portugal, he was soon recognized as an expert on the shipping routes to India. He was interested, too, in the idea of a North East passage until the failure of Willem Barentsz's third voyage in 1597 seemed to preclude the possibility of such a route. In 1602 he was appointed cartographer to the new Dutch East India Company.

Although Plancius produced no atlases his individual maps and charts, over 100 in all, exercised much influence on the work of other cartographers at the turn of the century. His very large wall map of the world dated 1592 was of particular significance.

1590	World Map: issued in an edition of the Bible by Plancius 1592, 1596, 1604, 1607 Re-issued
1592	World Map: wall map in 18 sheets 1600 (Arnoldo di Arnoldi)

c. 1640, 1669 (Pietro Petrucci) (Re-issued in Siena)

1594 World Map: twin hemisphere
1607 Re-issue by Pieter van den Keere

1596 World and other maps in Linschoten's *Itinerario* and subsequent editions

---

PIETER VAN DEN KEERE (PETRUS KAERIUS) 1571–c. 1646

Pieter van den Keere was one of a number of refugees who fled from religious persecution in the Low Countries between the years 1570 and 1590. He moved to London in 1584 with his sister who married Jodocus Hondius, also a refugee there, and through Hondius he undoubtedly learned his skills as an engraver and cartographer. In the course of a long working life he engraved a large number of individual maps for prominent cartographers of the day but he also produced an Atlas of the Netherlands (1617–22) and county maps of the British Isles which have become known as Miniature Speeds, a misnomer which calls for some explanation.

In about 1599 he engraved plates for 44 maps of the English and Welsh counties, the regions of Scotland and the Irish provinces. The English maps were based on Saxton, the Scottish on Ortelius and the Irish on the famous map by Boazio. These maps were not published at once in book form but there is evidence which suggests a date of issue (in Amsterdam) between 1605 and 1610 although at least one authority believes they existed only in proof form until 1617 when Willem Blaeu issued them with a Latin edition of Camden's *Britannia*. At this stage two maps were added, one of the British Isles and the other of Yorkshire, the latter derived from Saxton. To confuse things further the title page of this edition is signed 'Guilielmus noster Janssonius', which is the Latinized form of Blaeu's name commonly used up to 1619.

At some time after this the plates came into the possession of Speed's publishers, George Humble, who in 1627, the year in which he published a major edition of Speed's Atlas, also issued the Keere maps as a pocket edition. For these he used the descriptive texts of the larger Speed maps and thereafter they were known as Miniature Speeds. In fact, of the 63 maps in the Atlas, 40 were from the original van den Keere plates, reworked, 16 were reduced from Speed and 7 were additional. The publication was very popular and there were further re-issues up to 1676.

c. 1591–92 *Hiberniae novissima descriptio*: Boazio's map of Ireland, published by Jodocus Hondius

1593 Maps for *Speculum Britanniae* (John Norden)

1595 Charts for Willem Barentsz *Nieuwe beschryvinghe ende Caertboeck van de Midlandtsche Zee*

1595 Europe: wall map (Jodocus Hondius)

1599 Maps in *Caert Thresoor* (Langenes/Cornelis Claesz)

c. 1605–10 Maps for a miniature County Atlas of the British Isles: 44 maps probably issued in Amsterdam (no text)
1617 Re-issued in Amsterdam by W. J. Blaeu to accompany a Latin edition of Camden's *Britannia*: 46 maps (44 with Latin text)
1627 *England, Wales, Scotland and Ireland described and abridged from a farr Larger Voloume done by John Speed*
1631–76 Various re-issues
(For further detail see entry under John Speed.)

1607 World Map: twin hemisphere based on Plancius (1594)

1608 Charts in *Licht der Zeevaerdt* (W. J. Blaeu)

1614 *Americae Nova Descriptio*
Map of the American Continent with decorative borders of portraits and town views
1618 and later Re-issued

1617 *Germania Inferior* (Netherlands): Latin text, edited by Petrus Montanus
1622 (Latin), 1622 (French) Re-issued

1620 Maps in *Licht der Zeevaerdt* (Jan Jansson)

1628 Maps in *Atlas Minor* (Jan Jansson)

WILLEM BARENTSZ (BARENTZOON) c. 1560–97

Barentsz was a noted pilot who was convinced by the theorists of the day that it was possible to reach China and India via a North East passage through the Arctic. On his first voyage in 1594 accompanied by Jan van Linschoten he reached Novaya Zemlya but was forced back by ice: he failed again the following year. On his third voyage in 1596–97 his ship was trapped in pack ice and, although many of his crew survived in open boats, Barentsz himself died on the return voyage. He is noted for this chart book of the Mediterranean, the first of its kind, which was complementary to Waghenaer's charts of the Atlantic coasts, and which is sometimes found bound up with the later editions of Waghenaer.

1595   *Nieuwe beschryvinghe ende Caertboek van de*
        Midlandtsche Zee: 10 charts engraved by
        Pieter van den Keere
        1599, 1608 (Dutch) Re-issued
        1599, 1607, 1627 Re-issued with French
        text as *Description de la Mer Méditerranée* by
        Guillaume Bernard (Willem Barentsz)

1596–97 Charts of Ireland and Norway contained in
        Waghenaer's *Nieuwe Spiegel der Zeevaerdt*

JAN HUYGEN VAN LINSCHOTEN 1563–1610

Van Linschoten, born in Haarlem, is heard of in the
service of the Portuguese Archbishop of Goa where he
spent five years between 1583 and 1588. On his return
to Holland he produced a History of his travels,
important for the inclusion of maps from Portuguese
sources, at that time rarely available to Dutch – or any
other – cartographers. The maps (including a world
map by Petrus Plancius) engraved by van Langren, are
highly decorative with large cartouches, the arms of
Portugal, compass roses, rhumb lines and sea monsters. Some are illustrated with views of prominent
places or islands.

1596   *Itinerario*: 4 parts: 12 maps: Dutch text:
        Amsterdam (published by Cornelis Claesz)
        1598 (English), 1599 (Latin), 1605, 1614,
        1623, 1644 (Dutch), 1610, 1619, 1638
        (French) Re-issued with 15 maps

JAN BAPTIST VRIENTS 1552–1612

Vrients was the map engraver and publisher in
Antwerp who, after the death of Ortelius in 1598,
acquired the publication rights of the *Theatrum*.
Between 1601 and 1612 he issued a number of editions
which included some of his own maps and he was
responsible for printing the maps for the English
edition in 1606. He also published a number of
important individual maps and a small atlas of the
Netherlands.

1596   *Orbis Terrae Compendiosa descriptio*
        Double hemisphere world map with inset
        charts of the heavens

c. 1602 *Germania Inferior*
        19 maps of the Netherlands from the
        Theatrum Orbis Terrarum

CORNELIS WYTFLIET *fl.* 1597

Little is known of Wytfliet except that he was a native
of Brabant, but there is no doubt about the importance
of his only atlas, which was the first one printed to deal

exclusively with America. Although its title indicated
it to be a 'supplement to Ptolemy', Part I covered the
history of the discovery of America and its geography
and natural history and Part II consisted entirely of
contemporary maps of America and a world map based
on Mercator.

1597   *Descriptionis Ptolemaicae augmentum*:
        Louvain: Latin text: 19 maps
        1598–1615 Further editions printed in
        Louvain, Douai and Arnhem with Latin
        and French text: the French editions pub-
        lished under the title *Histoire Universelle des
        Indes Occidentales et Orientales* with 4 ad-
        ditional maps of China, Japan and the Far
        East

1598   Maps re-engraved and issued in Cologne
        by J. Christoffel to accompany a *Description
        of America* by José Acosta.

BARENT LANGENES *fl.* 1598–1610

Langenes was a publisher in Middelburg about whom
little is known except that he was probably the author
of the text and publisher of the first edition of a very
well known miniature atlas, the *Caert Thresoor*. After an
uneasy start – some maps were missing from the first
edition – the atlas acquired new life in Amsterdam with
a re-written text and eventually with re-engraved maps
which prolonged its use and popularity for about half a
century.

1598   *Caert Thresoor* (Miniature World Atlas)
        (8vo, approx. 85 × 120 mm)
        Maps engraved by Jodocus Hondius and
        Pieter van den Keere
        1599 Re-issued by Cornelis Claesz:
        Amsterdam (Dutch)
        1600–02   do   (French)
        1600 Re-issued by Cornelis Claesz and
        Jan Jansson the Elder with Latin text by
        Petrus Bertius
        1603   do   (Latin)
        1606 Re-issued by Cornelis Claesz (Latin)
        1609 Re-issue with revised 1598 text
        (Dutch)
        1612 Re-issue of 1600 edition in German
        1616 P. Bertii: *Tabularum geographicarum
        contractarum*: re-issue by Jodocus Hondius
        II with newly engraved, slightly larger
        maps (approx. 90 × 130 mm)
        1618 Re-issue of 1616 edition in Latin and
        French

1639 Re-issue by J. Blaeu (12mo)
1649 Re-issue of first edition by C. J. Visscher
1650 Petri Bertii: *Beschreibung der Ganzen Welt*: Re-issue by Jan Jansson of 1612 edition

PETRUS BERTIUS (BERT) 1565–1629

Petrus Bertius grew up in Beveren in Flanders and as a young man travelled widely in Europe. In company with so many of his compatriots he moved to Amsterdam as a refugee from religious persecution and after completing his studies there he was appointed a professor of mathematics and librarian at Leyden University. As well as being a prolific writer on mathematical, historical and theological subjects he is known as a cartographer for his editions of Ptolemy's *Geographia* (based on Mercator's edition of 1578) and for the miniature atlases detailed below. In 1618 he moved to Paris and became Official Cosmographer to Louis XIII. He was related by marriage to Jodocus Hondius and Pieter van den Keere.

1600   *Tabularum geographicarum contractarum* (Miniature World Atlas) (8vo) Latin text
This was a re-issue of the Caert Thresoor (1598) by Barent Langenes (see under Barent Langenes for detail of other editions).

1618–19 Ptolemy's *Geographia* (*Theatrum Geographiae Veteris*)
Edition containing 28 maps engraved by Mercator for his edition of 1578 plus 14 maps from Ortelius' *Parergon*: published by Jodocus Hondius II
(See also Appendix A.)

WILLEM JANSZOON BLAEU 1571–1638
JOAN BLAEU (son) 1596–1673
CORNELIS BLAEU (son) *d. c.* 1642

We have already written that at the beginning of the seventeenth century Amsterdam was becoming one of the wealthiest trading cities in Europe, the base of the Dutch East India Company and a centre of banking and the diamond trade, its people noted for their intellectual skills and splendid craftsmanship.

At this propitious time in the history of the Northern Provinces, Willem Janszoon Blaeu, who was born at Alkmaar in 1571 and trained in astronomy and the sciences by Tycho Brahe, the celebrated Danish astronomer, founded a business in Amsterdam in 1599 as a globe and instrument maker. It was not long before the business expanded, publishing maps, topographical works and books of sea charts as well as constructing globes. His most notable early work was a map of Holland (1604), a fine World Map (1605–06) and *Het Licht der Zeevaerdt* (The Light of Navigation), a marine atlas, which went through many editions in different languages and under a variety of titles. At the same time Blaeu was planning a major atlas intended to include the most up-to-date maps of the whole of the known world but progress on so vast a project was slow and not until he bought between 30 and 40 plates of the Mercator Atlas from Jodocus Hondius II to add to his own collection was he able to publish, in 1630, a 60-map volume with the title *Atlantis Appendix*. It was another five years before the first two volumes of his planned world atlas, *Atlas Novus* or the *Theatrum Orbis Terrarum* were issued. About this time he was appointed Hydrographer to the East India Company.

In 1638 Blaeu died and the business passed into the hands of his sons, Joan and Cornelis, who continued and expanded their father's ambitious plans. After the death of Cornelis, Joan directed the work alone and the whole series of 6 volumes was eventually completed about 1655. As soon as it was finished he began the preparation of the even larger work, the *Atlas Maior*, which reached publication in 1662 in 11 volumes (later editions in 9–12 volumes) and contained nearly 600 double-page maps and 3,000 pages of text. This was, and indeed remains, the most magnificent work of its kind ever produced; perhaps its geographical content was not as up-to-date or as accurate as its author could have wished, but any deficiencies in that direction were more than compensated for by the fine engraving and colouring, the elaborate cartouches and pictorial and heraldic detail and especially the splendid calligraphy.

In 1672 a disastrous fire destroyed Blaeu's printing house in the Gravenstraat and a year afterwards Joan Blaeu died. The firm's surviving stocks of plates and maps were gradually dispersed, some of the plates being bought by F. de Wit and Schenk and Valck, before final closure in about 1695.

It ought to be mentioned here that there is often confusion between the elder Blaeu and his rival Jan Jansson (Johannes Janssonius). Up to about 1619 Blaeu often signed his works Guilielmus Janssonius or Willems Jans Zoon but after that time he seems to have decided on Guilielmus or G. Blaeu.

Apart from the atlases and principal maps listed

CLAES JANSZ. VISSCHER *Daniae Regni Typum*. Published in Amsterdam in 1630, this is a fine example of the maps by the Visscher family.

below, the Blaeu family issued a large number of separate sheet maps, too numerous to list individually.

1604	Map of Holland
1605	Map of Spain
1605–06	World Map and the Continents issued separately without text
1608	The Continents (Wall Map)
1608	*Het Licht der Zeevaerdt*: 42 charts
	1608–30 Re-issued in 9 editions (Dutch)
	1612–22 Issued as *The Light of Navigation* (English)
	1619–25 Issued as *Flambeau de la Navigation* (French)

(See under Jan Jansson for editions by him.)

1617   William Camden's *Britannia*: abridged version with 46 miniature maps engraved by Pieter van den Keere: Latin text

1639 Re-issue with 22 maps from Petrus Bertius' *Tabularum geographicarum contractarum*: no text

1617   Maps of the Continents subsequently included in the *Atlantis Appendix* and the later Atlases

1623   *Der Zeespiegel*: 111 charts
        1623–52 10 re-issues (Dutch)
        1625–40 3 re-issues as *The Sea Mirrour* (English)
        1643–53 2 re-issues as *The Sea Beacon* (English)
        1655–66 Issued in enlarged form as *De Groote Zeespiegel*

1630   *Atlantis Appendix*: 60 maps: no text

1631   *Appendix – Theatri A. Ortelii et Atlantis G. Mercatori*
        2 editions in same year: 98–99 maps: Latin text

1635–55 *Theatrum Orbis Terrarum sive Atlas Novus*
        The following is a brief summary of the main editions of which there are many variants:
        1635–50 Vols I and II: editions with text in Latin, Dutch, French and German
        1640–50 Vol. III   do
        Volumes I, II and III covered maps of all parts of the world, except the Far East, the arrangement of contents varying greatly in different editions.
        1645–48 Vol. IV England and Wales (County Maps)
        (See Appendix B for further details.)
        1654 Vol. V Scotland and Ireland (County Maps): Latin, Dutch, French and German text
        1655 Vol. VI *Atlas Sinensis*: maps of China and Japan by Martino Martini: Latin, Dutch, French and German text

1648   *Nova Totius Terrarum Orbis Tabula*: World Map on 20 sheets

1649–51 *Toonneel der Steden van de Vereenighde Nederlanden* (Town Books of the Netherlands): 3 Latin, 3 Dutch editions with 220–26 town plans

1662–72 *Atlas Maior* (Grand Atlas)
        1662 Latin text: 11 volumes
        1663 French text: 12 volumes
        1667 Re-issued
        1664 Dutch text: 9 volumes
        1667 German text: 9 volumes
        1672 Spanish text: 10 volumes
        Printed between 1658 and 1672 but never completed owing to loss of plates in the fire of 1672. Some volumes made up with Spanish text pasted over sheets in other languages.

        Note: The number of volumes of the *Atlas Maior* varied in different editions and therefore the number of maps varied also but the contents of the French edition give a general indication of the arrangement:
        Vol. I Northern Europe, Norway, Denmark
        Vol. II Eastern Europe, Russia, Poland, Sweden and Greece
        Vol. III Germany
        Vol. IV The Netherlands
        Vol. V England
        Vol. VI Scotland and Ireland
        Vol. VII France and ⎫
        Vol. VIII Switzerland ⎭
        Vol. IX Italy
        Vol. X Spain, Africa
        Vol. XI Asia
        Vol. XII America

1663–1726 Town Books of Italy
        Between 1663 and 1726 many editions with varying contents, text in Dutch, French and Latin, were published by J. Blaeu and his heirs (Amsterdam), A. Moetjeus (The Hague), P. Mortier (Amsterdam) and R. C. Alberts (The Hague).

★

JAN JANSZOON (JANSSON) THE ELDER *fl.* 1597–1629
Jan Janszoon, a bookseller and publisher working in Arnhem, was responsible for issues of a number of important atlases. His publishing interests brought him and his son, the noted Jan Jansson, into touch with the Hondius family, an association which lasted for something like forty years.

1607–21 *Atlas Minor* (Mercator/Hondius)
        7 editions

1615   *Le Miroir du Monde* (Z. Heyns)

1615   *Discriptionis Prolemaicae augmentum* (C. Wytfliet)

1617   Ptolemy's *Geographia* (Magini)

NICOLAAS VAN GEELKERCKEN *fl.* 1610–35
Engraver, cartographer, publisher active in Leyden, Arnhem and Amsterdam in the early years of the seventeenth century. His maps, though few in number, were particularly elegant.

1610   World Map

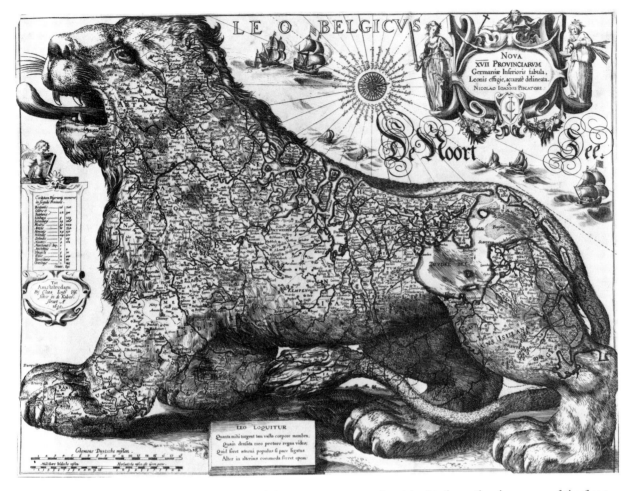

LEO BELGICUS   *The Low Countries.* An example of the numerous maps printed in this form; the above, one of the finest, was issued by Claes Jansz. Visscher in Amsterdam in 1630.

| 1617–18 | World Map: published by Jan Jansson 1632 Re-issued |
| 1618 | Switzerland: maps of Swiss Alpine regions 1630, 1645 Re-issued |

HESSEL GERRITSZ 1581–1632

Gerritsz was apprenticed to W. J. Blaeu as an engraver before starting in business on his own account. He worked closely with Petrus Plancius and his merit may be judged by the fact that he was appointed Cartographer to the Dutch East India Company in preference to Blaeu and subsequently held the same position in a newly formed West India Company. With the new company he came into touch with Johannes de Laet for whom he prepared a number of new maps of America in the latter's *Nieuwe Wereldt* published in 1625. His most important early work was a chart showing Henry Hudson's discoveries in his voyage of 1610–11: it is the first to give an outline of Hudson's Bay and indicates Hudson's belief that he had found a way to the North West Passage.

1612	Chart based on Henry Hudson's discoveries
1625–40	Maps in J. de Laet's *Nieuwe Wereldt*
1627–28	Charts of the South Seas showing the first discoveries in Australia (Eendracht's Land)

JAN JANSSON   *Norfolk.* A county map first published in Jansson's German Appendix to the Mercator/Hondius Atlas, 1638.

JAN JANSSON 1588–1664

Johannes Janssonius, more commonly known to us as Jan Jansson, was born in Arnhem where his father was a bookseller and publisher (Jan Janszoon the Elder). In 1612 he married the daughter of the cartographer and publisher Jodocus Hondius, and then set up in business in Amsterdam as a book publisher. In 1616 he published his first maps of France and Italy and from then onwards he produced a very large number of maps, perhaps not quite rivalling those of the Blaeu family but running a very close second in quantity and quality. From about 1630 to 1638 he was in partnership with his brother-in-law, Henricus Hondius, issuing further editions of the Mercator/Hondius atlases to which his name was added. On the death of Henricus he took over the business, expanding the atlas still further, until eventually he published an 11-volume

Atlas Major on a scale similar to Blaeu's *Atlas Maior.*

The first full edition of Jansson's English County Maps was published in 1646 but some years earlier he issued a number of British maps in the Mercator/Hondius/Jansson series of atlases (1636–44); the maps were printed from newly engraved plates and are different from the later 1646 issue and are now rarely seen (see Appendix B for further details). In general appearance Jansson's maps are very similar to those of Blaeu and, in fact, were often copied from them, but they tend to be more flamboyant and, some think, more decorative.

After Jansson's death his heirs published a number of maps in an *Atlas Contractus* in 1666 and later still many of the plates of his British maps were acquired by Pieter Schenk and Gerard Valck, who published them again in 1683 as separate maps.

1616   Maps of France and Italy

1620–37 *Het Licht der Zeevaerdt*
Charts copied from W. J. Blaeu's marine atlas of the same title issued in 1608
1620–34 Dutch: 1620–25 English: 1620–37 French editions
1650 *Le nouveau Flambeau de la Mer*: re-issue of the same charts with revised text

1626   *Nova Totius Terrarum Orbis*: decorative World Map based on earlier map by D. E. Lons
1632 Re-issued

1628   *Atlas Minor* (Mercator/Hondius/Jansson series)
Continuing the miniature atlas first issued by Jodocus Hondius and Jan Jansson the Elder in 1607: the maps were newly engraved by Pieter van den Keere and Abraham Goos: average size 180–190 × 230–245 mm (for further detail see under Gerard Mercator).
1628–51 9 editions in Latin, French, German and Dutch

1630   *Atlantis Maioris Appendix*: 80 maps

1631–32–36 *Theatrum Universal Galliae*
Theatrum Imperii Germanici
Theatrum Italiae
In an attempt to break away from their reliance on Mercator's maps, Henricus Hondius and Jansson issued the above atlas in 3 parts, using entirely new maps, but the experiment met with little success and few copies were issued: the maps, therefore, are now extremely rare.

1633   Atlas (Mercator/Hondius/Jansson series)
1633–41 In this period Jansson, in conjunction with Henricus Hondius, republished the series of Mercator atlases, first reprinted in 1606 by Jodocus Hondius. Apart from the English edition of 1636, there were editions in Latin, Dutch, French and German. From about 1638 under Jansson's direction the work developed into the *Atlas Novus* (see below)

1638   *Atlas Novus (Nieuwen Atlas)*
1638–66 Starting with an issue of 2 volumes in 1638, the atlas eventually expanded through many editions to 6 volumes (Vol. IV Great Britain 1646), (Vol. V Sea Atlas 1650). Finally, during the period

1650–60, the contents of the 6 volumes were used as the basis of a new *Atlas Major* (see Appendix B for further detail of Volume IV, Great Britain).

1647–62 *Atlas Major*: Dutch, 9 vols
1647–62 German: 11 vols
1658–66 Latin: 9 vols
1680–83 English: 4 vols
This English edition was started by Moses Pitt in association with Janssonius van Waesbergen but van Waesbergen died in 1681 and Pitt's hopes of issuing it complete were frustrated by financial difficulties.

1650   Petrus Bertius: *Beschreibung der Ganzen Welt* re-issue of the 1612 edition of the *Caert Thresoor* (Langenes)

1651   *De Lichtende Columne ofte Zee-Spiegel*
1654 Re-issue in English as *The Lighting Colomne or Sea Mirrour*
Both editions copied without alteration from the plates used by Pieter Goos/Anthonie Jacobsz

1652–57 *Theatrum Praecipuarum Urbium*
A series of plans of the principal cities and towns of Europe – about 500 in all in 8 volumes – which Jansson based on Braun and Hogenberg's *Civitates Orbis Terrarum*, the plates of which he acquired after the death of Abraham Hogenberg. Each volume bears a different title, depending on the area covered. The work was re-issued by Jansson's heirs in 1682, in abridged form.

1652   *Accuratissima orbis Antiqui Delineatio* (Atlas of the Antique World)
1653, 1654, 1660 Re-issued
1677, 1684, 1700 (English) Re-issued by Janssonius van Waesbergen and his successors
1740, 1741 (French): 1741 (English) Re-issued by P. de Hondt

1666   *Atlas Contractus*: 2 volumes (published by Jansson's heirs)

WILLEM CORNELIS SCHOUTEN 1567–1625
JACOB LE MAIRE *d.* 1617
The voyage of Schouten/Le Maire in the years 1615–17 was one of the most important in the seventeenth century; they were the first to sail round Cape Horn (named after their home town Hoorn in Holland),

disproving the long held theory that Tierra del Fuego was part of a southern continent.

Subsequent accounts of the voyage, with maps, were published by Schouten (1618) and Le Maire (posthumously, 1622).

CASPAR BARLÄEUS 1584–1648

Barläeus was an historian and theologian who compiled a small number of maps for historical works of his time. His maps of Brazil were particularly important and were used by Joan Blaeu.

1622	*Descripción de la Indias Occidentales* (Antonio de Herrera): 17 maps
1647	*Rerum in Brasilia Gestarum Historia*: 3 maps

JOHANNES DE LAET 1583–1649

1625	*Nieuwe Wereldt* (small folio): maps of the New World including a number by Hessel Gerritsz 1630 (Dutch), 1633 (Latin), 1640 (French) editions

---

PIETER VERBIEST *c.* 1607–74

An engraver and publisher active in Antwerp who produced a small number of maps including one of the British Isles based on an earlier map by N. Visscher.

1629–46	British Isles
1636	*Tabula Geographicarum Belgicae Liber* (Maps of the Low Countries) 1644, 1652 Re-issued
1636–56	Maps of the World, Germany, Italy, France and Spain

JACOB AERTSZ COLOM 1600–73
ARNOLD COLOM (son) *c.* 1624–68

Jacob Colom was a printer, bookseller, chart and globe maker who set out to challenge the virtual monopoly held by W. J. Blaeu, then the only chart maker in Amsterdam. His Pilot Guide *De Vyerighe Colom* published in various formats and languages (with exotic titles) to meet the demands of the time was highly successful and forced Blaeu to revise and enlarge his existing chart books. In spite of Blaeu's efforts, Colom's Guide remained popular with seamen for many years and although the charts were issued in great quantity, they are now extremely rare.

1632–71	*De Vyerighe Colom* 13 editions with Dutch text

{ *L'Ardante ou Flamboyante Colomne de la Mer*
Colom de la Mer Mediterannée

9 editions with French text

{ *The Fierie Sea Columne*
The New Fierie Sea Columne
True and Perfect Fierie Colom

12 editions with English text

Parts I, II and III issued in the above 34 editions in different sizes: folio, large folio and oblong. There were also editions in English (1648) and Dutch (1662) with the title *Upright Fyrie Colomne*

1663–69	*Atlas of Werelts-water-deel* (Sea Atlas) Various editions with numbers of maps increasing from 23 to 52: texts in Dutch, French, Latin, Portuguese, and Spanish

Arnold Colom

1654–58	*Zee Atlas ofte Water-wereldt* Three editions with 16–18 maps: text in Latin or Dutch
1660–61	*Lighting Colom of the Midland See* English text: 19 maps of the Mediterranean

---

CLAES JANSZ. VISSCHER 1587–1652
NICOLAES VISSCHER I (son) 1618–79
NICOLAES VISSCHER II (grandson) 1649–1702
ELIZABETH VISSCHER (widow of N. Visscher II) d. 1726

For nearly a century the members of the Visscher family were important art dealers and map publishers in Amsterdam. The founder of the business, C. J. Visscher, had premises near to those of Pieter van den Keere and Jodocus Hondius whose pupil he may have been. From about 1620 he designed a number of individual maps, including one of the British Isles, but his first atlas consisted of maps printed from plates bought from van den Keere and issued as they stood with some additions of his own, including historical scenes of battles and sieges for which he had a high reputation. Some maps bear the latinized form of the family name: Piscator. After Visscher's death his son and grandson, both of the same name, issued a considerable number of atlases, constantly revised and brought up to date but most of them lacking an index and with varying contents. The widow of Nicholaes Visscher II carried on the business until it finally passed into the hands of Pieter Schenk.

JOAN BLAEU *Dorset*. A typical county map from Volume 4 of Blaeu's *Theatrum Orbis Terrarum*, first published in Amsterdam in 1645.

Claes Jansz. Visscher

1634   *Belgium sive Germania inferior*: 43 maps
       1637, *c.* 1645 Re-issued with additional maps

1649   *Tabularum Geographicarum contractarum*
       Re-issue of the *Caert Thresoor* by Langenes (1598)

Nicolaes Visscher I

1656–79   *Atlas Contractus Orbis Terrarum*
       Several editions with varying contents

c. 1677   *Germania Inferior*: 52 maps
       Maps by the Visschers, Jansson, Blaeu and others

Nicolaes Visscher II

c. 1684   *Germania Inferior*: 21 maps

c. 1683–98   *Atlas Minor*
       In spite of its name this was a full-scale atlas in folio size.
       Several editions with numbers of maps varying from about 60 to 150.

Elizabeth Visscher

c. 1702–16   *Atlas Minor*
       6 editions with numbers of maps varying from 50 to 150, many bearing her name

c. 1702   *Atlas Major*: 2 volumes: 200 maps
       Enlarged edition of the *Atlas Minor*

PETRUS MONTANUS (Pieter van den Berg) *fl.* 1606–
A Dutch geographer, active in Amsterdam, who worked in association with his brother-in-law, Jodocus Hondius, for whom he prepared the text of the Mercator/Hondius Atlas (1606 and later editions). The map noted below, attributed to Montanus, is the first separately printed one of Maryland; known as 'Lord Baltimore's Map' it was published by him to attract settlers to the colony.

1635   *Nova Terrae-Mariae Tabula* (Maryland)
        Published in *A Relation of Maryland* by Lord Baltimore, London

ANTHONIE (THEUNIS) JACOBSZ *c.* 1606–50
JACOB JACOBSZ (LOOTSMAN) (son) *d.* 1679
CASPAR JACOBSZ (LOOTSMAN)(son) 1635–1711
Anthonie Jacobsz founded a printing and publishing business in Amsterdam in which he specialized in the production of pilot books and sea atlases. As he died at a comparatively early age most of the numerous editions of his works appeared after his death published by his sons, Jacob and Caspar, who took the name 'Lootsman' (sea pilot) to distinguish them from another printer of the name Jacobsz.

Following Blaeu and Colom, Anthonie Jacobsz was the most important compiler of sea charts in Amsterdam in the first half of the seventeenth century. In his new *Zee–Spiegel* issued in 1643 he increased the number of charts normally included in these books and enlarged them to folio size, which evidently proved popular. Editions in many forms appeared until 1715 and they were copied or reprinted by Pieter Goos, Hendrick Doncker and Jan Jansson, sometimes in competition with each other but usually in co-operation with the Lootsman brothers.

c. 1643– *De Lichtende Columne ofte Zee-Spiegel*
1717   *Nieuw en Groote Lootsmans Zee-Spiegel*
           Parts I and II Dutch text: about 23 editions under these and other titles
           1666–97 *Le Grand et Nouveau Mirrour ou Flambeau de la Mer*
           French text: 9 editions
           1649–92 *The Lightning Colomne – or Sea Mirrour*
           English text: 10 editions
           The number of charts in all these editions varied from about 33 to 70 depending on whether Parts I and II were issued together or separately.

1648–1704 *'t Nieuw Groot Straets-boeck*
           Part III of the *Zee-Spiegel* – the Mediterranean
           Dutch text: 9 editions: 14–20 charts
           1659–79 *Le Nouveau grand livre de l'Etroit*
           French text: 4 editions: 20–21 charts
           1678–c. 1703 *Lightning Colom of the Midland Sea*
           English text: 6 editions: 20–22 charts
1652–54   *'t Nieuwe en Vergroote Zee-boeck*
           Pilot guide in reduced format
           3 editions with 80–87 charts: average size 300 × 380 mm with a small number about 300 × 540 mm (folded)
1666–94   *Nieuwe Water-warelt ofte Zee Atlas* (The Sea Atlas of the Water World)
           L'Atlas de la Mer ou Monde Aquatique
           4 Dutch, 8 English, 1 French edition: 22 to about 40 charts
1692–1701 *The English Coasting Pilot*
           3 editions: 14–15 charts: 455 × 280 mm

ABRAHAM GOOS *fl.* 1614–43
PIETER GOOS (son) *c.* 1615–75
Abraham Goos was a noted engraver in Amsterdam who prepared plates for many maps published in well-known atlases of his time including Speed's *A Prospect of the Most Famous Parts of the World* (1627) and the 1632 edition of Speed's Atlas. He was related to the Hondius family by whom he was also employed as an engraver. In 1616 he issued a book of maps, the *Nieuw Nederlandtsh Caertboeck* (4to) which was re-issued in 1619 and 1625.

His son, Pieter, continued and extended his father's business and became one of the group of well-known engravers of sea charts active in Amsterdam in the middle years of the seventeenth century. In common with Colom, Doncker and Jacobsz he published a pilot guide, the *Zee-Spiegel*, basing it on plates obtained from Jacobsz. This went through many editions in different languages under the startling titles so popular at the time. In addition to publishing his *Zee-Spiegel* in the usual Parts I and II (Europe and Atlantic coasts) and Part III (Mediterranean) he broke new ground in preparing Parts IV and V, covering charts and sailing directions for the coasts of the West Indies and West Africa. The later editions of the *Zee Atlas* were published by his widow who eventually sold the publishing rights of the Atlas and of the *Zee-Spiegel* to Jacobus Robijn.

1650–85   *De Lichtende Columne ofte Zee-Spiegel*
De Nieuwe Groote Zee-Spiegel
The Lightning Colomne or Sea Mirrour
Lightning Colom of the Midland Sea
Le grand & Nouveau Miroir ou Flambeau de la Mer

Parts I, II and III issued in many editions in Dutch, English and French
1675 Part V: West Indies and American seaboard: 33 charts compiled by Arent Roggeveen for his *Het Brandende Veen* (The Burning Fen) Part I
c. 1685 Part IV: Atlantic Coasts of Africa: charts by Arent Roggeveen for Part II of the above work. Published by J. Robijn

1666–83   *De Zee Atlas ofte Water-Weereld*
41–44 maps in about 11 editions
1666–73 *L'Atlas de la Mer ou Monde Aquatique*
5 editions
1667–70 *Sea Atlas or the Water World*
5 editions
1668–76 *El Atlas de la Mar o Mundo de Agua*
2 editions

FREDERICK DE WIT 1630–1706

De Wit was one of the most prominent and successful map engravers and publishers in Amsterdam in the period following the decline of the Blaeu and Jansson establishments, from which he acquired many copper plates when they were dispersed at auction. His output covered most aspects of map making: sea charts, world atlases, an atlas of the Netherlands, 'town books' covering plans of towns and cities in the Netherlands and Europe, and wall maps. His work, notable for the beauty of the engraving and colouring, was very popular and editions were issued many years after his death by Pieter Mortier and Covens and Mortier.

c. 1654   (with Th. Jacobsz) *Zee Atlas*: 16 charts by de Wit and Jacobsz

c. 1670–
c. 1707   *Atlas* or *Atlas sive descriptio Terrarum Orbis* or *Atlas Maior*
Between these years, many editions of these atlases were published, the smallest with 17 maps, the largest under the title *Atlas Maior* with about 180: some included the charts from the *Zee Atlas* (below).
c. 1706–08 Re-issued in London by Christopher Browne as *Atlas Maior* (1706) and

Atlas Minor (1708)
c. 1710 Re-issued by Pieter Mortier as *Atlas Maior*
c. 1725 Re-issued by Covens and Mortier as *Atlas Maior*

c. 1675   *Orbis Maritimus ofte Zee Atlas* or *Atlas tabulae maritimae ofte Zee Kaarten*: 27 charts
c. 1680 Re-issued

c. 1680–90   *Germania Inferior*
Maps of the Netherlands in various editions

c. 1694–
1700   *Theatrum praecipuarum totius Europae urbium*
About 132 plans of European towns based on those of Jan Jansson

c. 1698   (*Theatrum ichnographicum*
(Town Book of the Netherlands
About 128 plans based on those of Blaeu, Jansson and others

GEORG HORN 1620–70

1652   *Accuratissima orbis antiqui delineatio*
Maps of the ancient world
1660–1740 Re-issued
1741 English edition – *A Compleat Body of Ancient Geography*

HENDRICK DONCKER *c.* 1626–99
HENDRICK DONCKER II (son) *c.* 1664–*c.* 1739

For about fifty years Hendrick Doncker ran a flourishing business in Amsterdam as a bookseller and publisher of sea atlases and textbooks on navigation. In a period when so many maps and charts were simply copied from other publishers, Doncker's charts were his own work and were noted for their accuracy and constant improvement. Apart from this work, he cooperated for many years with Pieter Goos and Anthonie Jacobsz in producing a pilot guide *De Zeespiegel*. Eventually his stock was sold to Johannes van Keulen.

1655   *De Lichtende Columne ofte Zee-Spiegel*
65 charts: the same as those issued by Goos and Jacobsz
1664–81 *Nieuw Groot Stuurmans Zee-Spiegel*
A number of editions containing about 64 new charts by Doncker
1682–93 *De Nieuwe Vermeerderde Stuurmans Zee-Spiegel*
A number of editions with new title and charts

1659–72   *De Zee-Atlas of Water-Waereld*
           The Sea Atlas of the Water World
           L'Atlas de Mer
           La Atlas del Mundo o El Mundo aguado
           Numerous editions, being enlarged from
           19 to 50 maps: text in Dutch, French,
           English and Spanish

1675–1705   *De Nieuwe Groote Vermeederde Zee-Atlas*
           Editions in Dutch, French and English
           with 50–70 enlarged charts

1685   *Nieuw Nederlandtsch Caertboeck*
           22 maps taken from atlas of the same name
           by Abraham Goos (1616)

c. 1700   (H. Doncker II) Atlas of the River Don
           17 maps by Cornelis Cruys

PIETER VAN ALPHEN *c.* 1632–91

A bookseller and publisher in Rotterdam, whose charts and maps were largely based on those of his father-in-law, Jacob Aertsz. Colom. His *Nieuwe Zee-Atlas* of 1660 was an important assembly of sea charts including many of South East Asia and Australia.

1660   *Nieuwe Zee-Atlas* (A New Sea Atlas)
           1660 (Dutch and Spanish), 1661 (English),
           1682 (Dutch) Re-issued

1662   *A new shining light or discovery of the Northermost and Westermost Waters* (Pilot Guide)

1691   Provinces of the Netherlands

JAN VAN LOON *fl. c.* 1649–86

Van Loon was a mathematician and engraver who contributed charts and maps to various pilot books and sea atlases by Jacobsz, Jan Jansson, Johannes Janssonius van Waesbergen and Robijn. In 1661 he published a sea atlas which was popular until the end of the century.

1661–1706   *Klaer-Lichtende Noort-Star ofte Zee-Atlas*
           1661 Issued with 35 charts
           1666, 1668, 1676, 1706 Issued by Janssonius van Waesbergen with 47–50 charts

---

JOHANNES JANSSONIUS VAN WAESBERGEN *fl.* 1661–81
(JAN JANSSON'S HEIRS)

Van Waesbergen, established as a bookseller in Amsterdam, acquired by inheritance from his father-in-law Jan Jansson many of Jansson's plates including those of the *Atlas Minor*, the *Civitates Orbis Terrarum* and the *Atlas of the Antique World*. These works were republished by him, or after his death in 1681 by his son, also named Johannes. For a time he was associated with Moses Pitt in the abortive attempt in 1680–81 to publish an English version of the major atlases by Blaeu and Jansson.

1666   *Atlas Contractus* (Jan Jansson's Heirs)

1673–1676   *Atlas Minor*

1677–1684   *Accuratissima Orbis Antiqui Delineatio* (Atlas of the Antique World)
           1700 English edition

1682   *Tooneel der Vermaarste Koop-steden* (Town Books)
           Re-issue in abridged form of the *Civitates Orbis Terrarum* (Braun and Hogenberg) with many plates re-engraved

---

JACOB VAN MEURS *c.* 1620–80

Publisher, active in Amsterdam, who produced *De Nieuwe en Onbekende Wereld* for Arnold Montanus, which was used by John Ogilby as the basis of his *Complete History of America*.

1670–71   *De Nieuwe en Onbekende Wereld*

c. 1677   Maps of Syria and Palestine by Dr O. Dapper

ARNOLD MONTANUS *fl.* 1671

Published a notable Atlas of America which was used by John Ogilby as the basis for his *An Accurate Description and Complete History of America*. The maps were extremely decorative and included a view of New Amsterdam as it appeared soon after its foundation.

1670–71   *De Nieuwe en Onbekende Wereld*: Amsterdam, published by Jacob van Meurs
           Maps of America including Virginia and New England, Central America and the Caribbean
           1673 German issue by Dr O. Dapper (1636–89)
           1729 Re-issued by Pieter van der Aa
           1761 Re-issued by Covens and Mortier

HUGH (HUYCH) ALLARD *fl. c.* 1645–91
CAREL ALLARD (son) 1648–1709
ABRAHAM ALLARD (grandson) *d. c.* 1730

The Allard family ran an active publishing business in Amsterdam in the latter half of the seventeenth century. Most of their publications consisted of atlases made up of maps and town plans by their more famous predecessors, Blaeu, Jansson, de Wit, Visscher and others, but one of their most attractive and interesting

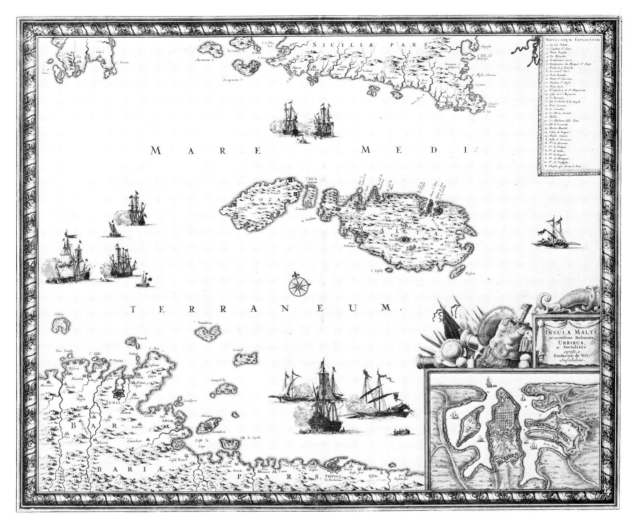

FREDERICK DE WIT   *Insula Malta*. De Wit produced a very large number of maps and charts of every part of the world as well as town plans. This map of Malta with inset of Valletta was published in Amsterdam about 1680.

sheet maps was of New England (Hugo Allard, 1656), based on Jansson, which included a view of New Amsterdam by C. J. Visscher.

1673   *New and Exact Map of All New Netherland*
          1675 and later re-issues
1697   *Atlas Minor* (folio)
          Re-issued by Covens and Mortier
c. 1698   *Orbis Habitabilis oppida*: town plans with
          costumed figures
1705   *Atlas Major*: 3 volumes: about 520 maps of
          various sizes
c. 1706   *Magnum Theatrum Belli*: maps and plans of
          forts and fortified cities

ARENT ROGGEVEEN *fl.* 1665–79

Roggeveen was a land surveyor and mathematician by profession, working in Middelburg where the Dutch East and West India Companies maintained collections of hydrographic manuscripts and charts, including Spanish portulans of the West Indies. No doubt through contacts there Roggeveen became interested in navigation and he compiled a pilot book of large-scale charts of the West Indies and parts of the American coasts, with a second volume of the coasts of West Africa. These were the first such charts printed in Holland.

1675 *Het Brandende Veen* (The Burning Fen)
Part I: West Indies and the American seaboard
33 charts published by Pieter Goos in English, French and Spanish as Part IV of his *Zee-Spiegel*.
1680, 1689, *c.* 1698 Re-issued by J. Robijn

c. 1685 Part II: Atlantic coasts of Africa
19 charts published by J. Robijn

CORNELIS DANKERTS THE ELDER 1603–56
JUSTUS DANKERTS (son) 1635–1701
THEODORUS DANKERTS (grandson) 1663–1727
CORNELIS DANKERTS II (grandson) 1664–1717

The Dankerts family, of whom the above were the most important, were prominent print and map sellers active in Amsterdam for nearly a century. Between the years 1680 and 1700 a number of atlases were produced with maps bearing the names Justus or Theodorus Dankerts. These are now very rare and as the title pages and maps are undated it is difficult, if not impossible, to place any map against any particular edition. The Dankerts were also noted for production of splendid wall maps of the world and the continents.

Their stock of plates was acquired by R. and J. Ottens who used them for re-issues, having replaced the Dankerts names with their own.

1680–1700 Atlas
Several editions with the number of maps varying from 26 to about 100: no text on reverse

c. 1690 Pocket Atlas of the Southern Netherlands: map in 32 numbered sections

1703 Planisphere Terrestre
A re-issue of J. B. Nolin's World Map (1696) based on J. D. Cassini's planisphere

JOHANNES VAN KEULEN 1654–1711
GERARD VAN KEULEN 1678–*c.* 1727
JOHANNES VAN KEULEN II *fl.* 1726–55
GERARD HULST VAN KEULEN *fl.* 1757–1801
CORNELIS BUYS VAN KEULEN *fl.* 1757–78
JOHANNES GERARD HULST VAN KEULEN *fl.* 1810–23

As we have noted in other biographies in this chapter, the Dutch produced a remarkable number of enterprising and prolific map and chart makers but not even the Blaeu and Jansson establishments could rival the vigour of the van Keulen family whose business was founded in 1680 and continued under their name until

1823 and in other names until 1885 when it was finally wound up and the stock dispersed at auction. Throughout the history of the family, the widows of several of the van Keulens played a major part, after their husbands' deaths, in maintaining the continuity of the business.

The firm was founded by Johannes van Keulen who was registered as a bookseller in Amsterdam in 1678. In 1680 he published the first part of his *Zee Atlas* which, over the years, was expanded to 5 volumes and continued in one form or another until 1734. More ambitious and with a far longer and more complicated life was his book of sea charts, the *Zee-Fakkel*, published in 1681–82 which was still being printed round the year 1800. A major influence in the development of the firm was the acquisition in 1693 of the stock of a rival map publisher, Hendrik Doncker.

Although the firm was founded by Johannes van Keulen, he was primarily a publisher; it was his son, Gerard, a talented engraver, mathematician, Hydrographer to the East India Company, who became the mainspring of the business which not only published charts but also books on every aspect of geography, navigation and nautical matters.

Set out below is a very brief detail of the issues of the *Zee Atlas* and *Zee-Fakkel*.

1680–1734 *De Groote Nieuwe Vermeerderde Zee Atlas ofte Water-werelt*
Between these years the *Zee Atlas* was published in about 34 editions with text in Dutch, French, English and Spanish: the number of maps varied from as few as 25 to a peak of 185 in 1707–08. Generally the size was approximately 540–550 × 340–350 mm although in 1706, 1710, 1718 and 1734 Gerard van Keulen issued editions with maps enlarged to about 600 × 1,000 mm

1681–1803 *De Nieuwe Groote Lichtende Zee-Fakkel*
Le Nouveau & Grand Illuminant Flambeau de la Mer
The Lightning Columne or Sea Mirrour
La Nueva y Grande Relumbrante Antorcha de la Mar
Della nuova e grande Illuminante Face del Mare
Part I (1681) North Sea and Baltic
Part II (1681) North Sea, the Channel, Coasts of England, Portugal and Spain
Part III (1682) Mediterranean
Part IV (1684) West Indies and Eastern

Seaboard of North America
Part V (1683) Atlantic coasts of Africa and Brazil (in later editions, charts of the Indian Ocean)
Part VI (1753) Indian Ocean and Far East
Average size: 500–510 × 580–590 mm: some editions incorporated larger charts – 600 × 1,000 mm
In all there were over 120 editions of the *Zee-Fakkel* with text in Dutch, French, English (1716, one edition of Parts I and III only), Spanish and Italian. The original charts were compiled by Claes Janszoon Vooght and frequently only his name appears, even on the atlas title pages. In later years, especially under the direction of Gerard van Keulen and his sons, the charts were constantly revised and increased in number. Until the founding of the Dutch Hydrographic Office in 1856 they were regarded as the 'official' Dutch sea charts.

CLAES JANSZ. VOOGHT *fl.* 1680–96
Not much is known of Vooght's personal life beyond his own description of himself as a 'surveyor and teacher of mathematics and the art of navigation' on which he was a prolific writer. He is noted as the author of charts in Johannes van Keulen's *Zee-Fakkel*; indeed, on some editions only his name appears and in consequence the *Zee-Fakkel* is often catalogued under his name.

JACOBUS ROBIJN 1649–*c.* 1707
About 1675, shortly before the van Keulen publishing business was set up in Amsterdam, Robijn practised there as a map 'illuminator' and chart seller. After a short association with Johannes van Keulen he acquired publishing rights covering the *Zee-Spiegel* and *Zee Atlas* from the widow of Pieter Goos and used the plates to produce his own pilot book and sea atlas. Apart from a small number of plates prepared to his own order, most of Robijn's work cannot be said to be original: he issued Goos's charts and those of Roggeveen with a variety of texts by J. and C. Jacobsz (Lootsman), Arent Roggeveen and even John Seller with the result that analysis of the various issues cannot easily be simplified. Robijn's stock was eventually taken over by Johannes Loots. The brief details given

below should be read in conjunction with our notes on Pieter Goos and Arent Roggeveen.

1682–96   *Zee Atlas*
9 editions with Dutch, French, English and Spanish text: the number of charts varied from 20 to 54, some by Robijn, others by Pieter Goos

c. 1680–98   *Nieuwe Groote Zee-Spiegel*
1680–98 Part V: three editions of 32–34 charts of the West Indies and the American seaboard compiled by Arent Roggeveen for his *Het Brandende Veen* (The Burning Fen) Part 1, first published by Pieter Goos (1675)
c. 1685 Part IV: 19 charts of the Atlantic coasts of Africa, compiled by Arent Roggeveen for Part II of the same work
1690–94 Parts I, II and III: charts copied from Pieter Goos's *De Nieuwe Groote Zee-Spiegel*

1688–   *Sea Mirrour*
Parts I, II and III: charts copied from Pieter Goos with English text 'borrowed' from Goos, Jacobsz and Seller.
c. 1717 Parts IV and V: charts from *The Burning Fen* (as above)
Re-issued by Joh. Loots

BERNHARD VAREN *fl.* 1622–50
Dutch physician and geographer whose work was used long after his death by Richard Blome and others.

1682–93   *A Compleat System of General Geography*
Translated and published by Richard Blome in his *Cosmography and Geography* containing charts and 24 maps of the world, the Continents and various countries and about 37 maps of the English counties
1733 Re-issued

PIETER SCHENK 1660–*c.* 1718
PIETER SCHENK (son) *c.* 1698–1775
PIETER SCHENK (grandson) 1728–*c.* 1784
Pieter Schenk was born in Germany but settled in Amsterdam where he became a pupil of Gerard Valck, the engraver. In 1687 he married Valck's sister and thereafter the Schenk and Valck families were active over a long period with a wide range of interests as

print sellers, publishers of books, maps, topographical and architectural drawings and globe makers. Although the Schenk family produced some original maps, most of their atlases consisted of printings from revised and re-worked plates originally by Jansson, the Visschers, the Sansons and others.

c. 1683–94	(with Gerard Valck) Re-issue of separate maps from the *Atlas Novus* by Jan Jansson
c. 1700	*Atlas Contractus* or *Atlas Minor* Maps by Jansson, de Wit, Visscher and others *c.* 1705, 1709 Re-issued 1719 Re-issued by P. Schenk II
1702	*Hecatompolis* 100 town plans and views, about half being taken from Carel Allard's similar publication 1752 Re-issued
c. 1702	(with Leonard Valck) *Atlantis sylloge compendiosa* or *Nova totius Geographia* Various issues covering 25 to 100 maps
1706	*Schouwburg van den Oorlog* Historical atlas 1707, 1709 Re-issued *c.* 1719, *c.* 1727, *c.* 1730 Re-issued by P. Schenk II
1715	(with Gerard Valck) *Atlas Anglois* 34 maps: published in London by D. Mortier with later issues by Covens and Mortier
c. 1752	(P. Schenk II) *Neuer Sächsischer Atlas* 1754, 1758, 1759, 1760, 1810 Re-issued
c. 1750	(P. Schenk II) *Atlas van Zuyd Holland*

GERARD VALCK *c.* 1651–1726
LEONARD VALCK (son) 1675–*c.* 1755

Gerard Valck and his son were printers, engravers and globe makers in Amsterdam, closely linked by marriage with the Schenk family with whom they also had a long business association in map engraving and publishing. For further detail see entry under Pieter Schenk.

c. 1683–94	(with Pieter Schenk) Re-issue of separate maps from the *Atlas Novus* by Jan Jansson
c. 1702	(with Pieter Schenk) *Atlantis sylloge compendiosa* or *Nova totius Geographia* Various issues covering 25 to 100 maps
1715	(with Pieter Schenk) *Atlas Anglois* 34 maps: published in London by D. Mortier with later issues by Covens and Mortier

FATHER LOUIS DE HENNEPIN 1640–1701

A Dutch missionary who was associated with the French explorer La Salle in searching for the course of the Mississippi. Although Hennepin's accounts of his adventures were often exaggerated and highly imaginative they were among the most widely read books of the time. He was the first to describe Niagara Falls and to use the name 'Louisiane' on a published map.

1683	*Carte de la Nouvelle France et de la Louisiane*
1697–98	*L'Amerique Septentrionale* Map of the Great Lakes and the Mississippi published in Hennepin's *A New Discovery of a Vast Country*.

PIETER (PIERRE) MORTIER 1661–1711
DAVID MORTIER 1673–*c.* 1728
CORNELIS MORTIER 1699–1783
(See also under Covens and Mortier)

Pieter and David Mortier were brothers of French extraction whose publishing interests covered a wide field embracing French and English works as well as Dutch. Pieter was probably trained in the bookselling business in Paris and David spent many years in England; in fact, he acquired British nationality and died there in about 1728. After Pieter's death, his widow continued the business until their son, Cornelis, was able to take over; then, in 1721, Cornelis entered into partnership with his brother-in-law, Johannes Covens, to form the famous name Covens and Mortier, a firm which continued in being with slight change of name until the middle of the nineteenth century. For details of their publications see under Covens and Mortier.

c. 1690– 1708	*Atlas Nouveau* Re-issue of Sanson/Jaillot maps originally published in Paris
1693–1703	*Le Neptune François* Charts engraved by H. van Loon in Paris (published by Jaillot) and re-engraved and published by Pieter Mortier in the same year, 1693 Other editions with Dutch/English text and additional volumes issued between 1693 and 1703
c. 1694	*Atlas Novum* (David Mortier) Maps by many different cartographers of the day, published in London *c.* 1708 Re-issued
c. 1700	Pocket Atlases in 6 volumes

c. 1710	*Atlas Maior* Re-issue of F. de Wit's *Atlas Maior* originally published from 1670 onwards
1715–28	*Nouveau Theatre de la Grand Bretagne/Atlas Anglois* (David Mortier) 3 volumes including 34 maps by G. Valck and P. Schenk

JOHANNES DE RAM 1648–93

c. 1690	*Atlas* Various issues containing 100–300 maps by earlier publishers

ROMAIN DE HOOGHE *c.* 1646–1708

A famous Dutch artist and engraver who produced a number of magnificent maps published in various atlases: some of the charts in Pieter Mortier's *Atlas Maritime* (part of *Le Neptune François*, 1693) were particularly splendid. For a time de Hooghe was in the service of King William III in England.

FRANÇOIS HALMA 1653–1722

A book publisher who started business in Utrecht and later moved to Amsterdam and finally settled in Leeuwarden. Included in his prolific output of historical and theological work were issues of the atlases detailed below.

1695	Ptolemy's *Geographia* Re-issues at Utrecht of Mercator's 1578 edition: further issues 1698 (Franeker), 1704 (Utrecht) (See also Appendix A.)
1704	*Geographia Sacra*
c. 1705–09	*Description de tout l'Univers* Re-issue of Sanson's *Description de l'Univers*
1718	Atlas of Friesland Re-issue of work by Schotanus van Sterringa (1698)

★ JOHANNES LOOTS *c.* 1665–1726

A mathematical and nautical instrument maker, Loots also published manuals on navigation. For a time he was in partnership with an engraver, A. de Winter, and an author of text books on charts, Claes de Vries, who had ambitions to publish a very large sea atlas of some 200 charts but this was never completed on the scale contemplated. Some of their charts were sold to Gerard van Keulen and others were used in a sea atlas published in 1697. Charts by Loots also appear in a number of other pilot books and sea atlases of the time.

1697	*Het Nieu en Compleet Paskaart-Boek* 11 charts of the North Sea and Baltic
c. 1707	Atlas The large sea atlas mentioned above containing 125–150 charts

PIETER VAN DER AA 1659–1733

Records show that van der Aa, born in Leyden in 1659, made an early start in life by being apprenticed to a bookseller at the age of nine and starting on his own in business as a book publisher by the time he was twenty-three. During the following fifty years he published an enormous amount of material including atlases and illustrated works in every shape and size, two of them consisting of no less than 27 and 28 volumes containing over 3,000 maps and plates. Most of his maps were not of the first quality and were certainly not original but they are often very decorative and are collected on that account.

c. 1707	{ *Zee-en land-reysen* { *Cartes des itineraires et voyages modernes* 28 volumes: average size of maps 240 × 360 mm
c. 1710	*Atlas Nouveau et Curieux* Average size of maps 160 × 240 mm 1714, 1728 Re-issued
1713	*Le Nouveau Théâtre du Monde* (N. Gueudeville) 2 maps to a page: av. size 230 × 300 mm
1714	{ *Nouveau petit atlas* { *Atlas Soulagé* 9 parts: average size of maps 140 × 200 mm
1714	*Nouvel Atlas*: average size of maps 140 × 200 mm *c.* 1735 Re-issued by Covens and Mortier
1729	*La Galerie Agréable du Monde* 27 volumes: 66 parts

EUGENE HENRI FRICX *fl.* 1706–*c.* 1740

Bookseller and printer in Brussels whose major work was a very large-scale map of Belgium and Luxembourg, much copied by other publishers.

1712	*Table des cartes des Pays Bas et des frontières de France* 73 maps and plans of fortifications and sieges including the large-scale 24-sheet map of Belgium which was also published separately
1744–92	A number of re-issues under the title *Atlas Militaire*

JOACHIM OTTENS 1663–1719

REINER OTTENS (son) 1698–1750

JOSHUA OTTENS (son) 1704–65

The family business of print and map selling was founded by Joachim Ottens but the active period of map publishing was concentrated in the years between 1720 and 1750 when the brothers, Reiner and Joshua, produced enormous collections of maps, some as large as 15 volumes. These, including copies of practically all maps available at the time, were made up to order and were magnificently coloured. Besides these specially prepared collections they also issued single-volume atlases with varying contents as well as pocket atlases.

1720–50	*Atlas Maior*
	Special collections, mentioned above, containing as many as 800 maps
1725–50	*Atlas/Atlas Minor*
	Single-volume atlases: contents varying from 24 to well over 100 maps
1739–45	*Atlas de la Navigation et du Commerce*
	Re-issue of work by L. Renard (1715)

JOHANNES COVENS 1697–1774

CORNELIS MORTIER 1699–1783

(See also under Pieter, David and Cornelis Mortier)

JOHANNES COVENS II 1722–94

CORNELIS COVENS 1764–1825

trading as

COVENS AND MORTIER 1721–78

J. COVENS AND SON 1778–94

MORTIER, COVENS AND SON 1794–*c.* 1862

Under the heading Pieter Mortier we give some details of the extensive publishing business which he built up in Amsterdam and which, after his death, was subsequently taken over by his son, the above-named Cornelis. In 1721 Cornelis married the sister of Johannes Covens and in the same year he and Johannes entered into partnership as publishers under the name Covens and Mortier which, with its successors, became one of the most important firms in the Dutch map publishing business.

Their prolific output over the years included re-issues of general atlases by Sanson, Jaillot, Delisle, Visscher, de Wit (whose stock they acquired) and others (often with re-engraved maps), atlases of particular countries including Germany, England and Scotland and others in Europe, pocket atlases, town plans and, from about 1730 onwards, a series under the title *Nieuwe Atlas*, some consisting of as many as 900 maps by various cartographers and publishers. As there is no conformity about these volumes they were presumably made up to special order and only general details of publication can be quoted in a work of this size.

c. 1725	*Atlas Maior*
	Re-issue of F. de Wit's Atlas (*c.* 1670 onwards)
c. 1730–	*Atlas Nouveau*
c. 1774	Re-issue of G. Delisle's Atlas (*c.* 1700)
1737	*A Map of the British Empire in America*
	Re-issue of Henry Popple's map (1733)
c. 1735	*Nouvel Atlas* (4to)
	Re-issue of Pieter van der Aa's atlas (1714)
c. 1730–	*Nieuwe Atlas*
1800	Maps by most of the noted cartographers from Sanson onwards made up in special collections: title pages not dated. This series included maps of the British Isles by Valck and Schenk.

JOHANNES RATELBAND 1715–*c.* 1791

| 1735 | *Kleyne en Beknopte Atlas* (8vo) |
| | Maps and town plans of various European countries based on the work of the La Feuille family |

ISAAC TIRION *c.* 1705–65

A successful publisher in Amsterdam who produced extensive volumes of Dutch town plans as well as a number of atlases with maps usually based on those of G. Delisle.

1739–57	Atlas of the Dutch Provinces: 35–40 maps
c. 1740–84	*Nieuwe en beknopte handatlas*
	Six editions with number of maps varying from 34 to over 100

HENDRIK DE LETH *c.* 1703–66

HENDRIK DE LETH (THE YOUNGER) *fl.* 1788

Engraver, publisher and painter, active in Amsterdam, worked for the Visscher family and eventually took over the business. De Leth is better known as an artist and engraver than as a cartographer although his historical atlas of the Netherlands was a very popular work. His son, Hendrik de Leth (the Younger), published a World Atlas in 1788.

c. 1740–66	*Nieuwe Geographische en Historische Atlas van de Zeven Vereengde Nederland* Several editions, some of which were sold as pocket atlases with folded maps
1743	A pocket map of London, Westminster and Southwark
1749	*Nouvel Atlas géographique et historique* 1770 Re-issued by S. J. Baalde

---

S. J. BAALDE *fl.* 1757–89
Publisher and bookseller in Amsterdam.

1770	*Nouvel Atlas géographique & historique* Maps of the Netherlands in 3/4 folds, based on atlas by Hendrik de Leth (1749) 1778 Re-issued
c. 1788	*Reis und Hand Atlas* Based on maps of the Netherlands by Hendrik de Leth (c. 1740)

JAN BAREND ELWE *fl.* 1785–09
A bookseller and publisher who reproduced a small number of maps copied from his predecessors.

1785–8	*Compleete Zak-Atlas* (with D. M. Langeveld *fl.* 1785–8): 29 maps of the Dutch provinces
1791	*Reisatlas van geheel Duitschland* Pocket atlas of Germany – 37 folded maps
1792	*Atlas de geheele Wereld*: 37 maps

PHILIPPE M. G. VANDERMAELAN 1795–1869
A Belgian publisher who produced one of the first atlases printed by lithography.

1827	*Atlas universel*

Specialist References

BAGROW, L., History of Cartography

HOWSE, D. and SANDERSON, M., *The Sea Chart*
Gives detailed examples of charts by Waghenaer, Goos, van Keulen and other Dutch chart makers

KOEMAN, D. C., *Atlantes Neerlandici*
Virtually complete analysis of all Dutch atlases and pilot books published in the Netherlands up to 1880

SCHILDER, G., *Australia Unveiled*
Gives the most detailed account available of the early Dutch maps of Australasia

THEATRUM ORBIS TERRARUM NV
Ortelius: *Theatrum Orbis Terrarum*, 1570 and 1606 (English edition)
de Jode, G.: *Speculum Orbis Terrarum*, 1578
Waghenaer: *Spieghel der Zeevaerdt*, 1585
    The Mariner's Mirrour, 1588
    Thresoor der Zeevaerdt, 1592
Barentsz: *Caertboek*, 1595
Wytfliet: *Discriptionis Ptolemaicae augmentum*, 1597
Blaeu, W.: *The Light of Navigation*, 1612
    The Sea Beacon, 1643–44
Van den Keere: *Germania Inferior*, 1617
Mercator/Hondius/Jansson: *Atlas for a Geographicke Description*, 1636
Blaeu, J.: *Le Grand Atlas*, 1663 edition
Van Keulen: *De Nieuwe Groote Zee-Fakkel*, 1716–53
Reproductions of complete atlases

TOOLEY, R. V., *Maps and Map Makers*
Detailed lists of editions of Ortelius, Mercator, Blaeu and Jansson atlases and Dutch sea charts

Chapter 14

FRANCE

In the turbulent times at the beginning of the sixteenth century a new king came to the throne of France, Francis I, young, ambitious and opposed at every turn to Charles V's designs to impose his will on Europe and the New World. Unable to obstruct Charles in Europe, Francis turned his attention to the New World and, in 1523, dispatched a Florentine seaman, Giovanni da Verrazano, to attempt to find a North West passage, followed a few years later by Jacques Cartier, who completed three voyages to the St Lawrence (1534–41) and staked France's claim to the lands bordering the great river. These discoveries were recorded on world maps made about 1544 by Pierre Desceliers, one of the leading figures of the Dieppe School of Cartographers which flourished in the years 1530–60.

Following the death of Francis I, France was plagued for half a century by religious wars of succession and a series of weak and unstable governments. Indeed, towards the end of the century Paris was in the hands of a revolutionary council and not until the Edict of Nantes in 1598 was any degree of stability achieved. In consequence, the orderly development of cartography which took place in Germany and England bypassed France until well into the next century. That is not to say, of course, that map production was entirely neglected. Apart from the work of the Dieppe map and chart makers, there were world maps by Oronce Fine and André Thevet which were copied by many cartographers and, some years before the issue of Waghenaer's sea charts, Nicolas de Nicolay, a widely travelled Frenchman, prepared navigational charts of many lands including one of the best maps to date of Scotland (1583).

The first printed national Atlas of the French provinces, the equivalent of Saxton's *Atlas of the Counties of England and Wales*, was produced in Tours in 1594 by Maurice Bouguereau, a printer and publisher, during the period of the Court's 'exile' there. The Atlas was not based on a general survey in the Saxton sense but was a collection of maps of different parts of the country made in earlier years and already produced by Ortelius and Mercator in their own atlases: it included only three maps published for the first time. Perhaps it is not surprising that this was the first national atlas published in France; printing there had a chequered history in the sixteenth century and such was the religious intolerance that, at one stage, it was regarded as a form of heresy to the extent that printers were burnt at the stake. The best-known printer of the time, Christopher Plantin, a Frenchman, fled from this persecution in the 1540s to Antwerp, where eventually he set up the establishment which produced or sold so many Ortelius atlases and other maps by most of the notable cartographers of the day.

The new century brought great political changes and under the absolutist rule of Louis XIII and XIV map makers were granted a degree of royal support and patronage unknown elsewhere. By the last years of the century Dutch maritime power was in decline and France became the centre of geographical science, her cartographers producing the most advanced and beautiful maps of the time. The first great name of the period, Nicolas Sanson, born in the year 1600, founded a map-publishing business which, in the hands of his sons and grandson, was to prosper for well over a century. Their early maps are noted for the elegance of their engraving and in later years, when they were able to take advantage of new scientific mapping methods, for their clarity and accuracy.

In France, map making and publishing was dominated by a small number of family names, Cassini, Jaillot, Delisle, as well as the Sansons. Brief biographical notes and details of their more important publications are given on the following pages but the Cassini family deserve special mention. The first of that name, Jean Dominique, an Italian, was an astronomer and mathematician who, having settled in France, was appointed in 1669 by Louis XIV as director of the Paris Observatory then recently founded. He was responsible for new astronomical methods of determining longitude and with Jean Picard and others he initiated a new survey of the French coasts which was completed about 1681. At the same time his methods enabled other cartographers to re-draw the map of the world far more accurately than hitherto. The projected survey of France by triangulation to which all Cassini's efforts and ambitions were directed was constantly delayed and postponed by political and practical problems until long after his death but, in 1733, his son Jacques was instructed by Louis XV to begin the survey and by 1745 a preliminary map was available. The continuation of the project, which had become known as the 'Carte de Cassini' and was now in the hands of César François Cassini de Thury, faced immense difficulties, not least the fickleness of the government in withdrawing financial support. Not to be deflected, César François formed a company to provide the necessary backing and with assistance from local government in the provinces, the work continued and was practically finished in 1784 when Cassini died of smallpox. The 'Carte de Cassini' or the 'Carte de l'Académie', as it was also known, was soon completed and, after engraving on 182 sheets, was published in 1789 by yet another member of the family, Jean Dominique. The most ambitious mapping project attempted up to that time, this work of the Cassini family served as a model to the map makers of the rest of the world and was not replaced in France until 1878–89. Even before the great survey was finished, their influence was being felt in the development of cartography in other countries, not least in England. In 1783, just before he died, Cassini urged on the British Government the advantages of linking the Paris and Greenwich Observatories by his method of triangulation, a suggestion which, rather surprisingly, was accepted. In 1784, as part of the agreement, an accurate baseline on Hounslow Heath was determined on which a few years later a 'combined operation' across the Channel linked the two systems of triangulation, an operation which was not without complications caused by the conversion of the different methods of ground measurement used in each country. The same baseline served as the starting-point for the general survey of the British Isles, soon to be co-ordinated under the control of the Ordnance Survey Office, of which an account is given in Chapter 8.

Whilst the members of the Cassini family were concentrating on the mapping of France, other French cartographers maintained and, indeed, surpassed the standards of excellence set by Sanson and his successors in the previous century. Prominent among the new generation of scientific cartographers were Guillaume Delisle, whose maps of Africa and America were especially influential, J. B. B. d'Anville with notable maps of Africa and the Far East, Robert de Vaugondy (*Atlas Universel*, 1757) and L. Renard, J. B. d'Après de Mannevillette and J. N. Bellin, famous for their sea charts. At the end of the eighteenth century and the beginning of the nineteenth, the explorers Comte de la Pérouse (1785–88), Louis de Freycinet (*c.* 1812) and others added to charts of the Pacific and the Australian coastline and Dumont d'Urville completed three voyages (1822–40) to New Zealand, and later issued a series of new improved charts of that country.

Biographies

ORONCE FINE 1494–1555

Oronce Fine, a professor of mathematics in Paris, was the most prominent French cartographer in the sixteenth century. Apart from compiling one of the first woodcut maps of France, he is best known for his maps of the world on heart-shaped projections which were frequently copied by other cartographers, including Peter Apian and Mercator.

1519	World Map: woodcut, single heart-shaped projection
	1536, 1566 (Venice) Re-issued
1525	France: woodcut
	1536, 1557 Re-issued
1531–32	World Map: woodcut, double heart-shaped projection
	c. 1535, 1541 Re-issued
1551	*Le Sphere du Monde*

★

NICOLAS DE NICOLAY 1517–*c.* 1583

A widely travelled Frenchman who prepared the first sea chart printed in France for his translation of the *Art of Navigation* by the Spanish navigator Pedro de Medina. He spent some years in England and, later in life, published an outline map, or chart, of Scotland which was the best available at that time. Ortelius used a map of Europe by Nicolay in his *Theatrum Orbis Terrarum*

1544	Chart of the Coasts of Europe

c. 1554–69   Chart of the New World in the *Art of Navigation*: Paris and Lyon
              1560 Reproduced in Venice
1570   Map of Europe used by Ortelius
1583   Scotland: *Navigation du Roy d'Ecosse*

PIERRE DESCELIERS 1487–1553

Desceliers was one of the leading figures in the Dieppe school of cartographers which was active in the years 1530–60. He produced several world maps, now very rare.

c. 1546   World Map with emphasis on Jacques Cartier's exploration along the St Lawrence and in New France

---

ANDRÉ THEVET 1502–90

1575   World Map (woodcut) in the shape of a fleur-de-lis, and maps of the Continents published in *La Cosmographie Universelle*
              1581 Re-issued

FRANÇOIS DE BELLEFOREST 1530–83

1575   *La Cosmographie Universelle de tout le Monde* French edition of Sebastian Münster's *Cosmographia* including map of the British Isles and a woodcut plan of London

---

MAURICE BOUGUEREAU *fl.* 1591–95

Little is known of Bouguereau except that he was a master printer and publisher in Tours, for a time the seat of the French government. There, in 1594, he published the first national atlas of France, basing its contents on a variety of regional maps which had appeared during the previous half century. The atlas is extremely rare, very few copies existing in various states. It was re-issued in later years by J. le Clerc and J. Boisseau.

1594   *Théâtre François*
              1620–31 Re-issued by J. le Clerc as the *Théâtre Géographique du Royaume de France*
              1642 Re-issued by J. Boisseau as *Théâtre des Gaules*

SAMUEL DE CHAMPLAIN 1567–1635

One of the great French explorers, de Champlain was sent to 'New France' in 1603 to survey the areas discovered by Jacques Cartier in his voyages between 1534 and 1541 and to report on the possibilities of colonial expansion there. As a result of his many expeditions as far inland as the Great Lakes he produced splendid maps of the region which were models for cartographers for many years to come.

c. 1607   Description of the Coasts and Islands of New France
1612   Map of the St Lawrence
1612–13   *Carte Géographique de la Nouvelle France*
              1632 Re-issued in Champlain's *Voyages de la Nouvelle France Occidentale* showing the latest discoveries

---

JEAN LE CLERC 1560–1621

Engraver, bookseller and publisher in Paris and Tours, le Clerc may have been associated with Maurice Bouguereau in the production of the *Théâtre François* in 1594, but whether that was so or not, he subsequently used the plates to republish the Atlas in 1620 under a new title. In addition to the maps of France, the atlas included a World Map, originally engraved by Jodocus Hondius in 1608 copied from Mercator's twin hemisphere map of 1595. He also issued in 1602 maps of Africa, America, Asia and Europe, engraved by Jodocus Hondius.

1620   *Théâtre Géographique du Royaume de France*
              1621, 1622, 1626, 1631 Re-issued

MELCHIOR TAVERNIER *c.* 1564–1644

Melchior Tavernier was a member of a large family involved in the publishing trade in Paris in the early years of the seventeenth century. He is probably best known for his publication of a map of the Post Roads of France which was copied many times until the end of the century. He also issued an atlas under the same title as J. le Clerc's *Théâtre Géographique*, using many of Lé Clerc's maps, but incorporating others from different sources. Apart from the maps noted below, he published works for other cartographers, including N. Sanson, N. Tassin, and P. Bertius. He is not to be confused with his nephew of the same name (1594–1665), who also engraved maps for Nicolas Sanson.

1632   *Carte Géographique des Postes qui traversent la France*
              1658 Re-issued by N. Sanson
1634   *Théâtre Géographique du Royaume de France*
1640–42   *Description de la Carte Générale de Tout le Monde*

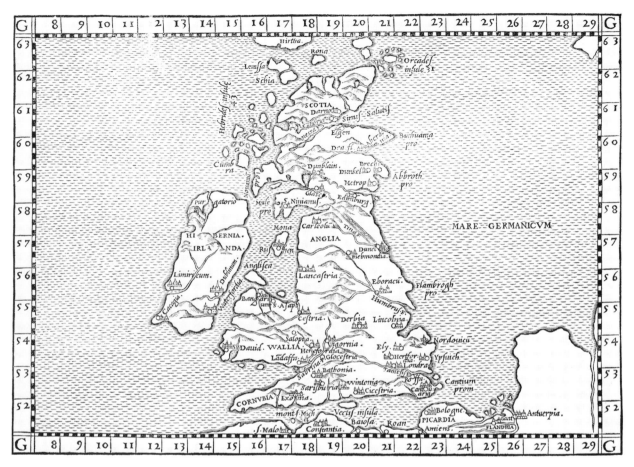

FRANÇOIS DE BELLEFOREST *Des Isles de Bretagne, La Grand' Albion* Paris 1575. Map of the British Isles published in *La Cosmographie Universelle*, a French translation of Sebastian Münster's *Cosmographia*; it was based on Girolamo Ruscelli's map published in the 1561 edition of Ptolemy's *Geographia*.

NICOLAS TASSIN *fl.* 1633–55

Tassin was appointed 'royal cartographer' at Dijon before setting up as an engraver in Paris where he issued various collections of small maps and plans of France, Switzerland, Germany and Spain.

1633–35	General maps of Germany and the Swiss Cantons (4to)
1634–44	*Les Plans et profils de toutes le principales villes . . . de France . . . du Pays des Suisses* (4to)
1634	*Cartes générales et particulières de toutes les costes de France*
1640–43	*Cartes générales de toutes les provinces de France*
1655	*Cartes générales de la Géographie royale* (miniature maps of the French and Spanish provinces) (4to)

JEAN BOISSEAU *fl.* 1637–58

Jean Boisseau was the last publisher to issue Bouguereau's *Théâtre François* using yet another title, *Théâtre des Gaules*, and adding a number of maps of other countries.

1637	World Map
1641–43	*Nouvelle France*
1642	*Théâtre des Gaules*
1643	*Trésor des cartes géographiques*

ANTOINE DE FER *fl.* 1640–52

| 1648 | World Map |
| 1652 | *Plans des Villes de France* |

NICOLAS SANSON (father) 1600–67
NICOLAS SANSON (son) 1626–48
GUILLAUME SANSON (son) –d. 1703
ADRIEN SANSON (son) –d. 1708
PIERRE MOULARD-SANSON (grandson) –d. 1730

Sanson was born in Abbeville where as a young man he studied history, particularly of the ancient world, and it is said that he turned to cartography only as a means of illustrating his historical work. For this purpose he prepared a number of beautifully drawn maps, one of which, after his move to Paris, came to the attention of Louis XIII. In due course the King appointed him 'Géographe Ordinaire du Roi', one of his duties being to tutor the King in geography.

In the preparation of his major atlas, *Cartes Générales de Toutes les Parties du Monde*, Sanson employed a number of engravers, one of whom, M. Tavernier, engraved important maps showing the Post Roads and River and Waterway system of France (1632–34) and a map of the British Isles (1640). In all, Sanson produced about 300 maps of which two of North America were particularly influential: *Amerique Septentrionale* (1650) and *Le Canada ou Nouvelle France* (1656), the first map to show all the Great Lakes. After Sanson's death the business was carried on by his two surviving sons and grandson, in partnership with A. H. Jaillot.

It is generally accepted that the great age of French cartography originated with the work of Nicolas Sanson but credit must go also to A. H. Jaillot and Pierre Duval for re-engraving his maps, many still unprinted at his death, and re-publishing them in face of strong competition from the Dutch, who continued to dominate the market until the end of the century.

| 1648–62 | *L'Europe, L'Asie, L'Afrique and L'Amerique en plusieurs cartes nouvelles* (issues in folio, 4to and 8vo sizes) 1683 and other re-issues |
| 1654 | *Cartes Générales de Toutes les Parties du Monde* 1658, 1664–66, 1667, 1670 Re-issued with increasing numbers of maps 1676 Re-issued under title *Cartes Générales de la Géographie Anciennes et Nouvelles* |

NICOLAS LANGLOIS (L'ANGLOIS) *fl.* 1650
A Parisian publisher and bookseller, Langlois produced a number of maps around the middle of the seventeenth century including one of the Post Roads of

France based on the famous map published by Melchior Tavernier in 1632.

| *c.* 1650 | Post Roads of France |

PIERRE DUVAL *c.* 1619–83
Son-in-law of Nicolas Sanson, Duval published a wide range of atlases, individual maps of the world and the continents and wall maps.

1651	*Tables géographiques de tous les pays du monde*
1653–55	Canada and America
1658	*Les acquisitions de la France par la paix* 1667 re-issued
1660–66	Maps of the World and the Continents
1662	*Cartes de Géographie* (12mo)
1670	*Le Monde ou la Géographie Universelle* (12mo) 1682 Re-issued
1672	*Cartes de géographie les plus nouvelles* (folio) 1677, *c.* 1688 Re-issued
1677	*La Géographie françoise*
1679	*Les XVII provinces en Holland et en Flandres* (12mo)
c. 1680	*Le Monde Chréstien* (12mo)
c. 1682	*Géographie Universelle* (12mo) 1691, 1694 Re-issued

MELCHISEDÉCH THÉVENOT 1620–92
A traveller and author of books on the early voyages of discovery, Thévenot produced some striking maps, perhaps not always his own work but no less interesting because of that. In particular, his map of Australia, the first by a Frenchman, showed the continent's uninterrupted eastern coastline and the latest information on Tasman's voyages.

| 1663–96 | Australia, Tasmania, New Zealand, (*Terre Australe découverte l'an 1644*) Kingdom of the Great Mogul Issued in *Relations de divers Voyages Curieux* |
| 1681 | *Recueil de Voyages* including 3 maps, one of which was the first printed map to show the approximate course of the Mississippi and the name Michigan (*Carte de la découverte faite l'an 1673*) |

CLAUDE JOLLAIN *fl.* 1667
| 1667 | *Trésor des cartes géographiques des principaux estats de l'univers* |

NICOLAS SANSON *Principauté de Galles.* Map of Wales published in Paris in 1658.

ALEXIS HUBERT JAILLOT *c.* 1632–1712
BERNARD JEAN JAILLOT (son) 1673–1739
BERNARD ANTOINE JAILLOT (grandson) *d.* 1749
JEAN BAPTISTE JAILLOT 1710–80

After Nicolas Sanson, Hubert Jaillot and Pierre Duval were the most important French cartographers of the seventeenth century. Jaillot, originally a sculptor, became interested in geography after his marriage to the daughter of Nicolas Berey (1606–65), a famous map colourist, and went into partnership in Paris with Sanson's sons. There, from about 1669, he undertook the re-engraving, enlarging and re-publishing of the Sanson maps in sheet form and in atlases, sparing no

effort to fill the gap in the map trade left by the destruction of Blaeu's printing establishment in Amsterdam in 1672. Many of his maps were printed in Amsterdam (by Pierre Mortier) as well as in Paris. One of his most important works was a magnificent sea atlas, *Le Neptune François,* published in 1693 and compiled in co-operation with J. D. Cassini. This was re-published shortly afterwards by Pierre Mortier in Amsterdam with French, Dutch and English texts, the charts having been re-engraved. Eventually, after half a century, most of the plates were used again as the basis for a revised issue published by J. N. Bellin in 1753.

1681	*Atlas Nouveau*
	1689, 1691, 1692 and others, including issues by Pierre Mortier and Covens and Mortier
1693	*Le Neptune François*
	1693–1703 Re-issued by Pierre Mortier in Amsterdam with French, Dutch and English texts
1695	*Atlas François*
	1696, 1700 and many other editions
1711	*Liste Générale des Postes de France*
	32 re-issues to *c.* 1778

ALAIN MANESSON MALLET 1630–1706

| 1683–88 | *Description de l'Univers* |
| | 1686, 1719 Re-issued with German text |

RÉNÉ BOUGARD *fl.* 1684

1684	*Le Petit Flambeau de la Mer* (8vo)
	1694, 1742 Re-issued
	1801 Re-issued in English as *The Little Sea Torch* with corrections and additions by J. T. Serres (1759–1825)

DES GRANGES

Apart from the fact stated on his map of Great Britain that he was 'Geographe du Roi' nothing is known of des Granges, not even his Christian name.

1688	Germany
1689	*Royaume d'Angleterre, d'Ecosse et d'Irlande*
1702	Greece

JEAN BAPTISTE NOLIN (father) *c.* 1657–1708
JEAN BAPTISTE NOLIN (son) 1686–1762

J. B. Nolin set up the family publishing business in Paris in the Rue St Jacques where he engraved and sold a wide variety of maps, on some of which he wrongfully used the titles 'Engraver to the King' and 'Geographer to the Duke of Orleans'. On a complaint by Guillaume Delisle he was accused and convicted of plagiarism but his business continued to flourish. Many of his maps were based on the work of Vincenzo Coronelli, the Italian cartographer and of another French geographer, Sieur de Tillemon (Nicholas de Tralage). His most notable work was the publication in 1696 of a World Map on one sheet based on J. D. Cassini's 24-ft planisphere housed in the Paris Observatory. His son continued the business for many years and prepared an *Atlas Général* which was published posthumously in 1783.

1688–89	Maps of America and Canada
1696	*Planisphere terrestre* (J. D. Cassini)
1718	*Nouvelle edition du théâtre de la guerre en Italie*
1720–56	(son) Maps of the Continents in various editions
1783	(son) *Atlas Général*

NICOLAS DE FER 1646–1720

Cartographer, engraver and publisher, Nicolas de Fer issued altogether rather more than 600 separate maps, including atlases, sheet maps and large wall maps. It has been said that he aimed at quantity rather than quality but he gained a great reputation in his lifetime and was appointed Geographer to the King. Today his maps are still popular, in spite of, or perhaps because of, their rather flamboyant decoration and even for their geographical errors.

1690	*Les Côtes France*
1693	*La France triomphante sous le règne de Louis le grand* (6 sheets)
1693–97	*Les Forces de l'Europe ou descriptions des principales villes*
	c. 1702 Re-issued by Pierre Mortier
	c. 1726 Re-issued by Pieter van der Aa
1695	*Atlas Royal*
	1699–1702 Re-issued
1697	*Petit et Nouveau Atlas* (4to)
1698	*Plusieurs Cartes de France aves les routes et le plan de principales villes*
	1726, 1730, 1756, 1760, 1763 Re-issued
1700–05	*Atlas curieux*: 2 parts: oblong folio
	1717 Re-issued
1700	*Les Postes de France et d'Italie*
	1728, 1760 Re-issued
1705	*Le Théâtre de la guerre aux environs du Rhein*
1709	*Atlas ou Recueil de Cartes Géographiques*
c. 1717	*Introduction à la Géographie* (8vo)

JEAN DOMINIQUE CASSINI 1625–1712

Of Italian parentage, Cassini studied in Genoa and graduated there with honours in theology and law. By chance he became interested in astrology which led him to take up astronomy and mathematics, and at the age of twenty-five his remarkable ability in these subjects prompted his appointment to the Chair of Astronomy at Bologna University. His fame there brought him numerous commissions from the Papal Office and provincial Senates to carry out surveys in various parts of Italy. Eventually his name came to the attention of Louis XIV of France who was seeking a scholar of

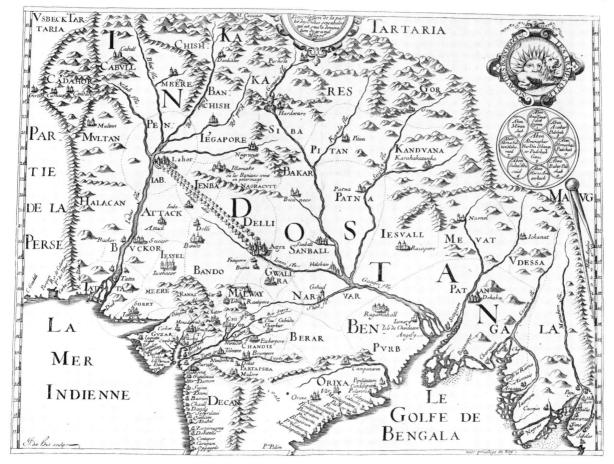

MELCHISEDECH THÉVENOT *Northern India* Paris 1663. Map of the Kingdom of the Great Mogul included in Thévenot's *Relations de divers Voyages Curieux* published in Paris, and derived from an earlier map by William Baffin, the English navigator, issued in 1619.

Cassini's eminence to direct the Paris Observatory; in due course, Cassini accepted the appointment and became a French citizen. There he introduced new astronomical methods of determining longitude and, in company with Jean Picard and others, established an accurate meridian of Paris on the basis of which a new survey of the French coasts was put in hand and completed about 1681. The World Map (1696) engraved by J. B. Nolin, based on Cassini's 24-ft diameter planisphere housed in the Paris Observatory is regarded as the first scientific map of the world. His work was continued by his son, Jacques Cassini de Thury, and grandson, César François Cassini de Thury.

1696   *Planisphere Terrestre* (J. B. Nolin)
      1703 Re-issued by Cornelis Danckerts

CLAUDE DELISLE (father) 1644–1720
GUILLAUME DELISLE (son) 1675–1726
SIMON CLAUDE DELISLE (son) 1675–1726
JOSEPH NICOLAS DELISLE (son) 1688–1768
LOUIS DELISLE (son) *fl. c.* 1720–45

The Delisle (de L'Isle) family followed the Sansons as a major influence in the development of French cartography at the very beginning of the eighteenth century at a moment when Dutch publishers were finally losing their control of the map trade. Like Nicolas Sanson, Claude Delisle was a geographer and historian and had four sons, all of whom made their mark in the life of the time, but Guillaume was the most remarkable member of the family. Said to have drawn his first map at the age of nine he was elected a member of the Académie Royale des Sciences by the time he was twenty-seven; later he was appointed to the highest honour as 'Premier Géographe du Roi'. His critical approach to the maps of his predecessors, backed by his training in mathematics and astronomy under J. D. Cassini, earned him early recognition as the 'first scientific cartographer' and the foremost geographer of his age. His maps were re-published long after his death in 1726.

Two of his brothers, Joseph Nicolas and Louis, spent many years in the service of Peter the Great in Russia where they organized a school of astronomy and carried out extensive surveys in areas hitherto hardly visited.

c. 1700	(Guillaume) *Atlas de Géographie* 1707, 1708, 1718 Re-issued c. 1730–c. 1774 Re-issued as *Atlas Nouveau* by Covens and Mortier, Amsterdam 1740–50 Re-issued as *Atlante Novissimo* in Venice
c. 1703	(Guillaume) *Carte du Mexique et de la Floride . . . et des Environs de la Rivière de Mississipi* The first printed map to show in detail the course of the Mississippi and the routes of its explorers
1718	(Guillaume) *Carte de la Louisiane et du Mississipi* 1730 Re-issued by Covens and Mortier
1745	(Joseph Nicolas) *Atlas Russicus* (large folio): St Petersburg
1757	(Joseph Nicolas) *Atlas Universel*

DANIEL DE LA FEUILLE (father) 1640–1709
JACOB DE LA FEUILLE (son) 1668–1719
PAUL DE LA FEUILLE (son) 1688–1727

Daniel de la Feuille, a Frenchman from Sedan, settled in Amsterdam about 1683 and built up a business there as an engraver, art dealer and book and map publisher. The maps listed below were published in Amsterdam.

Daniel de la Feuille

1702	*Atlas portatif ou le théatre de la guerre en Europe* 1706 and later re-issues in Dutch and German
1706	*Oorlogs tabletten* *Les Tablettes Guerrières* *The Military Tablettes* 1707–29 Various re-issues in Dutch, French and English

Jacob de la Feuille

c. 1710	Atlas (a collection of over 100 maps by Dutch and French cartographers)

HENRI ABRAHAM CHÂTELAIN 1684–1743

The *Atlas Historique* published by Châtelain was part of a major work of its time, an encyclopaedia in seven volumes, including geography as one of its main subjects. The text was by Nicholas Gueudeville and the maps by Châtelain. The Atlas included one of the finest maps of America (4 sheets) surrounded by vignettes and decorative insets.

1705–20	*Atlas Historique*: Amsterdam (maps by Châtelain based on G. Delisle) Further issues to 1739

NICHOLAS GUEUDEVILLE c. 1654–c. 1721

1705–20	*Atlas Historique*: Amsterdam (maps by Henri Châtelain) Further issues to 1739
1713	*Le Nouveau Théâtre du Monde*: Leyden (published by Pieter van der Aa)

MAURICE CASSINI *fl.* 1710

1710	*Hydrographia Gallia* (The Sea Coasts of France)

LOUIS RENARD *fl.* 1715–39

1715	*Atlas de la Navigation et du Commerce*: Amsterdam 1739, 1745 Re-issued by R. and J. Ottens: Amsterdam

LAURENT BREMOND and MICHELOT *fl.* 1715–30

c. 1718	*Ports et Rades de la Mer Mediterranée* 1730 Re-issued 1802 Re-issued in English by Wm Heather as *The New Mediterranean Pilot*

JACQUES CHIQUET *fl.* 1719

1719	*Nouveau Atlas Français* (8vo)
c. 1719	*Le Nouveau et curieux Atlas géographique et historique*

JEAN BAPTISTE BOURGUIGNON D'ANVILLE 1697–1782

Following the death of Guillaume Delisle, D'Anville continued the line of progressive French cartographers which had begun with Nicolas Sanson in the previous century. He is said to have designed his first map at the age of fifteen and in a long and active life he produced a

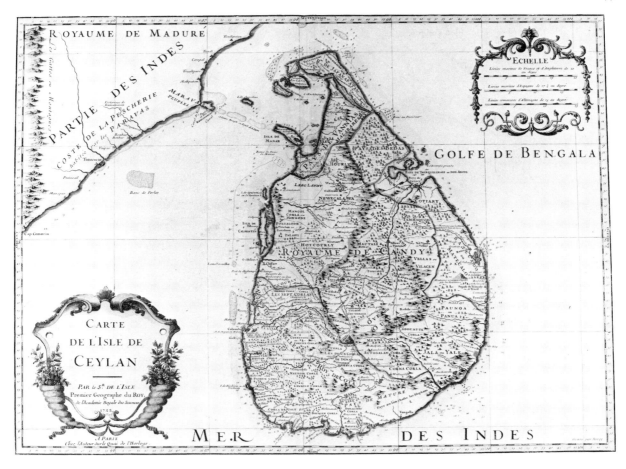

GUILLAUME DELISLE *Carte de l'Isle de Ceylan* Paris 1722. A good example of the elegant maps published by the Delisle family.

great number of elegantly engraved maps, noted for their scholarship and accuracy. If anything, he was even more critical of the work of his predecessors than Delisle and his exacting standards soon brought him international recognition as the finest cartographer of his time. In fact, during his whole life he never travelled outside Paris but he built up a vast collection of cartographic material which eventually was passed to the Bibliothèque Nationale. He was specially interested in the geography of the East and he designed maps for a *Description géographique de la Chine* by Père J. B. du Halde (1735), a notable work of the day based on surveys and reports of Jesuit missionaries. These maps were also issued in *Nouvel Atlas de la Chine* in 1737 and were the first to give a reasonably accurate picture of that remote land. From about 1740 onwards he published collections of maps under the title *Atlas Générale* which went through numerous expanding

editions in various languages; English editions were printed by Robert Sayer, Laurie and Whittle, and others into the next century.

1719	*France*
1727	*L'Ethiopie Orientale*
1735	Maps for *Description géographique de la Chine* by J. B. du Halde
1737	*Nouvel Atlas de la Chine*
c. 1740	*Atlas Générale*
	Numerous re-issues in various languages
1746–61	Maps of the Continents and the World North America (1746), South America (1748), Africa (1749), Asia (1751), World (1761). Numerous re-issues
1769	*Géographie Ancienne et Abrégée*
	1775, 1810 Re-issues in French
	1775–1820 Six re-issues by Laurie and Whittle

D. MARTINEAU DU PLESSIS *fl.* 1733

1733   *Nouvelle Géographie*

HENRI DU SAUZET *fl.* 1734–39

1734–38   *Atlas de poche*
           Atlas portatief
           Pocket atlases in two different versions
1739   Plans of European Cities

JEAN BAPTISTE DU HALDE 1674–1743

1735   *Description géographique de la Chine* (maps
           designed by J. B. B. d'Anville)
           1738–41 English edition
           Maps re-issued in 1737 in *Nouvel Atlas de la
           Chine* by d'Anville

PHILLIPE BUACHE 1700–73

Cartographer and publisher who succeeded his relative, Guillaume Delisle. He re-published many maps by Delisle and Jaillot but his own maps were not noted for their accuracy; in particular he let his imagination run riot on those of Australia and the South Seas. He was better known for his theoretical work on the physical aspects of geography, especially relating to mapping of the submarine world and devising methods of indicating underwater contours.

1739   Maps of Australia and the Southern
           Hemisphere
1745   (G. Delisle) *Carte d'Amerique*
1753–55   *Nouvelles Découvertes au Nord Amerique*
1754   *Cartes et Tables de la Géographie Physique*
1762   *Atlas Géographique et Universelle*
1769–99   *Atlas Géographique de Quatre Parties du
           Monde*

GEORGE LOUIS LE ROUGE *fl. c.* 1740–80

A military engineer by profession, le Rouge took up cartography and over a long period from about 1740 to 1780 produced many attractive works covering a wide range of subjects including plans of fortifications, military campaigns, town plans as well as the more usual atlases and sea charts.

1741–62   *Atlas Général*
1742   *Recueil des Cartes Nouvelles* (including a re-
           issue on reduced scale of Henry Popple's
           map of America of 1733)
1748   *Atlas Nouveau Portatif* (4to)
           1756, *c.* 1767 Re-issued
1755   *Recueil des Plans de l' Amerique* (8 vo)
1756   *Introduction de Géographie*

1758   *Atlas Prussien*
1759   *Recueil des Villes, Portes d' Angleterre* (8vo)
1760   *Topographie des Chemins d' Angleterre* (8vo)
1760   *Recueil des fortifications, forts et ports de mer de
           France* (8vo)
1778   *Atlas Amériquain Septentrional*
1778   *Pilote Americain Septentrional*

JEAN ROUSSET DE MISSY 1686–1762

1742   *Nouvel Atlas géographique et historique* –
           folding maps: average size 165 × 215 mm

JACQUES CASSINI DE THURY (father) 1677–1756
CÉSAR FRANÇOIS CASSINI DE THURY (son) 1714–84
COMTE JEAN DOMINIQUE CASSINI (grandson) 1748–1845
Elsewhere in this chapter we have set out in some detail the leading part played by the above-named descendants of the first Jean Dominique Cassini in compiling the geometrical and topographical surveys of France which occupied so much of the eighteenth century. Here it will suffice to summarize their publications.

1744–45   *Descriptions Géometrique de la France*
1789–91   *Atlas National de France*: also known as
           'Carte de Cassini' or 'Carte de l'Académie'
1818   *Atlas topographique, minéralogique et statist-
           ique de la France*

JEAN   BAPTISTE   NICOLAS   DENIS   D'APRÈS   DE
MANNEVILLETTE 1707–80
Born in Le Havre of a seafaring family d'Après de Mannevillette had a long and distinguished career as a navigator and one of the first French hydrographers. After studying mathematics in Paris, he gained early experience of the sea in a voyage at the age of nineteen to the Caribbean. During many subsequent voyages he assembled a collection of material for a projected hydrographic atlas which, with the support of the Académie des Sciences, was published in Paris in 1745 under the title *Le Neptune Oriental*. In spite of the popularity of the first issue, it failed to satisfy the author and he spent nearly thirty years, often with the assistance of his friend, Alexander Dalrymple, the English hydrographer, in the preparation of a revised and enlarged edition which eventually was issued in 1775.

1745   *Le Neptune Oriental*
           1775 Re-issued in expanded form
1781   *Supplement au Neptune Oriental*
           1821 Re-issued

GEORGE LOUIS LE ROUGE   *L'Ecosse*. Map of Scotland published in the Atlas Général in Paris *c.* 1746, a re-issue of a map by Bowles (London), 1735.

1795   *The East India Pilot* (Laurie and Whittle, London)

1797   *The Oriental Pilot* (Laurie and Whittle, London)

JACQUES NICOLAS BELLIN 1703–72

Bellin spent over fifty years at the French Hydrographic Service where he was appointed the first 'Ingénieur hydrographe de la Marine'. During his term of office there he was commissioned to carry out major surveys, first of the coasts of France and later of all the known coasts of the world. These tremendous undertakings resulted in the production of a very large number of sea charts of the highest quality which appeared in many editions with varying numbers of charts to the end of the century. He was appointed 'Hydrographer to the King' and was a member of the Royal Society in London.

1747–61   Maps for Prévost's *L'Histoire Générale des Voyages*

1751   *Atlas Maritime*

1753   *Neptune François*
Numerous re-issues

1755   *Partie occidentale et orientale de la Nouvelle France, ou du Canada*

1756–65   *Hydrographie Françoise*: 2 volumes
Numerous re-issues to 1802

1757   Guiana

1757   *Essai géographique sur les Isles Britanniques*

1764   *Petit Atlas Maritime*: 5 volumes (4to)

1769   Corsica

1771   Gulf of Venice

1773   Charts of the Caribbean

GILLES ROBERT DE VAUGONDY 1688–1766

DIDIER ROBERT DE VAUGONDY *c.* 1723–86

The Robert de Vaugondys were descended from the Nicolas Sanson family through Sanson's grandson, Pierre Moulard–Sanson; from him they inherited much of Sanson's cartographic material which they combined with maps and plates acquired after Hubert Jaillot's death in 1712 to form the basis for a very beautifully produced *Atlas Universel*. The old material was much revised and corrected with the addition of many new place names. The elder Robert de Vaugondy, Gilles, is also known as Le Sieur or Monsieur Robert.

1748–49   *Atlas Portatif* (small 4to)

1756   Pacific Ocean: maps for *Histoire des Navigations aux Terres Australes* (Charles de Brosses)

1757   *Atlas Universel*
1783, 1793 Re-issued

1761   (Didier) *Parte de l'Amerique septentrional*

1762   *Nouvel Atlas Portatif* (small folio)
1771–1813 re-issued

GASPAR BAILLEUL *fl.* 1750

c. 1750   The World and its Continents

JEAN DE BEAURAIN 1696–1772

1751   *Atlas de géographie ancienne et moderne*

1756   *L'Histoire militarie de Flandre* (1690–94)

1765   *Carte d'Allemagne*

ROBERT (?JEAN) JANVIER *fl.* 1746–76

A French cartographer who worked in Paris from about 1746. There is some confusion about his Christian name but his maps usually bore the inscription 'Le Sieur Janvier'. In addition to work published under his own name by Jean Lattré in Bordeaux and C. F. Delamarche in Paris, he collaborated with other cartographers and publishers in producing a considerable number of maps, many of which were used in general atlases by William Fadan, P. Santini and others.

1751   Map in *Atlas de Géographie ancienne et moderne* by Jean de Beaurain

1751   (with S. G. Longchamps) Map of France

1754   (do) Map of America

1759   *Les Isles Britanniques*
1779, 1791 Re-issued

c. 1760   Maps of the World, the Continents and France and Germany
1762 Re-issued on a reduced scale in *Atlas Moderne*
1763 Re-issued in *Atlas abrégé et portatif* by P. M. Gourné

1762   *Atlas moderne ou Collection de Cartes*
1771 Re-issued

1772   Map of America

1776–84   Maps in *Atlas Universel* by P. Santini

ROCH-JOSEPH JULIEN *fl.* 1751–68

1751   *Atlas géographique et militaire de la France*

1758   *Atlas topographique et militaire*

1758   *Nouveau théâtre de la guerre d'Allemagne*

1768   *Le Théâtre du Monde* including maps of the world and the continents by Gaspar Bailleul

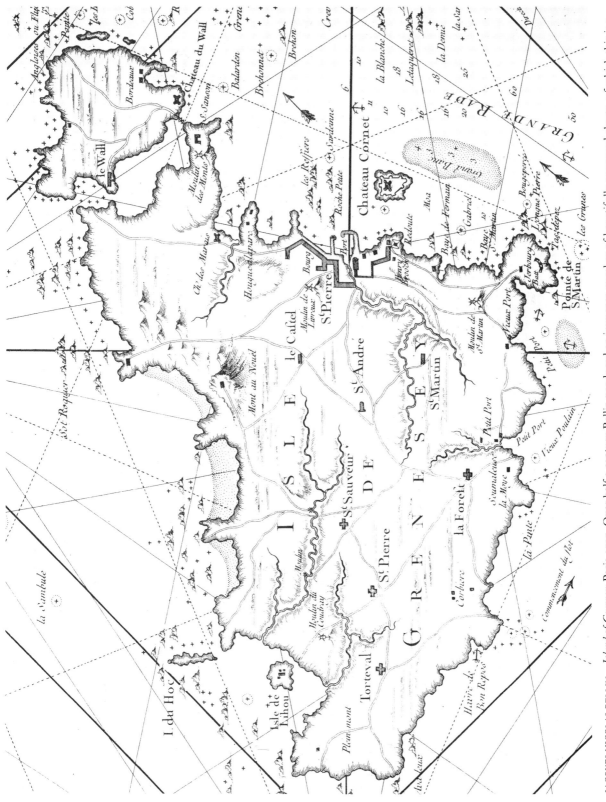

JACQUES NICOLAS BELLIN *Island of Guernsey* Paris 1757. Over half a century Bellin produced an immense number of beautifully engraved charts, of which this is a good example published in the Neptune François (Detail).

JEAN PALAIRET 1697–1774

1755   *Atlas méthodique*
        1775 Re-issued

1755   *Carte des Possessions Angloises et Françoises d'Amerique septentrionale*

1769   *A General Atlas of New and Current Maps* published in London by Carrington Bowles *c.* 1794 Re-issued

1775–80 Bowles Universal Atlas, published in London by Carrington Bowles

---

LOUIS BRION DE LA TOUR *fl.* 1756–1803

Beyond the fact that Brion de la Tour was an engineer by profession and held the post of Ingénieur-Géographe du Roi, little is known of his career. He published a wide range of statistical works and a number of atlases, of which the following are the most important:

1756   *Cartes des Places Fortes et des Principaux Ports des Isles Britanniques*

1757   *Côtes Maritimes de France*

1766   *Atlas Itineraire Portatif* (8vo)

1766   *Atlas Général*
        1776, 1786 Re-issued

1795   *Description générale de l'Europe etc* (4to)

1803   *Atlas géographique et statistique de la France* (4to)

CLAUDE BUY DE MORNAS *fl.* 1761–83

1761   *Atlas méthodique et élémentaire de géographie et d'histoire*
        1783 Re-issued

1762   *Atlas Historique et Géographique*

LOUIS CHARLES DESNOS *fl.* 1750–90

See entry under Denmark

RIGOBERT BONNE *c.* 1729–*c.* 1795

As Royal Hydrographer, Bonne's principal interest lay in the production of marine charts but he issued a number of other works, often including maps by fellow cartographers. He also provided maps for a notable atlas by Guillaume Raynal and for an Historical Atlas and Encyclopaedia published in association with Nicolas Desmaret (1725–1805).

1762   *Atlas Maritime* (folio)
        1778 Re-issued (8vo)

1764   *Petit Tableau de France*

1776   *Atlas Moderne* (4to)

1780   Maps for *Atlas de toutes les parties connues du globe terrestre* by Guillaume Raynal (4to)

c. 1783 *Atlas Portatif*

1783   (with Nicolas Desmaret) *Atlas de géographie ancienne*

1787–88 (with Nicolas Desmaret) *Atlas encyclopédique*
        1827 Re-issued

LOUIS DENIS 1725–94

Cartographer and engraver whose work included maps of the post roads of France and street plans of Paris.

1764   *Atlas géographique*

1768   *Guide des voyageurs* – Post Roads of France

1770   *Atlas de Normandie*

1774   *Routes de Paris*

1779   *Théâtre de la Guerre en Amerique*

1781   *Plan Geometral . . . de Gibraltar*

JOSEPH ROUX *fl.* 1764

1764   *Carte de la Mer Mediterranée*

1764   *Recueil des principaux plans des ports et rades de la Mer Mediterranée* (8vo)
        1779, 1804 Re-issued
        1817 Re-issued in expanded form by Jean-Joseph Allezard (*fl.* 1795–1817)

JEAN BAPTISTE LOUIS CLOUET 1730–*c.* 1790

1767   *Géographie Moderne*
        1780, 1787, *c.* 1793 Re-issued

1776–93 Maps of the Continents

ETIENNE ANDRÉ DE PRÉTOT 1708–87

A professor of History at the Académie Royale, Angers, de Prétot published two atlases containing decorative maps engraved by some of the most notable craftsmen of the time.

1768   *Cosmographie Universelle*

1787   *Atlas universel* (4to)

GUILLAUME THOMAS FRANÇOIS RAYNAL 1713–96

1773   *Atlas portatif*
        1775–80, 1783 Re-issued as *Atlas de toutes les parties connues du globe terrestre* (Rigobert Bonne)

1780   *Atlas des Deux Indes*

LOUIS STANISLAS D'ARCY DE LA ROCHETTE 1731–1802
A cartographer and engraver, active in London in association with the Bowles family and William Faden with whom be published a number of maps of America and Africa.

c. 1781–89 A Map of North America and the West Indies
1782 *Dutch Colony of the Cape of Good Hope* (published by W. Faden)
1795 Revised edition
1825–38 Revised and published by James Wyld
1803 Africa (published by W. Faden)
1823–60 Various editions, revised and published by James Wyld, the Elder and the Younger

EDMÉ MENTELLE 1730–1815
1788 *Atlas de la Monarchie Prussienne*
1790–1811 (with Pierre Gregoire Chanlaire) *Atlas National de la France*
c. 1797 (with Pierre Gregoire Chanlaire) *Atlas Universel*
1807 Re-issued
1798 *Atlas Èlémentaire*
c. 1804 *Atlas des tableaux et cartes*

PIERRE GREGOIRE CHANLAIRE 1758–1817
1790–1811 (with Edmé Mentelle) *Atlas national de la France*
1792 (with Dumez) *Atlas portatif de la France*
c. 1797 (with Edmé Mentelle) *Atlas Universel*
1807 Re-issued
1802 *Nouvel Atlas de la France*

CHARLES FRANÇOIS BEAUTEMPS-BEAUPRÉ 1766–1854
1792–93 Charts included in *Neptune des Côtes Orientales et du Grand Archipel d'Asie*
c. 1796 *Atlas de la Mer Baltique*
1807 *Atlas du Voyage de Bruny-d'Entrecasteaux*
1822 *Pilote Française (Environs de Brest)*

CHARLES FRANÇOIS DELAMARCHE 1740–1817
Successor to Robert de Vaugondy family, many of whose maps he republished.

1794 *Tableaux Géographiques*
1795 *Institutions géographiques ou description générale du globe terrestre*
1797 *Atlas d'Etude*

1806 *Nouvel Atlas portatif*
1820 *Atlas élémentaire*

JEAN FRANÇOIS GALAUP, COMTE DE LA PÉROUSE 1741–88
Noted explorer whose attempted round-the-world voyage in 1785–88 ended in disaster in the Pacific. The fate of the expedition was not established until 1825.
1797 *Voyage de la Pérouse autour du Monde*
1798 English edition

PIERRE LAPIÉ 1777–1851
ALEXANDER ÉMILE LAPIÉ *fl.* 1809–50
1811 (Alexander) *French Empire*
1813 Re-issued
1812 (Pierre) *Atlas classique et universel*
1829 (joint) *Atlas Universel de Géographie ancienne et moderne*
1837, 1841 and other re-issues
c. 1848 (Alexander) *Atlas Militaire*

LOUIS CLAUDE DESAULES DE FREYCINET 1779–1842
c. 1812 *Voyage de descouvertes aux Terres Australes* (4to)
1824 Re-issued
1824 *Voyage autour du Monde*
Further re-issues

EMANUEL, COMTE DE LAS CASES (A LE SAGE) 1766–1842
c. 1813 *Atlante storico, geografico*: Florence
1826 *Atlas historico*
Further editions in Italian, French, German and English (*Le Sage's Historical Atlas*)

ADRIEN HUBERT BRUÉ 1786–1832
1816 *Grand Atlas universel*
c. 1821 *Atlas de France*
1826 Re-issued
1826 *Atlas Universel*
Re-issued to 1846
c. 1826 *Atlas classique de Géographie ancienne et moderne.* Further editions

A. LORRAIN *fl.* 1836
1836 *La France et ses Colonies*

VICTOR LEVASSEUR *fl.* 1838–54
c. 1838 *L'Atlas National Illustré*
1847 and later editions
c. 1840 Pacific Ocean

JULES SÉBASTIEN CÉSAR DUMONT D'URVILLE 1790–1842
French geographer, navigator and naturalist who
carried out three voyages of exploration to Australia
and New Zealand between 1822 and 1840. The
following accounts of the voyages included a large
number of new maps and charts of those lands.

1833	*Voyage de la Corvette Astrolabe*
1834	*Voyage pittoresque autour du monde*
1841–54	*Voyage au Pole Sud et dans l'Oceanie*

Specialist References

BAGROW, L., *History of Cartography*

CARTES ET FIGURES DE LA TERRE, many examples of
early world and French Maps

FORDHAM, SIR GEORGE, *Studies in Carto-bibliography*
Although originally issued in 1914, this is still a
valuable reference book

LIBAULT, A., *Histoire de la Cartographie*
Concise history of cartography with special emphasis
on French mapping

THEATRUM ORBIS TERRARUM NV, Bouguereau: *Le
Théâtre François*
Reproduction of complete atlas

TOOLEY, R. V., *Maps and Map Makers*

Chapter 15

ENGLAND & WALES

When considering the work of English map makers we tend, perhaps, to think too much in terms of county maps, dominated by the names of Saxton and Speed, but we should not underrate the contribution to the sum of geographical knowledge made in other spheres, such as the sea charts of Edward Wright, Robert Dudley and Greenvile Collins, the discoveries of James Cook, the road maps of Ogilby and Cary, the meteorological and magnetic charts compiled by Edmund Halley, to mention only a few among the many whose work is covered in this chapter.

TWELFTH TO SIXTEENTH CENTURIES

We have written elsewhere of the thirteenth- and fourteenth-century maps of Matthew Paris, chronicler and historian, of St Albans, of the Hereford Cathedral *Mappa Mundi* by Richard of Haldingham and of the Gough Map in the Bodleian Library. Coming to the sixteenth century the first separately printed map of the British Isles was published by Sebastian Münster in 1540 and the first such map by an Englishman was that of George Lily, a Catholic exile at the Papal Court. This map, first issued in Rome in 1546 (with later editions up to 1589) was probably based on the Gough map, on Münster's map of 1540 and no doubt on the numerous estate maps then available. Few other maps of the time can approach it for clarity and elegance, and the compiler's use of conventional signs and symbols to show forests, hills, county towns, castles and episcopal sees was an innovation subsequently followed very closely by map makers for centuries.

In 1558 Queen Elizabeth came to the throne in the midst of a fast changing world. To a great extent England and Wales had been fortunate to escape the violent upheavals which afflicted so many European countries at the time. Despite the dissolution of the

monasteries and the religious persecution and doctrinal ferment of the middle years of the century, the country up to about 1540 and from 1570 onwards enjoyed long periods of comparative stability with consequent prosperity and a widening of intellectual attainments.

The break up and redistribution of monastic lands, which passed by royal favour to a new 'landed gentry', created a need for re-surveying and mapping on almost a countrywide scale and the times, therefore, seemed propitious for mapping the whole country in a uniform manner. In 1563 a nineteen sheet map, copies of which survive only in manuscript form, was completed by Laurence Nowell, and no doubt, the issue of Mercator's large-scale map of the British Isles in 1564 had an important influence on the thought of the period. A few years later a national survey was commissioned privately, although probably at the instigation of Lord Burghley, the Lord Treasurer, but subsequently was completed with royal encouragement. The outcome was Christopher Saxton's *Atlas of England and Wales*, started about 1570 and published in 1579 – the first printed set of county maps and the first countrywide atlas on such a splendid scale produced anywhere. It was immediately recognized as a work of national and, indeed, international importance and formed the basis on which nearly all county maps of England and Wales were produced until the mid eighteenth century, when Bowen, Kitchin and others carried out large-scale surveys for their new atlases. In later years, in 1583, Saxton published a large-scale map of England and Wales of which only two copies are known, although there were many later issues with considerable alterations including the addition of roads, town plans and other features.

Until the end of the century Saxton's maps faced little competition. In the 1590s John Norden planned a new set of county maps on the lines of Saxton's but including roads, grid references and a wider range of information; in the event his project failed through lack of support and only five maps were published in his lifetime. A Welsh antiquarian, Humphrey Lhuyd, was more successful and, even before Saxton's survey was complete, he had produced fine manuscript maps of England and Wales and of Wales separately which were used by Ortelius in editions of his Atlas from 1573 onwards. In the same period, in 1572, the first map engraved on copper in England was published. This was a map of Palestine by Humphrey Cole, a goldsmith and instrument maker. Town plans, also, were being drawn: of Norwich by William Cunningham in 1559, of London in 1560 by a Flemish artist and of Cambridge by Richard Lyne in 1572.

In the wider sphere, the English explorers, Drake, Chancellor, Frobisher, Hawkins, Raleigh, Davis and others were adding to the detailed knowledge of the geography of the world in spite of the lack of any satisfactory system of navigation. In an effort to solve their problems Edward Wright published in 1599 his treatise *Certaine Errors of Navigation* which enabled navigators to make fuller use of the charts drawn on Mercator's new projection. Wright's world map, published in the following year, set a pattern for ocean charts which in essence is still used today.

SEVENTEENTH CENTURY

The seventeenth century opened with a spate of new publications based largely on the original work of Saxton and Norden. Indeed, for much of the century, publishers, not least the Dutch, rather than cartographers, were to dominate the scene and many maps appeared in numerous editions with comparatively minor alterations to the maps themselves. The earliest maps of the new century, attributed to William Smith of the College of Heralds, covered only twelve counties based on Saxton/Norden and were presumably intended to be part of a complete new atlas. They were printed in the Low Countries in 1602–03 and were soon followed by maps for the Latin edition of Camden's *Britannia* dated 1607. In this series for the first time each county was shown on a separate sheet, being engraved by William Kip and William Hole on a reduced scale measuring about 355 × 255 mm. There is some evidence that the maps by Pieter van den Keere produced for a miniature atlas of the British Isles (subsequently known as 'Miniature Speeds') were first engraved in 1599, but more likely they were issued in

the period 1605–10. One authority, however, concludes that they were only issued in proof form until the issue by Blaeu in 1617. In 1610–11 the first edition of John Speed's famous county Atlas was published and immediately replaced Saxton's in popular appeal, an appeal which has remained to the present day. Speed, born in Cheshire in 1552, the son of a tailor, turned his life-long interest in history and antiquities to good account and soon after the year 1600 began the preparation of a national History and Atlas which was published in 1611 as *The Theatre of the Empire of Great Britaine*. The History left little mark but the Atlas which formed the appendix to the work brought him lasting fame!

Although Speed assembled much of his material from the earlier works of Saxton, Norden and others, a considerable part of the up-to-date information, especially relating to the inset town plans depicted on his maps, was obtained first hand; as he says in the preface to the Theatre 'by my owne travels through every province of England and Wales'. The maps undoubtedly owed much of their popularity to the splendid engravings of high quality made in the workshops in Amsterdam of Jodocus Hondius to whom Speed sent his manuscripts, the plates subsequently being returned to London for printing.

The issue of Speed's atlases continued through many editions into the next century but in the period we are considering here there were several other interesting publications. In 1612–13 Michael Drayton, an Elizabethan poet, published a book of poems with the title *Poly-Olbion* or *Chorographical Description of all the Tracts, Rivers, Mountains, Forests and other parts of the Renowned Isle of Great Britain*, containing 18 illustrative maps with a second part and 12 extra maps in 1622. A miniature atlas, based on Saxton, by John Bill, entitled *The Abridgment of Camden's Britania with the Maps of the Several Shires of England and Wales* was published in 1626. The engraver is not known but the latitude and longitude used is based on the island of St Michael's in the Azores following Mercator's custom. Only one edition was printed and the maps are, therefore, exceedingly rare.

In 1645, Volume IV of the famous Blaeu World Atlas covering the counties of England and Wales was published in Amsterdam, although, in fact, Jansson had produced some earlier County maps. The maps of both these publishers have always been esteemed as superb examples of engraving and design, the calligraphy being particularly splendid, but nevertheless they were nearly all based on Saxton and Speed and added little to geographical knowledge. In general appearance Jansson's maps are very similar to those of Blaeu and, indeed, were often copied from them but they tend to be more flamboyant and, some argue, more decorative.

Not until the latter part of the century do we find an English map maker of originality with the capacity to put new ideas into practice. John Ogilby, one of the more colourful figures associated with cartography, started life as a dancing master and finished as King's Cosmographer and Geographic Printer. After publishing a small number of county maps, somewhat on the lines of Norden, incorporating roads and extending the use of explanatory symbols, he issued in 1675 the *Britannia*, the first practical series of detailed maps of the post roads of England and Wales on a standard scale of 1,760 yards to the mile. These were copied extensively and, after Ogilby's time, roads were incorporated in practically all county maps, although due to the lack of detail, it is often difficult to trace accurately precise routes. Up to the end of the century and beyond, reprints and revisions of Saxton's and Speed's atlases continued to appear and the only other noteworthy county maps were Richard Blome's *Britannia* (1673), John Overton's *Atlas* (c. 1670) and Robert Morden's maps for an English translation of Camden's *Britannia* published in 1695.

In Chapter 6 we have written of another noted cartographer of the day, Captain Greenvile Collins, and of his work in surveying the coasts of Great Britain culminating in the issue in 1693 of the *Great Britain's Coasting Pilot*. There, too, will be found details of the earlier *Dell' Arcano del Mare* by Robert Dudley, published in Florence, and of the numerous sea charts of John Seller. Apart from these charts, English cartographers published during the century a number of world atlases, though it must be admitted that they fell short in quantity and quality of those coming from the Dutch publishing houses. Speed was the first Englishman to produce a world atlas with the issue in 1627 of his *A Prospect of the Most Famous Parts of the World*, which was combined with the edition of county maps in that year. Other atlases appeared later in the century by Peter Heylin, John Seller, William Berry, Moses Pitt and Richard Blome, whilst Ogilby found time to issue maps of Africa, America and Asia. Far more important, from the purely scientific point of view, was the work of Edmund Halley, Astronomer

Royal, who compiled and issued meteorological and magnetic charts in 1688 and 1701 respectively.

EIGHTEENTH TO NINETEENTH CENTURIES

At the beginning of the eighteenth century the Dutch map trade was finally in decline, the French in the ascendant and the English to a great extent still dominated by Saxton and Speed except, as we have shown, in the spheres of sea charts and road maps. Plagiarism was rife and until 1734 there were no laws of copyright; in 1710 Herman Moll on his map *Roads of the South Part of Great Britain* could write plaintively that 'this map has been copied four times very confused and scandalously'. New editions of Robert Morden's maps appeared; there were atlases by John Senex, the Bowles family, Emanuel and Thomas Bowen, Thomas Badeslade and the unique bird's-eye perspective views of the counties, *The British Monarchy* by George Bickham. In 1750–60 Bowen and Kitchin's *The Large English Atlas* containing maps on a rather larger scale than hitherto was published, the maps being annotated on the face with numerous highly entertaining descriptive notes.

About the time this atlas was issued the idea of preparing maps of the counties on a uniform scale of 1 in. to 1 mile was mooted, maybe inspired by Henry Beighton's splendid map of Warwickshire drawn in 1728. As a result, in 1759 the Society for the encouragement of Arts, Manufactures and Commerce offered an award of £100 for the best original surveys on this scale and by the end of the century about thirty counties had been re-surveyed, of which a dozen or more were granted the award. These maps, many of which formed, in later years, the basis for the first issues of county maps by the Ordnance Survey Office, were not only decorative but a tremendous improvement geographically on earlier local maps. In fact, they were symptomatic of the new approach to cartography engendered by the events of the times – the rise of Britain to naval and commercial supremacy as a world power, the expansion of the East India Company, the discoveries in the Pacific by James Cook, the colonizing of Canada and Australia and other parts of the world, the sea charts by Alexander Dalrymple and J. F. W. des Barres and, not least, the invention of the new Harrison chronometers which at last solved the major problem of accurate navigation at sea. Just as in the early 1600s Amsterdam had supplied the world of its time with maps and charts, so after 1750 London publishers and engravers were called on to provide every kind of map and chart for the vast new territories being opened up overseas. As a consequence, the skills and expertise of the new-style cartographers soon enabled them to cover the world as well as the domestic market. Thomas Jefferys was such a man; he was responsible for a number of the new 1 in. to 1 mile county surveys and he issued an edition of Saxton's much battered 200-year-old plates of the county maps, but he is better known for many fine maps of North America and the West Indies. After his death in 1771 his work was continued on the same lines by William Faden, trading as Faden and Jefferys. Other publishers such as Sayer and Bennett and their successors Laurie and Whittle published a prodigious range of maps, charts and atlases in the second half of the century. A major influence at this time was John Cary who, apart from organizing the first re-survey of post roads since Ogilby and subsequently printing the noted *Travellers' Companion*, was a prolific publisher of atlases and maps of every kind of all parts of the world. After starting work with Cary, and taking part in the new road survey, Aaron Arrowsmith set up in his own business and went on to issue splendid large-scale maps of many parts of the world. Both Cary's and Arrowsmith's plates were used by other publishers until far into the next century and, in turn, their work was taken up and developed by James Wyld (Elder and Younger) and Tallis and Co.

We have written in another chapter of the formation of the Ordnance Survey in 1791 and of the gradual decline during the first half of the nineteenth century in private map making, at least in so far as county maps were concerned, but a number of publishers fought a long rearguard action against the Board of Ordnance. The best known maps were by Henry Teesdale (1829–30), Christopher and John Greenwood, surveyors, who issued a very decorative atlas in 1834, Thomas Moule, a writer on heraldry and antiques (1830–36) and John Walker (1837) but by about the middle of the century few small-scale publishers survived and their business passed into the hands of large commercial concerns such as Bartholomews of Edinburgh and Philips of London who continue to this day.

Biographies

GEORGE LILY *fl.* 1528–59

George Lily, a Catholic exile living in Italy in the service of Cardinal Pole, is generally acknowledged to have been the author of the first map of the British Isles printed from a copperplate engraving. It was first issued in 1546 in Rome with an edition in London in 1555 when Lily, no doubt, returned to England after the accession of Queen Mary. In the following years, up to 1589, various derivatives appeared in Rome and Venice but all are extremely rare, some being known by only one copy.

1546	*Britanniae Insulae:* Rome
	1549 Re-issued: Antwerp (woodcut)
	1555 do : London
	1556 do : Venice (woodcut)
	1558 do : Rome
	1562 do : Venice
	1563 do : Venice
	1589 do : Rome

HUMPHREY COLE *c.* 1530–91

Goldsmith and instrument maker employed in the Royal Mint. Humphrey Cole is credited with producing the first map engraved in England, published in Archbishop Parker's *Bishop's Bible*, a notable edition of the day.

| 1572 | Map of Palestine |

HUMPHREY LHUYD 1527–68

Humphrey Lhuyd graduated at Oxford and, after studying medicine, became private physician to Lord Arundel, at that time a patron of learning and the arts. This position gave Lhuyd access to geographical publications of the period and, apart from publishing works on a wide range of other subjects, he undertook the compilation of up-to-date maps of Wales and the British Isles. Eventually his name was brought to the attention of Ortelius in Antwerp, who used information which Lhuyd passed to him in early editions of the *Theatrum*. Lhuyd unfortunately died before completing his major work but his notes and maps were sent to Ortelius who included the maps in the 1573 edition of his Atlas and in subsequent editions.

HUMPHREY LHUYD *Cambriae Typus – Wales* Antwerp 1587. The first printed map of Wales was published by Ortelius in the *Theatrum Orbis Terrarum* in 1573; there were many variants in the later editions.

1573–1612 *Cambriae Typus*: the first printed map of Wales

Included in editions of the Ortelius *Theatrum Orbis Terrarum*

1606–33 Revised, slightly smaller, version in Mercator/Hondius atlases engraved by Pieter van den Keere

c. 1636–41 Re-engraved version in Mercator/Hondius/Jansson atlases

1647 Re-issued in Jansson's *Atlas Major* and later editions

1573–1606 England and Wales

Included in editions of the Ortelius' *Theatrum Orbis Terrarum* until 1606

CHRISTOPHER SAXTON *c.* 1543–*c.* 1610

Saxton, a Yorkshireman, was probably born in Dewsbury although he grew up in the nearby village of Dunningley to which he often makes reference. Certainly the Saxton family had a strong connection with Dewsbury, whose vicar, John Rudd, was an enthusiastic and skilled cartographer. At one stage Rudd evidently planned to carry out a countrywide survey as a preliminary to the production of a map of England and records show that Saxton, as a young man, travelled with him as an assistant. Saxton is thought to have studied surveying at Cambridge but, whether that was so or not, he was fortunate enough to come into contact with a Thomas Seckford, a wealthy and influential lawyer and Court official who was himself in the employ of Lord Burghley, the Lord Treasurer.

Working under Seckford's patronage, Saxton began a survey of England and Wales sometime after 1570 and the first maps are dated 1574. In the early stages, after running into financial difficulties, he was granted by Queen Elizabeth a ten-year licence to make and market maps. The Privy Council order granting him this privilege instructed all Mayors and Justices of the Peace to 'See him conducted into any towre castle higher place or hill to view the country and that he may be accompanied with one or two honest men such as do best know the countrey'. Little is known of Saxton's methods of survey but much of the work must have been based on earlier manuscript estate maps and probably on larger maps, such as the Gough map, long since lost, and of course on the results of John Rudd's surveys, the extent of which cannot be judged as none of his work has survived. Boundaries of 'hundreds' were not outlined, nor was there any indication of

roads, although river bridges were shown. On completion of each county survey the maps were printed and sold separately (at fourpence each!), the complete atlas which eventually appeared in 1579 being the first printed set of county maps and one of the first national atlases produced anywhere. It was soon recognized as a work of major importance and formed, for the next two centuries, the basis on which practically all county maps of England and Wales were produced until the completion of the individual county surveys in the second half of the eighteenth century.

Having completed the County Atlas in 1579 it must have been only a short step to the publication in 1583 of the 20-sheet wall map of England and Wales of which only two copies are known, although there were later issues – details are given below. Thereafter, Saxton seems to have devoted himself to estate mapping, of which many manuscript records, but no printed maps, survive.

1579 *An Atlas of England & Wales*

1645 Re-issued by William Web

Date altered to 1642 but issued in 1645. Royal Arms of Queen Elizabeth replaced by those of Charles I and a number of other changes including alterations of map titles from Latin to English.

c. 1689 Re-issued by Philip Lea as *All the Shires of England and Wales*

c. 1693 Re-issued by Philip Lea as *The Shires of England and Wales*

c. 1693 Re-issued by Philip Lea as *Atlas Anglois*

The maps in the 1689–93 editions were much amended by the addition of town plans, roads, boundaries of hundreds and other lesser details. All the county titles shown in English.

c. 1730 Re-issued by George Willdey

Printed from the plates as amended by Philip Lea but bearing Willdey's imprint

c. 1749 Re-issued by Thomas Jefferys

George Willdey's imprint removed

1770 Re-issued by Dicey and Co.

1583 *Britannia: Insularem in Oceano Maxima*

England and Wales on 20 sheets

1687 Re-issued by Philip Lea

New title and roads added

c. 1760 Re-issued by T. and J. Bowles

c. 1763 Re-issued by Robert Sayer

1644–45   The Kingdome of England and Principality of Wales exactly described
A reduced version on six sheets of the 1583 map, known as the Quartermaster's Map, engraved by Wenceslaus Hollar, published by Thomas Jenner
1671, 1688, 1752, 1799 Re-issued

ROBERT ADAMS fl. 1588–90

An architect and surveyor who, apart from drawing a number of town plans, prepared famous charts showing the engagements day by day between the Spanish Armada and the English fleets. Subsequently the charts were used as the basis for the design of tapestries made for the House of Lords, but these, unhappily, were destroyed by fire in 1834. The charts are now best known from a 1739 publication by John Pine.

1588   *Expeditionis Hispanorium in Angliam vera descriptio*

1739   Charts re-engraved and published by John Pine (1690–1756) as *The Tapestry Hangings of the House of Lords representing the several Engagements between the English and Spanish Fleets in the ever memorable year 1588*

JOHN NORDEN 1548–1626

About the year 1590 Norden set out to prepare maps as part of a series of guidebooks for each county. His intention was to include roads, town plans, boundaries of hundreds, a gazetteer and grid references, all of which were lacking on Saxton's maps. In the event he was unfortunate in not getting adequate backing to cover so large a project and only two volumes of his work were published in his lifetime. Undeterred, he went on to draw a number of larger maps but again only three of these were printed. Even though so few of his maps reached publication, his techniques and methods of presentation made a lasting impression and later cartographers and publishers chose his work in preference to others whenever possible. Apart from maps Norden published a work entitled *England: an Intended Guyde for English Travailers* in which were included triangular tables showing distances between towns in each county. These were much copied and were used on the maps in *A Direction for the English Traviller* published by Matthew Simmons (1635).

1593–98   *Speculum Britanniae*
Maps of Middlesex and Hertfordshire
1723 Hertfordshire re-issued by John Senex

1840 Map of Essex
c. 1594–95   Surrey, Sussex, Hampshire: larger maps
c. 1650–60 Hampshire re-issued by Peter Stent (re-engraved)
c. 1665 Hampshire re-issued by John Overton in his Atlas (re-engraved)
1625   *An intended Guyde for English Travailers*
c. 1728   Cornwall
Descriptive text with maps of the county and its 9 hundreds

PHILIP SYMONSON fl. 1592–98

1596   Map of Kent
c. 1650 Re-issued by Peter Stent
c. 1665 Re-issued by John Overton

EDWARD WRIGHT c. 1558–1615

After studying mathematics at Cambridge Edward Wright took part in a voyage to the Azores during which problems of navigation arising from the use of the old plane charts led him to make a study of Mercator's new method of map projection. As a result, he wrote a treatise *Certaine Errors of Navigation* which provided mathematical tables enabling comparatively unskilled navigators to make full use of Mercator's ideas. Wright was dubious of the efficacy of his system but on finding that Hondius and others were claiming his formulae as their own he published his book in 1599 and followed it almost immediately with a world chart. In effect, charts now in general use are drawn on the projection laid down by Wright.

1599–1600   *True Hydrographical description of the World: A Chart of the World on Mercator's Projection* (with Emerie Molineux, published in Hakluyt's *Voyages*)
1610 Re-issued
1657 Revised and re-issued by Joseph Moxon in a new edition of *Certaine Errors of Navigation*

GABRIEL TATTON fl. c. 1600–21

Produced important maps of America which were magnificently engraved by Benjamin Wright, one of the earliest English engravers, who later worked in Italy on Giovanni Magni's Atlas of Italy. Apart from his printed maps, Tatton also compiled a number of manuscript charts in portulan form of the Mediterranean (c. 1600), the East Indies and the North Atlantic (c. 1602).

c. 1600   *Maris Pacifici* (Pacific Ocean and western coasts of America)

c. 1600–16 *Noua et rece Terraum et Regnorum Californiae* . . . (California and Central America)

WILLIAM SMITH *c.* 1550–1618

Following the publication of Saxton's maps in the last quarter of the sixteenth century, other cartographers planned atlases on the same lines. Among these was William Smith, an antiquarian and Rouge Dragon at the College of Heralds, to whom the 12 maps noted below are now firmly attributed. Until comparatively recently their authorship was in some doubt and they were known as the 'Anonymous Maps'. The series, probably engraved in Amsterdam, was clearly intended to be an improvement on Saxton and Norden but presumably was not thought good enough to compete with Speed's maps then being prepared.

1602–03   Chester, Essex, Hertfordshire, Lancashire, Leicester, Norfolk, Northamptonshire, Staffordshire, Suffolk, Surrey, Warwickshire, Worcester
c. 1652–60 Re-issued by Peter Stent
c. 1670, 1675, 1685, 1690, 1700, 1740, 1755 Re-issued by John and Henry Overton

PIETER VAN DEN KEERE 1571–*c.* 1646
See Chapter 13.

WILLIAM CAMDEN 1551–1623

Camden, historian and antiquarian, first published his *Britannia*, a description and history of Britain, in 1586. Written in Latin, the book contained only a general map of the country but it had a wide circulation and eventually in 1607 an edition (the sixth) was published with a series of county maps with Latin text on the reverse. Further editions in English were published in 1610 and 1637 but without text. The maps, mostly engraved by Wm Kip and Wm Hole, were based mainly on those of Saxton, but six were copied from Norden. The map of Pembroke is by George Owen and the general maps of England/Wales, Scotland and Ireland were probably taken from Mercator. Although not as decorative as Saxton's maps they are nevertheless very attractive with pleasing titles and ornament, but it should be noted that they are much smaller than Saxton's original maps.

Quite apart from containing these well-known maps, Camden's *Britannia* had a wide influence in its day on the work of other cartographers, not least in Holland. Miniature abridged versions were issued by W. J. Blaeu in 1617 and Joan Blaeu in 1639. Joan Blaeu also used the Latin text on the maps in his Atlas of Scotland issued in 1654. Later still, fresh translations appeared with new maps as far ahead as 1806.

1607   *Britannia*
57 maps: Latin text: average size 280 × 370 mm
1610 Re-issued: no text
1637 Re-issued: no text
Many of the maps in this edition have a plate number in the lower left-hand corner but there are several exceptions

1617   *Britannia*: abridged version: Amsterdam (W. J. Blaeu)
46 miniature maps engraved by Pieter van den Keere: Latin text
1639 Re-issued in Amsterdam (Joan Blaeu)
22 maps from Petrus Bertius' *Tabularum geographicarum contractarum*: no text

1626   *The Abridgement of Camden's Britania*
52 miniature maps by John Bill

1695–1772 *Britannia*
Editions with maps by Robert Morden

1789–1806 *Britannia*
Editions with maps by John Cary

JOHN SPEED 1552–1629

To all those interested in cartography the name of John Speed is synonymous with early county maps of Great Britain. The reasons why this should be so are not far to seek – his predecessors, Saxton, Norden and one or two lesser figures had laid the groundwork for the first mapping of England and Wales in the expansive days of Queen Elizabeth but by the end of the sixteenth century the rate of development was accelerating, increasing overseas trade was linking ports with inland towns, travel was becoming more commonplace and in consequence a need arose to replace the then outdated maps prepared thirty or forty years before. Speed's maps, with their detailed town plans, boundaries of 'hundreds' and descriptive texts filled the needs of the time and quickly replaced the Saxton atlases generally in use until then. Not only were they more up to date but undoubtedly the beauty of the engraving, the fine lettering and the elaborate ornamentation appealed to the original buyers as much as they do to us today. The

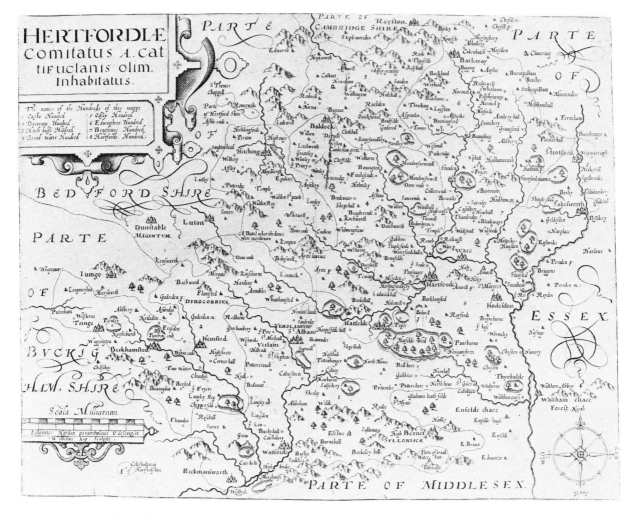

WILLIAM CAMDEN *Hertfordiae comitatus* London (1607) 1610. Map of Hertfordshire, engraved by William Kip, published in Camden's *Britannia*. This map was one of the half dozen based on the work of John Norden; most of the remainder were taken from Saxton's atlas of 1579.

popularity of the new maps was immediate and fresh editions appeared throughout the 1600s and, indeed, until about 1770 when the first moves towards a general 'Ordnance Survey' were being made.

John Speed was born at Farndon in Cheshire in 1552 and followed his father's trade as a tailor until about the age of fifty. He lived in London (probably in Moorfields) and his wife Susanna bore him twelve sons and six daughters! His passion in life, however, was not tailoring; from his early years he was a keen amateur historian and map maker, producing maps for the Queen and the Merchant Tailors Company, of which

he was a Freeman. He joined the Society of Antiquaries and his interests came to the attention of Sir Fulke Greville, who subsequently made Speed an allowance to enable him to devote his whole attention to his research. As a reward for his earlier efforts, Queen Elizabeth granted him the use of a room in the Custom House.

Although Speed assembled much of his material from the earlier works of Saxton, Norden and others, a considerable part of the up-to-date information especially relating to the inset town plans depicted in his maps was first-hand. He must have wasted little time in his preparatory work for the first individual maps engraved for the Atlas were printed in 1605-06 and were on sale between then and 1610–11, when the *Theatre of the Empire of Great Britaine* and the History which it accompanied, appeared in complete form. This seems all the more remarkable when it is remembered that all Speed's draft material was taken to Amsterdam, there to be engraved by Jodocus Hondius, the plates subsequently being returned to London for printing.

In 1627, just before he died, Speed published *A Prospect of the Most Famous Parts of the World* which, combined with the 1627 edition of the *Theatre*, became the first World Atlas produced by an Englishman.

CAPTAIN JOHN SMITH 1580–1631

A member and subsequently leader of the first successful party of English settlers in New England, Capt. Smith prepared accurate and very decorative maps of Virginia and New England which became the prototypes for numerous maps of the Colonies by Hondius, Jansson, Blaeu and others for more than half a century.

1612	Virginia
	Numerous re-issues in Smith's *Generall Historie of Virginia* and in *Purchas his Pilgrimes* by Samuel Purchas (1624–26)
1616	New England
	Issued in Smith's *A Description of New England* and later in his *Generall Historie*

Editions of John Speed's Atlases

PUBLISHED BY	THEATRE OF THE EMPIRE OF GREAT BRITAINE	A PROSPECT OF THE MOST FAMOUS PARTS OF THE WORLD	MINIATURE* 'SPEED ATLAS' (PIETER VAN DEN KEERE)	MINIATURE 'PROSPECT'
J. Sudbury & G. Humble	1611 (1st edn) 1614 1616 (Latin)			
George Humble	1623 1627 1631–32	1627 (1st edn) 1631–32	1627 (1st edn) 1631–32	
William Humble†	1646 1650–51–52–53–54	1646 1650–52–53–54	1646	1646 (1st edn)
Roger Rea	1662–65	1662–65	1662–65–66–68	1662–65–68
Bassett & Chiswell	1676	1676‡	1676	1676
Christopher Browne	*c.* 1690–95			
John & Henry Overton	*c.* 1710–43¶			
C. Dicey & Co	*c.* 1770			

Notes

1. As the maps were dated '1610' for many years after the first edition, the publisher's imprint and the different settings of the text on the reverse are a useful guide to the date of issue; at least the imprint narrows the field. But once an atlas has been split it is often very difficult indeed to date a single map with any certainty and in cases where accuracy is important we suggest reference to a specialist work containing map collations.

2. Normally, the earlier the edition, the more brilliant the impression, although a good impression may still have been obtained from an old retouched plate.

3. Minor alterations and additions to place names were made from time to time.

4. The text in English, except for the 1616 edition, was frequently re-set with different decorative 'woodcut' initials. (see Skelton, R. A., *County Atlases of the British Isles 1579–1703*)

5. Maps from the 1676 edition may be found without text and there is no text on issues after that date.

6. Roads were added to the 1743 edition.

* The purist may object to showing van den Keere's 'Miniature Speed' maps in this chart but the authors feel that their inclusion here sets them in context for those looking for all editions of Speed. A detailed history of these maps is given in Chapter 13 under Pieter van den Keere.

† As late as the 1662 editions maps still bore the imprint of John Sudbury and George Humble.

‡ Included new maps of Canaan, East Indies, Russia, Carolina, New England, Virginia, Jamaica/Barbados.

¶ Apart from 4 editions of the Atlas published between the years *c.* 1710 and 1743 (all extremely rare) Henry Overton also issued Speed's maps in other composite atlases.

JOHN SPEED   *The Countie Westmorland* London 1611 (1676). First published in Speed's *Theatre of the Empire of Great Britaine*. This copy is from the 1676 edition by Bassett and Chiswell.

MICHAEL DRAYTON 1563–1631

In 1612–13 Drayton, an Elizabethan poet and friend of Shakespeare, published his life's work, a book of songs called *Poly-Olbion or Chorographical Description of all the Tracts, Rivers, Mountains, Forests and other parts of the Renowned Isle of Great Britain* containing 18 illustrative maps; a second part bringing the number up to 30 followed in 1622. These regional maps, believed to be engraved by William Hole, are allegorical in nature and few geographical features are precisely shown. The whole emphasis is on the rivers of Britain from which nymphs and deities spring; in the countryside shepherds and huntsmen disport themselves. Here and there a few towns and cities are included symbolized by figures crowned with castles and spires. Although they are quite the most curious maps of the counties ever issued and have little geographical value they are very decorative and charmingly illustrate the romantic side of the Elizabethan age.

1612   *Poly-Olbion or Chorographical Description of all the Tracts, Rivers, Mountains, Forests and other parts of the Renowned Isle of Great Britain*: 18 maps (4to)
1613 Re-issued
1622 Enlarged edition with 12 extra maps

SAMUEL PURCHAS *c.* 1575–1626

Samuel Purchas wrote very popular accounts, accompanied by maps, of the travels and voyages of the early navigators and explorers based largely on the writings of his predecessors, Gian. Ramusio and Richard Hakluyt. His *Purchas his Pilgrimes* contained a *Treatise of the North West passage to the South Sea through the Continent of Virginia* by Henry Briggs (*fl.* 1625), a noted

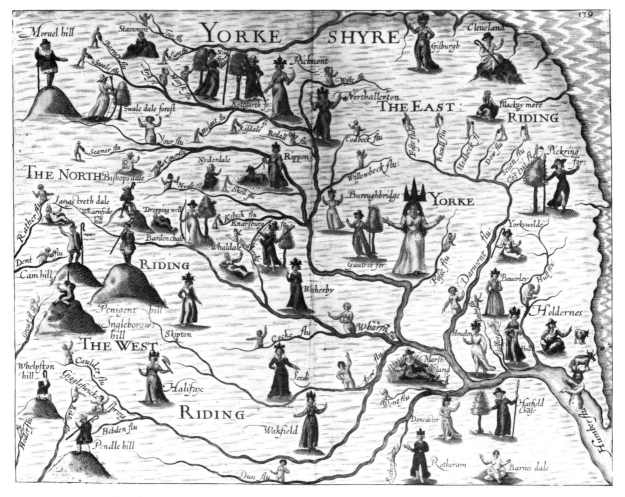

MICHAEL DRAYTON   *Yorkshire.* This was one of the additional maps included in the 2nd edition of Drayton's *Poly-Olbion* published in 1622.

scholar of the time. This was illustrated by a map, *The North part of America*, dated 1625, engraved by R. Elstracke which was famous as one of the first maps to show California as an island.

1613–26   *Purchas his Pilgrimage or relations of the World and the religions observed*
Described as 'a sort of religious geography'

1624–26   *Purchas his Pilgrimes*
Included maps printed by William Stansby from the Mercator/Hondius *Atlas Minor* as well as the Briggs map (above) and Capt. Smith's map of Virginia

---

PETER HEYLIN 1600–62

Heylin was a lecturer in geography who later became a

churchman and chaplain to the King. His *Cosmographie* was a popular work issued in several editions.

1621   *Geography*

1652   *Cosmographie*
Included maps of the four Continents bearing the names of Philip Chetwind, Robert Vaughan and H. Seile
1657–77 Six re-issues

JOHN BILL *fl.* 1591–1630

John Bill was a publisher and bookseller who worked in London from around 1591 until his death in 1630. He was apprenticed to John Norton who was three times Master of the Stationers Company. Born in Shropshire, Bill was commissioned by Sir Thomas Bodley (the founder of the Bodleian Library, Oxford) to travel abroad and purchase books. A frequent visitor to the Frankfurt Book Fair, he became a shareholder in the King's Printing House in about 1617, being succeeded by his son, also John Bill, at the time of his death on 5 May 1630.

The only two publications containing maps with which he seems to have been associated after establishing himself as a publisher in 1604, were the English text version of the Ortelius Atlas in 1606 (with John Norton) and *The Abridgement of Camden's Britania* in 1626. The maps in the latter book, based on the surveys of Christopher Saxton, are the first English and Welsh county maps to show latitude and longitude based on a prime meridian running through the island of St Michael's in the Azores following Mercator's custom. Although similar in size to the Pieter van den Keere county maps the engraver is not known; their scarcity is accounted for by the fact that the book was never re-published after its first appearance in 1626.

1626   *The Abridgement of Camden's Britania with the Maps of the severall Shires of England and Wales*: 52 maps (8vo)

MATTHEW SIMMONS *fl.* 1635–54

Printer and bookseller, notable for the publication of *A Direction for the English Traviller*, the earliest English road book with maps, which were engraved by Jacob van Langeren. The book contained 37 thumbnail maps, copied from the set of playing cards issued in 1590, combined with triangular tables showing distances between towns in each county, taken from Norden's *An Intended Guyde for English Travailers* (1625). Rivers form the main feature of the maps and in the first three editions towns were indicated only by initial letters. There were later editions on a larger scale from 1643 onwards by Thomas Jenner and John Garrett (*fl.* 1667–1718)

1635   A Direction for the English Traviller (small 4to) (map of Yorkshire omitted)
        1636 Re-issued twice: map of Yorkshire added

WENCESLAUS HOLLAR 1607–77

Born in Prague, Hollar spent some time in Frankfurt, where he was taught engraving by Matthäus Merian, before coming to England in 1636. In London, under the patronage of the Earl of Arundel, he became sufficiently well known to be appointed 'Iconographer' to the King and produced an enormous number of engravings on every kind of subject. In the field of cartography he is best known for the adaptation of Saxton's large map of England and Wales (1583) which he re-engraved on 6 sheets, published by Thomas Jenner in 1644 and known as the 'Quartermaster's Map'. Apart from this, he engraved plans of London before and after the Great Fire, and many maps for Blome, Stent, Overton, Ogilby and others, a few of which are detailed below.

c. 1643   Plans of Hull and Oxford
           c. 1700 Re-issued
1644   *The Kingdome of England and Principality of Wales exactly described in six maps, portable for every man's pocket* (the Quartermaster's Map)
           Published by Thomas Jenner
1655–75   London
           Plans drawn before and after the Great Fire. The map dated 1666 showing the destruction in the Great Fire is of particular interest.
1656   Warwickshire
           3 miles to 1 in. map for Sir William Dugdale
1666   *A New & Exact Map of America*
c. 1669–76 England and Wales
           Large road map, 620 × 790 mm, published by Wm Berry. Although it has not been possible to date this map precisely, it is one of the first road maps of England and Wales, possibly pre-dating Ogilby's *Britannia*.
1670–71   Maps for John Ogilby's *Complete History of America*

THOMAS JENNER *fl.* 1618–73

Printer and publisher, is well known for two cartographic works, the re-issue of Matthew Simmons' *A Direction for the English Traviller* and a map of England and Wales known as the Quartermaster's Map. The first he issued in 1643, having re-worked the plates used by Simmons in 1635–36, the maps being redrawn on double the original scale with place names shown in full. It seems likely that these maps were hurriedly issued to meet the demands of the armies in the Civil War: certainly the Quartermaster's Map was. This was based on Saxton's very large-scale map of 1583, reduced to six sheets, 'portable for every man's pocket', engraved by Wenceslaus Hollar.

1643   *A Direction for the English Traviller*
          1657, 1662, 1668. Maps re-issued as part of
          A Book of the Names of all the Hundreds
          contained in the Shires of the Kingdom of
          England
          1677–80 Re-issued by John Garrett

1644   *The Kingdome of England and Principality of*
          Wales exactly described in six maps, portable
          for every man's pocket (the Quartermaster's
          Map)
          1671 Re-issued by Thomas Jenner
          1688 Re-issued by John Garrett
          1752 Re-issued by John Rocque
          1799 Re-issued

1645   *A new booke of Mapps exactly describing*
          Europe

JOSEPH MOXON 1627–91
JAMES MOXON (the Elder) ⎱
JAMES MOXON (the Younger) ⎰ *fl.* 1646–1701

The Moxon family were active as engravers over a long
period and produced globes as well as maps. Joseph
was known especially for his work *A Tutor to
Astronomy and Geography* published in 1659 which went
through several editions.

1644   *Americae Septentrionale Pars*
(Joseph)

1657   *Book of Sea Plats* (charts) based on Edward
(Joseph)   Wright's *Certaine Errors of Navigation*

1670   *World Map*
(James)

1671   *A New Description of Carolina* (for John
(James)   Ogilby)

c. 1686   *New Map of America* (for Philip Lea)
(Joseph)

1688   *Sea Coasts of Scotland* (for John Adair)
(James)   *A New Map of the Kingdom of England* (do)

1701   *A New Sett of Maps* (for Ed. Wells)
(Joseph)

JOAN BLAEU 1596–1673
   See Chapter 13 and Appendix B.

SIR ROBERT DUDLEY 1573–1649
Even by the standards of his time, Sir Robert Dudley
was a remarkable character, whether as adventurer,
scientist, mathematician, naval architect or navigator.
He was the illegitimate son of one of Queen Elizabeth's
favourites, the Earl of Leicester, who was eventually

induced to acknowledge Dudley as heir. Dudley
claimed the titles of Duke of Northumberland and Earl
of Warwick and was known by them throughout his
years in Italy.

At the age of twenty-one he voyaged to the West
Indies with an expedition in the *Earwig* and the *Bear*,
which combined harassment of Spanish shipping with
exploration of the coast of Guiana. On return to
England he took a prominent part in the Earl of
Essex's raid on Cadiz in 1596 and received a knight-
hood for his services but, soon afterwards, matri-
monial problems led to loss of favour at Court and to
self-imposed exile. He spent the next few years travelling in Italy and finally, in 1605, settled in Florence
where his skills soon brought him fame and the
patronage of the Grand Dukes of Tuscany. In their
service he spent the following thirty years compiling
his monumental sea atlas *Dell' Arcano del Mare* (Secrets
of the Sea), a 6-volume work including 2 volumes of
maps and charts and 4 volumes covering the whole
field of navigation, astronomical tables, shipbuilding
and kindred subjects. Although produced in Italy it
was the first sea atlas by an Englishman and the first in
which all the charts were drawn on Mercator's projection. Material for so splendid a work must have been
drawn from many sources; in addition to his own
experience, it is known that he had at his disposal the
logs kept by his brother-in-law, Thomas Cavendish,
the circumnavigator, and other information on the
latest discoveries provided by John Davis and
Abraham Kendal, famous explorers of the time.

His charts were severely but beautifully engraved by
Antonio Lucini who stated that he spent twelve years
on the task and used 5,000 lb. of copper in the process.

1646–47   *Dell' Arcano del Mare*: Florence (published
        by Francesco Onofri)
        1661 Re-issued in Florence by Guiseppe
        Cocchini (the cartouches of all but 24
        charts in the 1661 edition carry the cypher
        'L°6°')

JAN JANSSON 1588–1664
   See Chapter 13 and Appendix B.

PETER STENT *fl.* 1642–65
Print and map seller, Stent made a notable contribution
to map history by acquiring and preserving a considerable stock of old map plates including many
prepared for William Smith (the 'Anonymous' series of
county maps), Speed, van den Keere and others, as well

JOHN BILL   *The Bishoprick of Durham*. A county map published in 1626 in Bill's *The Abridgement of Camden's Britania with the Maps of the severall Shires of England and Wales*.

as Symonson's Kent, Norden's *Hamshire* and engravings by William Hollar. Although he himself published comparatively few of them, his stock passed, after his death, to John Overton and formed the basis of the Overton Atlases which continued in use until the middle of the eighteenth century.

c. 1650   *Hamshire* by John Norden
c. 1650   Kent by Philip Symonson
1652–60   12 Counties by William Smith
1653   Ireland
1662   Flanders

JOHN FARRER *fl.* 1651

An officer in the service of the Virginia Company for many years, Farrer published a famous map of Virginia giving much new, although not very accurate, detail. The map is especially notable for its portrait of Sir Francis Drake set against the Pacific coast and the comment that the 'Indian Sea' could be reached 'in 10 days march with 50 foote and 30 hors-men from the head of Jeames River'.

1651   *A Mapp of Virginia*
       Engraved by John Goddard and sold by John Stephenson in London. Copies exist in several states.

       c. 1667–68 Re-issued by John Overton

ROBERT WALTON 1618–88

Printer, print and map seller, Walton was one of the first publishers to produce sheet maps of England and Wales showing the road system, even before the appearance of Ogilby's *Britannia*. Although he published comparatively few maps, his stock of plates was considerable and may have included those of Speed's county maps.

1655   Africa

PIETER VAN DEN KEERE *Lancaster: Pembrokeshire* London. Examples of the small county maps known as 'Miniature Speeds', originally compiled by van den Keere and subsequently published between 1627 and 1676 in *England, Wales, Scotland and Ireland described and abridged from a farr Larger Voloume done by John Speed.*

c. 1666   Maps of the Four Continents
1668   England and Wales by Thomas Porter
           Road Map
1676   Plan of London
c. 1680   *A New Map of England and Wales to which*
           the Roads or Highways are playnly layd forth
           (with 31 town profiles)

JOHN THORNTON 1641–1708
SAMUEL THORNTON (brother) *fl.* 1703–39

As a map engraver and hydrographer, Thornton was one of the best-known figures of his time, being appointed Hydrographer to the Hudson Bay Company and to the East India Company. He worked closely for many years with John Seller, William Fisher (*fl.* 1669–91), Richard Mount, Robert Morden and Philip Lea in preparing and publishing a number of well-known atlases and charts. In particular, when John Seller was beset by difficulties in completing the later volumes of the *English Pilot*, Thornton took over and subsequently published Book III (1703) and Book IV (1689), the latter in conjunction with William Fisher. He also assisted with the issue of Seller's *Atlas Maritimus* (*c.* 1675) and later issued an atlas of his own under the same title.

c. 1667   Charts of the East Coast of England
           onwards
1685   *Atlas Maritimus*
           1700 Re-issued
1689   *English Pilot*, Book IV
           1698–1789 About 37 editions
c. 1700   Atlas (without title)
1703   *English Pilot*, Book III
           1711 Re-issued by Samuel Thornton and
           further issues to about 1761

JOHN OVERTON 1640–1713
HENRY OVERTON *fl.* 1707–51

From about 1670 John Overton published a number of atlases without title made up from old and revised plates of maps by William Smith (the 'Anonymous Maps'), Blaeu, Jansson and some copies of Speed's maps. Later he acquired all the Speed plates then in existence and from these his son, to whom the business passed in 1707, produced several editions between about 1710 and 1743.

c. 1667–68   *A Mapp of Virginia* (John Farrer)
c. 1670   Overton Atlas
              c. 1675–1755 Six re-issues

1712   *England fully described*
c. 1710–43 Speed's *Theatre of the Empire of Great*
           Britaine

JOHN OGILBY 1600–76

Ogilby, one of the more colourful figures associated with cartography, started life as a dancing master and finished as the King's Cosmographer and Geographic Printer. In the course of an eventful life he built a theatre in Dublin, became the Deputy Master of Revels in Ireland, translated various Greek and Latin works and built up a book publishing business: in the process he twice lost all he possessed, first in a shipwreck during the Civil Wars and then in the Great Fire. Even this disaster he turned to advantage by being appointed to the Commission of Survey following the fire. Finally he turned to printing again and in a few short years organized a survey of all the main post roads in the country and published the first practical road Atlas, the *Britannia*, which was to have far-reaching effects on future map making (see also Chapter 5). The maps, engraved in strip form, give details of the roads themselves and descriptive notes of the country on either side, each strip having a compass rose to indicate changes in direction. He was the first to use the standard mile of 1,760 yards.

The *Britannia* was to have been part of a much larger project in 5 or 6 volumes, covering maps of all the counties, a survey of London and various town plans as well as maps of other parts of the world, but this proved too great a task and only the works detailed below were issued.

1670   *An Accurate Description and Complete*
           History of Africa
1670–71   *An Accurate Description and Complete*
           History of America
           Based on *De Nieuwe en Onbekende Wereld* by
           Arnold Montanus
           1673 German issue (Dr O. Dapper)
1672–73   Maps of Kent and Middlesex
1673   *An Accurate Description and Complete*
           History of Asia (Part 1)
1675   *Britannia – a Geographical and Historical*
           Description of the Principal Roads thereof
           1675–76 2 further re-issues
           1675 Re-issue as *Itinerarium Angliae* without
           text
           1698 Re-issue of first edition with shorter
           text

| 1676–77 | Survey of London (with Wm Morgan *fl.* 1676–81) |
| 1678 | Map of Essex |

JOHN SELLER *fl.* 1660–97

John Seller, appointed Hydrographer to Charles II in 1671, was a maker of mathematical instruments and globes as well as a publisher of marine and terrestrial atlases. His output was considerable and wide-ranging, covering individual charts and maps and complete atlases, but throughout his life he was beset with financial problems which limited the scope of his bigger projects. Of these, the *English Pilot*, the first part of which was published in 1671, was the most successful, but he was able to complete only the first volume without assistance. The details of issue of the later volumes and their subsequent editions are too complicated to be covered here; suffice to say that the work was continued in one form or another for over a century, being issued under many different names including John and Samuel Thornton, W. Fisher, C. Price, Richard and William Mount, Thomas Page and Davidson. Although the *English Pilot* was a popular work, Seller used Dutch sources and often actual Dutch copper plates which he adapted for the market by the use of English titles and details. As many of these plates were up to fifty years old their accuracy left much to be desired, a fact which directly inspired the call for a new coastal survey subsequently completed by Captain Greenvile Collins. Later, in 1695, Seller published an Atlas of County Maps, the *Anglia Contracta*.

English Pilot

1671–72	Books I and II: Northern/Southern Europe
1677	Mediterranean Sea (J. Thornton and W. Fisher)
	1690–1803 Issued in re-arranged form
1689–1789	Book IV: West Indies (J. Thornton and W. Fisher)
1701–80	Book V: West Coast of Africa (J. Matthews *fl.* 1701–02, Jeremiah Seller *fl.* 1698–1705 and C. Price)
1703–61	Book III: The Orient (J. Thornton) Numerous re-issues of each book
1672	*The Coasting Pilot* 1680 Re-issued
c. 1675	*Atlas Maritimus*

Further editions with varying contents to 1710

c. 1680–82	*Atlas Minimus* (24mo)
1680–85	*Atlas Terrestris*
1682–93	*Atlas Anglicanus* Six maps only completed
1685	*New System of Geography* (8vo) 1690, 1709 Re-issued
c. 1690	*Hydrographia Universalis* (4to)
1695	*Anglia Contracta* (average size 95 × 145 mm) 1696, 1701, 1703 Re-issued 1787 Re-issued in *The Antiquities of England and Wales* by Francis Grose

RICHARD BLOME *fl.* 1669–1705

Heraldic writer and cartographer, Blome flourished in the latter half of the seventeenth century. He was a prolific, but not at all an original, worker and indeed was frequently accused of plagiarism although it must be said for him that usually he made no attempt to hide his sources. His maps were attractive and quaintly designed and they still retain their charm.

His first series of county maps, the *Britannia*, based on the latest editions of Speed, was published in 1673 but was not a success; it was followed in 1681 by an issue of smaller maps entitled *Speed's Maps Epitomiz'd*. These, mostly engraved by Wenceslaus Hollar and Richard Palmer (*fl.* 1680–1700), are embellished with dedications to county dignitaries which were amended or sometimes erased in later editions.

1673	*Britannia, or a Geographical Description of the Kingdom of England, Scotland and Ireland* (average size 315 × 280 mm)
1681	*Speed's Maps Epitomiz'd* (average size 180 × 230 mm) 1685 Re-issued 1693 Re-issued in *Cosmography and Geography* 1715 Re-published by Thomas Taylor in *England Exactly described* *c.* 1750 Re-issued by Thomas Bakewell (1716–64)
1682	*Cosmography and Geography* (by Bernhard Varen) 1683–93 Re-issued
1687	*Isles and Territories of America* 1688 French edition

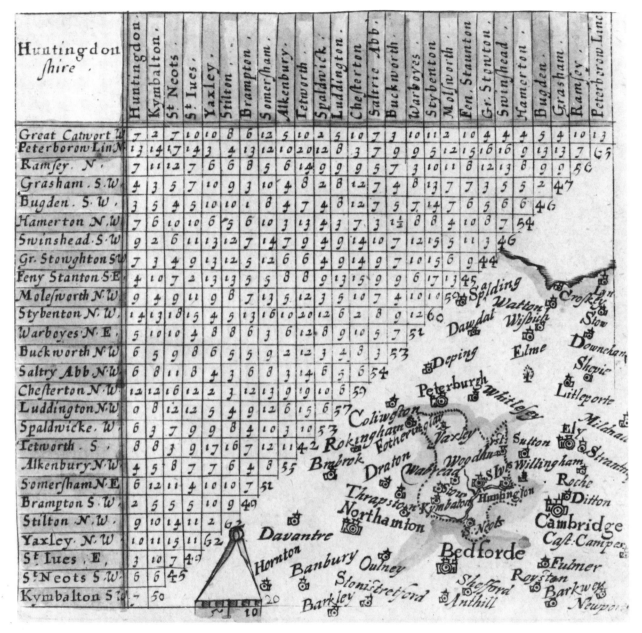

THOMAS JENNER *Huntingdonshire*. Map from *A Direction for the English Traviller* first published in 1643 using enlarged re-engraved maps originally issued in 1635–36 by Matthew Simmons.

ROBERT MORDEN *fl.* 1668–1703

Morden occupied premises in New Cheapside and Cornhill where he carried on business under the sign of 'The Atlas' as a map and book seller and maker of instruments and globes. It cannot be claimed that he was an outstanding cartographer and his work was often much criticized but he produced interesting sets of geographical playing cards (see Chapter 9), maps of various parts of the world and the county maps for Camden's *Britannia*, for which he is best remembered. These were issued in 1695 as part of a new translation of the *Britannia* by Dr Edmund Gibson and subsequently were re-issued a number of times up to 1772.

1673	*A New Map of the English Plantations in America* (with Wm Berry)
1676	Playing cards depicting the Counties (with Wm Berry)
1680	Re-issued without suitmarks as *A Pocket Book of All the Counties of England & Wales* (8vo)
	c. 1750 Re-issued as *A Brief Description of England & Wales*
1680	*Geography Rectified* (8vo)
	1688, 1700 Re-issued
1695	Camden's *Britannia*
	1715 Re-issued
	1722 Re-issued: some maps revised
	Watermark: figure of a horse in 3 in. diameter circle
	1730, 1753, 1772 Re-issued
	(There is no general agreement on how many editions of the *Britannia* were issued; some authorities quote only 4, i.e. 1695, 1722, 1753 and 1772.)
1701	*New Description and State of England*
	Maps similar to those in the 1695 *Britannia* but in miniature (average size 165 × 203 mm)
	1704 Re-issued
	1708 Re-issued by Herman Moll as *Fifty six New and Accurate Maps of Great Britain*
	1720–38 Re-issued as *Magna Britannia et Hibernia*
1708	*The Geographical Grammar* (P. Gordon)
	Miniature maps (average size 120 × 130 mm) of the Continents and European countries

WILLIAM BERRY 1639–1718

A publisher and seller of maps and globes who is known to have been in business at a number of London addresses between about 1671 and 1700. The son of a Warwickshire baker, his earliest known work was a book on Astronomy published in 1669 in conjunction with Robert Morden with whom he later published and sold the famous playing card maps. In his own right he became renowned as the publisher of a series of two-sheet maps based on the originals by the eminent French cartographer, Nicolas Sanson. He is also known for a very rare copy of a large road map (620 × 790 mm) of England and Wales by Wenceslaus

Hollar which has been tentatively dated between 1669 and 1676.

1673	*A New Map of the English Plantations in America* (with Robert Morden)
1676	Playing cards depicting the Counties (with Robert Morden)
c. 1679	*Grand Roads of England*
c. 1680	*A Mapp of All the World*
1689	Atlas
	Collections of maps with differing contents

JOHN ADAMS *fl.* 1670–96

Within two or three years of the publication of Ogilby's *Britannia*, John Adams compiled a 12-sheet road map showing distances between cities and market towns in England and Wales, which was based on Saxton's large-scale map of 1583. This was published between 1677 and 1679 and was followed by his *Index Villaris*, a gazetteer providing supplementary detail. Soon afterwards, no doubt influenced by the scientific projects of Jean Dominique Cassini and Jean Picard in France, Adams conceived the idea of carrying out a geodetic survey of England and Wales but, in spite of receiving encouragement from the Royal Society, he failed to obtain financial backing. However, in 1685, as a result of further surveying, he did issue a 2-sheet map, bordered with distance tables, which was much more manageable and accurate than the original 12-sheet map. His maps were important in their day and were used by Henry Overton and Philip Lea among others.

1677–79	England and Wales
	12-sheet road map
	1690–92 Re-issued by Philip Lea
1680	*Index Villaris, or an Alphabetical Table of all Cities, Market Towns, Parishes, Villages, Private Seats in England and Wales*
	1690, 1700 Re-issued
1685	*Angliae totius Tabula*
	2-sheet road map with distance tables

ROBERT PLOT 1640–96

Dr Plot, an Oxford historian, planned to write *A Natural History of England* but only the volumes for Oxfordshire and Staffordshire were completed; both include very decorative maps of the counties.

1677	Oxfordshire, engraved by M. Burghers
1686	Staffordshire, engraved by J. Browne

ROBERT MORDEN *Monmouth* London 1695. County map included in a new version of William Camden's *Britannia* published in several editions between 1695 and 1772.

MOSES PITT *fl.* 1654–96

A London bookseller who planned, in association with Joh. van Waesbergen, a large world atlas in 12 volumes on the basis of the Blaeu/Jansson atlases but in the event the task proved too costly and only 4 volumes with maps were completed; indeed, the undertaking ruined him and he was imprisoned for two years for debt. The only map by Pitt himself is of the Arctic regions, entitled *A Description of Places next to the North Pole.*

1680–83   Atlas
         Vol. I: English Atlas
         Vol. II: World and Northern Regions
         Vol. III: Germany
         Vol. IV: Netherlands

FRANCIS LAMB *fl.* 1670–1700

Lamb was an engraver working in Newgate Street in the City, employed by most of the map publishers of his time, including Blome, Ogilby, Seller and Morden. His most important work, the pocket atlas of Ireland, published by him in conjunction with Robert Morden and William Berry, was a straightforward reduction, with minor alterations, of Sir William Petty's atlas of 1685. It was as popular as the original work and further editions were issued until 1732.

c. 1689   *A Geographicall Description of the Kingdom of Ireland*: 39 maps (12mo)
1689, c. 1695 Re-issued
1720 Re-issued by Thomas Bowles with roads added
1728, 1732 Re-issue of the 1720 edition by John Bowles

WILLIAM HACK c. 1656–1708

Following a conventional apprenticeship as a map maker to a member of the Drapers' Guild, William Hack moved to a more adventurous life and is thought by some to have sailed with a notorious privateer, Bartholomew Sharpe. Whether this was so or not, Hack later made manuscript copies of a Spanish book of rutters – sailing instructions, sea charts and maps – covering South America, captured by Sharpe from the Spanish in the course of an expedition raiding the West Coast of South America. The Atlas was presented to Charles II and was subsequently of great value to English navigators. Apart from these copies, Hack also compiled a very large number of other manuscript charts and maps of America, the Indian Ocean and the Far East bound in 'atlas' form, possibly about 1,600 altogether, but none was engraved or printed.

c. 1682–83   *Waggoner of the Great South Seas* – 'the Buccaneer's Atlas'
Copied and adapted from the captured Spanish charts. The comparatively few surviving copies are to be found in museums and the great map collections, notably in the William L. Clements Library (University of Michigan), Ann Arbor.

PHILIP LEA *fl.* 1683–1700

A cartographer and map publisher with premises in Cheapside, particularly well known for his re-issue of Saxton's *Atlas of England and Wales*. Apart from this, Lea built up a very considerable business working in conjunction with his contemporaries, Robert Morden, John Overton, John Seller and others revising and re-engraving older maps as well as producing many new maps of his own.

c. 1686   New maps of America, Asia and Europe
1687   *The Traveller's Guide*
'A new map of England and Wales with the direct and crossroads'

c. 1689   *All the Shires of England and Wales*
1693 Re-issued as *Atlas Anglois* (French edition)
1693–94 English edition
These editions of Saxton's County Maps were completely revised with the addition of roads, town plans, boundaries of hundreds and new coats of arms

1690   *An Atlas containing the best maps of the World*
1690–92   A new map of Ireland
1690–92   *Angliae totius Tabula* (John Adams)
12-sheet map based on Saxton
c. 1693   *The Shires of England and Wales* (C. Saxton)
c. 1695   *A Travelling Mapp of England Containing the Principall Roads*
c. 1700   { *Hydrographia Universalis* (8vo)
{ *Hydrographia Galliae*

EDMUND HALLEY 1656–1742

One of the great names in the history of astronomy and cartography. A celebrated mathematician, Fellow of the Royal Society, Astronomer Royal in succession to Flamsteed, his name is perpetuated in the name of the comet, the orbit of which he calculated. As a young man he spent two years in St Helena taking observations and in the years 1698–1700 took part in voyages in the North and South Atlantic studying meteorology, magnetic variations and ocean currents. The charts he issued as a result of his studies were widely used and reproduced.

1688   *A Meteorological Chart of the Trade Winds*
1701   *A New and Correct Chart of the Western and Southern Oceans*
Chart of Magnetic Variations in the Atlantic Ocean
1702 *A Correct Chart of the Terraqueous Globe*
New edition to cover the whole world
1710 Re-issued with amendments by Pierre Mortier
1744–58 Revised editions
c. 1740–45 Re-issued by R. and J. Ottens
1702   *A New and Correct Chart of the Channel between England and France*
1728   *Atlas maritimus & commercialis*

CAPTAIN GREENVILE COLLINS *fl.* 1669–96

Captain Collins was an officer in the Royal Navy and during his service he took part in an expedition with Sir John Narborough to the Straits of Magellan and along the Chilean coast. He was master of the frigate *Charles* from 1676 to 1679 and saw service in the wars with Algiers, later being promoted to Commander. Although little more is known about him he must have been an outstanding personality for even before his great survey he was appointed 'Hydrographer to the King' and made a Younger Brother of Trinity House.

We have written in Chapter 6 of the events in the period from 1660 to 1680 when it became evident that a complete new survey of the coasts of great Britain was required and consequently in 1681 Charles II issued a proclamation appointing 'Captain Collins Commander of the Merlin Yacht to make a survey of the sea coasts of the Kingdom by measuring all the sea coasts with a chain and taking all the bearings of the Headlands'. This formidable and costly project, the first systematic survey of British coastal waters, was completed in about eight years and the resulting *Great Britain's Coasting Pilot* containing 48 charts was published in 1693 and finally replaced the old Dutch charts on which the English had relied for so long.

1693	*Great Britain's Coasting Pilot*
	1723–92 21 re-issues including French edition in 1757 by J. N. Bellin

RICHARD MOUNT *fl.* 1684–1722
WILLIAM MOUNT *d.* 1769
THOMAS PAGE *d.* 1762

The ramifications of the families and successors of Richard Mount and Thomas Page are too involved to concern us here; we need only say that the business founded by Richard Mount had a long history of chart publishing, first under his own name and later under the joint names of Mount and Page, continuing through the younger members of their families well into the nineteenth century. Richard Mount published the early editions of the *Great Britain's Coasting Pilot* (Greenvile Collins) and he and his successors were involved in the issue of many editions of the *English Pilot* (John Seller).

1693	(Greenvile Collins) *Great Britain's Coasting Pilot*
	Numerous re-issues
c. 1692–95	(John Seller/Wm Fisher) *Atlas Maritimus*
1698–	(John Seller/John Thornton) *English Pilot*
1789	Numerous re-issues

1702	*Atlas Maritimus Novus*
	1708, 1721, 1750, 1755 Re-issues
1705	World Map in Harris's *Complete Collection of Voyages*
1737	*Coasting Pilot*
1764	*A complete set of new charts of the coasts of Portugal and the Mediterranean Sea*

EDWARD WELLS 1667–1727

A mathematician and teacher of geography, Wells issued in 1700 *A New Sett of Maps* dedicated to William, Duke of Gloucester, who was then a student of geography at Oxford; unfortunately the Duke died, aged eleven, in July of the same year. The maps, highly regarded when issued for their accuracy, were bold and colourful but show comparatively little detail. His map of North America was one of the last to show California as an island.

1700	*A New Sett of Maps both of Antient and Present Geography*
	1701–38 Numerous re-issues

HERMAN MOLL *fl.* 1678–1732

A Dutch émigré who came to London about 1680 and worked there as an engraver, later setting up his own business and becoming, after the turn of the century, the foremost map publisher in England. His prolific output covered a wide range of loose maps of all parts of the world, varying from miniatures to very decorative large maps as well as atlases. His work enjoyed a high reputation and much of it was copied by other publishers, a fact of which he was always very conscious.

c. 1700	A General Atlas (no title) (large folio: maps in four folds)
	1730 Re-issued
1701	*A System of Geography* (small folio)
1708	*Fifty six New and Accurate Maps of Great Britain* (Morden)
1709	*Atlas manuale – A New Set of Maps of all parts of the Earth* (8vo)
	1723 Re-issued
1710	*The south part of Great Britain called England and Wales*
1711–17	*Atlas Geographicus* (4to)
1714	*The north part of great Britain called Scotland* (Thomas Bowles)
1715	*A new map of Great Britain*

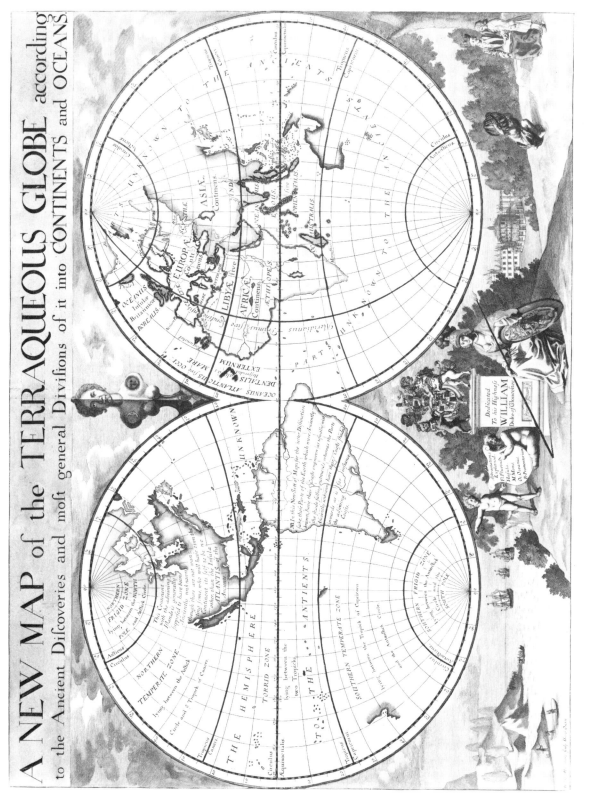

EDWARD WELLS   *A New Map of the Terraqueous Globe according to the Ancient Discoveries.* World map from *A New Sett of Maps* published in 1700 dedicated to the young Duke of Gloucester who died in the same year. The vignette at the bottom right depicts the Sheldonian Theatre in Oxford where the Atlas was printed.

1715   *A New and Exact Map of the Dominions of the King of Great Britain on ye Continent of North America* (on 2 sheets – the 'Beaver' map)
1726–40 Re-issued

c. 1719–36   *A New and Complete Atlas*
Re-issues entitled *The World Described*

1721   *Geographia Antiqua*

1724   *A New Description of England and Wales*
1724–26 Re-issued as *A Set of Fifty New and Correct Maps of England and Wales* (with T. and J. Bowles)
1728, 1739, 1747, 1753 Re-issued under original title

1727   *Atlas Minor*
Numerous re-issues

JOHN HARRIS *fl.* 1686–1746

c. 1700   *A View of the World in Divers Projections*

CHARLES PRICE *c.* 1665–1733

Price, a land surveyor and cartographer, seems to have had an unsettled career and he is known more by his association with other cartographers and publishers than for his own output. For a time he worked in association with John Senex, then in partnership with Jeremiah Seller and, later, for a short period with George Willdey. With all these he published a number of very decorative, and now quite rare, maps.

c. 1705   *A New and Correct Map of Great Britain & Ireland*: 2 sheets

c. 1710   (with John Senex) *A New Map of Great Britain*

c. 1714   *A New & Correct Map of the World*: published by George Willdey

---

GEORGE WILLDEY *fl. c.* 1695–1733

Map seller and publisher about whom comparatively little is known. Apart from publishing a number of maps and atlases at his premises known as 'The Great Toy Shop next to the Dogg Tavern, the corner of Ludgate Street near St Paul's', he also sold there globes, spectacles, snuff and 'other useful Curiosities'. For a time he was in association with Charles Price, a number of whose maps he used in his atlases. He is best known for the re-issue of Saxton's *Atlas of England and Wales*, the maps bearing his imprint. It is thought that this edition was intended primarily for travelling purposes, which may account for its extreme rarity.

1710   Map of Barbados

c. 1714   *A New & Correct Map of the World* (Charles Price)

1715   *Great Britain & Ireland*

c. 1717   *Atlas of the World*

1720   *A New & Correct Map of 30 miles round London*

c. 1730   *The Shires of England and Wales*
Re-issue of Saxton's Atlas from the plates amended by Philip Lea for the 1689–93 editions

---

CHRISTOPHER MAIRE *fl.* 1711

1711   Map of Durham (large scale)

JOHN SENEX *fl.* 1690–1740

Publisher and engraver, John Senex was a contemporary of Herman Moll and no doubt, to some extent, a rival, though his output was rather smaller. In conjunction with Charles Price and James Maxwell (*fl.* 1708–14) he produced some fine maps of the world and the continents as well as loose maps of various countries. Apart from these he seems to have had a particular interest in road maps and in 1719 he issued a corrected edition of Ogilby's *Britannia* in miniature form which went through many editions.

c. 1710   (with Charles Price) *A New Map of Great Britain*

1711   Atlas (20 maps published without title)

1712   Map of Ireland

1714   *The English Atlas*

1719   *An actual survey of all the principal roads of England and Wales* (8vo)
Numerous re-issues up to c. 1775 including a French edition in 1766

1719   World and the Continents

1721   *A new General Atlas of the World* (small folio)

1723   *Hertfordshire*
Re-issue of John Norden's map first published in 1593–98

THOMAS BOWLES *fl. c.* 1714–*c.* 1763
JOHN BOWLES 1701–79
CARRINGTON BOWLES 1724–93
BOWLES and CARVER *fl.* 1794–1832

The members of the Bowles family were publishers and map sellers rather than cartographers, their considerable output over a century or more covering many of the works of their contemporaries. A completely comprehensive list of these is beyond the scope of this volume but their best-known publications are listed below.

1714 (Thomas Bowles) *The north part of Great Britain called Scotland* (H. Moll)

1720 (Thomas Bowles) *A Geographicall Description of the Kingdom of Ireland*
1728, 1732 Re-issue of Francis Lamb's Atlas (*c.* 1689) with roads added
1728, 1732 Re-issue by John Bowles

1724–26 (T. and J. Bowles) *A Set of Fifty New and Correct Maps of England and Wales* (H. Moll)

1731 (T. and J. Bowles) *A new map of Scotland or North Britain*

1732 (T. and J. Bowles) *Kingdom of Ireland*
1765 Re-issued

1760 (T. and J. Bowles) Re-issue of Saxton's *Britannia* (1583)

1766 (Carrington Bowles) *Ellis's English Atlas* (John Ellis and William Palmer *fl.* 1766–1800

1769 (Carrington Bowles) *A General Atlas of New and Current Maps by Palairet and others*
1774 Re-issued

1772 (Carrington Bowles) *Atlas of Road Maps*

1775–80 (Carrington Bowles) *Bowles Universal Atlas* (Jean Palairet)

1782 (Carrington Bowles) *Bowles Post Chaise Companion*

1785 (Carrington Bowles) *New Medium English Atlas* (4to)

1785 (Carrington Bowles) *Pocket Atlas*

1785 (Carrington Bowles) *Paterson's British Itinerary* (Daniel Paterson)

1794–96 (Bowles and Carver) *New Traveller's Guide*

1794–98 (Bowles and Carver) *Universal Atlas*

EMANUEL BOWEN *fl.* 1714–67

THOMAS BOWEN *fl.* 1767–90

Emanuel Bowen, map and print seller, was engraver to George II and to Louis XV of France and worked in London from about 1714 onwards producing some of the best and most attractive maps of the century. He had plans for completing a major County Atlas but, finding the task beyond his means, joined with Thomas Kitchin to publish *The Large English Atlas*. Many of the maps were issued individually from 1749 onwards and the whole atlas was not finally completed until 1760. With one or two exceptions they were the largest maps of the counties to appear up to that time (690 × 510

mm) and are unusual in that the blank areas round each map are filled with historical and topographical detail which makes fascinating and amusing reading. The atlas was re-issued later in reduced size. Apart from his county maps and atlases of different parts of the world he also issued (with John Owen *fl.* 1720) a book of road maps based, as was usual at that time, on Ogilby but again incorporating his own style of historical and heraldic detail.

In spite of his royal appointments and apparent prosperity he died in poverty and his son, who carried on the business, was no more fortunate and died in a Clerkenwell workhouse in 1790.

c. 1714 Maps of the Continents

1720 (with John Owen) *Britannia Depicta or Ogilby Improved* (small 4to)
Numerous editions to *c.* 1764 in varying sizes

1744–47 *A Complete System of Geography*

1744–48 Maps for *Complete Collection of Voyages* (Harris)

1752 *Complete Atlas or Distinct View of the Known World*

1755–60 (with Thomas Kitchin) *The Large English Atlas* (average size 690 × 510 mm)
1763, 1767, 1777, 1785, 1787 Further editions and enlargements

1758 (with John Gibson) *Atlas Minimus* (24mo)
1774 Re-issued

1762 (with Thomas Kitchin) *The Royal English Atlas* (average size 215 × 315 mm)
1778, 1780 Re-issued
1794–1828 Re-issued as *The English Atlas*

c. 1763 (with Benjamin Martin *fl.* 1759–63) *The Natural History of England*

1766 *Universal History of the World*

1767 (with Thomas Bowen) *Atlas Anglicanus* (average size 225 × 320 mm)
1777 Re-issued

c. 1777 (Thomas Bowen) *The World showing the Discoveries of Capt. Cook and other circumnavigators*

c. 1784 (Thomas Bowen) Maps in Rapin's *History of England*

THOMAS TAYLOR *fl.* 1670–1721

1715 *England Exactly Described*
Maps from Richard Blome's *Speed's Maps Epitomiz'd* (8vo)
1716, 1718, 1731 Re-issued

EMANUEL BOWEN   *Rutlandshire* London 1756. County map published in the *Universal Magazine*.

1718	*Principality of Wales Exactly Described* The first separate atlas of Wales

THOMAS GARDNER *fl.* 1719

1719   *Pocket Guide for the English Traveller*: road maps (small 4to)

ADMIRAL SIR JOHN NORRIS *c.* 1660–1749

1723–28   *Compleat Sett of New Charts containing The North Sea, Cattegat and Baltick*

1756 Re-issued

HENRY BEIGHTON 1687–1743

1728   Warwickshire: 1 in. map
1750 Re-issued

HENRY POPPLE *fl.* 1732–33

Produced the best map up to that date (1733) of the North American continent, consisting of a key map and 20 individual sheets.

A Map of CUMBERLAND *North from London?*

Cumberland *sends* 6 *Memb?* *to Parliament, containing one City, one Borough,* 13 *Market Towns, &* 58 *Parish Churches, besides Chapels.*
Carlisle *is a City & Bishoprick, sends* 2 *Members, Market Saturday, Fairs August* 15. *Wednesday before Easter, and* 1*st Wednesday in June.*
Cockermouth *sends* 2 *Members, Market Monday, Fair September* 29.
Alstonmoor
Brampton *Market Tuesday.*
Egremont *Market Saturday.*
Holm
Ireby *Market Thursday.*
Keswick *Market Saturday, Fair July* 22.
Kirk Oswald
Longtown
Penrith *Market Tuesday, Fair Whitsun Tuesday.*
Ravenglass *Market Saturd: Fair July* 25.
Whitehaven *Market Thursd: Fair September* 1*st*
Wigton
Workington

THOMAS BADESLADE *Cumberland.* From a series of small county maps engraved by W. H. Toms issued in 1741–42 entitled *Chorographia Britannica*, said to have been produced for an intended royal tour by George II.

1733   *A Map of the British Empire in America with the French and Spanish Settlements adjacent thereto*

1737–47 Re-issues by Covens and Mortier, le Rouge and T. Bowen

---

THOMAS BADESLADE *fl.* 1719–45

Surveyor and engineer who prepared the maps for *Chorographia Britannica*, a series of small county maps produced for George II for an intended royal tour of England and Wales. Each map, engraved by W. H. Toms, has a column of historical and topical notes of great local interest.

1741–42   *Chorographia Britannica* (8vo)
Three issues
1743, 1745, 1747 Re-issued

GEORGE BICKHAM (Senior) 1684–1758

GEORGE BICKHAM (Junior) 1735–67

George Bickham (Senior) was a noted author and engraver of many works on penmanship including *The Universal Penman*, claimed to be the finest English book on calligraphy. His son was equally well known as an engraver and publisher and between them they published, in 1743, a very beautifully produced volume, *The British Monarchy*, consisting of descriptive text and historical notes illustrated with 5 rather sketchy 'maps'. The better known bird's-eye perspective views were engraved by George Bickham (Junior) between the years 1750 and 1754.

1743–   *The British Monarchy*: 5 maps engraved by
c. 1748   George Bickham (Senior)
(The King of Great Britain's Dominions in Europe, Africa and America; British Isles; Ireland; Scotland; Chart of the Sea Coasts)

c. 1754   *The British Monarchy*
43 bird's-eye views of the English and Welsh counties engraved by George Bickham (Junior)
1796 Re-issued as *A Curious Antique Collection of Bird's eye Views*

RICHARD WILLIAM SEALE *fl.* 1732–75

c. 1744–47 Maps of the Continents
c. 1745   Maps in *Mr Tindal's Continuation of Rapin's History of England*

ROBERT DODSWELL 1703–64

JOHN COWLEY *fl.* 1733–44

1744   *Geography of England*

1745 Re-issued as *New Sett of Pocket Maps of all the Counties of England and Wales*

SAMUEL SIMPSON *fl.* 1746

1746   *The Agreeable Historian or Compleat English Traveller* (miniature county maps)

JOHN ROCQUE *c.* 1704–62

Little is known of John Rocque's early life except that he was of Huguenot extraction and was living and working in London as an engraver from about 1734. His early experience in preparing plans of great houses and gardens for the nobility led him to take up large-scale surveying for which he developed a distinctive and effective style involving new ways of indicating land use and hill contours. He is best known for a very large-scale plan of London published in 1746 and for a pocket set of county maps, *The English Traveller*, issued in the same year. He spent some years in Ireland surveying for estate maps and in 1756 he published a well-known *Exact Survey of the City of Dublin*.

1746   *An exact survey of the Cities of London and Westminster*: 24 sheets, scale 26 in. to 1 mile
1747, 1748, 1751, 1769 Re-issued

1746   *The English Traveller* (8vo)
1753, 1762, 1764 Re-issued as the *Small British Atlas*

1748   *Environs of London*
1763, 1769 re-issued

1750   *Plan of Bristol*

1752   *The Quartermaster's Map* (Thomas Jenner)

1752–65 Large-scale maps of Shropshire, Middlesex, Berkshire, Surrey

1753   *Small British Atlas* (8vo)
1762, 1764 Re-issued
1769 Re-issued as *England Displayed*

1756   *An Exact Survey of the City of Dublin*: 4 sheets

1760   *County of Dublin*: 4 sheets
1799, 1802 Reduced versions issued by Laurie and Whittle

1761   *A general map of North America*

c. 1763–65 *A set of Plans and Forts in America* (published by Mary A. Rocque)

1764   *A collection of Plans of The Principal Cities of Great Britain and Ireland*

THOMAS JEFFERYS *c.* 1695–1771

An outstanding cartographer and publisher whose productions ranged from 1 in. to 1 mile county maps to some of the finest maps of the time of North America and the West Indies. These are regarded as his most important works although unfortunately many of them were only published after his death by Sayer and Bennett or by his business successor, William Faden. He was appointed Geographer to the Prince of Wales and to George III but, as so often happened in the eighteenth century, Jefferys enjoyed a very high reputation for his work and yet failed to obtain much material reward and, indeed, was bailed out of bankruptcy at one stage during the production of his American atlases

1747–79	County maps 1 in. to 1 mile Bedfordshire, Buckingham, Cumberland, Durham, Huntingdon, Northants, Oxfordshire, Westmorland, Yorkshire
1749	*The Shires of England & Wales* Re-issue of Saxton's *An Atlas of England & Wales* from the plates amended by Philip Lea for the 1689–93 editions with the imprint of George Willdey (*c.* 1730 edn) removed
1749	(with Thomas Kitchin) *Small English Atlas* (4to) 1751, 1775, 1785 Re-issued 1787 Re-issued as *An English Atlas or Concise View of England & Wales*
1755	*A Map of the Most inhabited part of New England* (4 sheets)
1760	*Natural and Civil History of the French Dominions in North and South America*
1761	*Description of the Maritime Parts of France*
c. 1762	*A general topography of North America and the West Indies*
1762	*Description of the Spanish Islands and Settlements on the Coasts of the West Indies*
1765	(with Benjamin Donn/e) Devonshire: 12 sheets and key map
1775–76	*North American Pilot* (Sayer and Bennett) 1777–84 5 re-issues 1799–1807 Re-issued by Laurie and Whittle in 2 parts
1775	*West India Atlas* (Sayer and Bennett) 1777 (French), 1780, 1783, 1794 Re-issued 1799 Re-issued by Laurie and Whittle
1775	*American Atlas* (Sayer and Bennett) 1776, 1778 Re-issued

THOMAS KITCHIN 1718–84

Working at premises at The Star in London's Holborn as an engraver and publisher, Kitchin produced a very wide range of books on many subjects as well as topographical work. For many years he worked in conjunction with Emanuel Bowen and Thomas Jefferys and apart from the atlases he published with them, he produced maps of every sort for magazines and books on history and the antiquities.

1747–60	Maps for *The London Magazine*
1749	(with Thomas Jefferys) *Small English Atlas* (4to) 1751, 1775, 1785 Re-issued 1787 Re-issued as *An English Atlas or Concise View of England and Wales*
1755–60	(with Emanual Bowen) *The Large English Atlas* 1763, 1767, 1777, 1785, 1787 Further editions and enlargements
1762	(with Emanuel Bowen) *The Royal English Atlas* 1778, 1780 Re-issued 1794–1828 Re-issued as *The English Atlas England Illustrated*
1764	*A General Atlas* 1773–1810 Numerous re-issues by Sayer and Bennett, and Laurie and Whittle
1769	*Kitchin's Pocket Atlas* (8vo)
1770	*Kitchin's English Atlas* (4to)
1786	(with Henry Boswell *fl.* 1786) *Antiquities of England and Wales*
c. 1789	*A New Universal Atlas* (Laurie and Whittle) 1796, 1799 Re-issued

T. OSBORNE *fl.* 1748

| 1748 | *Geographia Magnae Britanniae*: 63 maps, approx. 150 mm square 1750 Re-issued |

LEWIS MORRIS *fl.* 1737–48

| 1748 | *Plans of harbours, bars, bays and roads in St George's Channel* 1801 Revised and re-issued by his son, William Morris |

WILLIAM HERBERT 1718–95

1752	*Straits of Malacca*
1757	*Chart of the Western Atlantic*
c. 1758	*A New Directory for the East Indies* 1767 Re-issued

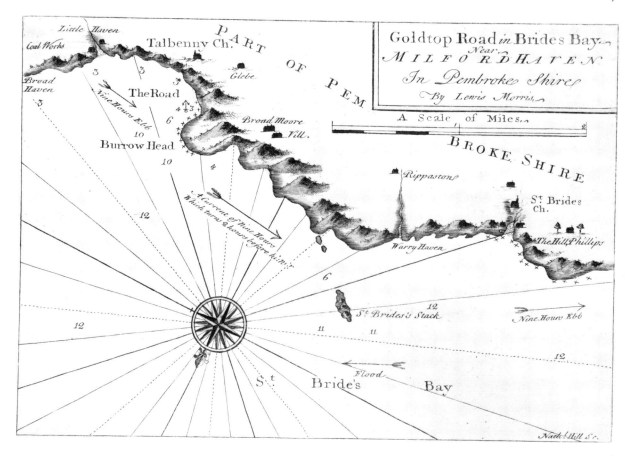

LEWIS MORRIS   *Coast near Milford Haven, Pembrokeshire.* A chart from *Plans of harbours, bars, bays and roads in St George's Channel* published in 1748. This work was revised and re-issued by Morris's son, William, in 1801.

ISAAC TAYLOR 1730–1807
1754–1800 Large-scale county maps:
        1754–86 Herefordshire
        1759 Hampshire
        1765–95 Dorsetshire
        1772–1800 Worcestershire
        1777–86–1800 Gloucestershire

JOHN GIBSON *fl.* 1750–92
1755   *A New Map of North America with the West India Islands*
1756   *Middle British Colonies*
1758   (with Emanuel Bowen) *Atlas Minimus* (24mo)
        1774 Re-issued

c. 1763   *A New & Complete Map of all America*
1772–94 Several re-issues with differing titles

JOHN MITCHELL 1711–68
Born in Virginia, John Mitchell studied medicine at Edinburgh, later returning to his birthplace where he practised as a physician, becoming well known not only as a doctor but also as a botanist and surveyor. About 1746 ill health forced him to return to England, where he compiled a map of the Colonies which, with official support, later became the famous *Map of the British and French Dominions in North America.* The map, showing the British and French Colonies, was used in the peace negotiations between Britain and the American colonies in 1782–83 and later in discussions

on the boundary settlement between the USA and Canada. Even as late as 1843 it was still accepted as an accurate and reliable map.

| 1755 | *A Map of the British and French Dominions in North America* (8 sheets) |
| | 1757–91 21 re-issues |

ROBERT SAYER 1735–94
JOHN BENNETT *fl.* 1770–84

From premises in Fleet Street, Robert Sayer traded as a print seller and map publisher either under his own name between the years 1751 and 1770 and 1784 and 1794, or in partnership with John Bennett as Sayer and Bennett in the intervening years. During his long business life he published a large number of maps by his contemporaries, Kitchin, Jefferys, Bellin, d'Anville and others as well as a re-issue of Saxton's *Britannia* of 1583. On his death his stock was taken over by Laurie and Whittle who re-issued his material in many varied editions.

c. 1763	*Large English Atlas* (Bowen and Kitchin)
c. 1763	Re-issue of Saxton's *Britannia* (1583)
1766	*Atlas Britannique*
1773–81	*General Atlas describing the whole universe* (Thomas Kitchin)
1775	*West India Atlas* (Thomas Jefferys)
1775–76	*North American Pilot* (Thomas Jefferys)
1775	*American Atlas* (Thomas Jefferys)
1775–81	*East India Pilot*
1776	*American Military Pocket Atlas* ('Holster Atlas')
1778	*Neptune Occidental: A Pilot for the West Indies*
	1782 Re-issued
1781–86	*Complete Channel Pilot*
c. 1784	*Oriental Pilot*
1787	*An English Atlas or Concise View of England and Wales* (4to)

G. ROLLOS *fl.* 1754–89

1764	(with W. Rider) *Atlas of the World*
1769	*England Displayed*
1779	*Universal Traveller*

W. RIDER *fl.* 1764

| 1764 | (with G. Rollos) *Atlas of the World* |

BENJAMIN DONN/E 1729–98

In 1759 the Royal Society of Arts, then known as the Society for the Encouragement of Arts, Manufactures and Commerce, offered an award of £100 for the best original 1 in. to 1 mile county surveys. Donn was the first successful applicant with a 12-sheet map of Devonshire, engraved by Thos Jefferys, published in 1765.

1765	*Devonshire:* 12 sheets and key map
	1799 Re-issued on one sheet by William Faden
1769	Eleven miles round Bristol: 4 sheets
1790	do Bath

JOHN ELLIS *fl.* 1750–96

1765	*New English Atlas*
1766	(with William Palmer) *Ellis's English Atlas* (8vo)
	1766 (French), 1768, 1773, 1777 Re-issued

CAPTAIN JOSEPH SPEER *fl.* 1766–96

1766	*West India Pilot*
	1771, 1773, 1785 Re-issued
1796	*General Chart of the West Indies*

JOHN ANDREWS *fl.* 1766–1809

1766–73	Large-scale maps of Hertfordshire, Wiltshire and Kent
c. 1772	*A Collection of Plans of the Capital Cities of every Empire*
1776	*A map of the country 65 miles round London*
1786	*England and Wales*
c. 1792	*Plans of the Principal Cities of the World*
1797	Maps in *Historical Atlas of England*

ALEXANDER DALRYMPLE 1737–1808

As hydrographer to the East India Company from 1779 to 1795 and then to the Admiralty, Dalrymple produced something like 1,000 maps and charts of the lands bordering the Indian Ocean and the Pacific. He was obsessed with the idea of the existence of a great southern continent and many of his charts reflected his determination to prove his case, even long after Captain Cook had shown that inhabited lands did not exist in the far south. It would not be practicable to attempt to list here all his work but the following are some of his more important collections of charts; many others were bound to meet special requirements.

| 1767 | *Account of Discoveries in the South Pacific before 1764* |
| 1771–72 | *A Collection of Charts and Memoirs* |

1774–75	*A Collection of Plans and Ports in the East Indies*
	1782, 1787 Re-issued
1791	*Oriental Repertory*
1792	*A Collection of Charts and Plans*
1792	*Atlas of Charts and Plans*

P. RUSSELL *fl.* 1769

| 1769 | (with Owen Price *fl.* 1769) *England Displayed* |

C. DICEY AND CO. *fl.* 1770

| *c.* 1770 | *The Shires of England and Wales* |
| | Final re-issue of Saxton's *An Atlas of England & Wales* from the plates amended by Philip Lea for the 1689–93 editions and subsequently used by George Willdey (*c.* 1730) and Thomas Jefferys (*c.* 1749) |

DANIEL PATERSON *fl.* 1771–91

1771–1832	*Paterson's Roads*
	18 re-issues
1772–99	*Paterson's Travelling Dictionary*
1785–1807	*Paterson's British Itinerary*
	4 re-issues
1786	*Direct and Principal Cross Roads in England & Wales*
1791	*Map of the Environs of London*

CAPTAIN JAMES COOK 1729–79

This is not the place to enlarge on the life of the greatest British navigator, but no list of cartographers would be complete without including details of his Pacific charts.

1773	*Volume I: An account of a voyage round the World in the years 1768–71*
1777	*Volume II: A voyage towards the South Pole and round the world*
1780	*Volume III: A voyage to the Pacific Ocean*
1784	Atlas

SAMUEL DUNN *fl.* 1774–94

1774	*A Map of the British Empire in North America*
1774	*A New Atlas of the Mundane System*
	1786, 1794, 1796, 1800, *c.* 1810 Re-issued

WILLIAM FADEN 1750–1836

Following the death of Thomas Jefferys in 1771 William Faden took over and continued the business, trading as Faden and Jefferys and producing excellent maps well into the nineteenth century. He was particularly interested in the mapping of North America for which he was as well known as his predecessor. In addition to the atlases mentioned below, he issued many special collections of large-scale and regional maps prepared for customers' individual requirements. All his work was of splendid quality and he was chosen to print the four sheets of the first Ordnance Survey map – of Kent – which was published in 1801. His business was taken over by James Wyld who re-issued many of his maps.

1775	*World Map*
c. 1777	*North American Atlas*
1777	*The British Colonies in North America*
	Numerous re-issues to 1820, and others by James Wyld until *c.* 1840
1778	*General Atlas* (large folio)
1781	*The Roads of Great Britain*
	Numerous re-issues to *c.* 1833
1785	*The United States of North America*
1793	*Petit Neptune Française*
1797	*General Atlas*
	Various re-issues containing collections of different maps
1798	*Atlases minimus universalis*
1799	Re-issue of map of Devonshire by Benjamin Donn

JAMES RENNELL 1742–1830

As the first Surveyor General of Bengal from 1767 to 1777 Rennell directed a comprehensive survey of the East India Company's lands and subsequently published maps of Bengal and other provinces followed by *The Bengal Atlas* in 1779. Considering the vastness of the areas covered, the difficulties encountered, and the speed with which it was accomplished, Rennell's mapping in India was a remarkable achievement and stood the test of time well into the next century. Indeed, he should be counted among our most able cartographers and, although ill health made it impossible for him to continue his practical survey work after 1777, he left his mark as adviser to the Indian Survey Office for something like half a century.

1779	*The Bengal Atlas*
	1780, 1781, 1783 Re-issued
1782	*Map of Hindoustan*
	1785 Re-issued
1788–94	*The Provinces of Delhi, Agra etc and the Indian Peninsula*

JOSEPH FREDERICK WALLET DES BARRES 1721–1824

Of Swiss extraction, des Barres became a British subject early in life and trained as a military engineer, subsequently serving with the British Army at the Seige of Quebec where he came to the attention of General Wolfe. After the fall of Quebec he surveyed parts of the coasts of Nova Scotia and the principal harbours in Newfoundland and then, on Admiralty orders, undertook a ten-year survey of the coasts of New England as well as Nova Scotia. Returning to England in 1773 he supervised the engraving and publication of his work which was issued about 1784 as *The Atlantic Neptune*, now recognized as one of the finest collections of charts and coloured views ever published. Copies vary very greatly in content from edition to edition. In later life des Barres was appointed Lieut. Governor of Cape Breton Province and Governor of Prince Edward Island. He died at the age of 103 in Halifax, Nova Scotia.

1784	*The Atlantic Neptune*, Vols I–IV: tall large folio
	Numerous re-issues

JOHN HARRISON *fl.* 1784–91

1784–89	Atlas to accompany Rapin's *History of England* (originally by Paul de Rapin-Thoyras published *c.* 1730–50)
1787	*Africa*
1791	*English Counties*
	1792 Re-issued
1815	*General Atlas*

GEORGE AUGUSTUS WALPOOLE *fl.* 1784

1784–94	(with Alexander Hogg) *The New British Traveller* (8vo)

ALEXANDER HOGG *fl.* 1778–1805

Published many works on antiquities which included re-issues of maps by Thomas Kitchin, Thomas Conder and others.

1784–94	(with G. A. Walpoole) *The New British Traveller* (8vo)
c. 1784	*A New Map of the Southern Part of Scotland*

ROBERT WILKINSON *fl.* 1785–1825

1785	Re-issue of Bowen and Kitchin's *The Large English Atlas*

1794	*General Atlas of the World*
	c. 1800, 1802, 1816 Re-issued
1820	*New Holland*
1823	*North America*
1825	*East India Islands*

THOMAS CONDER *fl.* 1775–1801

An engraver whose work is found in a number of historical works, particularly Henry Boswell's *Antiquities of England and Wales* (1786). He also engraved maps in Walpoole's *The New British Traveller* (1784).

JOHN CARY *c.* 1754–1835

Many writers regard John Cary as one of the finest of English cartographers. His maps, of course, are not decorative in the seventeenth-century sense but he came on the scene at a time when the large-scale county maps had recently become available, roads were being used as never before and accurate geographical information from distant countries was being received in greater and greater detail. His fine craftsmanship and ability as an engraver enabled him to make the fullest use of these sources and from them he produced a wide range of maps of great accuracy and clarity. His work covered not only county maps but world atlases, road maps, town and canal plans, sea charts and terrestrial and celestial globes. His business was eventually taken over by G. F. Cruchley (*fl.* 1822–75) who continued to use Cary's engravings throughout his life and it is believed that some plates were still in use in the present century. In this work we can give only a summary of his more important publications.

1786	*Actual Survey of the country fifteen miles round London* (8vo)
1787	*New and Correct English Atlas* (4to)
	1793–1831 Numerous re-issues
1789	Camden's *Britannia*
	1806 Re-issued
1790	*Cary's Travellers' Companion* (8vo)
	1791–1828 Numerous re-issues
1794	*New Maps of England and Wales with part of Scotland* (4to)
1798–1828	*Cary's New Itinerary*
	11 Re-issues
1805	(with J. Stockdale) *New British Atlas*
1808	*Cary's New Universal Atlas*
1809	*Cary's English Atlas*
	1811, 1818, 1828, 1834 Re-issued
1813	*New Elementary Atlas*

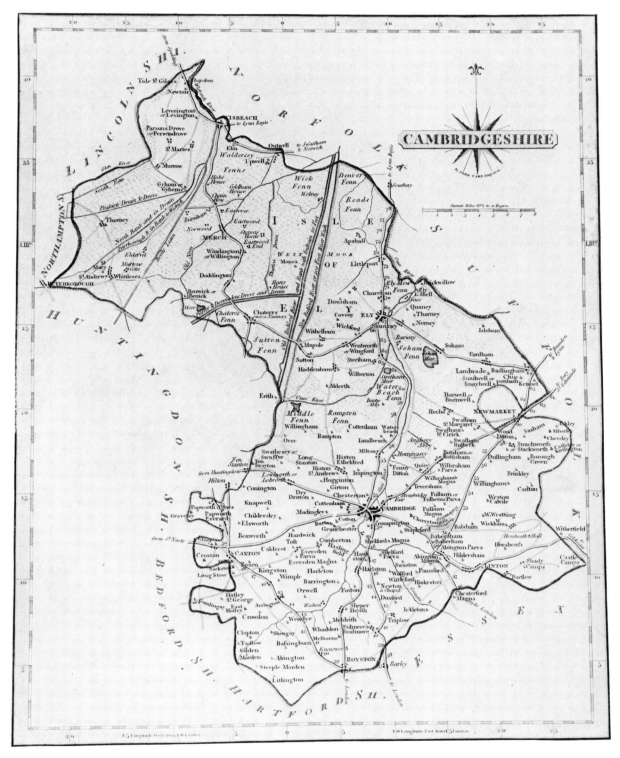

JOHN CARY *Cambridgeshire* London 1787. An example of the beautifully engraved maps in Cary's *New and Correct English Atlas* which was issued in many editions.

ROBERT LAURIE *c.* 1755–1836
JAMES WHITTLE 1757–1818
RICHARD HOLMES LAURIE *d.* 1858

Trading as:
LAURIE AND WHITTLE 1794–1812
WHITTLE AND LAURIE 1812–18
R. H. LAURIE 1818–*c.* 1903

Carried on business from about 1790, taking over the stock of Robert Sayer's publishing house in 1792–93. Their prolific output covered maritime atlases and charts as well as general atlases and sheet maps, including many revisions of works by Kitchin, Jefferys, Faden, Sayer and Bennett, and others.

c. 1789	*A New Universal Atlas* (Thos Kitchin)
	1796, 1799 Re-issued
1794	*A New and Correct map of the British Colonies in North America*
	1823 Re-issued (R. H. Laurie)
1795	*The East India Pilot* (B. d'Après de Mannevillette)
1795	*A complete body of Ancient Geography* (J. B. B. d'Anville)
	1820 Re-issued
1796	*A new and elegant Imperial Sheet Atlas*
	1798–1814 Re-issued
1797	*The Oriental Pilot* (B. d'Après de Mannevillette)
1798	*Universal Atlas*
1798	*The Complete East India Pilot*
	1800, 1802, 1803, 1806, 1810 Re-issued
1799	*North American Pilot* (Thomas Jefferys/ Sayer and Bennett)
	Many revisions throughout nineteenth century
1801	*African Pilot*
	1816 Re-issued
1801–04	*New and elegant General Atlas*
1805	(with Nathaniel Coltman *fl.* 1806–86) *Welsh Atlas*
1806	*New Traveller's companion* (8vo)
	1809, 1811, 1813 Re-issued
	1828 Re-issued (4to)
1807	*New and improved English Atlas* (4to)

AARON ARROWSMITH 1750–1823
AARON ARROWSMITH (son) *fl.* 1820–30
SAMUEL ARROWSMITH (son) *d.* 1839
JOHN ARROWSMITH (nephew) 1790–1873
Aaron Arrowsmith was the founder of one of the leading London map publishing houses in the early part of the nineteenth century. He came to London about 1770 from Durham, his birthplace, and worked as a surveyor for John Cary for whom he carried out some of the road surveys which subsequently appeared in *Cary's Travellers' Companion* in 1790. In that year he set up his own business in Long Acre and soon established an international reputation as a specialist in compiling maps recording the latest discoveries in all parts of the world. He produced, and constantly revised, a great number of large-scale maps, many issued singly as well as in atlas form. After his death the business passed to his sons, Aaron and Samuel, and later to his nephew John who maintained his uncle's reputation, becoming a founder member of the Royal Geographical Society. In all, the Arrowsmiths issued over 700 maps and it is possible, therefore, to quote only a few of their major works. Their maps of Australia and New Zealand were particularly noteworthy.

1790	*Chart of the World on Mercator's Projection* (11 sheets)
	Revisions to *c.* 1827
1795	*New Discoveries in the Interior Parts of North America*
	Numerous revisions to *c.* 1850
1796	*Map of the United States of America*
	Revisions to *c.* 1819
1798	*Chart of the Pacific Ocean* (9 sheets)
	Revisions to *c.* 1832
1798–1802	Maps of Europe, Asia and Africa
1804	America
	1808, 1811 Re-issued
1806	*A Pilot from England to Canton*
1817	*A new General Atlas* (4to)
	c. 1830 Re-issued
1822	*Atlas of Southern India*
1825	(Aaron & Samuel) *Outlines of the World*
1829–30	(Aaron & Samuel) *Arrowsmith's Comparative Atlas*
1834	(John) *The London Atlas of Universal Geography*
	Numerous re-issues
1838	(John) *Australia*
	Numerous revisions and re-issues of this map and maps of the Australian States.

BENJAMIN BAKER *fl.* 1766–1824
1791–97 *Universal Magazine*

JOHN STOCKDALE 1749–1814

1794	*The American Geography*
1805	(with John Cary) *New British Atlas*
1806	Large-scale map of Scotland
1809	do England

WILLIAM HEATHER *fl.* 1765–1812

For nearly fifty years from 1765 William Heather was a noted publisher and dealer in charts at a time when London had become the most important centre of map production. Charles Dickens wrote in *Dombey and Son* of the 'Navigation Warehouse' and 'Naval Academy', under which names Heather's business address in Leadenhall St was known. The business was eventually taken over by J. W. Norie and continued to prosper until late in the nineteenth century.

1795–1801	*A Pilot for the Atlantic Ocean*
1801	*Complete Pilot for the Northern Navigation*
1801	*New Set of Charts for harbours in the British Channel*
1802	*The New Mediterranean Pilot* (Bremond and Michelot)
	1814 Re-issued
1804–08	*The Maritime Atlas or seaman's complete pilot*
	1808 Re-issued
1805	*East India Pilot*
1811	*The New North Sea Pilot*, and others

JOHN LODGE *fl.* 1754–96

c. 1795	*Atlas of Great Britain & Ireland*
	Maps originally issued in 1782 in the *Political Magazine*

CAPTAIN GEORGE VANCOUVER 1758–98

1798	*A Voyage of Discovery to the North Pacific Ocean and round the World, with Atlas*

SAMUEL JOHN NEELE 1758–1824
JOSIAH NEELE (son) *fl.* 1826–45

c. 1800	*The Modern Royal Atlas*
1813	*Minor Atlas*

JOHN LUFFMAN *fl.* 1776–1820

1801	*Select Plans of the Principal Cities of the World*
1803	*New Pocket Atlas and Geography of England and Wales*: small circular maps (8vo)
	1805, 1806 Re-issued
c. 1809	*Luffman's Geographical and Topographical Atlas*
1815	*Universal Atlas*

CHARLES SMITH (and Son) *fl.* 1800–52

1804	*Smith's New English Atlas* (folio)
	1806–64 Numerous re-issues, some reduced to 4to size
1806	*England & Wales*
1808	*New General Atlas*
	1816 Re-issued
1826	*New Pocket Companion to the Roads of England & Wales* (8vo)

G. COLE and J. ROPER *fl.* 1801–10

1804–10	*The Beauties of England and Wales* – including town plans
1810	*The British Atlas* (4to)

EDWARD MOGG *fl.* 1804–48

A publisher and engraver who specialized in maps for guides of London and its surroundings. He also issued road maps of England and Wales.

c. 1805–36	*Twenty four miles round London* A circular map which was issued in a number of editions
1817–22	*A Survey of the High Roads of England and Wales* (4to)
1821–46	*Forty five miles round London*

ROBERT MILLER *fl.* 1810–21

1810	*Miller's New Miniature Atlas* (12mo)
	1820, 1825 Re-issued by William Darton as *Darton's New Miniature Atlas*

JAMES WALLIS *fl.* 1810–20

1810	*New Pocket Edition of the English Counties* (12mo)
	c. 1814 Re-issued
1811	Maps for Oddy's *New General Atlas of the World* (S. A. Oddy *fl.* 1810–11)
1812	*New and Improved County Atlas/New British Atlas*
	1813 Re-issued
1820	(with W. H. Reid) *The Panorama or Traveller's Instructive Guide*

CAPTAIN THOMAS HURD *c.* 1757–1823

1811	Charts of the English Channel
1814	Charts of Australia and Tasmania

JOHN THOMSON (and Co.) *fl.* 1814–69

1814–28	*A New general atlas of the World*
1820–32	*Atlas of Scotland*

ROBERT ROWE *c.* 1775–1843

1811–16   *English Atlas*
            1829–1842 Re-issued as Teesdale's *New British Atlas*

CAPTAIN MATTHEW FLINDERS 1774–1814

In association with the explorer, George Bass (*d.* 1812), Flinders surveyed the coasts of New South Wales and was the first to circumnavigate Australia. His remarkably accurate surveys still form the basis of many Australian coastal charts.

1814   *Atlas of Australia*
            1829 and other re-issues

WILLIAM SMITH 1769–1839

1815   *A delineation of the strata of England and Wales with part of Scotland* (14 sheets) – the first geological map of England and Wales
1819–24   *Geological Atlas of England and Wales*

JOHN WILLIAM NORIE 1772–1843

Norie, the most celebrated mathematician and hydrographer of his day, carried on business in Leadenhall Street, having taken over from William Heather as a publisher of naval books and dealer in maps and sea charts. The firm traded under the name of Norie and Wilson until about 1830 when Norie retired but it continued in business until the end of the century. Norie's books on navigation, particularly his *Epitome of Practical Navigation* (1805), became standard works and went through many editions.

1816   *Complete East India Pilot*
            Numerous editions
1824   *Complete North Sea and Baltic Pilot*
            1848 Re-issued
1825   *Complete North America and United States Pilot*
1830   *Complete British and Irish Coasting Pilot*
            1835, 1845 Re-issued
1833   *The Country trade or Free Mariners' Pilot*
c. 1845   *Complete Mediterranean Pilot*
c. 1850   *Brazil and South American Pilot*

EDWARD LANGLEY *fl.* 1800–35

1817–18   *Langley's New County Atlas of England and Wales* (with William Belch *fl.* 1802–20) (4to)
            1821 Re-issued

CHRISTOPHER GREENWOOD 1786–1855
JOHN GREENWOOD *fl.* 1821–40

The Greenwoods were among the notable firms of publishers in the period 1820–50 who attempted to produce large-scale maps of the counties in competition with the Ordnance Survey Office. In the long run their efforts were unsuccessful but before giving up the struggle they published between the years 1817 and 1830 a series of splendid large-scale folding maps of most of the counties based on their own surveys. Unfortunately, they were unable to complete the series and instead, in 1834, published an *Atlas of the Counties of England*, a very handsome work, often hand coloured, each map having a vignette of an important building in the county.

1817–30   Large-scale maps of all the counties except Buckinghamshire, Cambridgeshire, Herefordshire, Hertfordshire, Norfolk, Oxfordshire and Rutland
1834   *Atlas of the Counties of England*

JAMES ROBINS *fl.* 1819

1819   *Atlas of England and Wales* (4to)

G. ELLIS *fl.* 1819

1819   *New and Correct Atlas of England and Wales* (4to)
c. 1823   *General Atlas of the World*

JAMES WYLD (the Elder) 1790–1836
JAMES WYLD (the Younger) 1812–87

The Wylds, father and son, were highly successful map publishers in London for well over half a century. The Elder succeeded to William Faden's business, taking over his stock in 1823, and from then onwards he, and later his son, issued a large number of atlases and maps, including re-issues of Faden's maps – all noted for their excellence. In turn they both held the appointment of Geographer Royal, and the Elder was also a founder member of the Royal Geographical Society.

c. 1819–25 *A General Atlas*
1820   *Settlements in New South Wales*
c. 1824   *Map of North America* (6 sheets)
            Revised issues to *c.* 1856
1837   *Map of Australia compiled from nautical surveys*
1840   *Chart of New Zealand*
c. 1838–41 (the Younger) *A New General Atlas* (large folio)

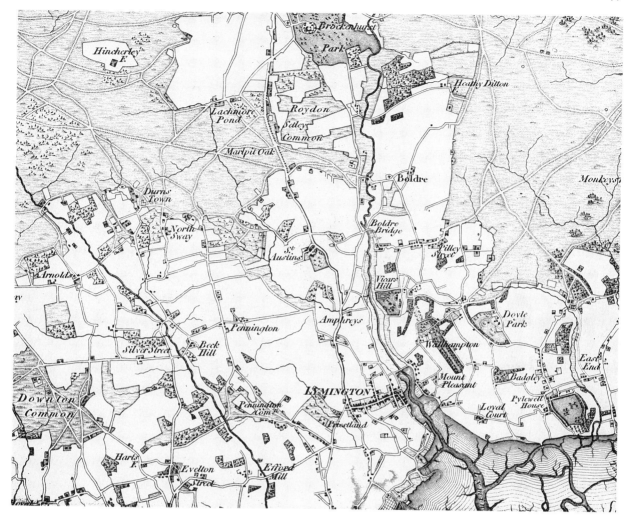

ORDNANCE SURVEY *Isle of Wight and part of Hampshire* Detail from the Ordnance Survey Map issued on 1 June 1810 by Lt.-Col. Mudge, Tower.

1842	(the Younger) *Atlas of Modern Geography*
1849	(the Younger) *Popular Atlas of the World*

WILLIAM LEWIS *fl.* 1819–36

1819	*Lewis's New Traveller's Guide* (12mo)
	1836 Re-issued

SAMUEL LEIGH *fl.* 1820–42

1820	*New Atlas of England and Wales* (12mo)
	1825–40 Numerous re-issues
	1842 Re-issued as *New Pocket Atlas of England and Wales*

WILLIAM DARTON *fl.* 1810–37

1820	*Darton's New Miniature Atlas* (maps from Robert Miller's *New Miniature Atlas*, 1810)
	1825 Re-issued
1822	(with Thomas Dix, *fl.* 1799–1821) *Complete Atlas of the English Counties*
	1830, 1833, 1848 Re-issued

W. H. REID *fl.* 1820

1820	(with James Wallis) *The Panorama or Traveller's Instructive Guide*

No. IV.

Price 1*s. plain, or* 1*s.* 6*d. coloured.*

·MOULE'S·ENGLISH·COUNTIES·

CHOROGRAPHIA

OXFORDSHIRE.

BRITANNIÆ

OXFORD CIRCUIT

THE ENGLISH COUNTIES DELINEATED;

OR

DESCRIPTIVE VIEW OF THE PRESENT STATE OF

England and Wales;

ILLUSTRATED BY A NEW MAP OF LONDON, AND A SERIES OF FORTY COUNTY MAPS,

WITH

VIGNETTE VIEWS OF REMARKABLE PLACES, AND ARMORIAL DECORATIONS, CHIEFLY FROM

THE SEALS OF COUNTY TOWNS.

Forming Two Volumes handsomely printed in Quarto.

BY THOMAS MOULE,

AUTHOR OF BIBLIOTHECA HERALDICA, AND EDITOR OF SEVERAL POPULAR TOPOGRAPHICAL WORKS.

T. CLERIHEW, Del.   MARY BYFIELD, S.

LONDON:

G. VIRTUE, 26 IVY LANE; SIMPKIN AND MARSHALL, STATIONERS' COURT;

JENNINGS AND CHAPLIN, 62 CHEAPSIDE;

AND MAY BE HAD OF ALL BOOKSELLERS.

1830.

RICHARD TAYLOR, PRINTER,   RED LION COURT, FLEET STREET.

THOMAS MOULE *Oxfordshire.* Title page dated 1830 from a part of Moule's *The English Counties Delineated,* one of the most popular atlases of the day.

A. BRYANT *fl.* 1822–35

1822–35	Large-scale maps of the Counties of Bedford, Buckingham, Gloucester, Hereford, Hertfordshire, Lincoln, Norfolk, Northants, Oxford, Suffolk, Surrey, Yorkshire (East Riding)

JOHN WALKER *fl.* 1759–1830
ALEXANDER WALKER
CHARLES WALKER } *fl. c.* 1820–*c.* 1890

1825–46	*Maps of India and The Provinces*
1833	*Topographical Dictionary of Wales*
1837	*British Atlas*
	1838–*c.* 1880 Numerous re-issues
1837	*Royal Atlas*
	Re-issues to 1873

JAMES DUNCAN *fl.* 1826–33

1826	*Lothian's Atlas of Scotland*
1833	*A Complete County Atlas of England and Wales*
	1837–65 6 re-issues

HENRY TEESDALE (and Co.) *fl.* 1828–45

1829	*New British Atlas* (Robert Rowe) (4to)
	1830–42 Various editions
1830	*New Travelling Atlas* (4to)
	1842 Re-issued
	1848 Re-issued as *Travelling Atlas of England and Wales*
	1850, 1852, 1860 Further re-issues of 1848 edition
1831–35	*A new general atlas of the World*
	1856 Re-issued

JAMES PIGOT AND CO. *fl.* 1829–35

1829	*British Atlas of the Counties of England*
	1831–44 7 re-issues
	1846 Re-issued by Isaac Slater as *British Atlas*
1835	*Pocket Topography and Gazetteer of England*
	1842 Re-issued

SOCIETY FOR THE DIFFUSION OF USEFUL KNOWLEDGE (SDUK) 1829–*c.* 1876

1829–43	About 200 maps of all countries of the world issued in separate parts, published by Baldwin and Cradock (1829–37) and the Society (1837–42)
1844–76	*World Atlas*, pub. by Chapman and Hall

SYDNEY HALL *fl.* 1818–60

1830	*A new General Atlas*
1833	*New British Atlas*
	1834, 1836 Re-issued
1842	*A Travelling County Atlas*
	1843–85 Numerous re-issues
1847	*New County Atlas*

THOMAS MOULE 1784–1851

Thomas Moule was a writer on heraldry and antiquities born in 1784 at St Marylebone in London. He carried on business as a bookseller in Duke Street, Grosvenor Square, from about 1816 until 1823, when he became Inspector of 'blind' letters in the General Post Office, his principal duties being the deciphering of such addresses as were illegible to the ordinary clerks. He also held, for many years, the office of Chamber-keeper in the Lord Chamberlain's Department which entitled him to an official residence in the Stable Yard of St James's Palace, where he died on 14 January 1851.

The well-known series of County Maps which are known as 'Moules' were first published in separate sections for each county in 1830–32 and they were then published in collected form in a two-volume work: *The English Counties Delineated: or a Topographical Description of England: Illustrated by a Complete Series of County Maps by Thomas Moule*: London: Published by George Virtue 1836. Further editions were brought out by Virtue (some with original hand-colouring of the maps) until about 1839. In 1841 the maps appeared in a publication entitled *Barclays Complete and Universal English Dictionary* with additions to the original plates showing the railways which had been constructed. Normally maps which come from this work are very close trimmed, often into the printed surface, as the format of the dictionary was slightly smaller than the original publication. They are the last series of decorative county maps to be published and are an elegant addition to any collection of maps.

1836	*The English Counties Delineated* (4to)
	1836–39 Re-issued
1841	Re-issued as *Barclays Complete and Universal English Dictionary*
	1842, 1848, 1850, 1852 Re-issued

THOMAS DUGDALE *fl.* 1835–60

1835	*Curiosities of Great Britain & Ireland* – maps by Cole and Roper
	1842–48 4 re-issues

A. FULLARTON AND CO. *fl.* 1840–70

1834	*Parliamentary Gazetteer of England and Wales* (8vo)
	1843, 1849 Re-issued
1864	*Royal Illustrated Atlas*
1870–72	*Hand Atlas of the World*

TALLIS AND CO. *fl.* 1838–51

London map publishers who traded under various names: L. Tallis, Tallis and Co., John Tallis, John Tallis and Co. (London and New York) between 1838 and 1851: after about 1850–51 their maps were published by The London Printing and Publishing Co., London and New York.

1838	*London Street Views*
1849–53	*Illustrated Atlas of the World*
	Steel-engraved maps decorated with attractive vignette views, issued in about 70 parts and including 26 town plans

REUBEN RAMBLE *fl.* 1845

c. 1845	*Travels through the English Counties* (4to)

ISAAC SLATER *fl.* 1846

1846	*Slater's New British Atlas*
	Maps from James Pigot and Co.'s *British Atlas*
	1847–62 Re-issued

Specialist References

BOOTH, J., *Antique Maps of Wales*

CHUBB, T., *The Printed Maps in the Atlases of Great Britain and Ireland*
In spite of its age still one of the first books to turn to for details of county maps

EVANS, I. M. and LAWRENCE, H., *Christopher Saxton: Elizabethan Mapmaker*
The definitive work on the life of Christopher Saxton

EVANS, O. C., *Maps of Wales and Welsh Cartographers*

SHIRLEY, R. W., *Early Printed Maps of the British Isles 1477–1650*
The definitive work on maps of the period

SKELTON, R. A., *County Atlases of the British Isles 1579–1703*
The best work available on county maps in the period covered

THEATRUM ORBIS TERRARUM NV
Speed: *A Prospect of the Most Famous Parts of the World,* 1627
Ogilby: *Britannia,* 1675
Seller, Fisher and Thornton: *English Pilot,* 4th book, 1689
Seller, Price: *English Pilot,* Part V, 1701
Seller, Thornton: *English Pilot,* 3rd book, 1703
Jefferys: *American Atlas,* 1775–76
Reproduction of complete atlases

TOOLEY, R. V., *Maps and Map Makers*
Apart from descriptive text contains listings of English Marine charts and county atlases issued up to about 1850

TYACKE, S., *London Mapsellers 1660–1720*

PLATE I

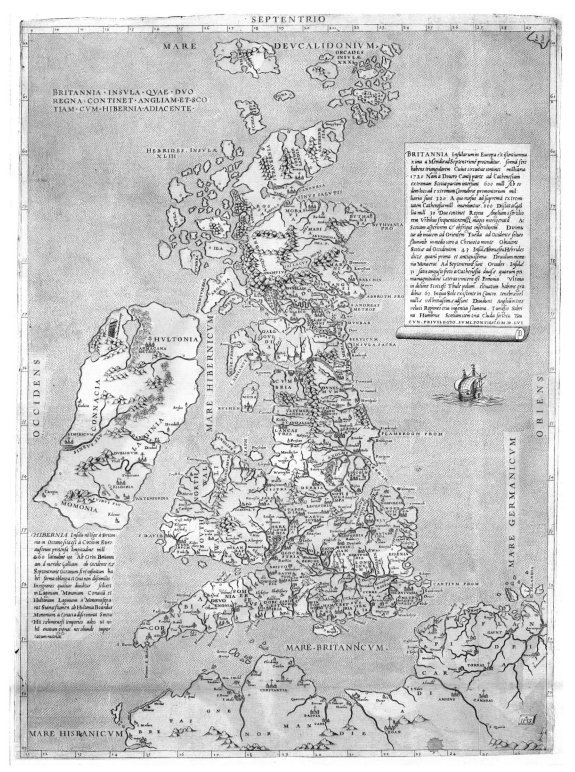

GEORGE LILY *British Isles* Rome (1546) 1556 This, the first map of the British Isles printed from a copperplate engraving, was published in Rome in 1546, followed by a number of other versions issued there and elsewhere.

PLATE II

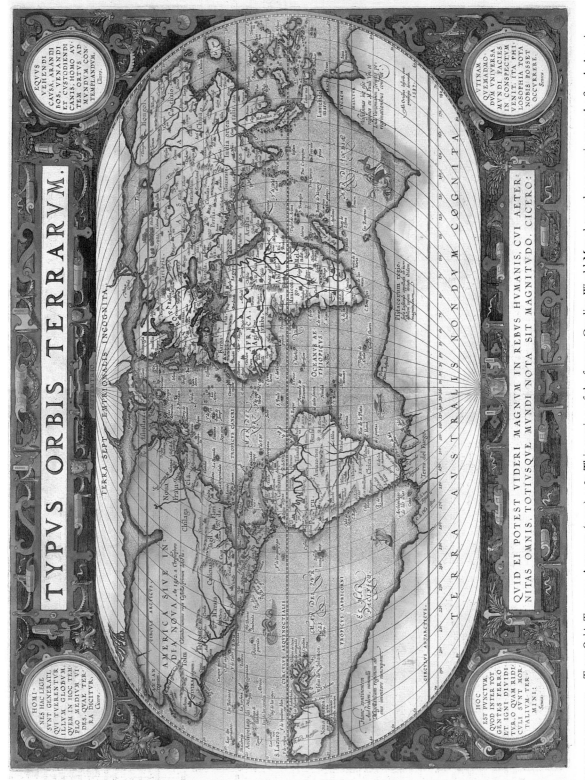

ABRAHAM ORTELIUS   *Typus Orbis Terrarum* Antwerp (1570) 1587 This version of the famous Ortelius World Map shows the corrections to the South American coastline and other alterations made after 1587.

PLATE III

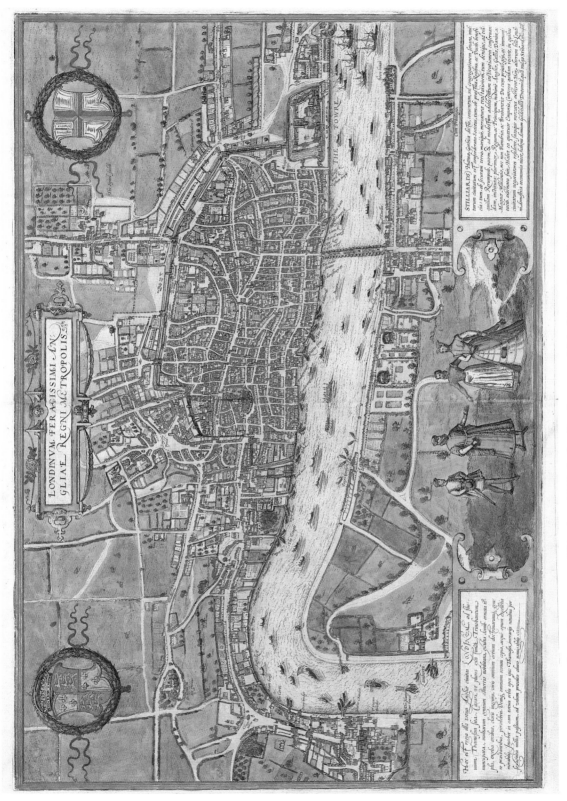

BRAUN AND HOGENBERG *London* Cologne 1572 This view of Elizabethan London was published in the first volume of the *Civitates Orbis Terrarum*.

PLATE IV

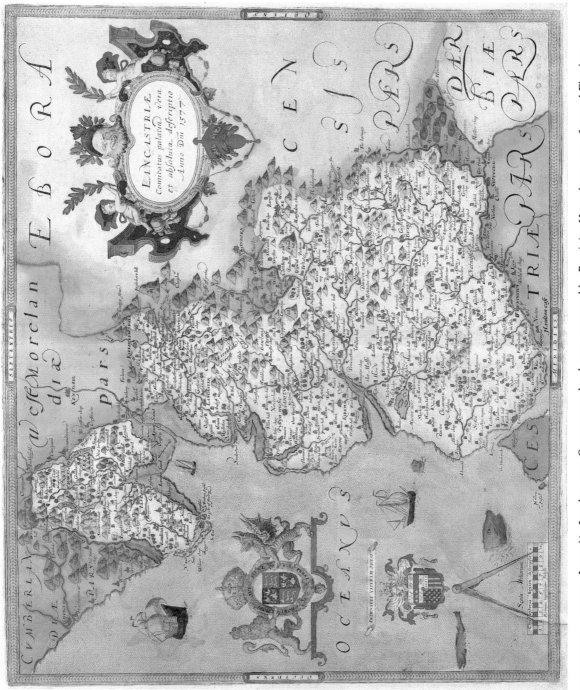

CHRISTOPHER SAXTON *Lancashire* London 1579 County map dated 1577, engraved by Remigius Hogenberg, one of several Flemings employed by Saxton, was published in the *Atlas of England and Wales* in 1579.

PLATE V

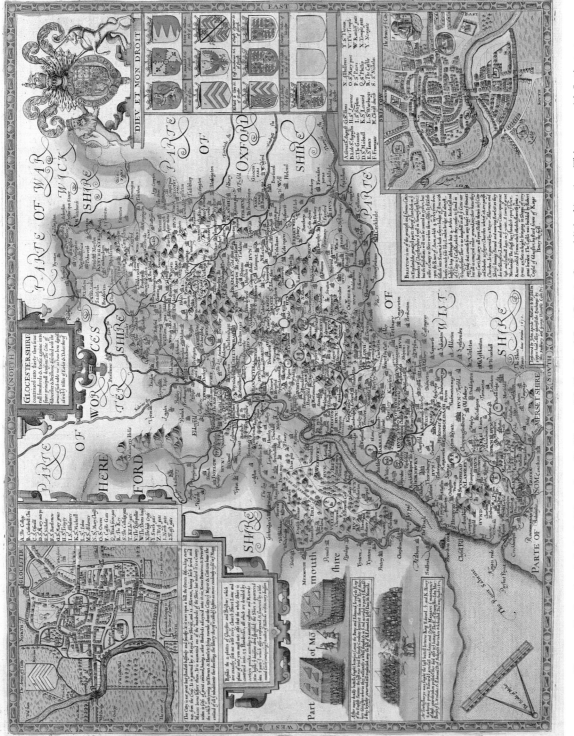

JOHN SPEED *Gloucestershire* London (1611) 1616 From Speed's *Theatre of the Empire of Great Britaine* first published in 1611. This copy, with Latin text, was issued in 1616.

PLATE VI

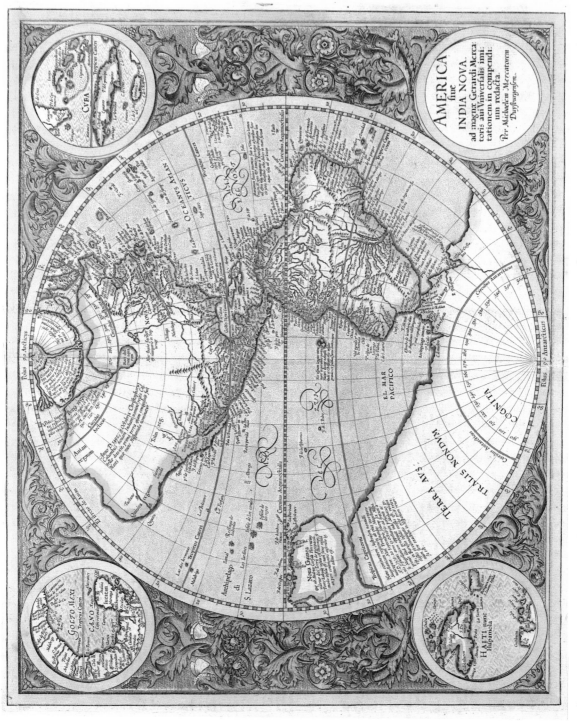

GERARD MERCATOR *America sive India Nova* Amsterdam 1595 Map of the American Continent compiled by Mercator's grandson, Michael, first issued in the third part of the *Mercator Atlas*.

PLATE VII

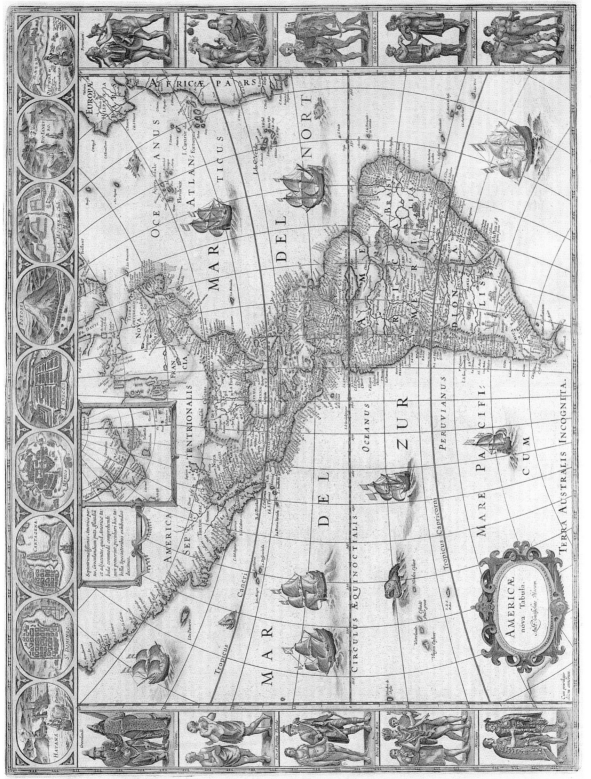

PLATE VIII

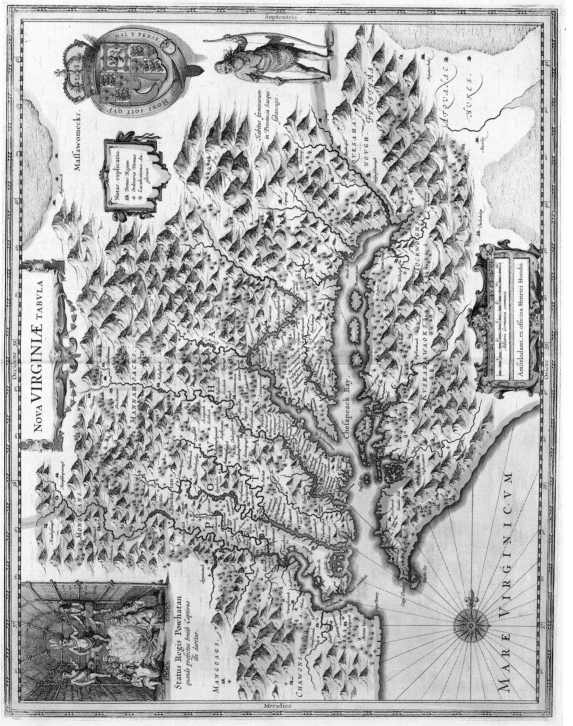

MERCATOR/HONDIUS/JANSSON   *Nova Virginiae Tabula* Amsterdam 1633 Map of Virginia derived from the famous map by Capt. John Smith (1612) with inset figure of Powhatan and showing Indian tribal names. Published by Henricus Hondius in conjunction with Jan Jansson.

Chapter 16
SCOTLAND

Both the Matthew Paris and Gough maps show an outline of Scotland, albeit unrecognizable, but for other early maps we have to look to the work of continental cartographers rather than to national sources; to rudimentary Italian and Catalan portulan charts of the fourteenth and fifteenth centuries, which are rare indeed, and to the various editions of Ptolemy from 1477 onwards. Up to 1508, the Ptolemaic maps show Scotland on an east–west axis, and although this is corrected in later editions, the general coastal outlines bear little relation to reality and we must turn to George Lily's map of the British Isles published in Rome in 1546 (with other editions up to 1589) to find a genuine representation of the coasts and islands. Lily's sources are not known with any certainty but presumably he used local manuscripts of some kind made, perhaps, during a voyage round Scotland by James V about 1540. Sebastian Münster's map of England and Wales (Basle 1540 and later editions) shows only the southern part of Scotland to just beyond Edinburgh with the national flag adjacent to it. Other maps, known from only one or two copies, include an anonymous one derived from Lily's map, printed in Italy about 1566, which was the earliest known separately printed map, and those of John Leslie, Bishop of Ross, compiled during exile in Italy and France in about 1578, based on the Lily and Ortelius maps and printed in Rome or Rouen in the last quarter of the century. The best outline map, or rather chart, of Scotland produced in this period was by Nicolas de Nicolay, printed in Paris in 1583. Nicolay, a much travelled Frenchman, claimed to have based his work on an earlier manuscript map drawn in about 1546 by Alex. Lindsay, pilot to King James V.

As might be expected, single-sheet maps were included in atlases by Ortelius, Mercator, Hondius, Camden, Speed, Blaeu and Jansson among others. Of these the best known is Speed's highly decorative map which, as well as being geographically realistic, shows full-length portraits of the Stuart reigning family. Speed's maps were re-issued in numerous editions until 1652 when the plate was re-engraved and four figures in national costume were inserted in place of the royal portraits.

Although these general maps were splendid in their way and often very decorative, there was no set of individual county maps comparable to Saxton's *Atlas of England and Wales* until 1654 when Part V of J. Blaeu's *Atlas Novus* was published in Amsterdam as the *Atlas of Scotland* containing 55 maps. This was the first comprehensive atlas of Scotland and the maps in it had a long and chequered history, having been prepared originally by a Scottish minister, Timothy Pont, who travelled widely and carried out surveys of much of Scotland from about the year 1583. Pont failed to find a patron or a publisher although his map of Lothian and Linlithgow was published in the Mercator/Hondius Atlas of 1630. His manuscript maps and drawings eventually came into the hands of Robert Gordon and his son James, who undertook the work of re-drawing and correcting the original maps, as well as adding a number of their own. After long delays the maps were published in 1654 with texts in Dutch, Latin, French and German. They were also included in the later *Atlas Maior* issued in the following years: 1658–72 (Spanish), 1662 (Latin), 1663 (French), 1664 (Dutch) and 1667 (German). As in the case of Blaeu's atlases of England and Wales, there were no issues with English text. In this instance Jansson did not attempt to compete with Blaeu in producing his own atlas but from 1636 onwards a small number of maps of Scotland and the Islands appeared in the Mercator-Hondius-Jansson atlases and in Jansson's own atlas of 1646 and its subsequent editions.

From this time onwards, maps of Scotland appeared in most atlases published by major cartographers of all nationalities. Although maps were published in great quantity, there was still a need for more accuracy and between 1747 and 1755 a detailed survey of the Highlands and part of the Lowlands was carried out by William Roy, who eventually became one of the founders of the Ordnance Survey Office.

Biographies

It would obviously be beyond the scope of this handbook to attempt to include details of all the maps printed in the seventeenth and eighteenth centuries but the following are of particular interest:

JOHN ADAIR *fl.* 1686–1718

A mathematician, living in Edinburgh, who embarked on a considerable number of cartographic enterprises but through shortage of money and ill luck few of them came to fruition. His maps of several Scottish counties, although completed in the 1680s, were not published until long after his death.

1688–93	*A true and exact hydrographical description of the Sea Coast and Isles of Scotland*: published in 1703
1727	*Nova Scotiae tabula*, published in Buchanan's *Rerum Scoticarum Historia*

HERMAN MOLL *fl.* 1678–1732

1701	Scotland, in *A System of Geography*
1708	*The north part of Great Britain*
1714	*The north part of Great Britain called Scotland*
1718	*A Pocket Companion of Ye Roads of ye north part of Great Britain called Scotland* 1727 and later editions
1725	*A set of Thirty Six New and Correct Maps of Scotland* 1745 Re-issued

CHRISTOPHER BROWNE *fl.* 1684–1712

1705	*North Britain or Scotland*

SUTTON NICHOLLS *fl.* 1695–1740

c. 1710	*A New Map of North Britain or Scotland*

THOMAS TAYLOR *fl.* 1670–1721

1715	*The North Part of Great Britain called Scotland*
1720	*A new Mapp of Scotland or North Britain* 1731–76 Re-issued

JOHN ELPHINSTONE 1706–53

A military engineer who served with the Duke of Cumberland at Culloden in 1746. His *New and Correct Mercator's Map* was criticized by Thomas Jefferys for its inaccuracies but it was generally recognized as a great improvement on all earlier maps of Scotland.

1745	*A New and Correct Mercator's Map of North Britain* 1746 Re-issued

EMANUEL BOWEN *fl.* 1714–67

1746	*A new and accurate map of Scotland or North Britain*
1747	*A new and accurate map of Scotland*

THOMAS KITCHIN 1718–84

Apart from the maps listed below, Thomas Kitchin produced a large number of other maps of Scotland for atlases by Wm Faden, Carrington Bowles, and Sayer and Bennett, among others.

1749	*Geographia Scotiae* (12mo) Pocket Atlas of 33 maps 1756 Re-issued
1771	*Scotland with the roads from the latest surveys*
1771	*Scotland from the best authorities*

JAMES DORRET *fl.* 1750–61

Little is known about Dorret except that, although employed as a valet by the 3rd Duke of Argyll, he claimed to be a land surveyor, evidently not without reason for at the Duke's order and expense he prepared a new large-scale map of Scotland which was so great an improvement on earlier maps that it remained the standard for the country for something like forty years.

1750	*A general map of Scotland and Islands thereto belonging* – in 4 sheets 1751, 1761 Re-issued on a smaller scale

MURDOCH MACKENZIE 1712–97

A notable hydrographer who carried out the first scientific marine survey on a measured baseline in this country. After completing a survey of the Orkneys begun in 1742 as a private venture he was commissioned by the Admiralty to survey the west coast of Britain and all the coasts of Ireland, the results of which were published in 1776. He was succeeded as Admiralty Surveyor by his nephew, also Murdoch MacKenzie (1743–1829).

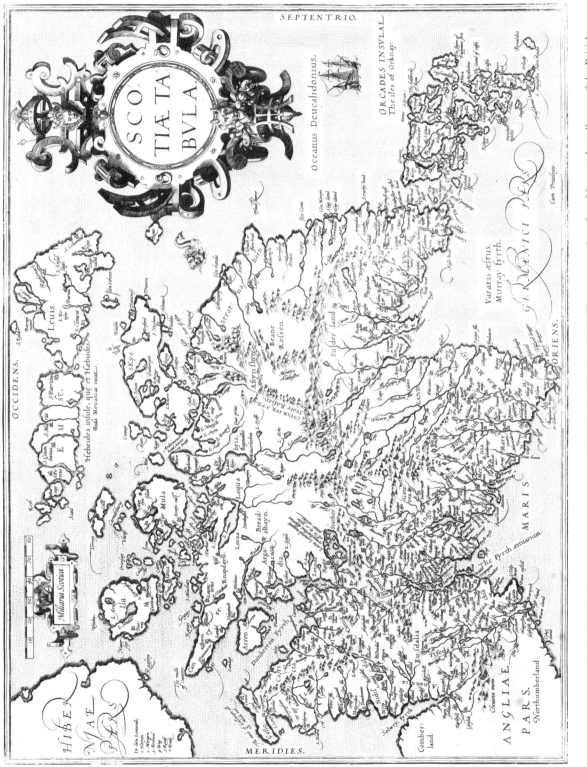

ABRAHAM ORTELIUS *Scotiae Tabula* Antwerp 1573. This map, published in the *Theatrum Orbis Terrarum*, was based on Mercator's wall map of the British Isles compiled in 1564 and remained the standard map until 1611, when Speed's new map was issued.

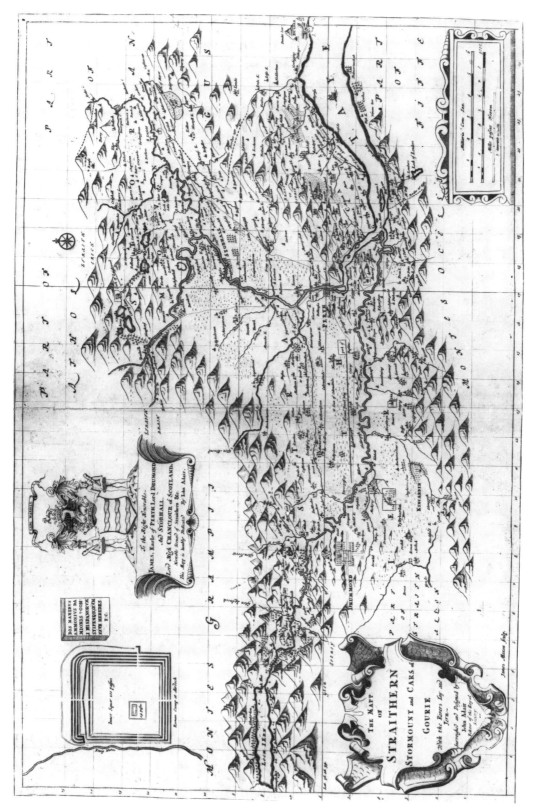

JOHN ADAIR   *Mapp of Straithern, Stormount and Cars of Gourie.* Although this map by John Adair was engraved by James Moxon probably about 1685–86, it was not published until after Adair's death in 1718.

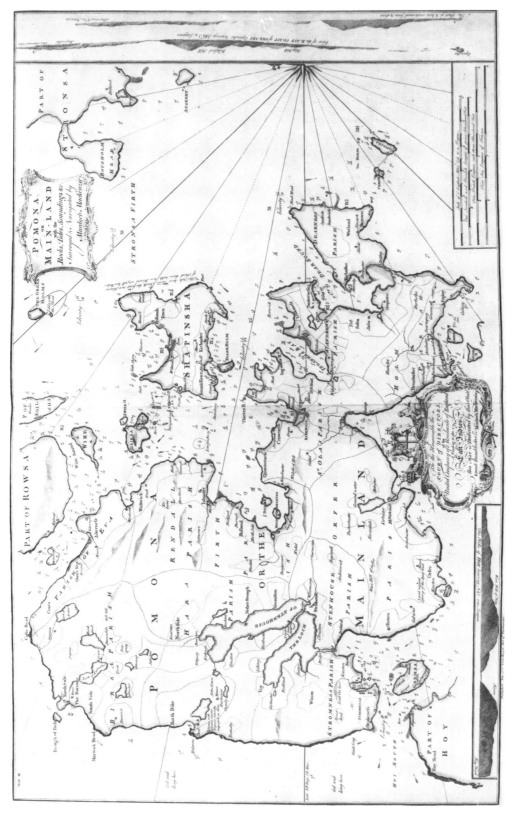

MURDOCH MACKENZIE *Pomona or Mainland (The Orkneys).* Published in 1750 in Mackenzie's *Orcades, or a Geographic and Hydrographic Survey of the Orkney and Lewis Islands.*

1750   *Orcades, or a Geographic and Hydrographic Survey of the Orkney and Lewis Islands*

1776   *A Maritime Survey of Ireland and the West Coast of Great Britain*

DANIEL PATERSON *fl.* 1771–91

1771   *A New and Accurate Description of all the Direct and Principal Cross Roads of Scotland*

ANDREW ARMSTRONG *fl.* 1768–81

Traded with his son Mostyn Armstrong (below) as Captain Armstrong and Son. Surveyed and published a number of maps of Scottish and English Counties.

1775   *A New Map of Scotland*

1775   *Bowles New Pocket Map of Scotland*: published in *Bowles Universal Atlas*

MOSTYN JOHN ARMSTRONG *fl.* 1769–91

1776   *An Actual Survey of the Great Post Roads between London and Edinburgh*

1777   *A Scotch Atlas or Description of the Kingdom of Scotland*
        1787 Re-issued by John Sayer
        1794 Re-issued by Laurie and Whittle

GEORGE TAYLOR
ANDREW SKINNER } *fl.* 1772–85

1776   *Survey and Maps of the Roads of North Britain or Scotland*

1776   *The Traveller's Pocket Book*

CARRINGTON BOWLES 1724–93

1782   *Bowles's new and accurate Map of Scotland*

1782   *Bowles's new pocket Map of Scotland*
        1795, 1806 Re-issued

MARCUS ARMSTRONG *fl.* 1782

1782   *A new Map of Scotland* (road map)

JOHN AINSLIE 1745–1828

Worked with Thomas Jefferys on surveys of a number of English counties before setting up business in Edinburgh as a bookseller and land surveyor. His output of county and coastal surveys and estate plans

was prolific: he is best known for his large-scale map of Scotland published in 1789.

1783   *Ainslie's travelling Map of Scotland*
        1789 Re-issued

1789   *Scotland Drawn and Engrav'd from a Series of Angles and Astronomical Observations* (9 sheets)
        Numerous re-issues to *c.* 1840

JOHN CARY *c.* 1754–1835

1789   Wm Camden's *Britannia: New and correct maps of the South and North parts of Scotland*
        1806 Re-issued

1790   *The Travellers' Companion: A Map of Scotland*
        Numerous re-issues

1808   *Cary's New Universal Atlas: A new Map of Scotland*

AARON ARROWSMITH 1750–1823

1807   Map of Scotland
        1810, 1840, 1841, 1849 Re-issued

JOHN THOMSON (AND CO.) *fl.* 1814–69

1820–32   *Atlas of Scotland* (large folio)

Specialist References

ROYAL SCOTTISH GEOGRAPHICAL SOCIETY, *The Early Maps of Scotland to 1850 with a history of Scottish Maps*
Contains detailed listing of maps of Scotland

SHIRLEY, R. W., *Early Printed Maps of the British Isles 1477–1650*
Although covering maps of the British Isles much of the detail contained in this book also covers the history of Scottish maps

SKELTON, R. A., *County Atlases of the British Isles 1579–1703*
Includes detailed description and collations of the Blaeu/Jansson atlases of Scotland

TOOLEY, R. V., *Maps and Map-Makers*
Includes detail of large-scale surveys

Chapter 17

IRELAND

The earliest maps of Ireland up to the year 1500 or so share the shortcomings of those of the rest of the British Isles especially as represented on world maps. It was not to be expected that lands literally on the very edge of the known world could be depicted with any accuracy; very often one feels that the cartographers or engravers placed the islands in the nearest available space consistent with their imagined position. Even in the first printed Ptolemaic map there is still much distortion in Ireland's shape and geographical position but, on the other hand, a quite surprising number of place names and other details are shown, as many, in fact, as in the rest of Britain put together. This detailed knowledge is not as puzzling as it might appear, for the Ptolemy maps, at least the later editions from 1513 onwards, were based on Italian portulan charts and these, in turn, reflected knowledge gained during the long commercial relationship which had existed between Italy and Ireland ever since the thirteenth century. The distortions on land-surveyed maps remained uncorrected until late in the seventeenth century but a quite accurate coastal outline was given in the marine atlases of Waghenaer, Dudley, Blaeu and later Dutch chart makers.

Apart from a few manuscript maps and very rare maps printed in Rome and Venice (George Lily, 1546, and others in the period 1560–66) Ireland is shown on Mercator's large map of the British Isles (1564), and in his Atlas (1595) and as a separate sheet in the Ortelius atlases (from 1573). The most important map, however, was compiled by an Italian, Baptista Boazio, probably in the 1580s. This has survived in manuscript form and may have been used by Pieter van der Keere for a map published by Jodocus Hondius in 1591. Boazio's map was subsequently published by John Sudbury, who later sold Speed's maps, and this version was included in editions of the Ortelius atlases from 1602 onwards. The Boazio map is a quite splendid map, very decorative, some copies even showing an Eskimo

complete with kayak and hunting spear. Thereafter the trend is familiar: Camden, Speed, Blaeu, Jansson, Sanson and others of the Dutch and French schools all included a general map or maps of the Irish provinces in their atlases. Speed's map of the whole of Ireland was based at least partly on surveys by Robert Lythe (*c.* 1570) and Francis Jobson (*c.* 1590) and included figures in national costume; it was for long regarded as the best map available and was much copied by publishers in other countries.

In 1685 the first atlas of Ireland to match Saxton's *Atlas of England and Wales* was published by Sir William Petty as *Hiberniae Delineatio*, the result of a highly organized and detailed survey (the 'Down' survey) carried out in the years following 1655. Re-issued in miniature form soon afterwards by Francis Lamb, Petty's Atlas was widely used as the basis for practically all maps of Ireland produced by English, French, Dutch and German publishers in the following century. Apart from re-issues of Petty's Atlas and its many copyists there were maps by George Grierson, a Dublin publisher, John Rocque, the Huguenot surveyor and engraver who spent some years in Dublin, and Bernard Scalé, Rocque's brother-in-law. Details of their principal works are noted in the listing below.

Towards the end of the century many large-scale maps were published but, as in England, private mapping was gradually overtaken and eventually replaced by the Ordnance Survey maps produced between the years 1824 and 1846.

Biographies

SIR WILLIAM PETTY 1623–87
William Petty, after studying mathematics and the sciences in France and Holland, qualified as a doctor and before the age of thirty was appointed Physician General to the Army in Ireland. However, his interests

lay outside medicine and he acquired the job of surveying a large area of Ireland for valuation and demarcation purposes. In the event, he persuaded his superiors to permit him to embark on a wider survey covering the whole country and with an organization consisting of over one thousand surveyors, assistants and others, the work was completed in about five years. For various reasons the final engraving and printing was not completed until 1685 when the Atlas consisting of 36 maps was published by Petty himself. Its popularity was immediate and a version on a reduced scale was soon issued by Francis Lamb. Petty was a founder member of the Royal Society.

1685   *Hiberniae Delineatio*: 36 maps (4to)
        1690, 1732 (Grierson) Re-issued
        c. 1795 Re-issued by Laurie and Whittle

FRANCIS LAMB *fl.* 1670–1700

c. 1689   *A Geographicall Description of the Kingdom of Ireland*: 39 maps
        1689, *c.* 1695 Re-issued
        1720 Re-issued by Thomas Bowles with roads added
        1728, 1732 Re-issue of the 1720 edition by John Bowles

PHILIP LEA *fl.* 1683–1700

1689   *An Epitome of Sir William Petty's Large Survey of Ireland*
1690   (with Herman Moll) *A New Map of Ireland According to Sir Wm Petty* (2 sheets)

HERMAN MOLL *fl.* 1678–1732

1728   *Set of Twenty New and Correct Maps of Ireland* (4to)

THOMAS and JOHN BOWLES *fl. c.* 1714–79

1732   *Kingdom of Ireland*
        1765 Re-issued

GEORGE GRIERSON 1709–53

A Dublin printer and publisher who, apart from his own publications, re-issued Sir William Petty's Atlas in 1732.

1732   *Hiberniae Delineatio* (Petty)
1746   *The World Described or a New and Correct Sett of Maps*
1749   *The English Pilot: Northern Navigation*
c. 1772   do   : *Southern Navigation*

JOHN ROCQUE *c.* 1704–62

1756   *An Exact Survey of the City of Dublin*: 4 sheets
        1757 Re-issued on one sheet
1760   *County of Dublin*: 4 sheets
        1799, 1802 Re-issued by Laurie and Whittle in reduced form
1760   *County Armagh*: 4 sheets
1764   Plans of various other towns
1765   *A Map of the Kingdom of Ireland*: 4 sheets

BERNARD SCALÉ *fl.* 1760–87

1773   *City and Suburbs of Dublin*
1776   *Hibernian Atlas*: Sayer and Bennett (4to)
        1788 Re-issued by Robert Sayer
        1798   do   Laurie and Whittle

GEORGE TAYLOR ⎫ *fl.* 1772–85
ANDREW SKINNER ⎭

c. 1778   *Roads of Ireland*
        1783 Re-issued

CARRINGTON BOWLES 1724–93

1791   *New Pocket map of the Kingdom of Ireland*

DANIEL AUGUSTUS BEAUFORT *fl.* 1792

1792   *A new Map of Ireland – Civil and Ecclesiastical*

ROBERT LAURIE *c.* 1755–1836
JAMES WHITTLE 1757–1818

1794   *Kingdom of Ireland* (John Rocque)
1795   *The Irish Coasting Pilot*
1798   *Hibernian Atlas* (Bernard Scalé)
1799–1802 *County of Dublin* (John Rocque)

Specialist References

ANDREWS, J. H., *Irish Maps*
A short but very useful booklet on Irish maps

SKELTON, R. A., *County Atlases of the British Isles 1579–1703*
Includes description and collation of Sir Wm Petty's *Hiberniae Delineatio* and Francis Lamb's *A Geographicall Description of the Kingdom of Ireland*

TOOLEY, R. V., *Maps and Map Makers*
Apart from the usual information, includes detail of large-scale surveys

ABRAHAM ORTELIUS   *Eryn: Hiberniae, Britannicae Insulae, Nova Descriptio* Antwerp 1573. Highly decorative map of Ireland copied by Ortelius from Mercator's large map of the British Isles published in 1564. This remained the standard map of Ireland until the end of the sixteenth century.

Chapter 18

MAPS OF THE BRITISH ISLES

The works of many British cartographers have been described in other chapters without any attempt to specify the contents of their atlases in detail; this task, however desirable, is beyond the compass of this work. It is obvious that a high proportion of the maps in the atlases of the national cartographers will be of the counties and these are well documented elsewhere. In recent years, however, interest has grown in maps of the British Isles (as an entity) and of England and Wales, and accordingly in this chapter will be found brief details of some of these maps, most of them still obtainable by collectors. Some are rare but the parameter for inclusion is that it would have been possible to purchase each of them readily during the 1970s.

In writing this chapter the surprising fact emerges that probably more maps of the British Isles were issued in European atlases than in those produced in this country. It is to be expected, therefore, that the names of many of the cartographers included will not be familiar to collectors of English county maps. To avoid repetition, biographical details of the European cartographers will not be given here – this information will be found in the preceding chapters – and special emphasis will be given to the 'modern' geographic content. This excludes, by definition, the Ptolemaic maps, which were known to be only of academic and historic interest at the time of publication, and means that the earliest 'modern' map of the British Isles is that first published in 1513 at Strassburg by Martin Waldseemüller, which is our starting-point.

Whilst many of the available books on cartographic subjects include information on maps of the British Isles, Rodney Shirley's *Early Printed Maps of the British Isles 1477–1650* must be mentioned as the definitive work on this subject; it would be quite impossible to write credibly about (or collect) these maps without reference to it.

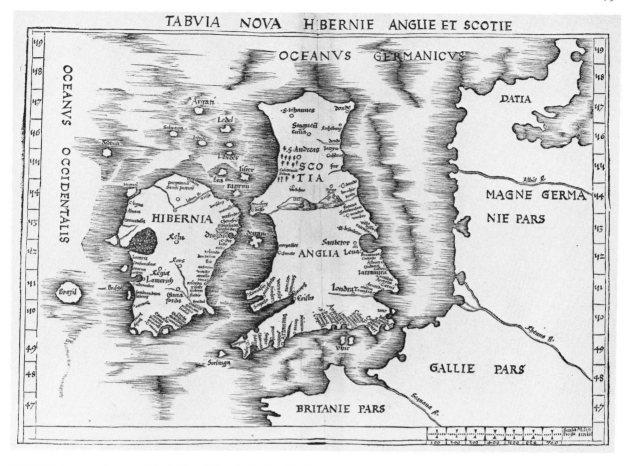

MARTIN WALDSEEMÜLLER   *Tabula Nova Hibernie Anglie et Scotie* 1513

MARTIN WALDSEEMÜLLER

Tabula Nova Hibernie Anglie et Scotie: Strassburg 1513
360 × 510 mm, woodcut

Martin Waldseemüller undoubtedly used Italian portulans as a source for this woodblock map but apparently did not include the most recent available information. The basic outline was used on manuscript charts of the late fourteenth century and it is difficult to identify some of the names on the map, probably due to errors made in copying from other maps but despite this it may still be described as the first 'modern' map of the British Isles. The extensive naming of ports, especially on the Irish coastline and Eastern and Southern England, reveals the extent of trading and cultural connections which are known to have been established by the Phoenicians as early as 200 BC and continued in medieval times by the Genoese, amongst others.

Amongst the identifiable towns are Dover, Portsmouth, Southampton, Plymouth and Bristol. Following earlier traditional marine charts Ireland is pear-shaped and the 'Purgatorium of St Patrick' is shown. The myth about the island off the west coast of Ireland called 'Brazil' is described in Chapter 10. Despite its German origins the scale on this map is in Italian miles! There was only one further issue, again at Strassburg, in 1520.

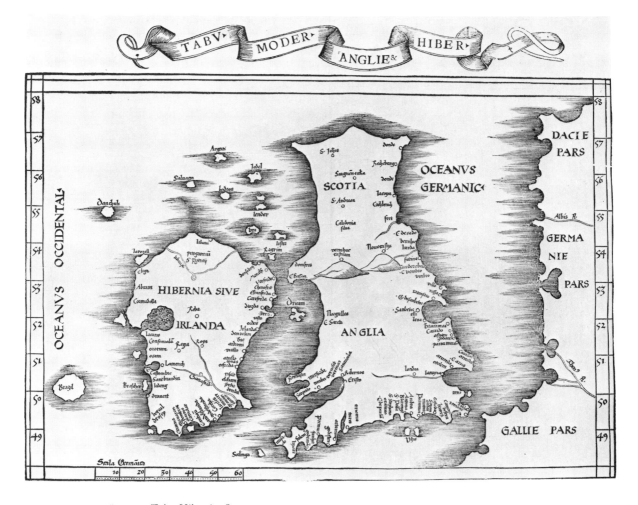

MARTIN WALDSEEMÜLLER   *Tabu. Hiberniae Sco.* 1522

MARTIN WALDSEEMÜLLER
Tabu. Hiberniae Sco.: Strassburg 1522
280 × 410 mm, woodcut
A re-drawn version of the 1513 map which, despite the 25 per cent reduction in overall size, includes all of the information from its predecessor with only minor changes in the lettering and coastline. The scale is now given in German miles and as less of the European mainland is shown the actual printed size of the British Isles is very little smaller than on the earlier map.

There is reason to believe that the decorative Renaissance panels enclosing the text on the back of this map were from designs by Albrecht Dürer, who was known to have produced designs used elsewhere in this atlas. The printer was Johannes Grüninger.

Further issues, with varying titles, were made in 1525 (Strassburg), 1535 (Lyon – illustrated) 1541 (Vienne, a town on the Rhône just south of Lyon).

BENEDETTO BORDONE   *Inghilterra Secodo Moderni* 1528

BENEDETTO BORDONE

Inghilterra Secōdo Moderni: Venice 1528

140 × 150 mm, woodcut

Bordone's woodcut map was published in an *Isolario* or Book of Islands, a very popular form of atlas, the first of which was printed between 1477 and 1485, although earlier manuscript versions are known. The outline uses the traditional curved shapes from the portolani and the medieval cartographers' error of showing Scotland separated from the mainland betrays the map's early origins. This is the first printed map of the British Isles to use the new conventional symbol of a small towered building to represent a town but only Dover, Southampton and London are specifically named.

There were three later issues of the map in 1534, 1547 and *c.* 1565, some of which have the Ptolemaic map of the British Isles on the reverse.

SEBASTIAN MÜNSTER

Anglie Triquetra Descriptio: Basle 1538

135 × 110 mm, woodcut

The first of the five maps of the British Isles by the eminent Sebastian Münster, this woodcut map is scarcer than the other four, due probably to the fact that there was only one other issue, in 1543, and that it was published in Münster's version of the works of Pomponius Mela, a classical Spanish geographer working in Italy around the first century AD.

Despite its small size this is an informative map, the outline probably being derived from the Gough map dating from the time of Edward I. It is the first map to show Anglesea separate from Wales and is also the first to show the existence of the six major rivers: the Tweed, Humber, Trent, Severn, Wye and Thames.

SEBASTIAN MÜNSTER   *Anglie Triquetra Descriptio* 1538

SEBASTIAN MÜNSTER *(opposite page)*

Anglia II Nova Tabula: Basle 1540

240 × 335 mm, woodcut

The second of Münster's maps of the British Isles, this important woodcut has North at the left-hand side of the page enabling a larger scale to be used than would have been possible with North at the top. A very considerable advance on any of the earlier maps, it had a very wide circulation, being issued in over twenty-five separate publications of Münster's *Geographia* and *Cosmographia* from 1540 until 1588, when an entirely new block was cut for the later editions. More than fifty rivers and some seventy or more named towns are shown, most for the first time on a printed map.

The panel in the top left corner gives 'Interpretationes' of the Latin names into English whilst the Scottish flag is shown firmly planted in the sea! On the first edition of the map the text on the verso was contained within two pillars surmounted by a decorative archway. Identification of various issue dates is practically impossible without comparing loose maps with the complete dated atlases. In the late 1970s this map was still easily obtainable.

Surprise is often expressed that North is not always shown at the top of the sheet on this, and various other, maps. Two reasons have been suggested for this: many of the very early maps were drawn in religious foundations and it is to be expected that East would be given prominence at the top – the Hereford World Map being an example of this type; latterly the more prosaic reason that it was sometimes possible to use a larger scale on a given piece of rectangularly-shaped, handmade paper was given as the justification – the British Isles map by Ortelius with West at the top is an example of this category. Navigators on ships even today have their charts displayed on chart tables of a size sufficient to enable the chart to be turned so that the ship is always going 'up'. This avoids errors in turning 'left' or 'right' (to use the more easily understood terms for Port and Starboard). Conventional usage makes us always expect to find North at the top of a map but really there is no geographic justification for this long-established habit.

SEBASTIAN MÜNSTER *Anglia II Nova Tabula* 1540

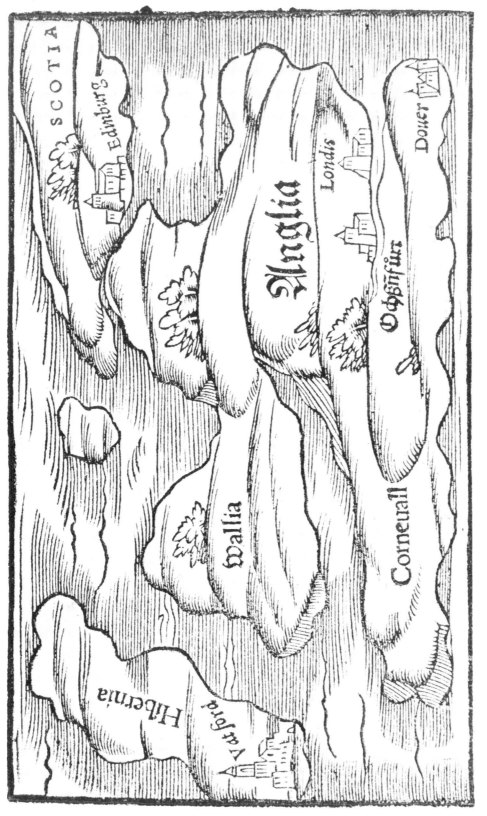

SEBASTIAN MÜNSTER   *Von Den Britannischen Inseln Albione das ist Engelland und Hibernia* 1550

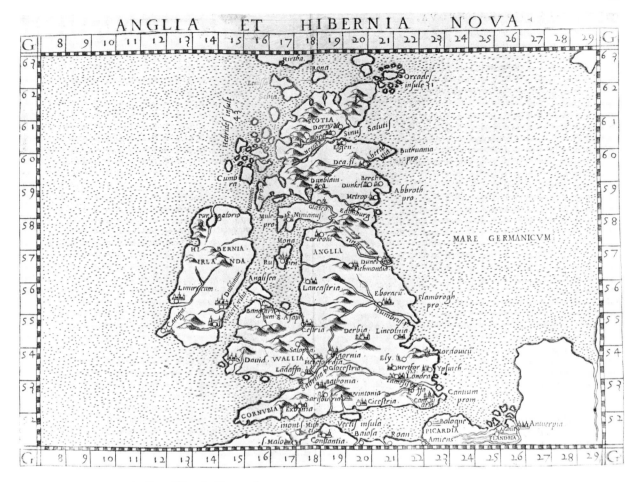

GIROLAMO RUSCELLI *Anglia et Hibernia Nova* 1561

SEBASTIAN MÜNSTER *(opposite page)*
Von Den Britannischen Inseln Albione das ist Engelland und
Hibernia . . .: Basle 1550
80 × 130 mm, woodcut

This small Münster map appeared set in the text of
various editions of the *Cosmographia* from 1550 onwards. Considerably less advanced geographically than
his two earlier maps it reverted to the Ptolemaic
distortion of Scotland and fewer names were included
than previously, the type setting of the names being
changed in different editions. The map illustrated is
from an edition dated 1552.

The inclusion of this map in some of the editions of
the *Cosmographia*, which also included the double-page
map of 1540 can, perhaps, be explained by regarding it
as an *aide mémoire* for readers, saving them the necessity
of finding the other larger map which is normally
bound in a totally different part of the book.

GIROLAMO RUSCELLI
Anglia et Hibernia Nova: Venice 1561
180 × 250 mm, copper engraving

This elegant copperplate map is apparently based on
the 1546 Lily map but because of the considerably
reduced size much detail has been omitted. No scale is
given, but latitude and longitude are shown.

A number of later issues of this map are found
including 1562, 1564, 1574, 1598 and 1599; these last
two constituting State II of the map with a ship and
two sea monsters added to the plate.

ABRAHAM ORTELIUS

Angliae, Scotiae et Hiberniae Sive Britannicar. Insularum Descriptio: Antwerp 1570

345 × 495 mm, copper engraving

The publication of Ortelius's atlas *Theatrum Orbis Terrarum*, from which this map comes, was the start of the epic 100-year period when the Dutch cartographers were the supreme exponents in all aspects of cartographic production. Based on the famous large wall map by his friend, Gerard Mercator, a number of errors have occurred in this reduction, many of the copied names being quite different from the original. More than thirty separate issues of this map were made, both coloured and plain, with the descriptive text on the back in a variety of languages including Latin, German, Dutch, French, Spanish, Italian and even English (this being very scarce). It is sometimes possible to date individual examples exactly with reference to Koeman's *Atlantes Neerlandici* but often it is difficult to be precise due to the complicated printing history; for example, there were four printings in the year of publication alone! For many years it was supposed that the various issues were printed from only one plate, until in 1981 it was discovered that two states existed. (See illustrations on following pages.) It is known that the first state was used in the first edition of 1570 and in a number of later editions. At the time of writing the earliest recorded usage of the second state is from 1583 onwards.

This is probably the earliest map of the British Isles still readily available in the early 1980s, and the collector will at once see that the proportions of Ireland and Scotland compared with England and Wales are not correct; but, nevertheless, it was an influential map with a very wide circulation. Many of the names betray its ecclesiastical sources; it was issued only about thirty years after the Dissolution of the Monasteries and quite a number of the religious institutions shown on it no longer existed when it was published. No roads, rivers or bridges are shown, although towns where fords would have been are indicated, but it would have been practically useless as a route map. It should be remembered, of course, that speeds were so much slower when travelling in the sixteenth century that exact directions could easily be obtained by word of mouth provided the general route was known.

Examples of this map may be found with original colour or uncoloured and whilst an early coloured example is preferable for a collection, the extra premium on the price may put this beyond many collectors' pockets.

ABRAHAM ORTELIUS   *Angliae, Scotiae et Hiberniae Sive Britannicar. – Insularum Descriptio* 1570

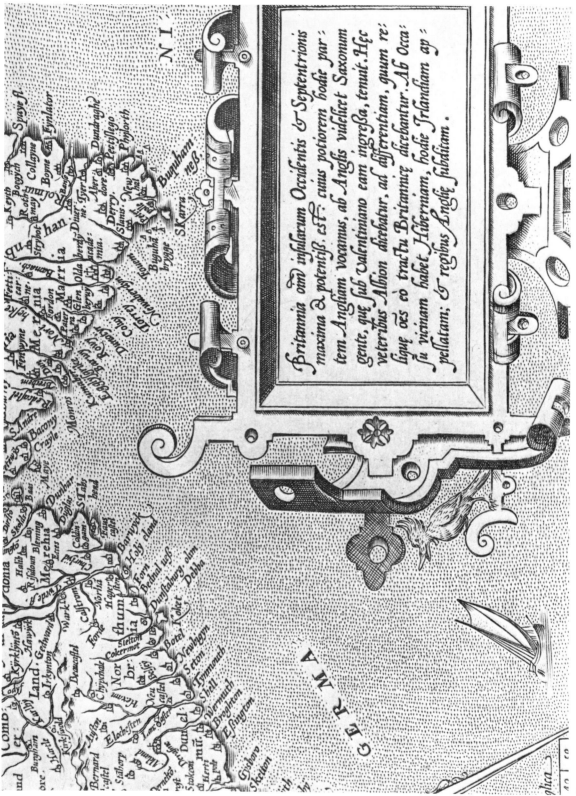

Britannia omn̄ insularum Occidentis & Septentrionis
maxima & potentiß. est, cuius potiorem hodie par=
tem Angliam vocamus, ab Anglis videlicet Saxonum
gente, quæ sub Valentiniano eam ingreßa, tenuit. Hæc
veteribus Albion dicebatur, ac differentiam, quum re=
liquæ ōs eo tractu Britanniæ dicebantur. Ab Occa:
su vicinam habet Hiberniam, hodie Irlandiam ap=
pellatam; & reginæ Angliæ subditam.

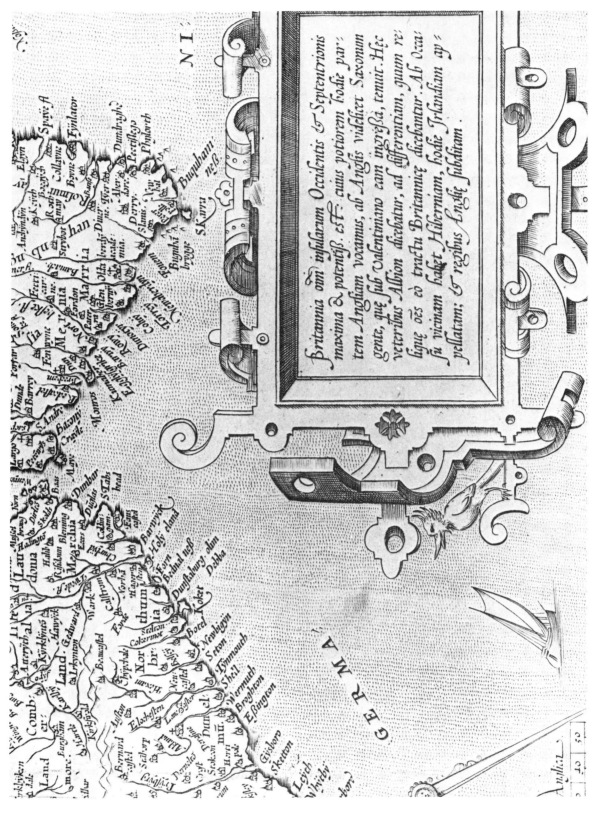

Britannia om insularum Occidentis & Septentrionis
maxima & potentiß. est: cuius potiorem hodie par=
tem Angliam vocamus, ab Anglis videlicet Saxonum
gente, quæ sub Valentiniano eam ingreßa, tenuit. Hæc
veteribus Albion dicebatur, ad differentiam, quum re:
liquæ oēs eo tractu Britanniæ dicebantur. Ab Occa:
su vicinam habet Hiberniam, hodie Irlandiam ap=
pellatam; & regibus Lystiæ subditam.

Second state 1583 onwards

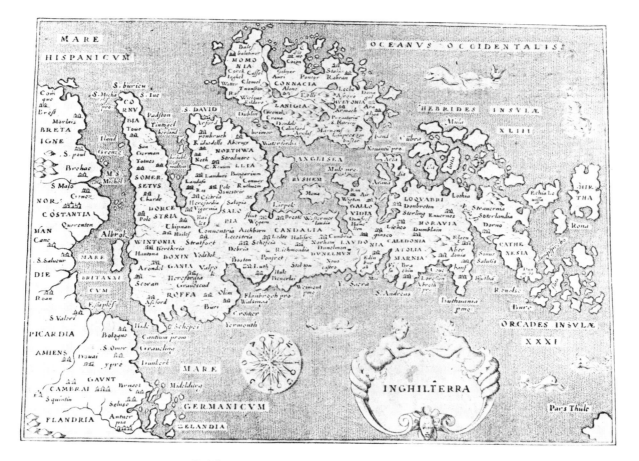

TOMASO PORCACCHI DA CASTILIONE   *Inghilterra* (1572) 1620

TOMASO PORCACCHI DA CASTILIONE
Inghilterra: Venice (1572) 1620
100 × 140 mm, copper engraving
Taken from an 'Island' book entitled *L'Isola piu Famose del Mondo* . . . this quaint map has West at the top and is unusual in not showing London!

There is evidence to suggest that Girolamo Porro, the engraver, copied manuscript sources and early Lafreri maps for the outlines of this map. A number of further issues were made, all in Venice, notably in 1576, 1590, 1604, 1605, 1620 and 1713. There was also a complete re-engraving of the maps published in 1586, of which many issues were made over a period of about a hundred years in a wide variety of travel books.

HUMPHREY LHUYD and ABRAHAM ORTELIUS   *Angliae Regni Florentissimi Nova Descriptio Auctore Humfredo Lhuyd Denbygiense* 1573
(a later edition)

HUMPHREY LHUYD – ABRAHAM ORTELIUS
Angliae Regni Florentissimi Nova Descriptio Auctore Humfredo Lhuyd Denbygiense 1573: Antwerp 1573
380 × 470 mm, copper engraving
Humphrey Lhuyd died in 1568 and therefore the information on this map must have been five years old when Ortelius published it in the first supplement to his atlas. It is difficult to understand why Ortelius had not used information from it for his British Isles map of 1570, as it shows a considerable geographic advance on the Mercator sources which he had used, especially relating to the southern Welsh coast and the Devon and Cornwall peninsula. The names included come from sources unique to Lhuyd although counties are not marked.

The map appeared in more than seventeen of the later editions of the Ortelius Atlas from the date of its first appearance until 1606, when the sole English version was published in London.

SEBASTIAN MÜNSTER
Beschreibung Engellandts und Schottlandts: Basle 1578
250 × 170 mm, woodcut

The fourth of Münster's representations of the British Isles, this map shows a considerable geographic regression compared to his first two. Scotland is again shown using the traditional Ptolemaic projection, similar to his 1550 map, although many more names of towns and rivers are included.

A later version of a Münster map, entitled *Engellandt mit dem anstoffenden Reich Schottland* (310 × 360 mm) published by Sebastian Petri in Basle in 1588 with later editions in 1592, 1598, 1614 and 1628, is described as a woodcut 'engraved in the copper plate manner'. It may be speculated that the blocks from the 1544 *Cosmography* had worn out by this time (the world map had been completely re-cut for the publication of *c.* 1555) and by producing another set of maps the market for this very popular work would have been considerably extended.

West is shown at the top of the map and many of the rivers are shown as emanating from lakes – a geographic regression compared with the important 1540 map. Many of the names included on this earlier production are now left out and altogether this is rather a poor production. It must, however, be pointed out that due to its pedigree this would have been an influential map with a wide distribution and is, therefore, worthy of inclusion in any collection, being one of the more readily obtainable sixteenth-century maps.

It should be noted that the illustration numbers in the written descriptions of these maps in Rodney Shirley's *Early Printed Maps of the British Isles* are incorrect: the 1578 edition is shown on Plate 32; the 1588 edition on Plate 28.

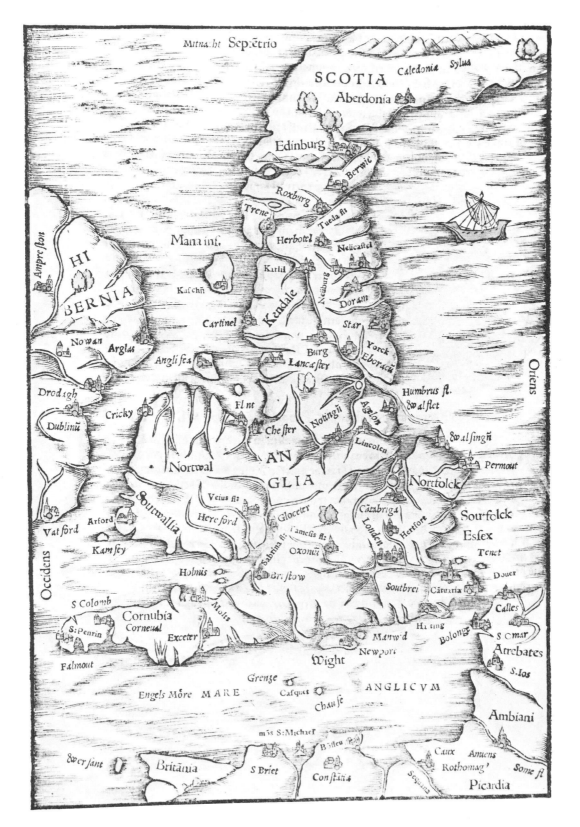

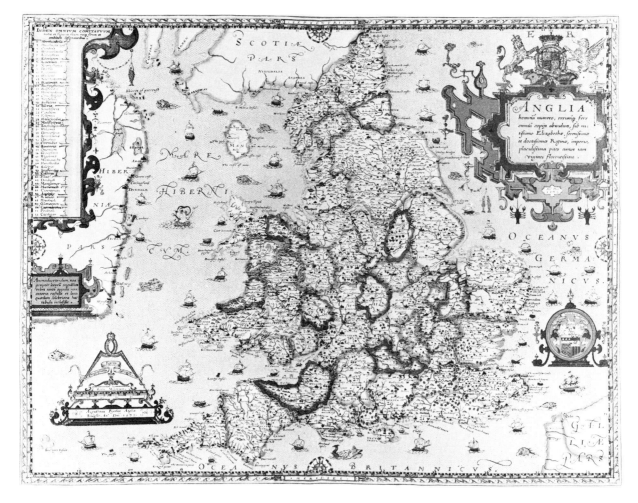

CHRISTOPHER SAXTON *Anglia* 1579

CHRISTOPHER SAXTON

Anglia: London 1579

380 × 495 mm, copper-plate engraving

The first map of England and Wales published in England, this map is probably the most difficult (and expensive) to find of all the maps described in this selection and is only included because of its importance. Most of the known examples have original colouring, the magnificent engraving being the work of Augustine Ryther, the most accomplished of the three English engravers used by Saxton.

Geographically it is a very significant advance on all previous maps, all the place names being shown in English; the basic outline was later used by Mercator, Speed, Blaeu and Jansson besides many other cartographers for nearly two hundred years.

The plate was altered for the only variant issue after 1583 when indications of latitude and longitude were added. Later issues, all with alterations to the original plate, were made in 1645, 1665, 1689–93, *c.* 1730, *c.* 1749 and *c.* 1770. No issues of this map are known with text on the back. It has been reproduced by the British Museum (along with the county maps) and the authors have seen 'doctored' copies purporting to be genuine antique maps of both the England and Wales and county maps.

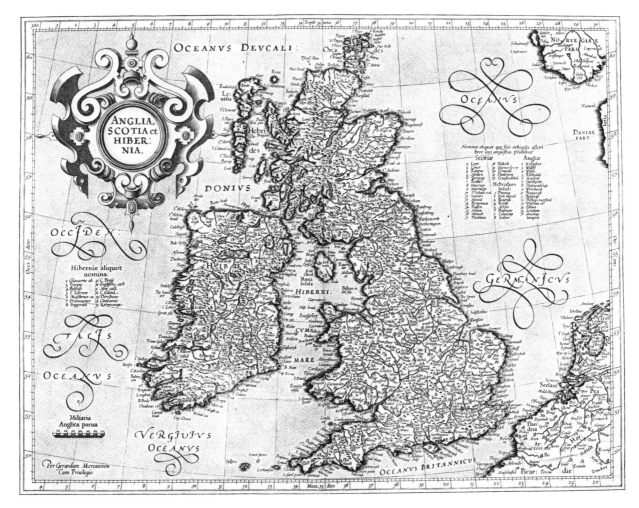

GERARD MERCATOR   *Anglia, Scotia et Hibernia* 1595

GERARD MERCATOR
Anglia, Scotia et Hibernia: Duisburg 1595
325 × 410 mm, copper engraving
Although this map was published a year after Mercator's death (by his son Rumold) there seems little doubt that he was personally responsible for its compilation. Signed 'Per Gerardum Mercatorem . . .', the quality of workmanship prevented speedy publication. Part III of the Atlas, in which this map was issued, was dedicated to Queen Elizabeth I of England.

The outline is a composite one, being derived from at least three separate sources. The outline of Scotland became the standard – although slightly improved by Speed – until the Robert Gordon map was published in the Blaeu atlas of Scotland in 1654.

The publishing history of the Atlas is complicated and this map was issued in a number of editions between 1595 and 1630. There is also evidence to suggest that it appeared in the three French editions of 1639, 1640 and 1641 although it was generally replaced after 1630 by other maps. The descriptive text verso was printed only in Latin and French, but note that examples, including some in the first edition, were issued with blank backs.

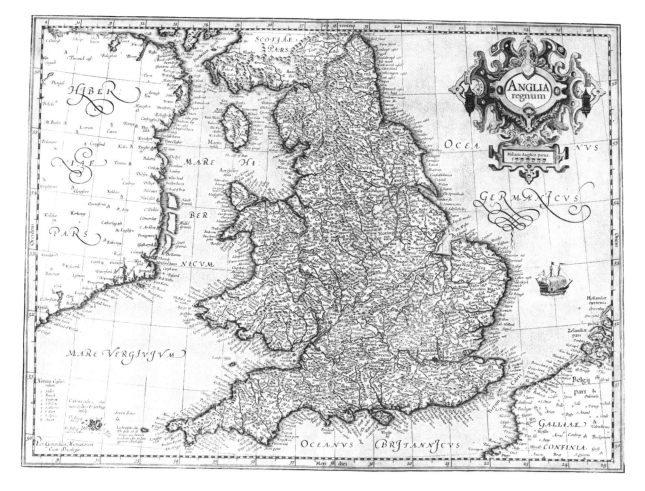

GERARD MERCATOR   *Anglia Regnum* 1595

GERARD MERCATOR
Anglia Regnum: Duisburg 1595
350 × 470 mm, copper engraving
Issued in the same atlas as the last map this is on a considerably larger scale as a result of the smaller area shown and includes many more names copied from Christopher Saxton's map of 1579. County boundaries and the Latinized names of counties are shown.

Although it initially appeared in the same atlas, the life of this map was rather longer than the previous one and the last edition was in 1641. The descriptive text on the verso was published in Latin, French, German, Dutch and English. The original plate was considerably altered for the later publications.

GIOVANNI MAGINI   *Britanicae Insulae* 1596

GIOVANNI MAGINI
Britanicae Insulae: Venice 1596
130 × 170 mm, copper engraving
This elegant map comes from one of the many editions of Ptolemy published during the late Renaissance, containing Ptolemaic and 'modern' maps. The engraving was probably by Girolamo Porro under the supervision of Giovanni Magini, one of the most prominent Italian cartographers of the time.

It is one of the earliest maps to show a river bridge at London: latitude and longitude are also included. The lettering is a fine italic script and despite geographical shortcomings this is a good example of Italian map production.

There is a Latin text on the back of the map and further issues were made in 1597, 1598 and 1621, all in Italy. Some almost identical maps were issued in 1597, 1608 and 1617 in a German-inspired version of the Magini *Ptolemy*.

WILLIAM HOLE   *Englalond Anglia Anglosaxonum Heptarchia* 1607

WILLIAM HOLE

Englalond Anglia Anglosaxonum Heptarchia: London
1607

290 × 335 mm, copper engraving

This unjustly neglected map is the earliest obtainable
(at a modest price) of England and Wales, printed in
England. It was first published in the sixth edition of
William Camden's *Britannia*, the first book to contain a
complete series of individual maps of the English and
Welsh counties.

Designed to illustrate the Anglo Saxon Kingdom
for the historical section of the *Britannia* – a complete
description, both historic and modern, of the British
Isles – the names are given in a script which purports to
be 'Anglo-Saxon', a key being given in the top left
corner. Derived from an earlier map of 1600 by
William Rogers, this map was issued again in 1610 and
1637. The back of each issue is blank and no plate
changes were made to the issue of 1610, but a plate
number '1' was added in the lower left corner for the
1637 edition. (First issues of the county maps have
Latin text on the verso, later issues are blank with plate
changes including the adding of a number on most of
the maps.)

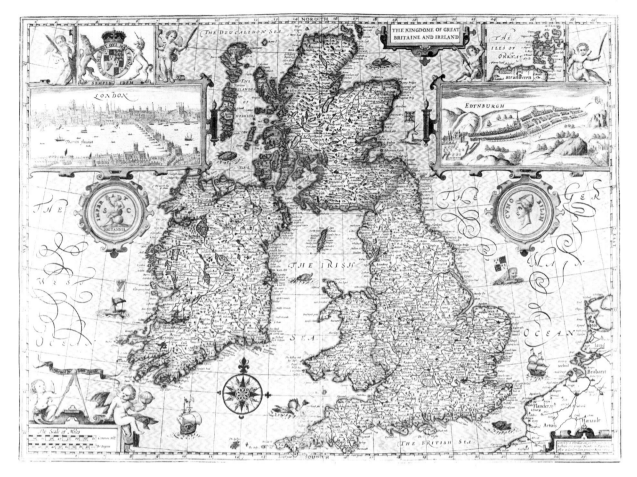

JOHN SPEED   *The Kingdome of Great Britaine and Ireland* 1611

JOHN SPEED
The Kingdome of Great Britaine and Ireland: London 1611
380 × 510 mm, copper engraving
This famous map by Speed was engraved by Jodocus
Hondius in Amsterdam. Although proofs from the
plates are known to have been made in 1608, publication was delayed until 1611–12, perhaps caused by
Hondius's illness. Finally dated 1610, the outline of the
map is based on original work by Saxton, Hondius and
Mercator and on the excessively rare 'Battles' map of
1603 compiled by Speed himself.

Panoramas of London and Edinburgh decorate the

top of the map, whilst the skill of the engraver in
incorporating a profusion of decorative detail – ships,
sea monsters, putti etc. – is evident. The lettering is
especially fine and the sea is portrayed in the famous
shot silk style; in later editions this fine effect is lost as
delicate engraving of this type soon wore smooth. For
some curious reason no river bridges are shown except
those crossing the Thames! The map was re-issued
many times in Speed's atlases and as a separate
publication. The text on the reverse, if present at all, is
in English, except for the Latin version of 1616.

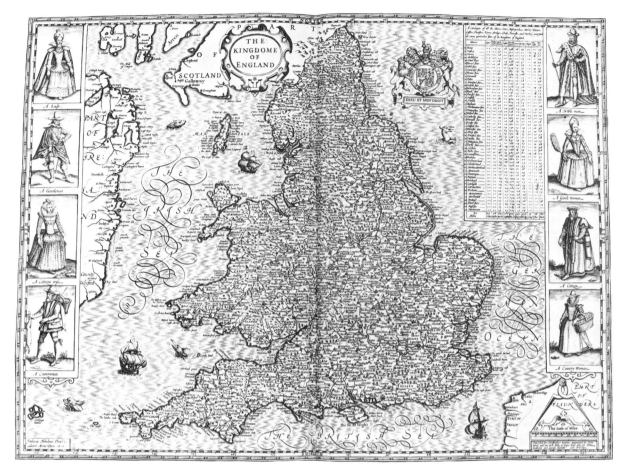

JOHN SPEED   *The Kingdome of England* 1611

JOHN SPEED

The Kingdome of England: London 1611

380 × 510 mm, copper engraving

Speed acknowledges that Saxton's maps (and their derivatives) provided most of the information on this map. The outline and place names came from this source as does the panel containing 'A Catalogue of all the Shires . . .' alongside the costume vignettes at the top right-hand side of the map. Hondius was one of the first engravers to introduce vignettes on his maps and the eight on this one show A Nobleman, A Gentleman,

A Citizen, A Countryman, and their wives, in characteristic costumes.

The text on the verso is normally in English, but one issue, that of 1616, has it in Latin. Included in all editions of Speed's atlas until (and including) 1627, this map was replaced, as the plate was worn, by another engraved by Abraham Goos for later editions. Although very similar to the original, this may be identified by the imprint 'Abraham Goos' contained in a box beneath the scale in the bottom right-hand corner.

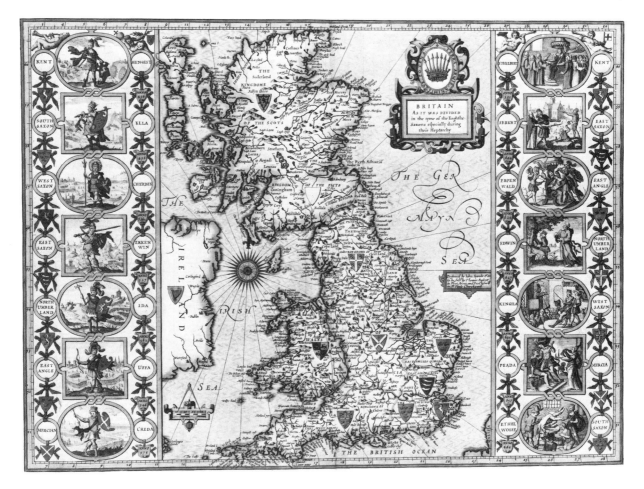

JOHN SPEED   *Britain as it was devided in the tyme of the Englishe-Saxons especially during their Heptarchy* 1611

JOHN SPEED
Britain as it was devided in the tyme of the Englishe-Saxons especially during their Heptarchy: London 1611
380 × 510 mm, copper engraving
This highly decorative map, often described as the 'Speed Heptarchy', was the original from which both the Blaeu and Jansson maps on the same theme were copied. Arguably one of the masterpieces included in the Speed *Theatre*, seven vignettes on the left side show various Saxon kings, whilst the right-hand side depicts the conversion to Christianity of seven others – the forcible nature of the tactics depicted on two of these vignettes giving the impression that the conversion was hardly voluntary!

Later issues were made, as for the atlas, the text on the verso being in English except for the Latin version of 1616.

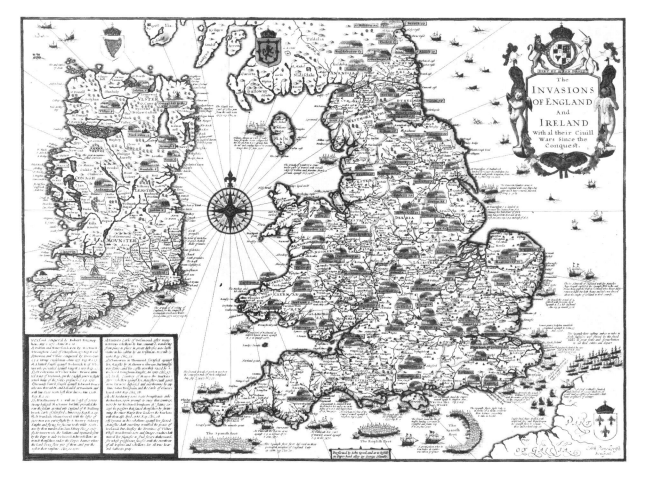

JOHN SPEED   *The Invasions of England and Ireland with al their Civill Wars since the Conquest* 1627

JOHN SPEED

The Invasions of England and Ireland with al their Civill Wars since the Conquest: London 1627

380 × 510 mm, copper engraving

This interesting map is derived from the earliest known printed map by Speed of which only three sections have survived. Engraved by Cornelius Dankerts, it was first included in the last edition of Speed's Atlas to be published in his lifetime. Usually found between the *Theatre* and the *Prospect* there are four pages of separate text describing the battles depicted. The map was subsequently issued in all editions of the Atlas until 1676 and for this last issue descriptions of the Civil War conflicts were included in the text, but no alterations were made to the map to show where they had taken place. Text on the verso (and accompanying sheets) was only in English.

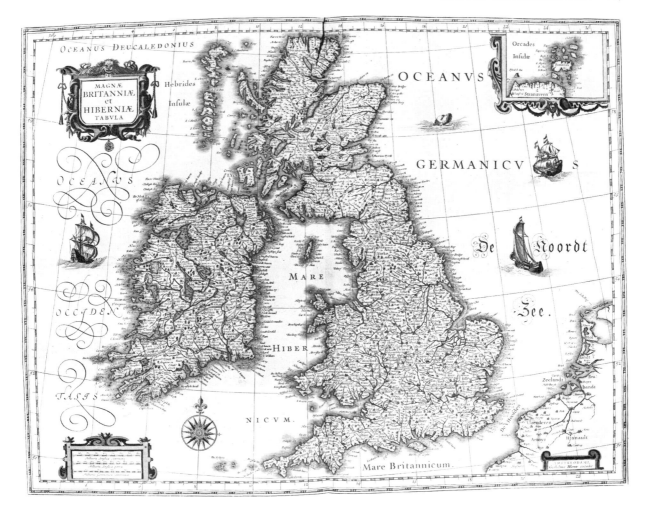

WILLEM BLAEU   *Magnae Britanniae et Hiberniae Tabula* (1631) 1662

WILLEM BLAEU

Magnae Britanniae et Hiberniae Tabula: Amsterdam (1631) 1662

385 × 500 mm, copper engraving

This fine production from the firm of Blaeu is believed to be printed from a cut-down plate of a map which first appeared in 1630. A number of map plates which had previously belonged to Jodocus Hondius had come into Blaeu's possession and as they were rather larger than his standard size it is presumed that he cut them down. On some examples of the map traces may be seen of alterations which have been made in erasing the figures and town panoramas of the earlier map.

The map appeared in many of the Blaeu atlases between 1634 and 1672 and was included in all editions of the Blaeu atlas of England and Wales from 1645 onwards. Examples may be found with the text verso in a number of languages including Dutch, French, Latin, German and Spanish, besides issues with blank backs. The text on the Blaeu and Jansson maps (unlike Speed's) is not complete in itself and collectors should enquire whether the remaining text sheets are available if they wish to have the complete descriptive text which is, incidentally, a translation of William Camden's *Britannia*.

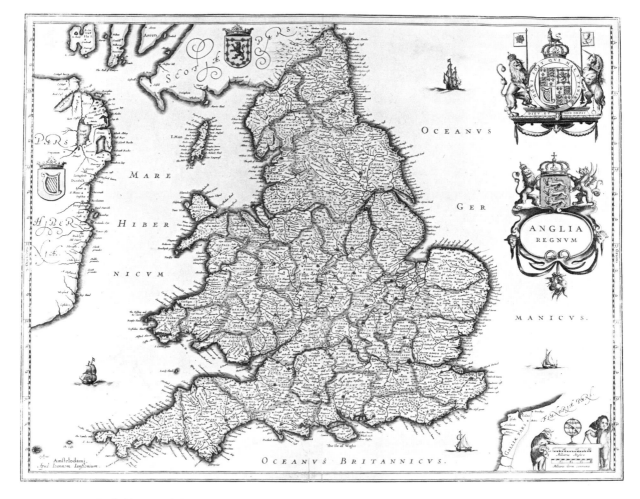

JAN JANSSON   *Anglia Regnum* 1636

JAN JANSSON
Anglia Regnum: Amsterdam 1636
385 × 500 mm, copper engraving
It is considered likely that when preparing this map
Jansson copied directly from the Blaeu map of
England and Wales of 1634, rather than from the Speed
of 1611, which Willem Blaeu had utilized. It can be
distinguished at a glance from the Blaeu map as the
national crests of Scotland and Ireland are included and
there are, in addition, many other less significant
changes of detail.

Many issues of Jansson's atlases included this map –
some 20 or so before 1650 – with the descriptive text on
the back (which is not complete in itself) in Dutch,
Latin, German or French, besides issues from 1646
onwards without any text. It is difficult to identify the
date of individual loose examples of the earlier issues,
but some of the editions by later publishers (including
Visscher, Overton and the partners Peter Schenk and
Gerald Valck) can often be attributed to specific dates.

MATTHÄUS MERIAN   *Magnae Britanniae et Hiberniae Tabulae. Die Britannischen Insulen* 1638

MATTHÄUS MERIAN

Magnae Britanniae et Hiberniae Tabulae. Die Britannischen Insulen: Frankfurt 1638

270 × 355 mm, copper engraving

This map of Great Britain was copied from the Bleau map of 1631 by Merian himself as his signature in the lower right-hand corner shows. The studio employed a number of prominent seventeenth-century engravers – including Wenceslaus Hollar – to produce an important 21-volume illustrated descriptive and historical text about seventeenth-century Europe, which contained nearly 700 maps, some 250 portraits and 34 large panoramas of towns! A standard reference work on the European mainland, it is rarely found in Great Britain and few copies can have come here at the time of publication.

The map is approximately one third smaller than Blaeu's and the Stuart coat of arms has been added in the North Sea. The map was published again in 1646 and a re-engraved version, lacking Merian's signature, appeared *c.* 1649.

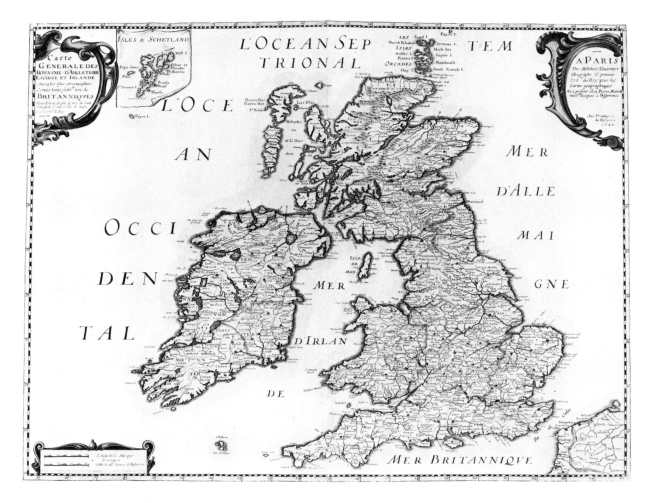

NICOLAS SANSON   *Carte Générale des Royaume d' Angleterre Escosse et Irlande 1640*

NICOLAS SANSON

*Carte Générale des Royaume d' Angleterre Escosse et Irlande
. . . Nouvellement Dressée & Tirée . . . par N. Sanson . . .
à Paris par Melchior Tavernier 1640*

405 × 530 mm, copper engraving

This rather sparse map was a production of the Sanson
workshops and it is typical of their output. Lacking the
visual beauty and appeal of the Dutch maps of the same
period, it was engraved by Melchior Tavernier.
Examples are usually found with original outline
colouring which is often quite attractive. The distortion of Ireland and the condensed size of Scotland is, in
part, caused by the projection used by Sanson.

Nicolas Sanson (1600–67) was an influential cartographer who is described by many authorities as the
founder of the French School of Geography. In his
early days he was tutor to Louis XIII and after his
death in 1667 the business was continued by his three
sons, Nicolas, Adrian and Guillaume. Latterly his
grandson, Pierre Moulard-Sanson and then his
nephew, Gilles Robert de Vaugondy, continued the
firm until the end of the eighteenth century.

This map was much copied by other French publishers around the 1640s and also by Richard Blome (in
London) in 1669. Blome's map was engraved by
Francis Lamb and – unusually for Blome – acknowledged its source as being Sanson.

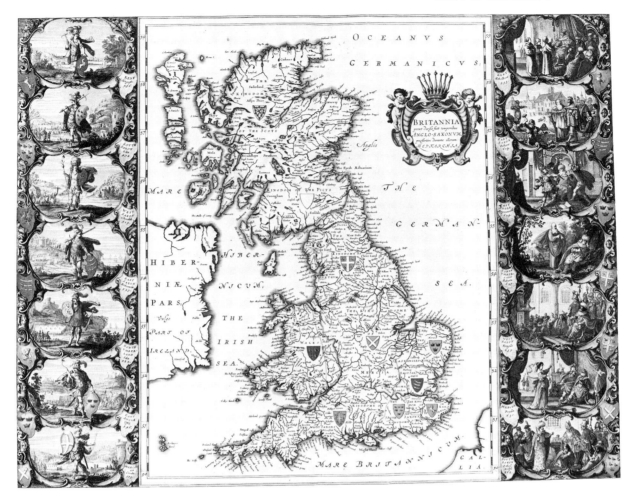

JOAN BLAEU   *Britannia prout divisa fuit temporibus Anglo-Saxonum, praesertim durante illorum Heptarchia* 1645

JOAN BLAEU

Britannia prout divisa fuit temporibus Anglo-Saxonum, praesertim durante illorum Heptarchia: Amsterdam 1645
425 × 530 mm, copper engraving

This is the only map of the British Isles published under the aegis of Joan Blaeu, who took over the publishing house upon the death of his father, Willem, in 1638. Arguably one of the finest maps published anywhere in the seventeenth century, Blaeu used Speed's map of 1611 for source material. It is generally accepted that the copy is far finer than the original. Each of the fourteen vignettes – seven on each side of the map – is a work of art in its own right; miniatures in the style of renowned Dutch painters of the day. The original coloured examples of this map are often exceptionally beautiful, showing seven Saxon kings down the left-hand side and the conversion to Christianity of a further seven down the right-hand side.

This map appeared on a number of occasions in each issue of Blaeu's atlas of England and Wales until the destruction (by fire) of the Blaeu workshops in 1672. The text verso may be in Latin, Dutch, French, Spanish or German; issues were also made with blank backs. The text, when present, is not complete in itself and is a translation from William Camden's *Britannia*.

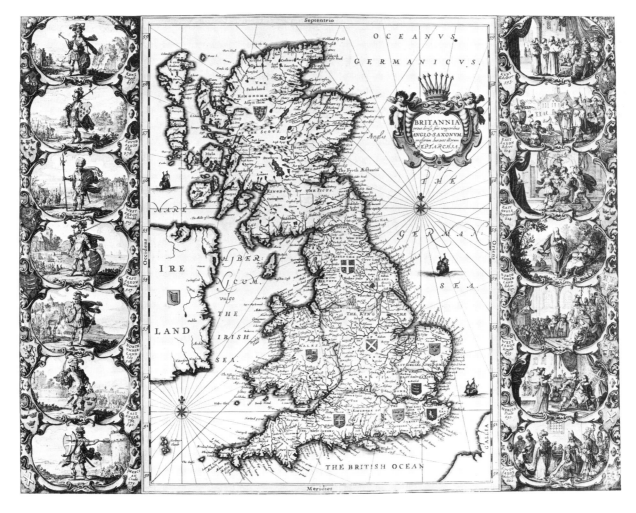

JAN JANSSON   *Britannia prout divisa fuit temporibus Anglo-Saxonum, praesertim durante illorum Heptarchia 1646*

JAN JANSSON
Britannia prout divisa fuit temporibus Anglo-Saxonum, praesertim durante illorum Heptarchia: Amsterdam 1646
420 × 530 mm, copper engraving

Jansson copied the 1645 map by Blaeu for his version of Anglo-Saxon Britain. It may be identified at once by noticing the compass lines radiating through the seas. Issued in various publications for very nearly a hundred years this map is less often found than the Blaeu. It is difficult to understand why this is so and, perhaps, the fact that the paper used by Jansson for his atlases was inferior to that used by Blaeu has some bearing on this matter. As a generalization it is harder to find fine examples of Jansson's maps than those of almost any other of the popular seventeenth-century cartographers; the colouring is often faded or foxed and in consequence extensive restoration and preservation is needed. It is possible that the general lack of care in original production is responsible for this state of affairs.

Each issue of Jansson's atlas of England and Wales contained this map until 1649 when it was published in the 1652 Jansson classical atlas which had a text by Georg Horn. The plate was then passed on to the various heirs and successors of Jansson until at least the 1740s. The map may be found with the text verso in Dutch, Latin, German and French; issues were also made with a blank back.

Specialist References

SHIRLEY, R. W., *Early Printed Maps of the British Isles 1477–1650*
Descriptive detail of virtually every map of the British Isles published in the period covered

SKELTON, R. A., *County Atlases of the British Isles 1579–1703*
Although basically concerned with county maps, much of the information in Skelton's book also applies to maps of the British Isles

Chapter 19

PORTUGAL, SPAIN, SCANDINAVIA, SWITZERLAND, RUSSIA & POLAND

In this chapter we record some of the more important names associated with the development of cartography in Portugal, Spain, Scandinavia, Switzerland, Russia and Poland. As a matter of historical interest details of a number of famous manuscript maps and charts from Portuguese and Spanish sources are included as well as later printed maps from those countries. The rarity of manuscript maps needs no emphasis but early printed maps by Portuguese and Spanish cartographers are also scarce and although those of Scandinavia and Switzerland are perhaps not quite so rare the appearance on the market of an early edition of Olaus Magnus's map of Scandinavia or of maps of Switzerland by Johann Stumpf is an unusual event.

PORTUGAL AND SPAIN

Portuguese and Spanish manuscript maps

As we have already shown few of the charts and maps drawn by the first Portuguese and Spanish navigators have survived for the very good reason that, on completion of their voyages, pilots were obliged to hand over their manuscript notes to the Casa da India (founded 1500–04) in Lisbon or to the equivalent Casa de Contratación de las Indias (founded 1504) in Seville. The clear intention was to maintain secrecy over new discoveries and control over the distribution of cartographic material, not always successfully, as it happened; pilots and navigators seem to have changed allegiance with impunity and, in consequence, many of the earliest and most informative charts were compiled as far away as Genoa, Venice, Florence and Ancona, presumably from sources outside the Portuguese and Spanish 'Casas'.

It will be apparent from the foregoing that few manuscripts reached the printing stage and, indeed, are so rare that any study of them must be regarded as a specialist subject far beyond the scope of this work. The accompanying notes do no more than give the briefest introduction to names which our 'general collector' may wish to follow up elsewhere. This short list of manuscript maps is followed by details of the more conventional, though still not very common, printed maps by Portuguese and Spanish cartographers.

PEDRO REINEL *fl. c.* 1485–1522
JORGE REINEL *fl. c.* 1510–40
Manuscript charts and maps of the west coast of Africa (*c.* 1485), the North Atlantic (*c.* 1504–06), the South Atlantic (*c.* 1519), World Map (*c.* 1522).

JUAN DE LA COSA *fl.* 1492–1500
Manuscript map of America (*c.* 1500) – the first surviving map of the New World.

ALBERTO CANTINO *fl.* 1502
Manuscript world map (1502) showing America.

LOPO HOMEN 1497–1572
Manuscript maps of Brazil (*c.* 1519), World Map (1554).

DIOGO RIBEIRO *fl.* 1519–33
Manuscript map (1527) recording Magellan's voyage of circumnavigation. Maps of Africa (*c.* 1529) and America (*c.* 1532).

Biographies of Portuguese cartographers

FERNANDO ALVAREZ (SECCO) *fl.* 1560–65
c. 1560–61 *Lusitania*
          The first modern map of Portugal, published in Rome and later used by Ortelius and de Jode.

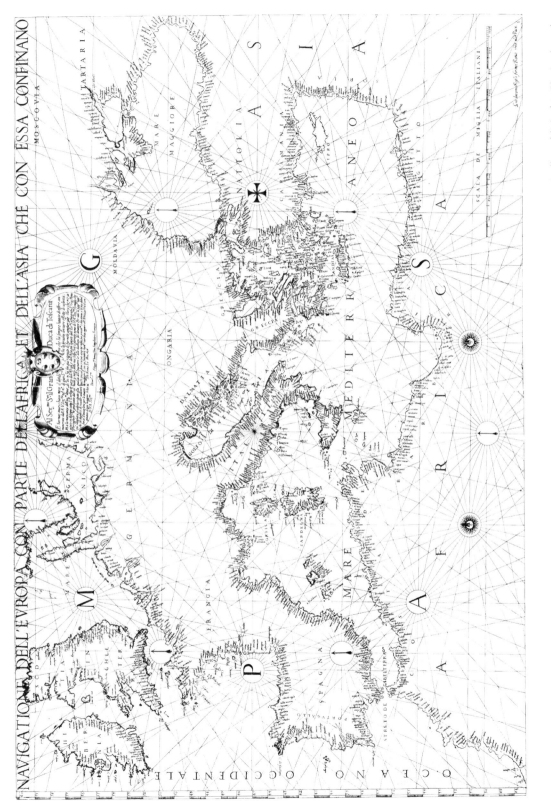

DIOGO HOMEN   *Navigatione dell'Europa.* The Giacomo Rossi (Rome 1648) version of the first sea chart engraved on copper, originally published in Venice in 1569.

LUIZ JORGE DE BARBUDA/ORTELIUS   *Chinae* Antwerp (1584) *c.* 1598. Compiled by Barbuda, a Portuguese Jesuit missionary, this famous map remained the standard map of China for about half a century. Barbuda used the signature 'Ludovico Georgio'.

DIOGO HOMEN *fl.* 1530–76

Homen, one of the most important portulan chart makers of his time, engraved the plates for what is claimed to be the first printed sea chart (1569), showing the Mediterranean and most of Europe as far north as Denmark. Homen had an uneasy life, being exiled for political reasons from his native country, from which he went to England where he was even less fortunate. He eventually settled in Venice where his sea chart was published.

1569–71   *La Carta del navigar dell' Europa*: Venice, published by Paolo Forlani

       c. 1572 Re-issued by Lafreri

       c. 1606 Re-issued in Rome

       *c.*1648 Re-issued by Giacomo Rossi, Rome

FERNÃO VAZ DOURADO *c.* 1520–80

1568–71   Maps of the Indies including a World Map

1568–80   Sea Atlas

LUIZ JORGE DE BARBUDA (LUDOVICO GEORGIO) *fl.* 1584

Barbuda, for many years a Jesuit missionary in China, related his experiences there in a work, *A Description of China*, with a map of the country which was subsequently used by Ortelius from 1584 onwards. The map was signed 'Ludovico Georgio'.

1584   Map of China

LUDOVICO (LUIZ) TEIXEIRA 1564–1604

Ludovico Teixeira, a mathematician and map maker in the service of Spain, was appointed cartographer to the

Spanish crown. Apart from manuscript maps relating to the Azores and voyages to Brazil he is remembered for his map of Japan (1592), used by Ortelius in 1595. This was the first separately printed map of the country and remained the standard map until those compiled by Martini were published in Amsterdam in 1655. His world maps issued probably in 1598 and 1604 have not survived.

1592   Japan

JOÃO TEIXEIRA *c.* 1602–66

João Teixeira, as Cosmographer to the King of Portugal, compiled important manuscript maps and sea charts on which Portugal's territorial claims against Spain were based. In spite of the terms of the Treaty of Tordesillas drawn up in 1494, argument between Spain and Portugal as to the division of the 'new world' still continued after 150 years and in that context these maps are of historical importance.

c. 1630   Atlas (of the whole world)
           Maps of Brazil, India, Portugal and the world

★

ANTONIO DE MARIZ CARNEIRO *fl.* 1639–42

c. 1639   *Recimento de Pilotes e roteiro de navegacem . . .* (4to)
           Charts and sailing directions covering the coasts and harbours of West Africa and South America

Biographies of Spanish cartographers

PEDRO DE MEDINA *c.* 1493–*c.* 1567

Medina, who took part in expeditions with Cortez in the New World, was famous in his time for a treatise called *The Art of Navigation*, one of the first practical books on seamanship. His work was held in high esteem and was widely read in many languages throughout Europe. A particularly important translation was made by the French traveller, Nicolas de Nicolay, who made a number of additions including an engraved sea chart of his own.

1545   *Arte de Navegar*: Valladolid, published in Spanish, containing woodcut illustrations and chart showing America
           1549 onwards: many re-issues
           1554–69 Nicolas de Nicolay: Paris and Lyon

JERÓNIMO GIRAVA *fl.* 1556

Cosmographer to Charles V, Girava is known for a book published in 1556 in Venice which contained a woodcut world map, now very rare.

1556   *La Cosmographia y Geographia*
          1570 Re-issued

DIEGO GUTIÉRREZ 1485–1554

Gutiérrez was a chart maker and pilot in the Casa de la Contratación de las Indias in Seville where he was associated with Sebastian Cabot. Apart from manuscript maps, his large map of America, published posthumously in Antwerp, showed the Spanish possessions in the New World, named California for the first time, and gave a much exaggerated picture of the course of the Amazon which influenced other cartographers for a century or more.

1562   *Americae sive quartae orbis partis nova et exactissima descriptio*

BENEDICTUS ARIAS MONTANUS *c.* 1527–98

Montanus, a Spanish theologian, compiled maps issued with a Polyglot Bible published in Antwerp by Plantin in 1571–72. It included a map of the Holy Land, now very rare, and a double-hemisphere world map on which there is a clear indication of an Australian Continent.

1571–72   *Biblia Polyglotta*

ANTONIO DE HERRERA Y TORDESILLAS 1559–1625

Herrera, a writer and official historian to the King of Spain, compiled a history of the Indies accompanied by maps of the West Indies and Central and South America. This was first published in Madrid in 1601 and was re-issued in several editions and languages, the most important of which were in 1622; the map of South America in that edition indicated the track of the Le Maire/Schouten voyage round Cape Horn and the title page shows the western seaboard of North America with California as an island, probably the first map to do so.

1601   *Descripción de las Indias Occidentales*: Madrid: 14 maps
          Various editions including 1622 in Amsterdam in French and Latin

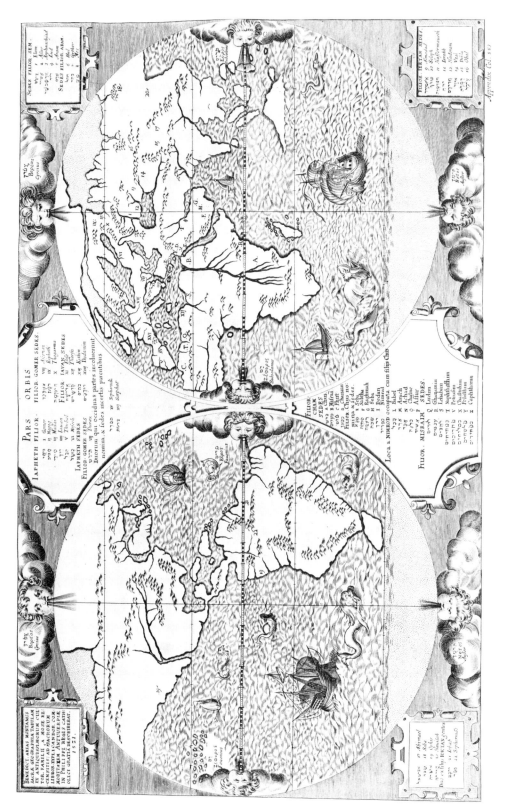

BENEDICTUS ARIAS MONTANUS *Sacrae Geographiae Tabulam* Antwerp 1571–72. Double-hemisphere world map included in the Polyglot Bible edited by Arias Montanus and published by Plantin This is one of the earliest maps to give a hint of an Australian continent.

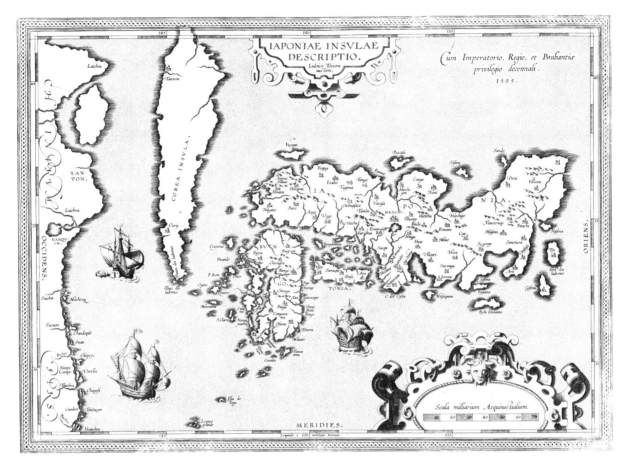

LUDOVICO (LUIZ) TEIXEIRA *Japonia Insulae Descriptio*. The first map of Japan published in a European atlas. Compiled by Teixeira, a Portuguese Jesuit in the service of the Spanish Crown, it was used by Ortelius in 1595 and in later editions of the *Theatrum Orbis Terrarum*.

TOMÁS LÓPEZ (DE VARGAS MACHUCA) 1730–1802

López, as Geographer to the King, compiled and published in Madrid a considerable number of town plans, maps and atlases, of which those noted below were the most important.

c. 1757	*Atlas geográfico de España*
	Later editions into nineteenth century
1758	*Atlas geográfico de la América septentrional y meridional*
1778	Map of Portugal
1792	*Atlas elemental*
c. 1798	Atlas (without title)
	Maps dated between 1765 and 1798

MIGUEL COSTANSÓ (COSTANZO) *fl.* 1769–1811

c. 1771	*Carta Reducida del Océano Asiático*
	Map of the west coast of America made during a Spanish expedition in 1769–70
1777	*Nueva España*

VICENTE TO(R)FIÑO DE SAN MIGUEL *c.* 1732–95

Spanish marine cartographer whose charts were noted for their accuracy and excellence of engraving.

c. 1786	*Cartas maritimas de la costa de España*
c. 1789	*Atlas Maritimo de España*: Madrid, 2 vols (large folio)
	Vol. I Spain (Atlantic Coast), Portugal, Azores
	Vol. II Spain (Mediterranean Coast) and Balearics
1807	Re-issued

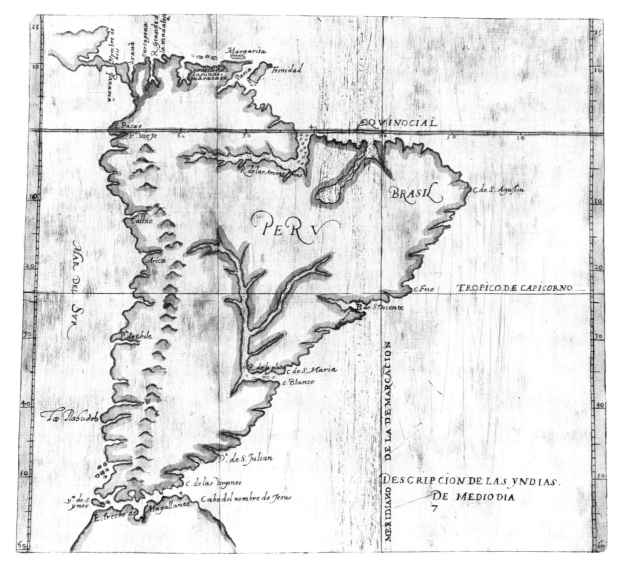

ANTONIO DE HERRERA   *South America*. Map of South America first published in Madrid in 1601 showing the demarcation line between the Spanish and Portuguese 'spheres of influence' laid down by the Pope in the Treaty of Tordesillas in 1494. On this copy, place names have been added in manuscript in a very early hand.

c. 1805   Atlas (without title)
Maps of the West Indies and South America

JOSÉ DE ESPINOSA *c.* 1753–1815
A Spanish traveller and hydrographer, de Espinosa compiled charts of the west coast of North America and the Indies. Active at a time when Spain was at last

breaking away from the secrecy imposed for so long on her map and chart makers he founded the Spanish Hydrographical Survey Office (Depósito Hydrográfico) in 1797.

1800–06   Atlas
Included the first charts (Vancouver Island 1795–98) published by the new Hydrographical Survey Office

Specialist references (Portugal and Spain)

BAGROW, L., *History of Cartography*

CRONE, G. R., *Maps and their Makers*

HOWSE, D. and SANDERSON, M., *The Sea Chart*

TOOLEY, R. V., BRICKER, C. and CRONE, G. R., *Landmarks of Map Making*
Throughout the chapters on the Continents contains much information about Portuguese and Spanish cartographers

SCANDINAVIA

Before the fifteenth century the peoples of Southern Europe had little geographical knowledge of the Scandinavian world except from sketchy detail shown in the Catalan Atlas (1375) and on a number of 'portolani' embracing Denmark and the southern tip of Norway. It was not until 1427 that a manuscript map prepared about that time by Claudius Clavus (*b.* 1388), a Dane who had spent some time in Rome, made available to scholars a tolerable outline of the northern countries and Greenland. That was to remain the best map available for the rest of the century and it was used as the basis for maps of Scandinavia in early printed editions of Ptolemy. Others by Nicolaus Cusanus (1491) and Ehrhard Etzlaub (*c.* 1492) followed but, needless to say, these are extremely rare; even the later maps by Olaus Magnus and Marcus Jordan, where they have survived at all, are known only by very few examples. In fact, apart from the rare appearance of an early Ptolemy map, the oldest of Scandinavia which a collector is likely to find are those in Münster's *Cosmography* published in 1544 with many later editions. In the following centuries the comparatively few maps and charts compiled in Scandinavia were usually published in Amsterdam, Antwerp, Paris or Nuremberg, the more important maps often being incorporated in the major Dutch, French and German atlases.

Biographies of Danish cartographers

MARCUS JORDAN (MARK JORDEN) 1521–95

Jordan, a professor of mathematics in Copenhagen, was an important figure in the history of Danish cartography. His original map of Denmark, said to have been made in 1552, has not survived but is known from its later use by Ortelius and Mercator. There is only one copy of a map of Holstein also made by him, but another map of Denmark (1585) was included in Braun and Hogenberg's *Civitates Orbis Terrarum* (1588), the only map included in that collection of town plans.

1552	Kingdom of Denmark
	Used by Ortelius from 1570 onwards (in various states)
1559	Holstein
1585	Kingdom of Denmark
	With coats of arms, allegorical figures and globes

LIEVEN ALGOET *fl.* 1562

1562	*Terrarum septentrionalium*
	Map of Scandinavia published in Antwerp

TYCHO BRAHE 1546–1601

A mathematician, scientist and, above all, the most noted astronomer of his time, Tycho Brahe built an observatory at Uraniborg on the island of Hven off Elsinore, where for twenty years he carried out a prolonged series of observations of the movement of the sun, moon, stars and the planets. These, and his discoveries of a new star Cassiopeia in 1572, affected profoundly the approach to astronomy and the prevailing ideas of the nature of the universe.

Late in life he was exiled from Denmark and settled in Prague where he came in contact with Johannes Kepler (1571–1630), the German scientist who eventually, after Brahe's death, edited and published his work.

The most famous of Brahe's pupils was the young Willem Blaeu who spent two years at Uraniborg before setting up in business in Amsterdam as a globe maker, later to become the most celebrated map publisher of his time. Blaeu's famous engravings of the Observatory were published in the *Atlas maior* in 1660.

JOHANNES ISAKSEN PONTANUS 1571–1639

As 'royal historian', Pontanus compiled a history of Denmark which included maps of Denmark and Schleswig.

1631	*Rerum Danicarum Historia*: Amsterdam, published by Jodocus Hondius and Jan Jansson

JOHANNES MEJER 1606–74

As mathematician and geographer to the Court, Mejer compiled important maps, some of which were subsequently used by Blaeu in the major atlases.

c. 1649–52   Atlas of Schleswig Holstein, published by Caspar Danckwerth

c. 1650   Map of Denmark

PEDER RESEN 1625–88

1677   *Atlas Danicus*

1684   Faroe Islands

JENS SÖRENSON 1646–1723

1679   Sea charts of the Baltic
Copied by Jaillot and van Keulen

ERIK PONTOPPIDAN 1698–1764

Pontoppidan, a noted theologian, naturalist and geographer, was Bishop of Bergen before being appointed to Copenhagen University in 1755. There, in association with Christian Fester (1732–1811), he compiled a comprehensive Danish Atlas, which was published in 7 parts between 1763 and 1781.

1730   *Theatrum Daniae veteris et modernae* (4to): town plans and views

1763–81   *Den Danske Atlas*
Various re-issues

VITUS JOH. BERING 1680–1741

A Danish seaman in the service of Peter the Great, Bering undertook arduous journeys across Siberia followed by voyages of exploration in the Northern Pacific, during which he proved the existence of the Strait (bearing his name) between the Asiatic mainland and Alaska. His manuscript maps and charts were used as the basis for maps in the *Nouvel Atlas de la Chine* (1737) by the French cartographer J. B. B. d'Anville.

LOUIS CHARLES DESNOS *fl.* 1750–90

Desnos was appointed globe maker to the King of Denmark but he spent most of his life as a globe maker and map publisher in Paris, often in association with Brion de la Tour.

1761   *Atlas Méthodique*

1761   *Routes des Postes*

c. 1764   *Atlas Historique et Géographique*

1766   *The Roads through England or Ogilby's Survey* (after Senex)

1767   *Nouvel Atlas d'Angleterre*

1768   *Atlas Général Méthodique* (with Brion de la Tour)
c. 1790 Re-issued

1786   *Atlas Général et Elémentaire*

THOMAS BUGGE 1740–1815

Thomas Bugge, mathematician and surveyor, completed the first survey of Denmark by triangulation.

c. 1780–89   Kingdom of Denmark

PAUL DE LÖVENÖRN 1751–1826

A noted hydrographer who founded the Danish Hydrographic Office in 1784.

1800   Kattegat: Sailing directions

1807   Chart of the Baltic Straits

1815   Charts of the coasts of Norway

CONRAD MALTE BRUN 1775–1826
VICTOR MALTE BRUN 1816–89

A Danish geographer, Conrad Malte Brun settled in Paris about the year 1800 where he collaborated with the French historian Edmé Mentelle in the publication of a Universal Atlas and other works.

1804   *Géographie Mathématique*

1812   *Atlas Complet*

1816   *Atlas de Géographie Universelle* (with E. Mentelle)
Further editions by Victor Malte Brun

Biography of Norwegian cartographer

CHRISTIAN JOCHUM PONTOPPIDAN 1739–1807

Pontoppidan served for many years in the Danish Army earning a high reputation as a skilful surveyor and cartographer. At a time when official map making in Norway was in its infancy, his accurate and detailed maps were used in boundary settlements when Norway was ceded by Denmark to Sweden in 1814.

1781   Denmark, Norway and Sweden

1785–95   Southern and Northern Norway
Separate large-scale maps

Biographies of Swedish cartographers

JOHANNES MAGNUS *fl.* 1534

A former Archbishop of Uppsala, exiled in Rome with his brother, Olaus Magnus, Johannes wrote a *History of the Swedish People*, accompanied by a map of

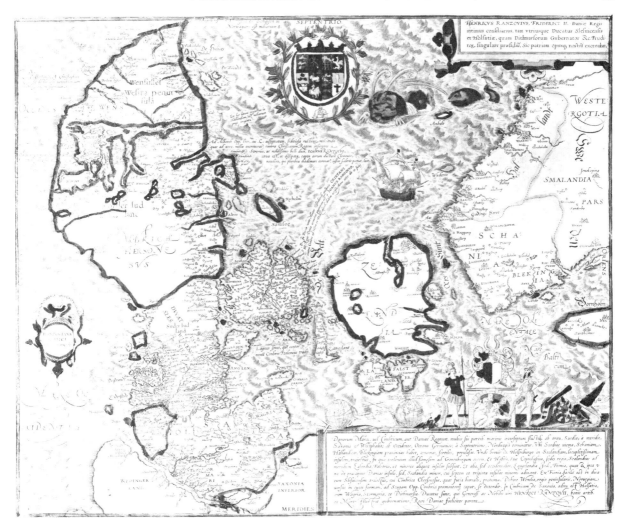

MARK JORDEN   *Danorum marca* . . . Cologne 1588. This was the only map published in Braun and Hogenberg's collection of town plans, the *Civitates Orbis Terrarum*.

Scandinavia.

1534   *History of the Swedish People*: Rome, with
           large woodcut map of Scandinavia

OLAUS MAGNUS 1490–1558

Olaus Magnus, a celebrated churchman, was born in Linköping and studied at Uppsala, then a famous centre of learning. As a devout Catholic he became involved in the convulsions of the Swedish Reformation and in consequence spent many years in Italy, where he probably compiled his very famous large-scale map of Scandinavia, the *Carta Marina*, published in Venice in 1539, of which only one copy is known. Fortunately, reduced versions were printed in his later

Historia which went through many editions.

1539   *Carta Marina* (9 sheets): Venice
           1572 Reduced version in Lafreri (Rome)
           atlases

1555   *Historia de gentibus septentrionalibus – A
           Treatise concerning the Northern People*:
           Rome (small folio)
           Contained woodcut map of Scandinavia –
           a simplified version of the 1539 map
           20 re-issues over the next century

ANDREAS BURE (BURAEUS) 1571–1661

A surveyor and mathematician who compiled an important map of the northern part of Sweden and the

WILLEM BLAEU/ANDREAS BURE   *Suecia, Dania et Norvegia* Amsterdam (1634) 1642. Map of Scandinavia based on Bure's map of 1626. Bure was an important figure in the history of Swedish cartography and set up a land surveying office which continued for over 200 years.

first separately printed map of the country, both of which were used extensively by Dutch and other publishers. Original copies are now extremely rare. Bure wrote a historical geography of Sweden and set up a land surveying office which continued in being for over 200 years.

| 1611 | Northern Provinces of Sweden |
| 1626 | *Orbis Arctoi Nova* (Scandinavia) (6 sheets) |

JOHAN MANSSON *fl.* 1644–59

Swedish hydrographer who compiled some of the earliest sea charts of the Baltic.

| 1644 | First printed chart of the Gulf of Finland |
| 1645 | Sea Atlas |

COUNT ERIK DAHLBERG 1625–1703

A Swedish field marshal, military engineer and cartographer, Count Dahlberg was the author of a number of topographical works including the maps and plans in a famous account of the military exploits of Gustavus Adolphus by Samuel Pufendorf

1660	Kingdom of Denmark
1667	*Suecia Antiqua*
	Nearly 500 topographical views republished over a long period
1696–99	*History of the reign of Gustavus Adolphus* by Samuel Pufendorf: Nuremberg
	Maps and plans by Dahlberg
1698	Atlas of Sweden

★ PETTER GEDDA *c.* 1661–97

Gedda published the first Swedish sea charts, which were widely copied by Hendrick Doncker, van Keulen and others.

1694–95	Chart Book of the Baltic: published in Swedish and Dutch
1695	Charts of the Skager Rack

★ DANIEL DJURBERG 1744–1834

A cartographer at Uppsala University, Djurberg compiled a notable map of the Pacific showing Cook's voyages. He used the name 'Ulimaroa', the Maori name for Australia, which appeared on a number of maps for thirty or forty years.

1780	Map of Polynesia (Australia, New Zealand and the Pacific Ocean): Stockholm

★ JOHAN NORDENANKAR 1722–1804

1788–90	Charts of the Baltic
1795	Sea Atlas

COUNT SAMUEL GUSTAF HERMELIN 1744–1820

1796–1812	*Geografiske Kartor ofver Swerige* – Atlas of Sweden and part of Finland (large folio)

GUSTAV KLINT 1771–1840

1832	Swedish Sea Atlas

Specialist References (Scandinavia)

BRAMSEN, BO, *Gamle Danmarkskort*
A history of Danish cartography with biographies of prominent map makers

NORDENSKIÖLD, A. E., *Facsimile Atlas to the Early History of Cartography*

TOOLEY, R. V., *Maps and Map-Makers*
Contains much useful information, not readily available elsewhere, on Scandinavian cartographers

SWITZERLAND

By comparison with her larger neighbours, Germany and Italy, it may not be considered that Switzerland has made a major contribution to the history of cartography, but in the sixteenth century especially Swiss influence was by no means negligible. Certainly the first printed map of Switzerland was published in Martin Waldseemüller's edition of Ptolemy at Strassburg in 1513, but the manuscript map by Konrad Türst (1497) drawn to scale was a splendid achievement for its time and the researches of Vadianus at St Gallen University produced notable work; the Germanic influence in Basle, which became part of the Swiss Confederation in 1501, and the highly developed wood engraving skills there were important factors in European map publishing. The almost endless editions of Münster were published there from 1540 onwards for nearly a century and Zurich can claim to have published the first national atlas produced anywhere – that of Johann Stumpf in 1548–52.

In the second half of the sixteenth century many maps of the cantons in manuscript or woodcut appeared but the mountainous nature of the country produced its own mapping problems and imposed a need for large-scale surveys as well as practical and effective methods of showing land surfaces in relief. Early in the seventeenth century Hans Gyger perfected new ways of doing this but although he published a wide range of very large-scale maps of the cantons and of Switzerland as a whole his techniques did not receive the acceptance they deserved. On the other hand his countrymen followed his precedent of compiling large-scale maps for which they have always been noted until the present day.

Biographies

JOACHIM VADIANUS (JOACHIM VON WATT) 1484–1551
A mathematician and scholar, active in St Gallen in Eastern Switzerland, Vadianus wrote a treatise *Epitome trium terrae partium*, published in Zurich, which included a noted woodcut world map.

1534	*Epitome trium terrae partium* Included a world map, *Typus Cosmographicus Universalis*, on oval projection probably based on Bordone 1546 Re-issued: 13 woodcut maps by Joh. Honter
1540	*De situ Orbis* (Pomponius Mela): Paris: included double heart-shaped world map by Orance Finé (small folio)

AEGIDIUS TSCHUDI 1505–72 ★
A Swiss cartographer who compiled a number of manuscript maps, the most important being a map of

MARTIN WALDSEEMÜLLER   *Tabula Helvetia* Strassburg 1525. This map is a later edition of the first printed map of Switzerland which appeared in 1513.

Switzerland which was subsequently printed and used by Münster, Forlani, Ortelius and others.

1538   Map of Switzerland: Basle
        1555 Re-issued in Rome

JOHANN STUMPF 1500–77

Swiss historian who published in 1548 a Swiss Chronicle, a history and geographical description of Switzerland which included 23 woodcut maps. The maps, re-issued as an Atlas in 1552, can be claimed to form the first national Atlas, pre-dating Lazius's maps of Austria (1561) and Saxton's *England & Wales* (1579). Town plans by Stumpf were used by Braun and Hogenberg in the *Civitates Orbis Terrarum*.

1544   Map of Canton Valais
1545   Map of Canton Zürich

1548   *Chronicle*: Zurich
        History of Switzerland with 23 woodcut maps including maps of Germany and France – some maps by Johannes Honter
        1552 Re-issued as *Landtaffeln*: Zurich, Ch. Froschauer

---

HANS KONRAD GYGER (GEIGER) 1599–1674

Gyger was a mathematician who devised new and very effective means of showing land surface in relief, but his methods were never generally accepted.

c. 1634–85   Swiss Cantons: large-scale maps

MATTHÄUS MERIAN (father) 1593–1650
MATTHÄUS MERIAN (son) 1621–87
See entry in Chapter 12

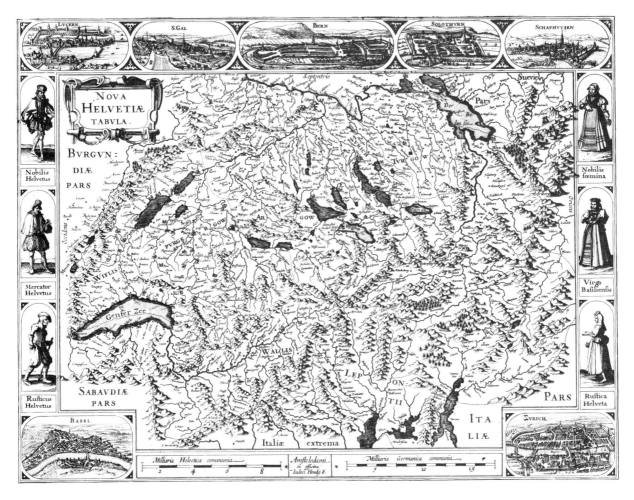

JAN JANSSON *Nova Helvetiae Tabula* Amsterdam 1630. This is a rare map, engraved by Jodocus Hondius II, from an 'experimental' Atlas issued by Jansson to test the market for a proposed new work.

JOHANN JAKOB SCHEUCHZER 1672–1733
Mathematician, physician and geographer who produced one of the first large-scale maps of Switzerland.

1712   *Nouvelle Carte de la Suisse* (4 sheets)
            1716 Re-issued by Pieter Schenk
            1730–35   do   Covens and Mortier
            1765 Further re-issue
            (His map was also used by R. and J. Ottens.)

JOHANN GASPAR SCHEUCHZER *fl.* 1727
A Swiss naturalist who is known for his compilation of a series of 11 maps of the provinces and main cities of Japan based on the work of a German physician and naturalist, Engelbert Kaempfer, who spent some years in Nagasaki in the service of the Dutch East India Co.

1727–29   Maps, plans and itineraries of Japan
            1740 Re-issued by R. and J. Ottens

ISAAC BRUCKNER 1686–1762
Bruckner was a cartographer, engraver and instrument and globe maker who was appointed a Geographer to Louis XV of France.

1749   *Nouvel Atlas de Marine*: Berlin
            1759 Re-issued in The Hague

LEONHARD EULER 1707–83
Physician and cartographer, born in Basle, Euler spent

many years in Germany and Russia where he was associated with the preparation of the Atlas of Russia (J. N. Delisle) published in St Petersburg in 1745

1753   *Atlas Geographicus*: Berlin
            1756, 1760 Re-issued

★

★ JOHANN HEINRICH WEISS 1759–1826
JOHANN RUDOLF MEYER 1739–1813
Weiss and Meyer published the first Atlas of engraved maps of Switzerland as well as a large-scale relief map.

c. 1786–   *Atlas Suisse*
1802
c. 1788–96 *Carte de la Suisse*: 16-sheet map

★ GUILLAUME HENRI DUFOUR 1787–1875
c. 1832–64 Switzerland: 25-sheet map – the first complete topographical survey of the country

★

Specialist References (Switzerland)

BAGROW, L., *History of Cartography*

CRONE, G. R., *Maps and their Makers*

RUSSIA

It is scarcely necessary to look at a map of Russia – with which we must include Siberia – to visualize the daunting task facing Russian map makers. Indeed, considering the vastness of their territory and the lack of skilled cartographers, it is surprising that relatively good maps were available for engraving and printing in most of the well known sixteenth and seventeenth century atlases. Generally, maps of that time were based on material brought back from Moscow by visitors from the West. Notable among these were the following:

PAOLO GIOVIO (1483–1552)
Map of European Russia (1525) based on detail provided by a Muscovite ambassador to Rome, Demetrius Gerasimov (c. 1465–c. 1525). It appeared in manuscript form and was subsequently used by Giacomo Gastaldi in his 1548 edition of Ptolemy's *Geographia* and also by later publishers.

SIGISMUND HERBERSTEIN (1486–1566)
Map of Muscovia (1549) compiled by Herberstein, who was ambassador from the Habsburg Emperor, Maximilian I to Moscow. The map, based on material by a Lithuanian, Ivan Lyatsky (*fl. c.* 1526–1555) was used by Sebastian Münster and others. Lyatsky himself also produced a map of Russia dated 1555.

ANTHONY JENKINSON (*fl.* 1545–1577
The first English ambassador to Russia, Jenkinson made a remarkable journey as far as Bokhara in Asiatic Russia and subsequently compiled a famous map of his travels. Unfortunately, no actual copy of the map has survived but it was used by Ortelius in 1570 and Gerard de Jode in 1578 as the basis for maps in their atlases.

ISAAC MASSA (1587–1635)
A Dutch traveller, Massa compiled a map of Russia (*c.* 1612) which was used in the Blaeu/Jansson atlases.

CORNELIS CRUYS (1657–1727)
A Dutch Admiral, in the service of Peter the Great, compiled and published an atlas of the River Don and the Sea of Asov (*c.* 1704).

The first map of any real importance known to have been produced in Russia was the manuscript 'Great Map' compiled in the time of Tsar Boris Godunov (1598–1605), followed by later versions covering the expansion of the Empire southwards and eastwards. In the second half of the seventeenth century a start was made on the mapping of Siberia (1667) by Peter Godunov (*fl.* 1667–69) and an atlas of Siberia was published (*c.* 1698–1701) by Semyon Ulanovitch Remezov (1642–1720). Evidently the printing of maps in Russia presented difficulties which Peter the Great (1689–1725) attempted to overcome by licensing a Dutch publisher in Amsterdam specifically to print Russian maps. This was about 1699 but soon afterwards a private printing house was established in Moscow by the cartographer, Vasily Kiprianov (*fl.* 1706–17) who published maps of Russia and the World.

During this same period, Peter the Great ordered a comprehensive survey of his country and the training of a corps of professional surveyors. In charge of this immense undertaking was an employee of the State Chancellry, Ivan Kyrilov (1689–1737). He planned a 3

anks for your order!

garding this order, please contact us at sales@halcyonbooks.co.uk

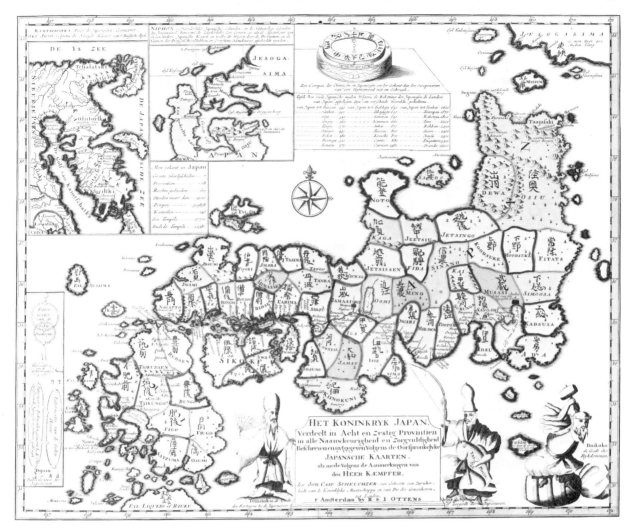

R. and J. OTTENS/JOH. CASPAR SCHEUCHZER   *Het Koninkryk Japan* Amsterdam (1728) *c.* 1740. Based on a work by the Swiss scholar Scheuchzer, this map is one of the few to use Japanese names as well as their westernized forms.

volume atlas of Imperial Russia to consist of something like 300 to 400 maps, but it soon became evident that advice and assistance by foreign cartographers was required if the project was to be completed in a reasonable time. In consequence, following a visit to France by the Tsar and the subsequent founding of the Imperial Academy of Sciences in 1724, the French cartographers Joseph Nicolas and Louis Delisle (brothers of Guillaume Delisle) were invited to St Petersburg to set up a School of Astronomy and to train teams of surveyors. Unfortunately, Kyrilov and the Delisles totally disagreed on the methods of surveying needed to map the country and, in the event,

Kyrilov pursued his own course and, in 1734, published the first part of his planned atlas consisting of a general map of Russia and 14 regional maps. Meanwhile, the Delisles travelled throughout Russia and Siberia gathering geographical data, compiling maps with the assistance of Swiss mathematician Leonhard Euler (1707–83) and the Danish explorer Vitus Joh. Bering (1680–1741) who traversed Siberia on at least two occasions and explored the Northern Pacific. No doubt the Delisles also used much of Kyrilov's material for, after Kyrilov's death in 1737, his atlas was suppressed, possibly because of inaccuracies but more likely as a result of jealousies and intrigue; only two copies of the atlas are known to exist. Eventually, in 1745, following further disagreements between Joseph Nicolas Delisle (who felt the work was still incomplete) and the Academy of Sciences the *Atlas Russicus* was published containing a general map and 19 regional maps. Thereafter, further work and revision of the atlas was in the hands of Michael Lomonosov (1711–65), director of the Geographical Department of the Academy. In due course, as in so many countries, official mapping was taken over by the military and, in 1816, a new survey by triangulation was undertaken, which eventually included Poland, most of which country was then occupied by Russia.

★

Specialist References (Russia)

BAGROW, L., *History of Cartography*

BROWN, LLOYD A., *The Story of Maps*

TRUSTEES OF THE WALTERS ART GALLERY
World Encompassed

POLAND

In a turbulent history it was Poland's fate in the second half of the eighteenth century to be the victim of powerful and aggressive neighbours. Frederick the Great's ambition to extend the boundaries of Prussia along the Baltic coast led to the first partition of the country in 1772; at the same time Maria Teresa of Austria and Catherine II of Russia needed little persuasion to join in the destruction of an ancient enemy so that, in 1795, after the second and third partitions, Poland ceased to exist as a separate country until its sovereignty was restored at the end of the first World War in 1918. In consequence, Poland's cartographic history is fragmented, but, at least in the fifteenth and sixteenth centuries knowledge of the subject was far more firmly based there than in Russia. It was in Poland that scientific knowledge was given its greatest stimulus of the time by the writings of astronomer and mathematician, Nicolaus Copernicus (1473–1543), born in Cracow. After a lifetime's study, his work, *De Revolutionibus Orbium Coelestium*, published in Nuremburg in the last year of his life, confirmed and extended the Pythagorean theory that the sun is the centre of the planetary system. In the field of practical cartography he produced maps of Poland and Lithuania, neither of which has survived.

Manuscript maps are known to have been drawn in the fifteenth century and there were printed maps of Eastern Europe in the *Nuremberg Chronicle* (1493) and in the early editions of Ptolemy's *Geographia* but the first 'modern' map, used by Münster and Mercator, was a woodcut compiled about 1526 by Bernard Wapowski (1475–1535) in Cracow. This may well have been based on the work of Copernicus. Other names which appear later in the century were Wenceslaus Godreccius (*d.* 1591) and Andreas Pograbius (*d.* 1602) whose maps of Poland were used by Ortelius. Following the Treaty of Lublin in 1569 with Lithuania (then a vast country covering great areas of present day Russia), a number of maps of the whole area were compiled by Polish cartographers, amongst them Maciej Strubicz (*c.* 1520–89) and Tomasz Makowski (1575–*c.* 1620). Makowski's map was published by W. J. Bleau from 1613 onwards.

Over the next 150 years the whole of Poland was gradually mapped in considerable detail, often with the aid of foreign surveyors such as Guillaume Le Vasseur de Beauplan (1595–1685) whose maps were used by Nicolas Sanson. Finally, in the year of the first partition, 1772, a 24 sheet map was published in Paris by G. A. Rizzi Zannoni, the noted Italian cartographer, who spent many years assembling earlier manuscript and printed maps on which his work was based. This was a high point in the history of Polish cartography; the publication of Rizzi Zannoni's map inspired the preparation of new maps, atlases and town plans but this activity was shortlived and for about 125 years after 1795 mapping was in the control of the occupying powers, whose authority, rarely given, was required if original cartographic work of any kind was contemplated. In spite of that, the spirit of independence was kept alive by emigrés such as Joachim Lelewel (1786–1861) who spent much of his life in France publishing atlases and cartographic work.

Specialist References (Poland)

BAGROW, L., *History of Cartography*

TOOLEY, R. V., *Map Collectors' Circle*
Papers No. 25, 31, 43, 56 and 57.

Chapter 20

MAPS OF THE WORLD & THE CONTINENTS

In the various chapters in which we have outlined the history of map production in Western European countries, we have set out in some detail the work of the better known national cartographers and publishers. It is true to say that practically all the general atlases listed included maps of the world, the continents and their principal regions and it would be tedious now to repeat that detail; this chapter therefore only seeks to draw attention to the more interesting maps of this kind. Many of the fifteenth- and sixteenth-century maps in these categories are, of course, unique copies or at best are only available in the great libraries or collections but nevertheless early maps may still be found by the assiduous collector.

THE WORLD

Elsewhere we have touched upon the historical changes wrought by Henry the Navigator and the Portuguese and Spanish adventurers who eventually found their way to the Orient and the New World. We have noted that few of the charts and maps made during, or even after, their voyages have survived for, apart from being working documents, vulnerable to day-to-day wear, their manuscripts were reproduced only on a very limited scale, closely controlled by Portuguese and Spanish officialdom. In consequence it fell to the Italians, Germans, Dutch and other European cartographers to prepare and produce printed maps in any quantity.

By the beginning of the seventeenth century the world was assuming a more recognizable shape. True, until 1605–06, firm knowledge of Australia was lacking and the voyages of the later explorers, Tasman, Dampier, Cook, Flinders and others, were still far ahead but, during the century, enthusiasm for the search for a North East or North West passage waned, the Indies and the Spice Islands became reality rather

than myth and fleets of trading vessels took over the sea routes opened up by the early explorers. In the Americas, colonists were making a new life but were still dependent on regular sea traffic for their lifeline with Europe. Around the year 1700 aids to navigation, such as Halley's magnetic and meteorological charts, Cassini's methods of determining longitude and, later, Harrison's chronometer permitted ever more detailed and accurate surveys. World maps naturally reflected these changes and there is endless scope for the collector with special interests to make his own selection from the material available.

World maps of the sixteenth century are not common but the following are available from time to time: Waldseemüller (1513–41), Peter Apian (1520 onwards), Bordone (1528–c. 1565), Grynaeus (1532 onwards) Münster (1540–44 and many later editions), Ortelius (1570–1612), Plancius (1590–96 and later editions), de Jode (1593), Mercator (1595) and the later Hondius/Jansson editions well into the next century.

From the first part of the seventeenth century there are magnificent maps by the Blaeu family (1606 onwards), van den Keere (1608), Jansson (1626), Speed (1627), N. Visscher (1639) and, in the second half, the still rare maps by Sanson (1651), Duval (1660), Jaillot (1668), de Wit (1680), Morden (1680), Dankerts (1680–90), van Keulen (1682), Coronelli (1695), Delisle (1700), Wells (1700); all these and others were usually issued in a number of editions and with many variants.

As we have already seen the first half of the eighteenth century was dominated by the French cartographers, Delisle, de Vaugondy, d'Anville, le Rouge, but at the same time the Dutch publishers van der Aa, R. and J. Ottens, the Mortier family, and Covens and Mortier published very large atlases made up of maps either by their predecessors or by noted cartographers of the day. To these the German map trade, revitalized by Homann, added its quota with

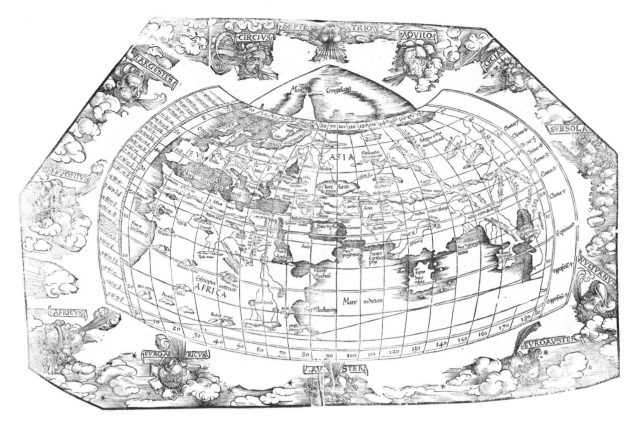

MARTIN WALDSEEMÜLLER   *World Map.* This version of the Ptolemaic World Map was published in Waldseemüller's *Geographia* in the 1525, 1535 and 1541 editions.

maps by Homann himself and his successors and by Seutter, Weigel and Lotter; and finally the English map publishers, Kitchin, Faden, Sayer and Bennett, Laurie and Whittle, Cary, Arrowsmith and the Wylds took over with atlases of every type, most of them containing the latest world maps.

For those collectors who have a special interest in World Maps we can do no better than refer them to *The Mapping of the World* by Rodney W. Shirley.

THE AMERICAS

No account of cartography on a world scale would be complete without considering in some detail not only maps of the New World as a whole but also the many splendid regional maps, especially of the North American continent, which illustrate its history; in any case, the links between the Old and New Worlds are so close that it is hardly possible to consider one without the other.

For fifty years or so after the first voyage by Columbus the Spaniards concentrated on Central America, Peru and the Caribbean, the emphasis being on conquest and plunder rather than settlement in any peaceful sense. But that phase passed; after a number of abortive colonizing expeditions in the middle of the 1500s and in the face of intense rivalry from the French and British, the Spanish succeeded, in 1565, in establishing a permanent colony at St Augustine in Florida where they retained their hold until 1819 when Florida was ceded to the United States. Otherwise their main sphere of interest, inspired originally by their search for the mythical Seven Cities of Cibola but in later years based more solidly on Jesuit, Dominican and Franciscan missions, continued to lie around the Gulf of Mexico and in the American South West.

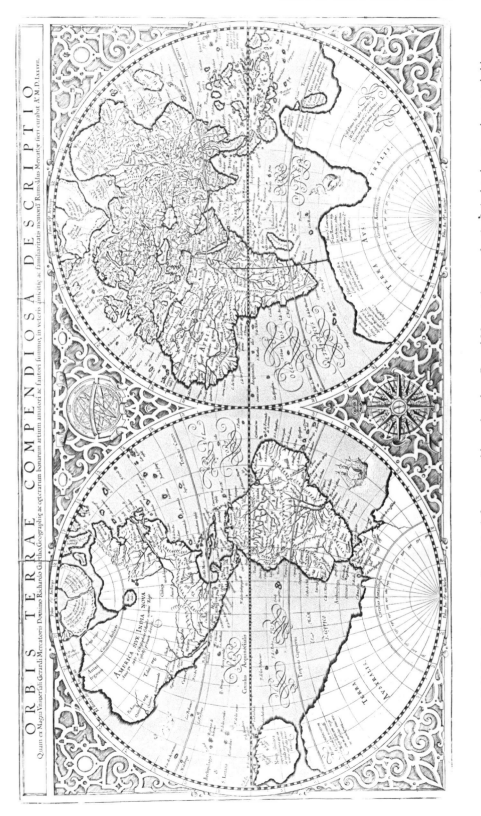

RUMOLD MERCATOR   *Orbis Terrae Compendiosa Descriptio.* A famous world map based on Gerard Mercator's map of 1569. It is dated 1587 and was probably issued as a separate sheet map before appearing in the Mercator Atlas in 1595.

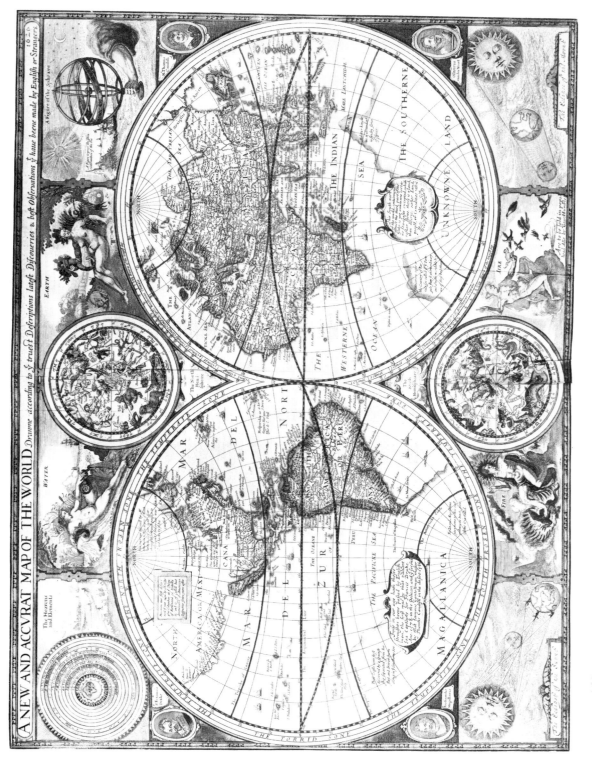

JOHN SPEED   *A New and Accurate Map of the World.* Published from 1627 to 1676 in Speed's *Prospect of the Most Famous Parts of the World,* the first World Atlas produced by an Englishman. This map illustrates the misconception of California as an island.

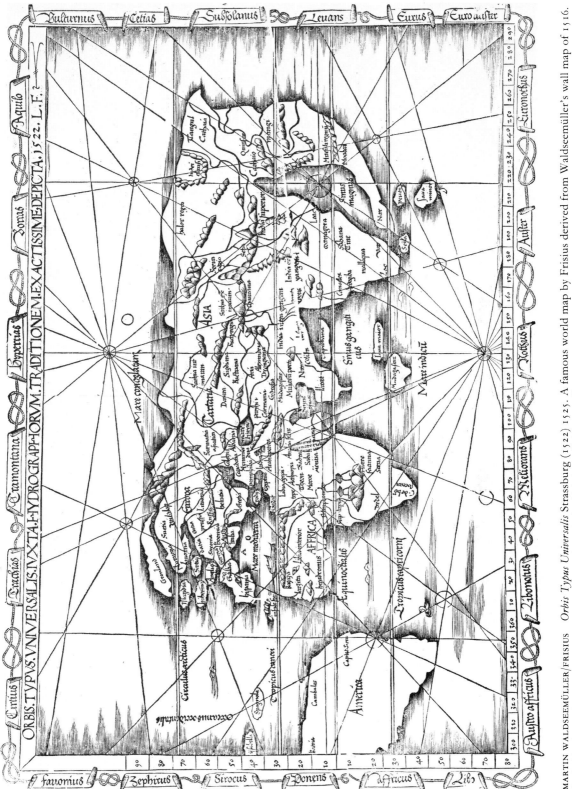

MARTIN WALDSEEMÜLLER/FRISIUS   *Orbis Typus Universalis* Strassburg (1522) 1525. A famous world map by Frisius derived from Waldseemüller's wall map of 1516. Probably the earliest map mentioning the name 'America' which is available to collectors.

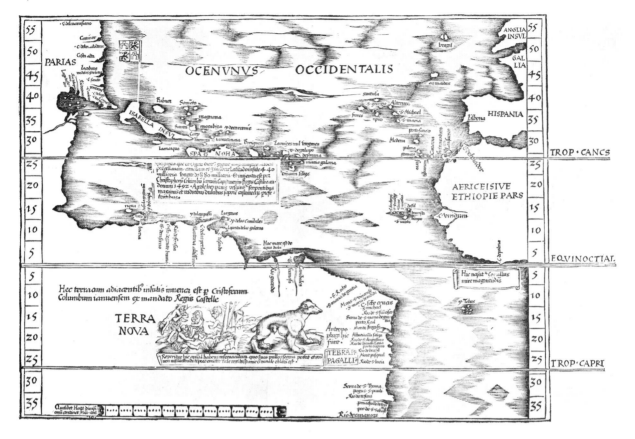

MARTIN WALDSEEMÜLLER   *Oceani Occidentalis seu Terre Nove* Strassburg (1522) 1525. This map of the Atlantic and the New World was based on a similar map in the 1513 edition of Waldseemüller's *Geographia* but included additional information giving credit to Columbus for discovering America. Sometimes known as the 'Admiral's Map'.

Lower California and parts of Arizona were colonized in the seventeenth century but, in the face of Indian tribal resistance, their efforts were sporadic and never wholly successful, even under the inspiration of Father Kino who, as an explorer, finally disposed of the idea that California was an island. As late as 1766–68 the last Spanish exploratory expedition through New Mexico was beset with difficulties and achieved no lasting benefits.

Within a few years of Columbus's first landfall, England had staked a claim directly on the American mainland by virtue of John Cabot's voyage to New-foundland in 1497. At the time there was no successful follow-up to Cabot's voyage but, in later years, English interest in the Caribbean was, of course, very much alive; Hawkins, Drake, Raleigh and Hakluyt saw to that and after Drake's world voyage the urge to set up colonies in the New World was not be to denied. As is well known, the first English attempt at settlement,

directed by Raleigh in 1585–86 on the coast of Carolina, failed, but an account of the expedition published soon afterwards by Thomas Hariot, illustrated by John White, included a map of Virginia. This was said to be the inspiration for Theodore de Bry's major work, the *Grands Voyages* (1590) in which the map of Virginia and many others appeared. That was followed soon afterwards by Wytfliet's *Descriptionis Ptolemaicae augmentum*, the first printed atlas to consist entirely of maps of America. The next century saw the second English attempt at colonization, organized more successfully this time by the Virginia Company (1606) under the governorship of Captain John Smith, whose famous map of Virginia, published at Oxford in 1612, was the precursor of a whole series of beautiful maps of the Eastern States. Even though the settlement was successful, English exploration inland was on a limited scale. The colonists needed time to break in their new lands and attune themselves to the

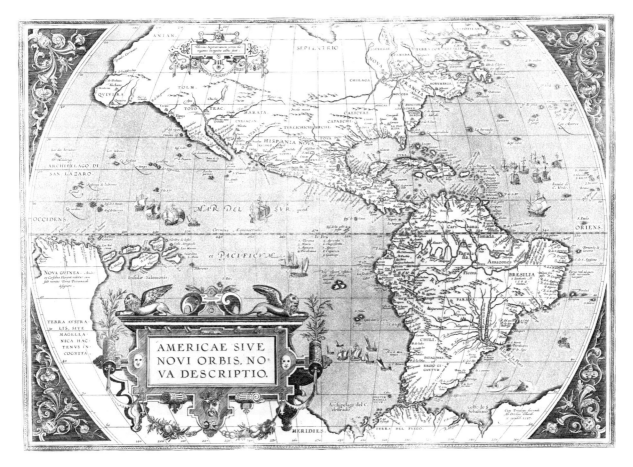

ABRAHAM ORTELIUS   *Americae sive Novi Orbis Nova Descriptio*. This Ortelius map is regarded by many as the most beautiful map of the Western Hemisphere produced in the sixteenth century. First published in 1570, the above example is from an edition dated 1587 (or later) printed from a re-engraved plate which corrects the coastal outline of South America and includes the Solomon Islands.

unaccustomed climate and conditions but by the end of the century the realization of the vastness and resources of the Continent on which they had established themselves had become clearer as pioneer traders and explorers penetrated the interior.

The French in the north were more adventurous; their interest in a North West Passage had been roused in the first decades of the sixteenth century by Breton fishermen who crossed the Atlantic regularly to the fishing banks off Nova Scotia, and by Giovanni da Verrazano (1523) with his hints of a passage in the region of Pamlico Sound or Chesapeake Bay, for long known as the Sea of Verrazano. A few years later Jacques Cartier, in his three voyages between 1534 and 1541, explored the St Lawrence and staked France's claim to Quebec and New France. After the long

interval of some sixty years caused by the internecine troubles in France itself, Samuel de Champlain was dispatched in 1603 to survey the areas already reached by Cartier with a view to future colonization. After completing his first surveys, he devoted thirty years to fostering good relations with the Indians, developing the fur trade and exploring the complex river systems and the Great Lakes. His map of 1632 was the first to show all the lakes except Michigan. While the English remained in the coastal belt, de Champlain's successors, Louis Joliet and La Salle, penetrated still further into the interior and in 1682 René La Salle, after many false starts, sailed the length of the Mississippi, naming its watershed 'Louisiana' and claiming it for France. The British and French, of course, were not alone in their ventures across the Atlantic; the Dutch set up a trading base at New Amsterdam around 1624–26 backed by the small hinterland of New Netherlands and there were shortlived Swedish settlements, all of which eventually merged by conquest into the coastal states.

While these events were taking place in the East, map makers had to contend with a bewildering mixture of fact and fiction when attempting to draw remoter parts of the continent; the question whether California was an island or a peninsula, did the Strait of Anian really exist and, of course, the ever present problems presented by the concept of a North West Passage. The first maps of the Pacific coast, including those of Ortelius, Mercator, Wytfliet and Tatton, were not only beautifully drawn but were also remarkably accurate in showing California as a peninsula although, even at that time, legends cast doubt in some minds. It can be understood that map makers were sceptical but not entirely surprised when a captured Spanish chart drawn about 1602 indicated that it had been proved to be an island and within a very few years maps were being redrawn. Those published by Henry Briggs in 1625 and Speed in 1627 set the pace and Nicolas Sanson seems to have accepted the new outline without question. Not until about 1700, following exploration by Father Kino, an Austrian Jesuit priest, was the story disproved and cartographers could settle again for the original coastline although, even then, not without some hesitation. Herman Moll, in particular, was reluctant to accept the new version, claiming that he knew of seamen who had actually sailed round the 'island'.

Speculation about the shape of the continent far to the north of California and the stretch of water dividing it from Asia led Gastaldi, the Italian geographer, to declare that the continents were divided by the Strait of Anian, a name he took from the Kingdom of Anian which Marco Polo had placed more or less where Alaska lies. From about 1566 the name appeared on maps well into the next century and for many years it was thought that the strait could be reached from the Atlantic through the North West Passage and was therefore a vital link in the route to India. We need not dwell here on the valiant attempts to find that passage; apart from those already mentioned, the voyages of Frobisher, Davis, Baffin and Hudson were inevitably to end in failure but each added his quota to knowledge of the far north.

Questions such as these time would answer but more important were the changing relations between the colonial powers in the eastern part of the continent. The expansion of the British colonies over the Appalachians towards Ohio, the consolidation of the French hold on the Mississippi and the Seven Years War in Europe inevitably led to conflict between the British and French colonists and eventually to the fall of Quebec and the French loss of the St Lawrence and Canada (1763). Another twenty years brought the War of Independence and the end of colonial ambitions in the East and North, but it was not until 1846 that the Mexican War ended the influence of the Spanish missions in the South West.

The final stages of exploration across the North American continent turned out to be rather more prolonged and hazardous than John Farrer's blithe estimate in 1651 of a 10-day 150-mile journey would have suggested. In Canada, rivalry between the North West Company and the Hudson's Bay Company led to remarkable journeys by Samuel Hearne (1769–72) to the Arctic, by Alexander Mackenzie down the river bearing his name (1780–90) and a year or two later over the Rockies to the Pacific making him the first man to complete the overland journey north of Mexico. In 1805–08 Simon Fraser also reached the Pacific, having followed the Fraser river to its mouth near present-day Vancouver in an area of coastline which had already been surveyed and charted by Capt. Vancouver during a world voyage in 1791–94.

In the United States, President Jefferson's purchase of Louisiana from the French in 1803 more than doubled the area of the country, adding vast new unknown territories, and almost immediately the President set about organizing exploration of the new lands. Expeditions led by Meriwether Lewis and William Clark (1803–06) to the Pacific coast, by Lieut. Pike (1805–07) to the Upper Mississippi and the South West and by others too numerous to mention here provided sufficient new geographical knowledge to keep such publishers as Arrowsmith and Wyld in London, and Carey and Lea, and Tanner in New York and Philadelphia, occupied for years to come.

In South America, as in the Gulf of Mexico, the search for gold and silver was the prime objective of the first Spanish and Portuguese adventurers. The Spanish were lucky in finding Peru and the silver mines of Potosí on their side of the demarcation line laid down in the Treaty of Tordesillas in 1494; the Portuguese less so in their allotted country, Brazil, which for centuries yielded them only the red dyewood (from which the name 'Brazil' derives) and sugar, although there was a

THEODORE DE BRY   *Central and South America*. One of the most splendid maps by de Bry, first published in 1592 in Frankfurt-am-Main. Although this highly decorative map was published in 1592, the west coast of South America still retains the projecting outline which Ortelius had corrected in 1587.

shortlived 'gold rush' during the early years of the eighteenth century. On the other hand, of course, the Treaty also gave the Portuguese exclusive rights to the sea route to the Spice Islands via Africa and the Indian Ocean, thereby limiting Spanish ambitions to Central America and the Pacific Ocean. The ocean crossing to Asia proved to be too great a barrier for commercial purposes and eventually Spain sold its rights in the spice trade to the Portuguese.

Within very few years of the first landing of Columbus, Spanish colonists settled successfully in Peru (*c.* 1535), in Paraguay (*c.* 1537) and later in Buenos Aires (*c.* 1580). The conquest of Peru made way for an

astonishing journey down the River Amazon in 1541–42 which was recorded on Sebastian Cabot's map of 1544 and for journeys across the continent to the River Plate, already discovered in 1516 and further explored by Cabot in 1526–30 when he sought a 'South West' passage to the Pacific. Before this, in 1519, Magellan, a Portuguese in the service of Spain, had sailed south-westwards and eventually through the Straits bearing his name in the hope of forestalling Portuguese claims to the Spice Islands, and although his ship, the *Victoria*, completed the three-year circum-navigation of the world, Magellan with many of his crew perished *en route*. For a century his discoveries,

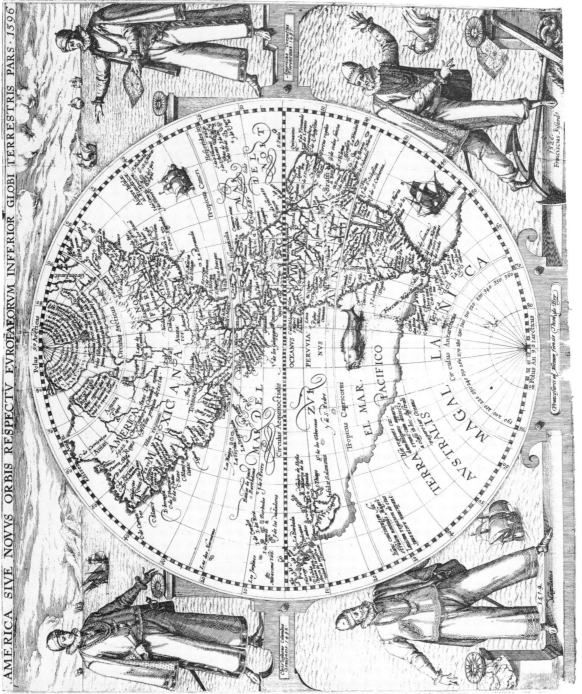

THEODORE DE BRY   *America sive Novus Orbis.* Map of the Western Hemisphere published in 1596 in Frankfurt-am-Main. A rare and decorative map showing Terra Australis named 'Magellanica'.

CORNELIS WYTFLIET   *Utriusque Hemispherii Delineatio* Louvain 1597–1615. The World Map (copied from Mercator's map of 1584) included in the earliest Atlas devoted entirely to America.

mapped by the cartographer Diogo Ribeiro in 1527, were accepted by the world until the voyage of the Dutchmen Cornelis Schouten and Jacob Le Maire in 1615–17 pioneered the passage round Cape Horn into the Pacific, a change very quickly reflected in maps by Blaeu, Jansson and others.

After the first spectacular journeys across the Continent, development and exploration in the southern part of the New World lost momentum; the Spanish colonies in particular were closed to all but officials and Roman Catholic missions and it was over 200 years before Alexander von Humboldt made his epic journeys in the rain forests of Venezuela following the course of the Orinoco and tributaries of the Amazon, a journey which was recorded in his *Voyage de Humboldt et Bonpland* published in 1805.

The secrecy surrounding the Spanish colonies applied also to mapping, especially of the coastline and harbours, and only on rare occasions did information become available to navigators of other nations. Of

great value to English navigators was a book of rutters – sea charts and sailing directions – captured by Bartholomew Sharpe about 1680, subsequently copied in manuscript form by William Hack and entitled *Waggoner of the Great South Seas* (c. 1682–83).

Leaving aside the very earliest manuscript maps showing America by Juan de la Cosa (1500) and Nicolay Caneiro and Cantino (c. 1502) and the unique copy in the British Library of the Contarini/Rosselli printed map (1506), the earliest maps bearing representations of America, or the name itself, which are likely to come the way of a collector are those of Waldseemüller, Peter Apian, Grynaeus and Münster. These and other maps are listed below but it must be said that although the maps detailed have been chosen in a very general sense to illustrate the development of cartography of the New World, the volume of material available is so great that any choice must be arbitrary. Examples of the work of numerous cartographers are included but the authors are only too well aware that a

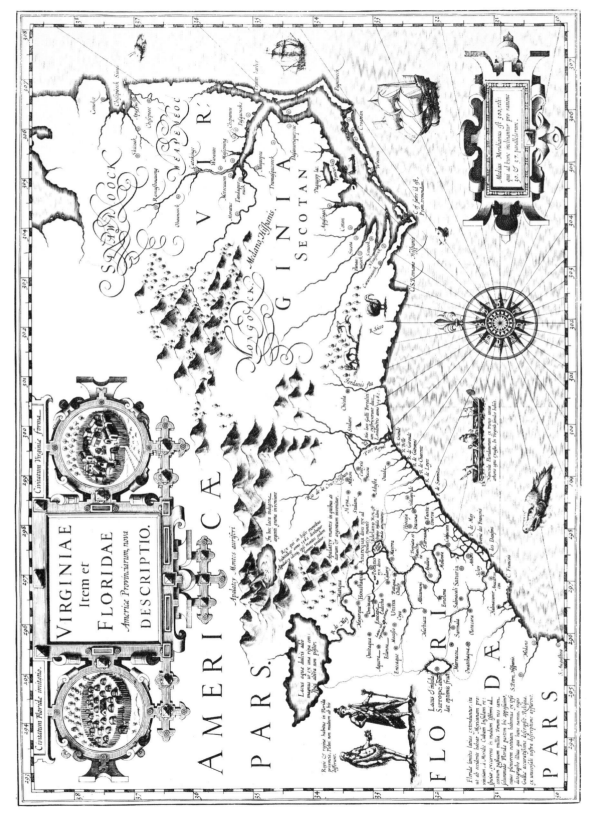

GERARD MERCATOR/JODOCUS HONDIUS *Virginiae item et Floridae* Amsterdam (1606) 1611. One of the most important maps of the region, which influenced the work of other cartographers and publishers for the rest of the century.

number of interesting maps are not even mentioned, especially those in the period 1650–1750, e.g. by Duval, Jaillot, de Wit, Ogilby, Homann, the Visschers and many others. To a great extent the choice has been personal but perhaps more important is the fact that, with one or two exceptions, the maps noted are still available to a collector.

For the Third Edition of this book, the listing of American cartographers has been greatly expanded, and in addition to those listed below on pp. 253–62, a new section on the most important indigenous map makers of the period 1612–*c.* 1800 is to be found in the supplement (pp. 293–300).

A selection of Maps of the Americas

MARTIN WALDSEEMÜLLER

1513–41   Ptolemy's *Geographia*
The 'Admiral's Map' showing the American seaboard and islands
1522 and later: World Map: the earliest map showing the name 'America' which is likely to be available to collectors

PETER APIAN

1524   *Cosmographia*: containing World Map on
and later   heart-shaped projection showing America

BENEDETTO BORDONE

1528–   *Isolario* containing world map on oval
c. 1565   projection showing America

SIMON GRYNAEUS

1532   World Map showing America: an extreme-
and later   ly elegant map

SEBASTIAN MÜNSTER

1540–52   *Geographia*
1544–1628 *Cosmographia*
Münster was the first to introduce separate maps of the Continents; that of the New World is particularly fanciful

GIOVANNI BATTISTA RAMUSIO 1485–1557

c. 1556   Bird's-eye view of Nuova Francia (Canada)
Brazil: highly decorative, showing the Rio de la Plata in the far south

DIEGO GUTIÉRREZ

1562   *Americae sive quartae orbis partis nova et exactissima descriptio*
Map of the Spanish possessions in North America

BOLOGNINO ZALTERIUS

c. 1566   North America with emphasis on Canada and showing the Strait of Anian (very rare)

ABRAHAM ORTELIUS

1570–1612 *Theatrum Orbis Terrarum*
North and South America: particularly splendid map engraved by Frans Hogenberg. Up to 1584 South America is shown with a projecting 'hump' on the western seaboard and Tierra del Fuego is part of the imagined southern continent: California is shown as a peninsula
1589   *Maris Pacifico*: the Pacific Ocean showing the western seaboard with the 'hump' in South America straightened out

THEODORE DE BRY

1590   *Grands Voyages* and *Petits Voyages*
and later   Virginia, based on a manuscript map by John White who accompanied Raleigh's unsuccessful attempt at colonization in 1585
Florida, based on a map made about 1564 by a French artist, Jacques le Moyne, who accompanied a French colonizing expedition
America sive Novus Orbis
A rare and decorative map of the Western Hemisphere showing 'Terra Australis' named 'Magellanica'
Central and South America
One of the most splendid maps by de Bry, first published in 1592

CORNELIS DE JODE

1593   Polar projection showing a short route to Cathay with numerous large islands in the Arctic
Americae Pars Borealis, Florida, Baccala, Canada
One of the earliest detailed maps

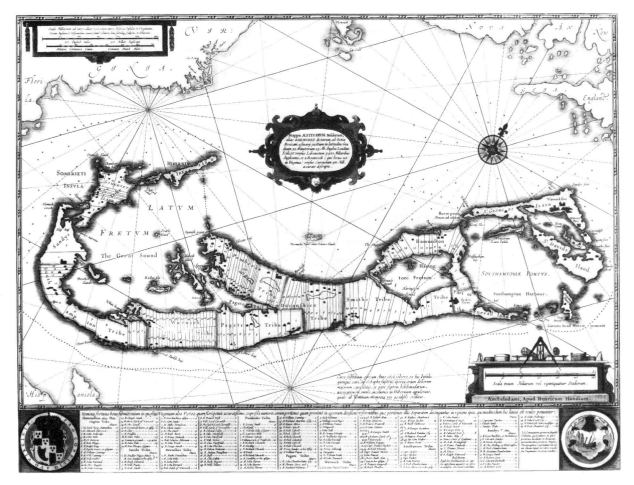

HENRICUS HONDIUS   *Mappa Aestivarum Insularum alias Barmudas* Amsterdam 1630. An elegant map of Bermuda, very similar to one published by Willem Blaeu in the same year but with different decoration.

GERARD MERCATOR

1595 and later	Western Hemisphere with inset maps of Gulf of Mexico, Cuba and Haiti
1606 and later	Hondius/Jansson series Western Hemisphere with a profusion of ships, sea monsters and illustrations of natives
	Virginia and Florida: one of the most beautiful of all regional maps
	America Meridionalis (South America)
1630	Western Hemisphere with decorative borders

JAN VAN LINSCHOTEN

1596 and later	*Itinerario* South America: extremely decorative and fanciful map
	Polar Regions: showing Scandinavia, Greenland and the Strait of Anian

CORNELIS WYTFLIET

1597 and later	*Descriptionis Ptolemaicae augmentum* The first atlas devoted to maps of America: maps of California, as a peninsula, the St Lawrence, Virginia and Quivira and Anian are especially interesting

GABRIEL TATTON

1600–16	Beautifully engraved maps of 'New Spain', California and the Pacific coast, still showing California as a peninsula

JAN JANSSON   *Freti Magellanici*. A decorative but not very accurate map of the Straits of Magellan, first published in Amsterdam in 1630. It describes the Patagonians as 'giants of vast magnitude'.

★ CAPTAIN JOHN SMITH

1612   Virginia: famous map by the Governor of the colony, with Indian tribal names and inset figure of Powhatan – this beautiful map was widely copied for the following half century

Capt. Smith also drew a map of New England, published in 1616

SAMUEL DE CHAMPLAIN

1612   *Nouvelle France*: map of the St Lawrence embellished with drawings of Indians and the flora and fauna of the area

1632   *Nouvelle France*: showing the extent of Champlain's explorations and including the Great Lakes (except Michigan)

HESSEL GERRITSZ/JOHANNES DE LAET

1612   Chart of Henry Hudson's ill-fated voyage into Hudson's Bay

1625   New maps of America in *Nieuwe Wereldt*
and later   by de Laet

PIETER VAN DEN KEERE

1614   *Americae Nova Descriptio*
and later   One of the finest maps of North and South America, the first to be decorated with borders showing costumed figures and town views, an idea much copied by later publishers

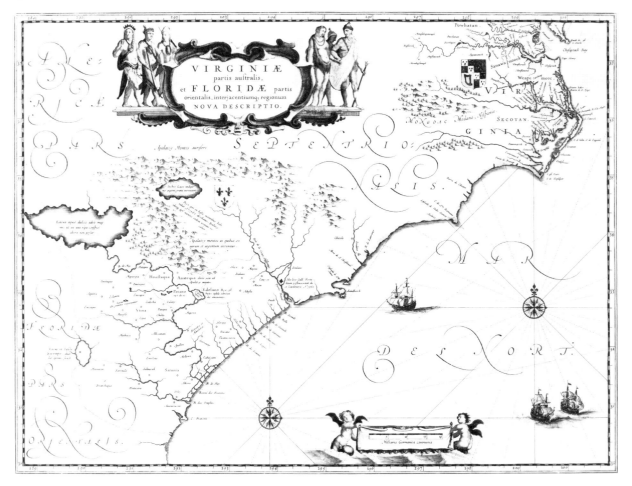

JOAN BLAEU   *Virginiae partis australis et Floridae* . . . Amsterdam 1640–72. One of the many elegantly engraved maps of the Eastern seaboard of North America published by Blaeu or Jansson which influenced other cartographers for most of the seventeenth century.

WILLEM JANSZOON BLAEU

1617
and later

Americae nova Tabula: a beautiful map with decorative borders – the first issue still shows only the Straits of Magellan but from 1618 Tierra del Fuego is shown as an island with Cape Horn, the result of the discoveries of Cornelis Schouten and Jacob La Maire

1635
and later

Nova Belgica and *Anglia Nova*: one of the most beautiful and decorative maps of the time and one of the earliest to chart the coastline accurately – widely copied by later publishers. The later atlases of the Blaeu family contained a very large number of maps of the Western Hemisphere

HENRY BRIGGS

1625

The North part of America: the map, engraved by R. Elstracke, based on Spanish charts which popularized the idea of California as an island, was published in *Purchas his Pilgrimes* by Samuel Purchas

JOHN SPEED

1627
and later

A Prospect of the Most Famous Parts of the World included a fine decorative map of the Western Hemisphere; a much later edition in 1676 included extra maps of Carolina, Jamaica and Barbados, New England and New York, Virginia and Maryland

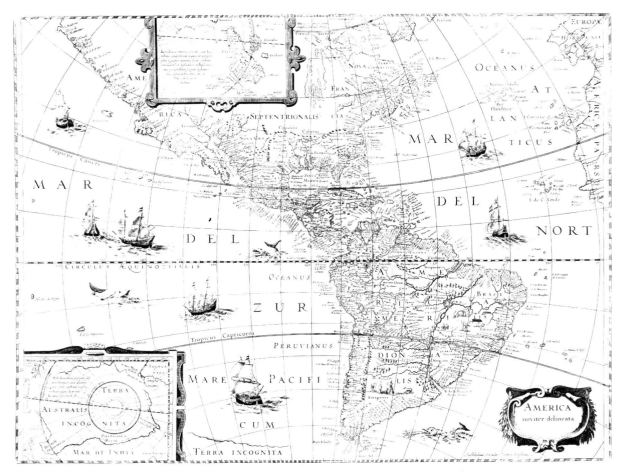

JAN JANSSON   *America noviter delineata.* Published about 1647, this close copy of an earlier Hondius map has interesting insets of the polar regions.

JAN JANSSON

1633
and later

From about this time, Jansson produced numerous maps of the Americas, often very similar to those of Blaeu: of particular note is his map *Nova Anglia Novum Belgium et Virginia* (1636) which was much copied

ROGERT DUDLEY

1646–61   *Dell' Arcano del Mare*
The first printed sea charts of the Virginia coastline and of the western coasts and California

JOHN FARRER

1651   *A Mapp of Virginia*
A map of great interest combining new details about Virginia and Maryland with

the fanciful idea, even then still widely held, that the South Sea was only 'ten days march over the hills'

NICOLAS SANSON

1650   *Amerique Septenrionale*
1656   *Le Canada ou Nouvelle France*
The first maps to show all the Great Lakes
1656   *Le Nouveau Mexique et La Floride*
An important map showing California as an island

PIETER GOOS

c. 1666   *Nova Granada and the Island of California*
Magnificent chart showing the Strait of Anian to the north

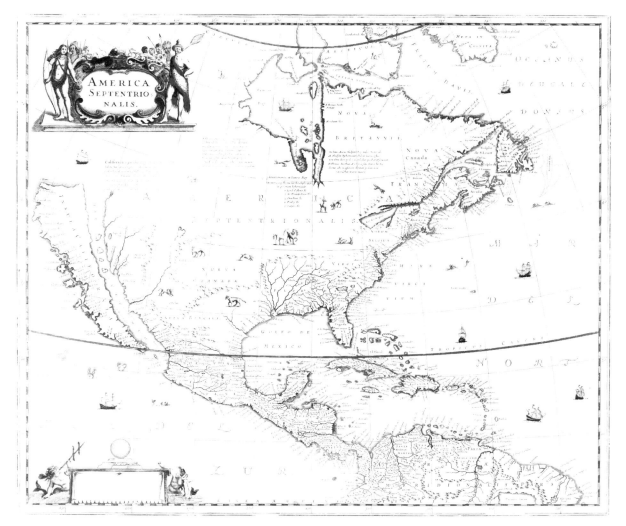

JANSSON-HONDIUS *America Septentrionalis* Amsterdam (1636) *c.* 1666. Decorative map with many interesting notes. California clearly shown as an island, following the lead given by Henry Briggs in 1625.

HUGO ALLARD

1673 *New and Exact Map of All New Netherland* Very decorative map with inset of New Amsterdam issued to celebrate the recapture of the town from the English

JOHN FOSTER 1648–81

1677 *A Map of New-England* The first map, a woodcut, to be printed in America – it was included in an edition of a book by William Hubbard *Narrative of the troubles with the Indians in New England*

LOUIS DE HENNEPIN

1683 *Carte de la Nouvelle France et de la Louisiane*

1697–98 Map of the Great Lakes and the Mississippi Father Hennepin, a Dutch missionary, was associated with the explorer, La Salle, who was the first to follow the course of the Mississippi

VINCENZO CORONELLI

1690 *America Settentrionale* (1688) Splendid representation of the Great Lakes and California as an island

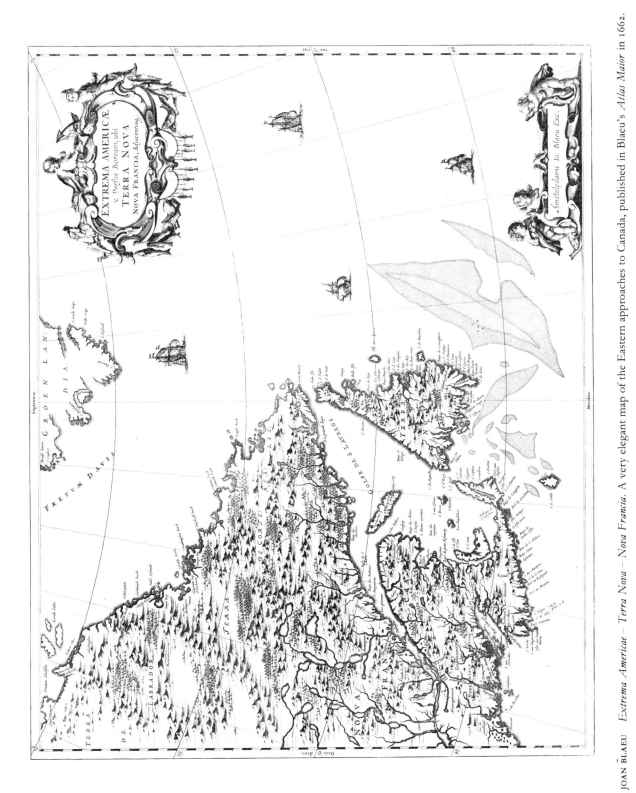

JOAN BLAEU   *Extrema Americae – Terra Nova – Nova Francia.* A very elegant map of the Eastern approaches to Canada, published in Blaeu's *Atlas Maior* in 1662.

GUILLAUME DELISLE

c. 1703   *Carte du Mexique et de la Floride . . . et des Environs de la Riviere de Mississipi*
The first printed map to show in detail the course of the Mississippi and the routes of its explorers

1718   *Carte de la Louisiane et du Cours du Mississipi*
The most influential map of its time, widely copied by Senex, Covens and Mortier, Bellin, Homann and others

HENRI CHÂTELAIN

1705–20   *Atlas Historique*
and later   Containing one of the finest maps of America (4 sheets) surrounded by vignettes and decorative insets

1719   *Carte de la Nouvelle France*
With inset plan and view of Quebec

HERMAN MOLL

1715   *A New and Exact Map of the Dominions of the King of Great Britain on ye Continent of North America* – the 'Beaver' map
A beautifully designed and very popular map

1720   *A Map of North America*
Very decorative map still showing California as an island

★ HENRY POPPLE

1733   *A Map of the British Empire in America with the French and Spanish Settlements adjacent thereto*
The finest and most detailed map of its time consisting of a key map and 20 individual sheets
Re-issued on one sheet by Covens and Mortier, le Rouge and others

JOHN MITCHELL

1755–91   *A Map of the British and French Dominions in North America* (8 sheets)
A most important map re-issued many times, which was used in fixing boundary settlements in the 1782–83 treaty between Great Britain and the United States

★ LEWIS EVANS *c.* 1700–56

1755   *A general Map of the Middle British Colonies in America*

One of the most influential maps of the time with many derivatives: published in London and Philadelphia

DENIS DIDEROT 1713–84

c. 1770   *Carte de la Californie*
Composite map setting out the various stages in the mapping of California from 1604 to 1767

THOMAS JEFFERYS

1775–76   *American Atlas* (published by Sayer and Bennett)
The best-known atlas of its time containing large-scale maps, town plans and James Cook's charts of the St Lawrence, Newfoundland etc.

1775   *West India Atlas* (published by Sayer and Bennett)
Maps of the Caribbean

WILLIAM FADEN

c. 1777   *North American Atlas*

ABEL BUELL 1742–1822

1783–84   *A New and correct Map of the United States of North America*
First map of the United States compiled, engraved and printed by an American: published in New Haven

J. F. W. DES BARRES

1784   *The Atlantic Neptune*
and later   Magnificent collection of charts of the East coasts of America with coloured plates

AARON ARROWSMITH

1795   *New Discoveries in the Interior Parts of North America*

1796   *Map of the United States of America*
Both these maps and others were re-issued many times, being constantly revised as new information became available

CAPTAIN GEORGE VANCOUVER

1798   *Survey of the Pacific coast*
Charts included in *A Voyage of Discovery to the North Pacific Ocean and round the World*

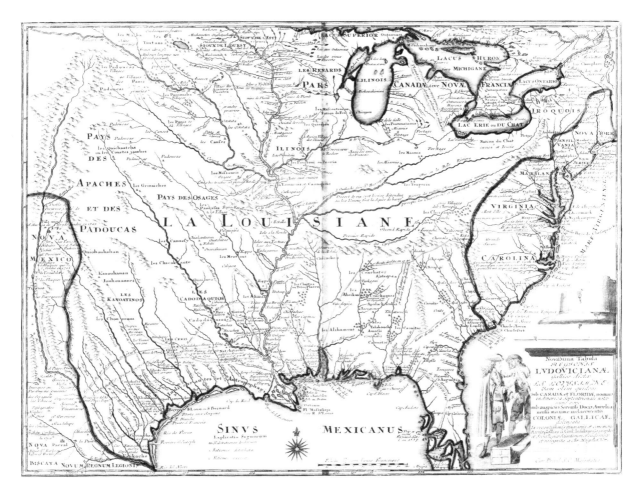

CHRISTOPH WEIGEL   *Novissima Tabula Regionis Ludovicianae* Nuremberg *c.* 1734. Derived from the famous map of Louisiana by Delisle which was the first printed map to show Texas.

ALEXANDER VON HUMBOLDT

1805–14   Maps in *Voyage de Humboldt et Bonpland*

1811–12   *Atlas Géographique et Physique du Royaume de la Nouvelle Espagne*

JAMES WYLD

c. 1824   *Map of North America* (6 sheets)
An important detailed map, re-issued many times to about 1856 with constant revision

TALLIS AND CO

1849–53   *Illustrated Atlas of the World*
Contained many maps of the American Continent: published in London and subsequently in New York

Important Atlases and Maps produced by American cartographers and publishers in the period 1795–c. 1855

MATTHEW CAREY 1760–1839

1795–1809   *The American Atlas*
The first Atlas published in America

1796–   *General Atlas*
c. 1818

1796–1814   *American Pocket Atlas* (8vo)

1817   *Scripture Atlas*
All published in Philadelphia

JEDIDIAH MORSE 1761–1826

1795   *American Geography*: London

further editions in 1825–27

1832–36   *Family Cabinet Atlas*

JOHN REID *fl.* 1796

1796   *The American Atlas*
Published in New York to accompany Wm Winterbotham's *An Historical, Geographical, Commercial and Philosophical View of the United States*

ABRAHAM BRADLEY (JR) *fl.* 1796–1817

1796   *Map of the United States exhibiting the Post Roads etc.*

1797–1804   Separate maps of the Northern and Southern Parts of the United States

---

EDMUND MARCH BLUNT 1770–1862
GEORGE WILLIAM BLUNT 1802–78

1796   *The American Coast Pilot*
c. 1867

1830   Charts of the North and South Atlantic Oceans

★

JOHN MELISH 1771–1822

1813–15   *A Military and Topographical Atlas of the United States*

1816   *Map of the United States with the contiguous British and Spanish Possessions* (wall map)

1822–32   *Map of Pennsylvania*: Philadelphia

FIELDING LUCAS (JR) 1781–*c.* 1852

1814   *A New Elegant General Atlas containing maps of each of the United States* (Samuel Lewis) Baltimore:

1823   *A General Atlas*: Baltimore

★

HENRY SCHENK TANNER 1786–1858

1818–23   *A New American Atlas*

1823–28   *A New Pocket Atlas of the United States*

1828–46   *New Universal Atlas*

1834   *The American Traveller*
These and other atlases published in Philadelphia under the names Tanner and Marshall, and Tanner, Vallance, Kearny and Co.

HENRY CHARLES CAREY 1793–1879
ISAAC LEA 1792–1886

1822   *A Complete historical, chronological, and geographical American Atlas*: Philadelphia
A London edition published in 1823 –

1822–28   (with S. E. Morse) *Modern Atlas*: Boston and New York

---

★

SIDNEY EDWARDS MORSE 1794–1871

1823   *Atlas of the United States*

1825   *A New Universal Atlas of the World*

1842–45   (with Samuel Breese) *Cerographic Atlas of the United States* – maps produced by means of new wax engraving technique: New Haven

---

ANTHONY FINLEY *fl.* 1824–*c.* 1840

1824–33   *A new General Atlas*: Philadelphia

1826   *A New American Atlas*: Philadelphia

ROBERT MILLS 1781–1855

1825–38   *Atlas of the State of South Carolina*: Baltimore, the first state atlas produced in the United States

---

DAVID H. BURR 1803–75

1829–38   *An Atlas of the State of New York*

1835   *Universal Atlas*: New York

1839   *The American Atlas, exhibiting the Post Roads (etc.) of the United States*
Published by J. Arrowsmith, London, the maps bearing Arrowsmith's name

---

SAMUEL AUGUSTUS MITCHELL 1792–1868

1835   *Travellers Guide through the United States* (J. H. Young): Philadelphia

1839   *Atlas of Outline Maps*: Philadelphia

1846–   *New Universal Atlas*: Philadelphia
c. 1890

THOMAS GAMALIEL BRADFORD 1802–87

1835   *A Comprehensive Atlas*: Boston and New York

1838   *An illustrated atlas of the United States and the Adjacent Countries*: Philadelphia

1842   *A Universal illustrated Atlas*: Boston

★

JOSEPH HUTCHINS COLTON 1800–93
GEORGE WOOLWORTH COLTON 1827–1901

1855   (J. H. Colton) *World Atlas*

1855   (G. W. Colton) *Atlas of America*: J. H. Colton and Co., New York
The Colton family produced a large number of maps and atlases until the end of the nineteenth century

Specialist References

CUMMING, W. P., *The South East in Early Maps*
Although covering a particular area of America, the information given here is of the greatest interest in considering all early American maps

PHILLIPS, P. L., *A List of Geographical Atlases in the Library of Congress*
As nearly a complete list of maps of America (among others) that it is possible to compile

SCHWARTZ, S. I., and EHRENBERG, R. E., *The Mapping of America*

THEATRUM ORBIS TERRARUM NV
Wyfliet: *Descriptionis Ptolemaicae Augmentum*, 1597
Jefferys: *The American Atlas*, 1775–76
Reproductions of complete atlases

TOOLEY, R. V., *The Mapping of America*
This volume and *Landmarks of Map Making* (below) give an immense amount of detailed information on maps of America

TOOLEY, R. V., BRICKER, C. and CRONE, G. R., *Landmarks of Map Making*
Apart from the general historical portion of the book, the chapters on the Continents are particularly interesting and informative

AFRICA

Being part of the Mediterranean world, the northern coasts of the African continent as far as the Straits of Gibraltar and even round to the area of the Fortunate Isles (the Canaries) were reasonably well known and quite accurately mapped from ancient times. In particular, Egypt and the Nile Valley were well defined and the Nile itself was, of course, one of the rivers separating the continents in medieval T-O maps. Through Arab traders the shape of the east coast, down the Red Sea as far as the equator, was also known but detail shown in the interior faded into deserts with occasional mountain ranges and mythical rivers. The southern part of the continent, in the Ptolemaic tradition, was assumed to curve to the east to form a land-locked Indian Ocean. The voyages of the Portuguese, organized by Henry the Navigator in the fifteenth century, completely changed the picture and by the end of the century Vasco da Gama had rounded the Cape enabling cartographers to draw a quite presentable coastal outline of the whole continent, even if the interior was to remain largely unknown for the next two or three centuries.

The first separately printed map of Africa (as with the other known continents) appeared in Münster's *Geographia* from 1540 onwards and the first atlas devoted to Africa only was published in 1588 in Venice by Livio Sanuto, but the finest individual map of the century was that engraved on 8 sheets by Gastaldi, published in Venice in 1564. Apart from maps in sixteenth-century atlases generally there were also magnificent marine maps of 1596 by Jan van Linschoten (engraved by van Langrens) of the southern half of the continent with highly imaginative and decorative detail in the interior. In the next century there were many attractive maps including those of Mercator/Hondius (1606), Speed (1627), Blaeu (1630), Visscher (1636), de Wit (*c.* 1670), all embellished with vignettes of harbours and principal towns and bordered with elaborate and colourful figures of their inhabitants, but the interior remained uncharted with the exception of that part of the continent known as Ethiopia, the name which was applied to a wide area including present-day Abyssinia. Here the legends of Prester John lingered on and, as so often happened in other remote parts of the world, the only certain knowledge of the region was provided by Jesuit missionaries. Among these was Father Gerónimo Lobo (1595–1678), whose work *A Voyage to Abyssinia* was used as the basis for a remarkably accurate map published by a German scholar, Hiob Ludolf in 1683. Despite the formidable problems which faced them, the French cartographers G. Delisle (*c.* 1700–22), J. B. B. d'Anville (1727–49) and N. Bellin (1754) greatly improved the standards of mapping of the continent, improvements which were usually, although not always, maintained by Homann, Seutter, de la Rochette, Bowen, Faden and many others in the later years of the century.

Thereafter, in broad terms, the story of cartography in Africa in the nineteenth century is the story of the search for the sources of the great rivers, the Nile – and the lakes associated with it –, the Niger, the Congo and the Zambesi, to which may be added the quota of knowledge provided by missionaries of many nationalities and by the Voortrekkers in South Africa.

The results of these explorations, the naming of

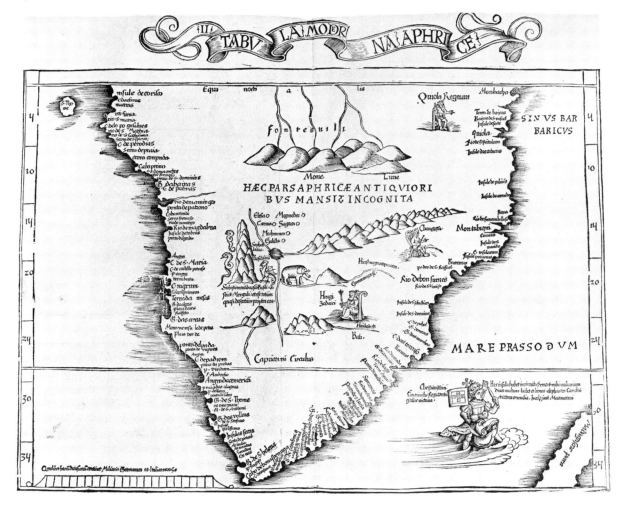

MARTIN WALDSEEMÜLLER *Tabula Moderna Aphrice* Strassburg (1522) 1525. This map, included in a new edition of Waldseemüller's Ptolemaic atlas, first issued in 1513, was revised by Laurent Fries with the inclusion of decorative but geographically inaccurate detail from earlier maps. In spite of its inaccuracies in the interior, it was an important map, which influenced cartographers for a century or more.

newly discovered lakes, rivers and mountain ranges, the establishment of new settlements, were soon recorded on maps which appeared in constantly revised editions by such publishers as Cary, Arrowsmith, the Wylds, and Tallis and Co. in London, Thomson and Co. in Edinburgh, Levasseur, P. and A. Lapié, Brué in France, and Vandermaelen in Brussels.

Specialist References

THEATRUM ORBIS TERRARUM NV
Sanuto: *Geografia dell' Africa*, 1588

Reproduction of complete atlas

TOOLEY, R. V., *Collector's Guide to Maps of the African Continent and Southern Africa*
Invaluable reference book to maps of the Continent
— *Maps and Map Makers*

TOOLEY, R. V., BRICKER, C. and CRONE, G. R., *Landmarks of Map Making*
The chapters in this book on the Continents are particularly interesting and informative

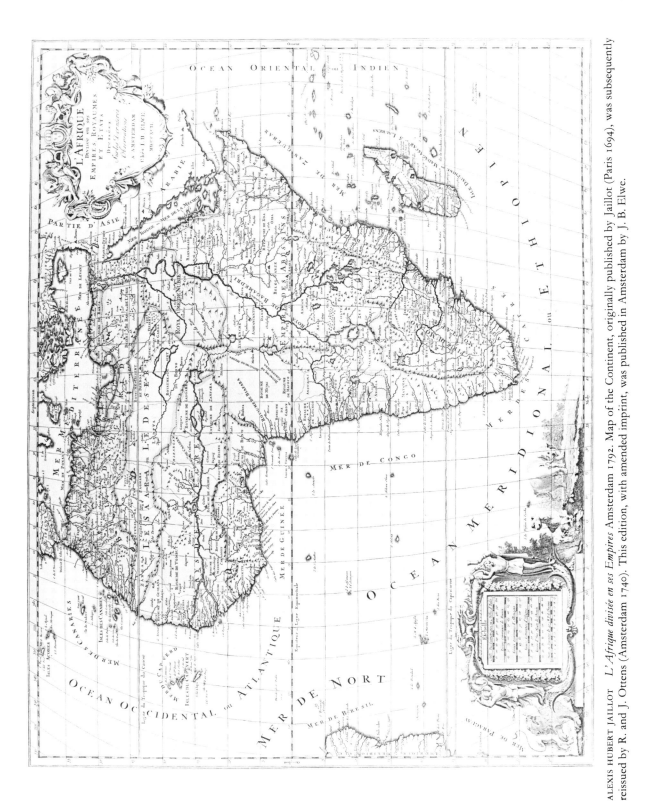

ALEXIS HUBERT JAILLOT   *L'Afrique divisée en ses Empires* Amsterdam 1792. Map of the Continent, originally published by Jaillot (Paris 1694), was subsequently reissued by R. and J. Ottens (Amsterdam 1740). This edition, with amended imprint, was published in Amsterdam by J. B. Elwe.

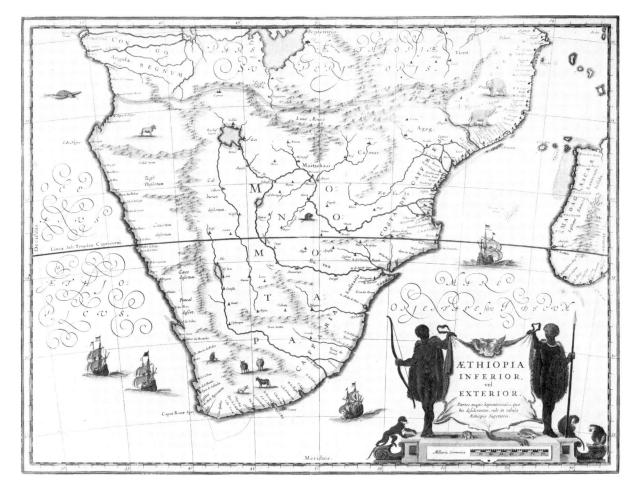

JOAN BLAEU *Aethiopia Inferior vel Exterior* Amsterdam 1635. Considered to be the finest map of Southern Africa of its time; much copied by other publishers until the end of the seventeenth century. Continued use of Portuguese names on the coastline betrays the map's origins from the old nautical charts used by the early explorers.

ASIA

Although Arabia, Persia, the Silk Road to China and those parts of Northern India conquered by Alexander the Great were known to the classical world, it was not until the year AD 1375 that a map giving some idea of the real shape and size of the Continent was compiled. This was the famous Catalan Map, based on reports of Franciscan missionaries and the writings of Marco Polo. A century or so later, in the first Ptolemaic atlases, there were altogether 12 maps of Asia which, of course, revealed no more or less than Ptolemy's view of the ancient world, but in the expanded Waldseemüller editions of 1513 and 1522 there were 'modern' regional

maps including much information from Marco Polo's travels. Later sixteenth-century maps continued to show many of the distorted outlines copied from Ptolemy although by this time India, Ceylon and the Indies were gaining a more recognizable shape. Münster was again the first publisher to print a separate map of the Continent and later Ortelius issued the first separately printed maps of China (1584) and Japan (1595). In the next century highly decorative maps of the Continent were published by van den Keere (1614), Speed (1627), Blaeu (1630), de Wit (1660), Visscher (*c.* 1680) and others too numerous to list.

Perhaps because the vast areas of the continent made it difficult to include interesting detail on general maps,

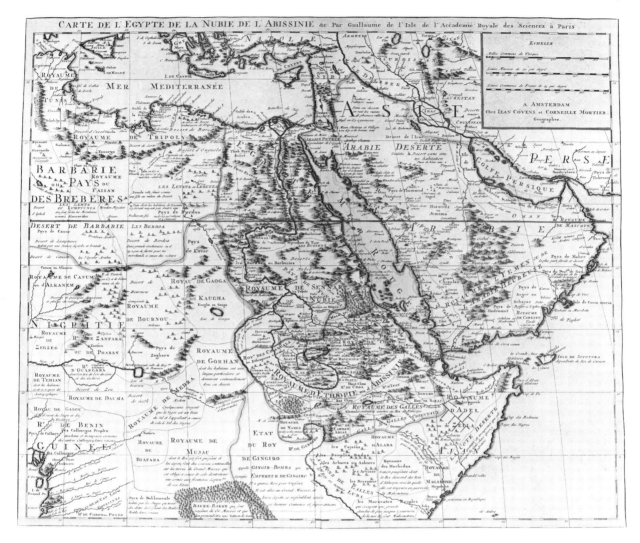

GUILLAUME DELISLE   *Carte de l'Egypte de la Nubie de l'Abissinie* Amsterdam 1735. This edition of a very elegant map of the Middle East by the noted French cartographer, G. Delisle, was issued by the Dutch publishers, Covens and Mortier.

it is usually found that maps of the major regions, e.g. Muscovy, Tartary, China, Japan, India and the Holy Land make a greater appeal to most collectors. The Ortelius and Mercator maps, especially, of these countries are all fascinating examples of the beliefs of the time, not only in their geographical content but also in their decoration, recording the customs and habits of little-known lands.

A brief outline of the history of map making in the more important countries of Asia is given in the following paragraphs.

China

In contrast to the history of the mapping of America, Africa and India where European influence was all-important, the story in China is a different matter altogether and the first maps appeared there long before those in Europe. It seems that the whole of China and its regions had been mapped in some form as far back as 1100 BC but, as in Europe, cartographic development had an uneven growth. Almost 100 years after Ptolemy produced his *Geographia* in Alexandria,

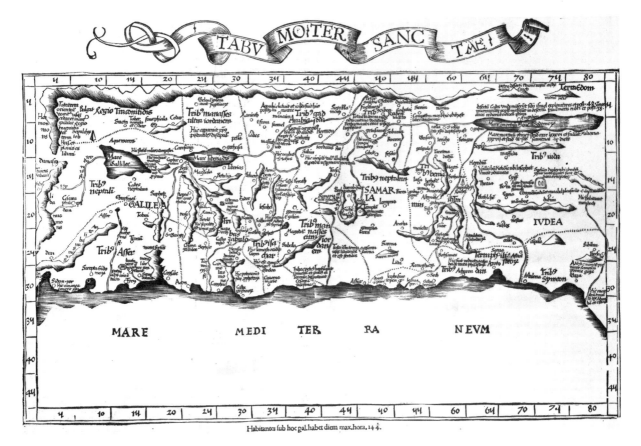

MARTIN WALDSEEMÜLLER   *Tabula Moderna Terra Sanctae* Strassburg (1522) 1525. Derived from a map by Pietro Vesconte, a Genoan cartographer working in Venice in the early fourteenth century, this map has East at the top as is often the case with maps of the Holy Land.

and about the same time as the invention of paper in China, an 18-sheet map of that country was made by P'ei Hsui (AD 224–71) who was the first recorded Chinese map maker of note. This map has not survived, nor have others which followed it, but two engraved on stone in the twelfth century are still in existence.

In the following century the remarkable journeys of Marco Polo between the years 1271 and 1295 and his predecessors, Carpini (1245), Rubruquis (1252) and other Franciscan missionaries renewed the contacts between Europe and China which had existed in nebulous form long before Ptolemy's day. Although Marco Polo was not in the usual sense a cartographer, the account of his travels enabled scholars to revise their ideas of the shape of Cathay and the myriad islands of the Indies. Later still, in the sixteenth and seventeenth centuries new generations of missionaries,

especially the Jesuits, following in the wake of Portuguese explorers and traders, exerted a considerable influence on Chinese map making. Certain names have already been mentioned elsewhere: Father Matteo Ricci who compiled the first European map of the world printed and circulated in China (1584–1602); Ludovico Georgio (Jorge de Barbuda), whose map of China was used by Ortelius (1584) and subsequently by other Dutch publishers; Father Martino Martini, an Italian Jesuit who compiled the first European atlas of China, the *Atlas Sinensis* (1655), which was used by Blaeu and others, J. B. du Halde's *Description Géographique de la Chine* (1735) used in 1737 by J. B. d'Anville in his *Nouvel Atlas de la Chine*. Other maps, usually based on those mentioned above, were issued by all the cartographers and publishers we have named so often, Mercator, Speed, Blaeu, Jansson, Sanson and so on.

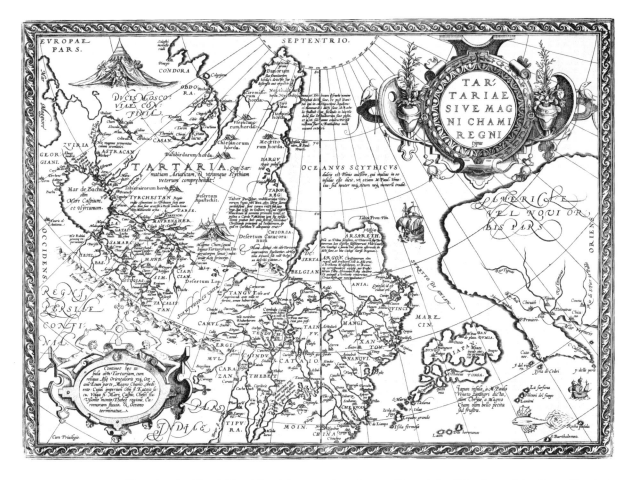

ABRAHAM ORTELIUS   *Tartariae sive Magni Chami Regni* Antwerp (1570) 1598. Map of the 'Kingdom of the Great Khan'. An important map, much copied by other cartographers, still showing California as a peninsula.

Japan

In Japan the history of map-making covers a shorter, though still considerable, span of time. As early as the seventh century AD the Japanese acquired knowledge of surveying and map engraving through their cultural links with Korea and China; their earliest surviving map dates from the fourteenth century. The first uncertain attempts to show Japan on European maps were not made until the mid fifteenth century (Fra Mauro, 1459) and even in 1540 Münster's map of the New World still shows 'Zipangu' and the 7,448 Spice Islands of Marco Polo, but as in China, Jesuit influence was responsible for providing the first reasonably accurate map of the country which was compiled by Ludovico Teixeira (1592). This was used by Ortelius

and later by Hondius, Jansson and others as the basis for their maps of the country.

From 1640 Japan closed its frontiers (except the Port of Nagasaki) to the 'barbarians' from the West and consequently there was little opportunity for compiling more accurate maps but over the years there was a noticeable improvement on maps generally in the orientation of the country in relation to mainland China and Korea. Maps by a French Jesuit, Père Briet (1650), Schenk and Valck (*c.* 1700) and Robert de Vaugondy (*c.* 1750) all showed a better outline than their predecessors. Interesting maps of the country using names in Japanese characters as well as their westernized forms and a plan of Nagasaki were published by Johann Scheuchzer, a Swiss scholar, in 1727. These were based on the work of a German,

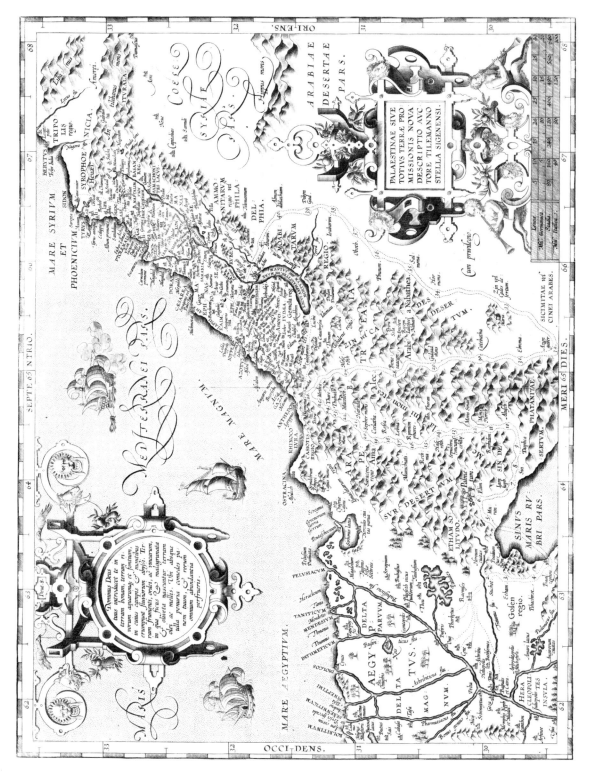

ABRAHAM ORTELIUS   *Palaestinae sive totius Terrae Promissionis (Typus Chorographicus)* Antwerp (1570) 1595. The first of three maps of the Holy Land by Ortelius issued in many variants.

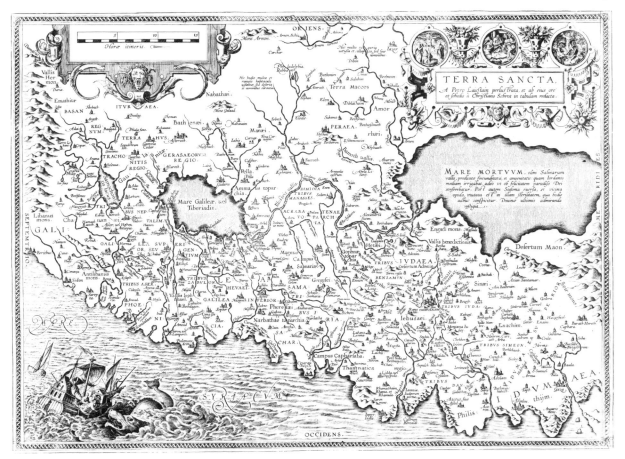

ABRAHAM ORTELIUS *Terra Sancta* Antwerp (1584) 1606. A beautifully engraved map of the Holy Land, again with East at the top. Jonah and the Whale are depicted in the lower left corner. The scale is shown in 'Hours of travel'.

Engelbert Kaempfer, who spent some time in the 'open' port of Nagasaki in the service of the Dutch East India Co. In the isolationist period, maps of Japan by the Japanese themselves were numerous, accurate and highly artistic but it was not until the end of the eighteenth century, and indeed well into the nineteenth, that European maps could be compiled with complete accuracy.

India

Maps of India, much distorted in shape, appear in most world atlases from the time of Ptolemy, the earliest usually showing India as a relatively small extension of Southern Asia, dominated by the very large island of Taprobana (Ceylon). In later sixteenth-century maps de Jode, Ortelius and Mercator gave a much improved outline of both lands but India was still shown too small in relation to the whole continent. Most publishers in the seventeenth century continued to issue maps but with little improvement in detail until about 1719 when a French Jesuit priest, Father Jean Bouchet, compiled an accurate map of South India, subsequently used by G. Delisle (1723), Homann Heirs (1735) and by J. B. B. d'Anville, then the French East India Company's cartographer, as the basis for his greatly improved maps in 1737 and 1752.

In the next decade Alexander Dalrymple published a collection of newly surveyed coastal charts and plans of ports and, about the same time, in 1764, James Rennell, a young British Army officer who showed a remarkable aptitude for surveying, was appointed – at the age of 21 – Surveyor General of Bengal; he immediately set in motion a comprehensive survey of the Company's lands, subsequently publishing maps of Bengal and

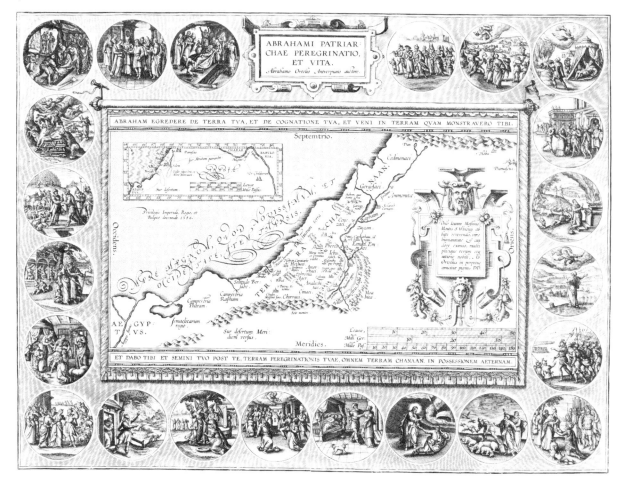

ABRAHAM ORTELIUS *Abrahami Patriarchae Peregrinatio, et vita* Antwerp (1590) 1595. The last of three Ortelius maps of the Holy Land, showing the wanderings of the Tribes of Israel.

other provinces which eventually formed *The Bengal Atlas* (1779). His other works included a *Map of Hindoustan* (1782–85) and *The Provinces of Delhi, Agra etc and the Indian Peninsula* (1788–94). These maps by Rennell provided the basis for a Trigonometrical Survey of India which was initiated in 1802 and for splendid maps published in London by Cary, the Arrowsmiths (1804–22) and the Wylds.

The Holy Land

Although the Holy Land may be regarded geographically as part of Asia, its proximity to Europe provided a quite different background where map making was

concerned. It was very much part of Ptolemy's world and there is no shortage of maps in the editions of his 'atlases' from 1477 onwards. From the earliest days of Christianity religious pilgrimages to Jerusalem were frequent, culminating in the mass movements of the Crusades, but records are scanty; such maps as have survived are predominantly religious in conception with Jerusalem at the centre of the world as in the Hereford World Map (*c.* 1300) or in the form of 'itineraries' such as Bernhard von Breydenbach's *Sanctarum Peregrinationum* (1486). In Palestine itself, at Madaba, there exist the remains of the famous multi-coloured tesserae 'map', laid down in the sixth century, which depicts a plan view of Jerusalem and other geographical features of the Eastern Mediterranean.

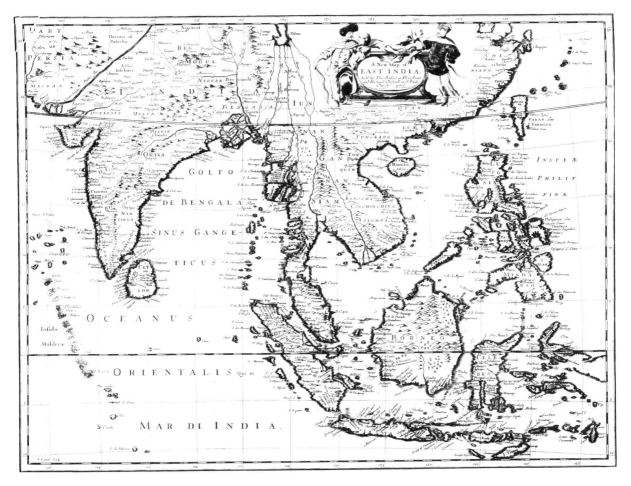

JOHN SPEED   *A New Map of East India.* One of the seven additional maps included in the final edition of Speed's *Prospect of the Most Famous Parts of the World* published by Bassett and Chiswell in 1676

In the sixteenth century, apart from the Ptolemaic maps and the world maps with Jerusalem at the centre such as Heinrich Bünting's 'clover-leaf' map it was not unusual to find printed editions of the Bible containing maps of the Holy Land. A famous example known as the Polyglot Bible by a Spanish theologian, Benedictus Arias Montanus, was published in Antwerp by Plantin in 1571–72 and, in the following year, another published in London contained a map by Humphrey Cole which is claimed to be the first map engraved by an Englishman. From then onwards maps by Ortelius appeared in their various versions in 1570, 1584 and 1590, by de Jode (1578), C. van Adrichom (*c.* 1584), Speed (*Canaan*, 1611–76, in a number of versions), Blaeu (1629), Jansson (*c.* 1658), Visscher (*c.* 1659), Dapper (*c.* 1677), de Wit (1680) and many others.

Specialist References

BAGROW, L., *History of Cartography*

CRONE, G. R., *Maps and their Makers*

GOLE, S., *Early Maps of India*

NATIONAL MARITIME MUSEUM, Catalogue of the Library: Volume 3

TOOLEY, R. V., *Maps and Map Makers*

TOOLEY, R. V., BRICKER, C. and CRONE, G. R., *Landmarks of Map Making*
Contains details of many early maps of the Continent

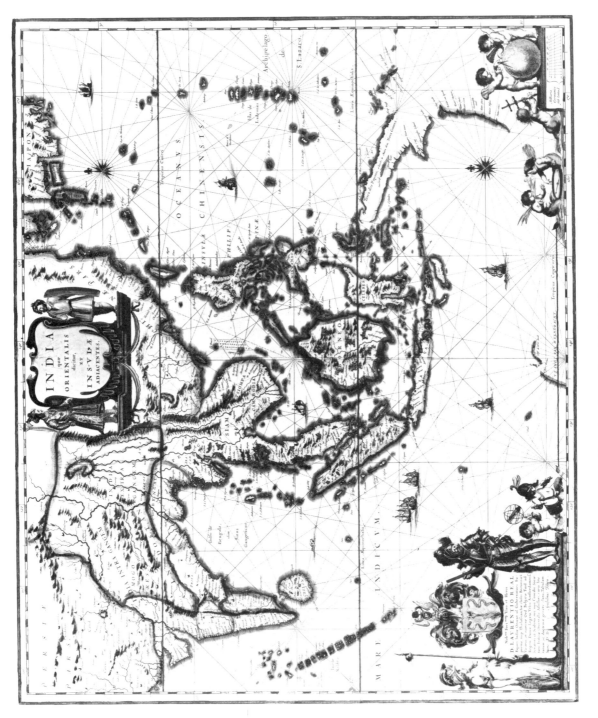

WILLEM BLAEU   *India quae orientalis dicitur et insulae adiacentes.* Published in Amsterdam in 1636, this map appeared in many editions of the Blaeu atlases: the first popular map to show the early discoveries in Australia.

AUSTRALASIA

Australia

In the history of cartography nothing underlines more profoundly the influence of Ptolemy and the Greek mathematicians and geographers before him than the plain fact that the existence of a New World across the Atlantic was never even contemplated by their successors, whereas the possible existence of a Southern Continent was a source of constant speculation for 1,500 years or more. Admittedly, in medieval times, enthusiasm for the idea of a populated world below the equator waned in the face of religious scepticism and ridicule but by the fifteenth and sixteenth centuries the successful voyages of the Portuguese into the Southern Hemisphere brought about a revival of interest in the ancient theories.

Late in the sixteenth century the Portuguese, Spanish and Dutch explorers, looking for guidance at their world maps and charts, must often have suspected the existence of a land mass lying in the Pacific somewhere to the south of the Dutch Indies, and it is more than likely that the northern shores of Australia had been sighted a number of times even though no record of a landing has come down to us. Indeed, some maps, especially those by members of the Dieppe School, among whom were Jean Rotz (later chart maker to Henry VIII) and Pierre Descelier, give a clear indication as early as 1542–46 of such a land area. Other maps by Ortelius (1570), Arias Montanus (1571) and Cornelis de Jode (1593) add their support, albeit uncertainly, to the notion of an undiscovered continent. By the end of the century the Portuguese and Spanish had exhausted their efforts and it was finally a pinnace of the Dutch East India Company from Java, the *Duyfken*, which in 1605–06 sailed into the Gulf of Carpentaria to make the first recorded landfall in Terra Australis, later to become known as the Land of Eendracht after another Dutch ship which made a landing in 1616, and later still to be called New Holland. These discoveries were recorded by Hessel Gerritsz on charts dated 1627–28, by Philipp Eckebrecht on a world map of 1630, by Henricus Hondius in 1630–33, by Jan Jansson in 1633 on a map which shows 'Duyfken's Eyland' to the south of New Guinea, and by Willem Blaeu in 1636. The first chart by an Englishman showing the northern coastline is that of Robert Dudley from *Dell' Arcano del Mare* (1646–61).

Until the results of Tasman's discoveries in his voyages of 1642–44 became available most map publishers continued to issue maps such as those mentioned above showing vague outlines of the northern shores of the Continent, with perhaps a dozen names or so. Even after Tasman it could not be claimed that any of the maps of the time were very informative, but Joan Blaeu's map of 1648 was an improvement on that of 1636. There was not much to show, of course, except an extension of the coastal outlines and French geographers, particularly, were adept at supplying imaginary detail, although Thévenot published in Paris in 1663 a sparse and elegant map showing all the western half of the Continent with a hint of New Zealand. A close copy of that map was engraved by Emanuel Bowen for publication in 1744 in Harris's *Collection of Voyages*. New Guinea, Tasmania and New Zealand were not infrequently shown as part of the main continental land mass but gradually knowledge and accuracy improved; the voyages of Dampier in 1686–91 and 1699, of Cook between 1768 and 1778, Flinders in 1801–03 and the French explorers Comte de la Pérouse and Louis de Freycinet and others ensured that the coastal outline at least was acceptably mapped, but still the interior remained a void well into the nineteenth century. In consequence, even up to about the year 1800 there were few separate maps of Australia and the continent was usually included as part of, or an extension of, the East Indies.

After that date the most interesting and the most sought after maps are those showing the early development of the separate states usually published in London. Apart from those by the major publishers, Cary, Arrowsmith, Wyld and Tallis, there were others by less well-known names:

JOHN BOOTH (*c.* 1801–10)
A New and accurate map of New South Wales
Plan of the Settlements in New South Wales

MATTHEW CAREY (1817)
A new and accurate map of New South Wales: Philadelphia

JOHN OXLEY (1818–25)
Charts of the Interior of New South Wales

GEORGE EVANS (1822)
Description of Van Diemen's Land

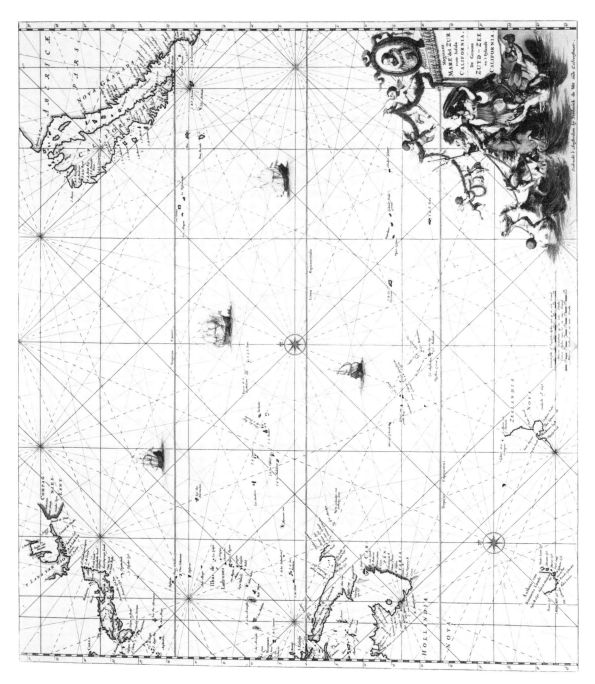

FREDERICK DE WIT *Mare del Zur cum Insula California.* De Wit's beautifully engraved map of the Pacific issued *c.* 1680 in Amsterdam makes an interesting comparison with Coronelli's map of the same area published in 1696.

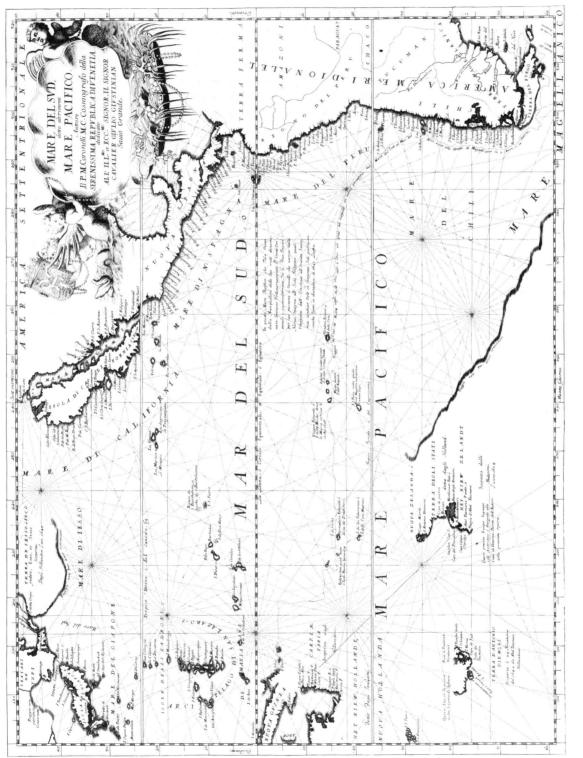

VINCENZO CORONELLI   *Mare del Sud . . . Mare Pacifico.* First published in Venice in 1696, this splendid map of the Pacific shows the early discoveries in Australia and New Zealand as well as illustrating California as an island.

SDUK (1833–59)
Maps of New South Wales and the other states when they became independent

T. L. MITCHELL (1834)
Map of New South Wales

T. HAM (1856)
Map of Queensland
These in turn were gradually superseded by official surveys and by the work of local publishers.

New Zealand

Although New Zealand was certainly populated by Polynesian peoples many centuries ago, the first Europeans known to have seen the islands were the seamen of Tasman's expedition in 1642 during which Tasmania was also discovered. From about 1646 when Blaeu showed the new discoveries on a world map for the first time, there was controversy about the separate existence of the islands and another century passed before James Cook surveyed the coastline and disposed of any argument that New Zealand might be part of the Australian continent. Cook's charts published in the period 1773–80 naturally had a wide circulation and were extensively copied by French, German and Italian cartographers and publishers among whom were Rigobert Bonne/Nicolas Desmaret (1787), Antonio Zatta (1775–85) and G. M. Cassini (1792–1801). For many years after Cook's voyages the British Government took only a passing interest in the islands and the main contribution to improved knowledge of the coastline was made by French expeditions, notably in 1822, 1827 and 1840 under command of Dumont d'Urville whose later accounts of his voyages included many fine maps.

After 1840, when organized settlement began, the demand for better maps was met first by the private publications of firms such as the Arrowsmiths, the Wylds, and Tallis and Co., eventually augmented and then gradually replaced by official surveys of the interior and detailed charting of the coastline by survey ships of the Royal Navy.

It might be thought that building up a more or less complete collection of maps of New Zealand would be relatively easy but this is far from being the case and even maps issued after 1850 are difficult to find.

Specialist References

SCHILDER, G., *Australia Unveiled*
A most detailed account of the early Dutch maps of Australia

TOOLEY, R. V., *The Mapping of Australia*
Detailed descriptions of a very large number of maps of Australia

TOOLEY, R. V., BRICKER, C. and CRANE, G. R., *Landmarks of Map Making*

EUROPE

All the atlases by the well-known sixteenth-century cartographers, such as Münster, Mercator and Ortelius, contained maps of Europe in one form or another. There were, of course, many others by, for example, Bordone, Gastaldi, de Jode, Waghenaer and Hondius, to name only a few, which are now becoming very rare and which a collector would count himself lucky to find. The greater output of publishers in the next century presents the collector with wider opportunities; more atlases by Dutch, French and English cartographers, often in numerous editions, mean that far more copies have survived and although it cannot be said that they are readily available, most dealers will have a good selection from time to time. Moreover, maps of the seventeenth century such as those by Speed, Blaeu, Jansson, Sanson and Jaillot, frequently embellished with decorative borders and vignettes, are often more attractive than issues of earlier years.

By the eighteenth century the range becomes wider still and, apart from the tremendous output by French and English publishers, includes issues by the Germans Homann, Seutter and Lotter and the Italians Rizzi-Zannoni, Zatta and G. M. Cassini, so that a collector has an extremely wide base on which to build a collection.

Specialist References

BAGROW, L., *History of Cartography*

TOOLEY, R. V., *Maps and Map Makers*

TOOLEY, R. V., BRICKER, C. and CRONE, G. R., *Landmarks of Map Making*

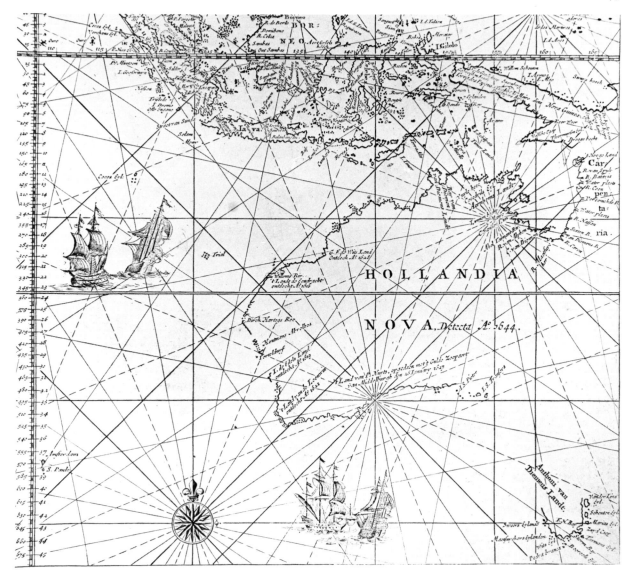

JOANNES VAN KEULEN   *Oost Indien* (Detail) Amsterdam (1680) *c.* 1689. Chart of the East Indies giving a splendid representation of the Australian Continent – Hollandia Nova, as it was then known – with New Guinea still attached to the mainland, and Anthoni van Diemens Landt, later to be known as Tasmania.

Part III

MAP COLLECTING

Chapter 21

BUYING MAPS & FORMING A COLLECTION

'How do I know I am buying an original map?'
'How can the map you are selling me be an "original" when you have another one exactly the same in stock?'
'How do I know it isn't a reproduction?'

In the nature of things many map purchasers are first-time buyers to whom antique maps simply make a visual and perhaps local appeal and these questions, among many which dealers are asked, are indeed understandable, especially when we think of current prices; none of us likes to be 'taken for a ride'. In fact, the more we probe into the subject the more questions, many of them affecting the value of a map, arise, so let us set some of them out and suggest some answers.

What is an original map?

In Chapter 2 we have given a brief outline of early methods used for printing maps but, having done that, we have still to decide when a map is 'original'. One would be tempted to say that only the manuscript map from which the engraver made the block or plate could be considered an original. In the case of a painting there would be no doubt about it but, in the map trade, from the earliest times, a print made from a particular woodblock or copper plate has been regarded as an 'original' and until that block or plate was destroyed 'originals' could be printed from it.

Different editions – alterations to blocks or plates. How can you date maps?

Having agreed the definition of an 'original' map we are immediately led to subsidiary but much more difficult questions. A printing block or plate might well be in use for a century or more and detail could obviously be added or deleted; the plates themselves might pass from the original publisher to others who made their own alterations and issues; some copies might be issued coloured and others left plain black and white. It will be readily understood that as today, it was necessary for map publishers to keep their products up to date as new discoveries were made or new geographical information became available. Generally publishers were not noted for their initiative in this direction, but even so, reference to a few of the biographies in Part II will show that most atlases and maps were re-issued, some once or twice, others often a dozen times or more. Dating an atlas from a title page is usually straightforward (although even here dates of successive editions were not always altered) but our problems begin when individual maps are sold separately. Essentially the purchaser has to rely on his own knowledge and on the reputation of the seller, although certain details can be checked without too much difficulty. If the impression is strong and clear, the map could be from an early edition; a weak impression would probably indicate the opposite. Geographical evidence can be a useful guide to dating, i.e. new discoveries being shown. Watermarks offer some help but batches of paper were often in use for a long time, sometimes forty or fifty years! Alterations to text, publisher's names, heraldic devices or cartouches can all have an important bearing on dating. In considering some or all of the above points it should be remembered that most dealers have available specialist works in which may be found details of maps in various editions with their distinguishing characteristics, and although the process of tracking down precise detail is often laborious, no one can be blamed for wishing to know exactly what he is buying. For examples of long-running series of maps illustrating these points the reader need only refer to those of Christopher Saxton and John Speed.

Condition

As with all antiques, whether furniture, china, paintings or maps, condition is important and obviously a collector having decided on a purchase should buy a map in the best obtainable condition. The ideal map, coloured or uncoloured, should have a strong, clear impression with wide margins, be printed on good quality watermarked handmade paper of the right size, free from foxing, water stains, worm holes or repair (except perhaps to the centre fold or outside the printed surface), with an undoubted date and provenance. Plenty of such maps exist of course, but our advice here implies that the buyer is offered a choice; it would be a fortunate occurrence indeed to be offered a choice of two Münster maps of America, two Blaeu world maps or two van Keulen charts, and so, more often than not, the decision depends on the collector's urge (and pocket) to possess a particular map, perhaps irrespective of condition. After all, if a map is one of only three or four known copies, who is going to reject it, even if it has damage to the centre fold – especially if it happens to be the very last map to complete a collection! Paper is a comparatively fragile medium and obviously maps printed three or more centuries ago will generally have suffered some damage, so the collector should expect to be asked to pay a premium for flawless maps.

Rarity

At this point our collector may well ask in what quantities maps were printed; if there were so many re-issues it is hard to understand the rarity on which so much emphasis seems to be placed.

As to the numbers of maps printed it is generally accepted that an edition consisted of a few hundred examples. Compared to the number of postage stamps printed the production was miniscule; it is known that some 68 million Penny Blacks (the first stamp) were printed during 1840 – using the same method of printing as had been first used for maps some four centuries earlier! In the case of maps by Mercator or Ortelius and those of such publishers as Bleau or Jansson, who issued numerous editions, even 500 maps per edition would imply a quite large number of individual maps. This is true, of course, but as soon as we begin to look at the hazards to which maps were subjected, their survival in any quantity over the centuries comes almost as a surprise.

Leaving aside maps drawn on vellum (which is exceptionally durable) and other manuscripts (which were probably preserved with special care) maps printed on paper could scarcely be on a material less likely to endure. We need look no further than our own present-day treatment of current maps to realize that hard usage and obsolescence are their main enemies. Even in atlases we tend to use maps roughly and our canvas-backed sheet maps survive only a few years of constant use – but obsolescence is the really destructive element. There is nothing more irritating than an out-of-date map which no longer reflects accurate detail; on replacement, the old map is almost certainly thrown away to avoid unintentional use. How true this must have been of sea charts for example, or of maps of America or Australia as new information became available. Wall maps, especially, must have been prone to rough handling and rarely survived long unless bound as atlases in sheet form for library use.

Apart from these mundane reasons for the short life of maps, other more unpredictable hazards existed. Obviously fire, and probably simultaneous water damage, was likely to be the most destructive; wars and looting played a part in the destruction of great libraries. A number of unique maps were lost in the wars of the present century. Portuguese charts of the fifteenth and sixteenth centuries preserved in the Casa da India were lost in the Lisbon earthquake in 1755, a fact which accounts for their extreme rarity. Today, survivors are to be found in museums, libraries and national collections and not least, of course, in the hands of the present generation of private collectors, which alone must amount to a formidable total.

Should maps be coloured or uncoloured and how can original colour be recognized?

Whether a collector 'prefers' maps coloured or un-coloured is entirely a personal matter, although it can be said immediately that it is generally accepted that woodcuts are really best left in their original state, i.e. uncoloured. Exceptionally, the maps in the Ptolemy edition issued at Ulm in 1482 were usually coloured. Maps from copper-engraved plates are a different matter and here personal preference does play a large part. What proportions of engraved maps were sold originally plain or coloured it is not possible to say but no doubt price and usage entered into the matter. Plain maps were probably bought for practical purposes at perhaps half or even a quarter of the price of a coloured example which may have been wanted only for ornament or as a 'good buy' even in those days.

The practice of colouring varied greatly. In the case of Saxton's maps, for example, there is a uniformity of colour which strongly suggests that they were worked by the same hands, or at least in the same workshops, and it is very rare to see an uncoloured copy. A large number of Blaeu's maps are also beautifully coloured, which we would expect from their highly organized workshops in Amsterdam. On the other hand, many by Blaeu, Jansson, Speed and innumerable others were issued uncoloured or have been coloured in recent years which brings us to what may well be the most difficult question of all to answer: how do we distinguish between original and recent colour? The short answer, which is no help at all to the new collector, is experience and familiarity with the subject. Those handling maps frequently will ask themselves if the colours are appropriate to the time and subject and does the appearance of the map generally accord with others from the same source; have the colours been carefully and artistically applied; do the elusive browns, greens and orange reds strike an authentic note; in fact, does it all look 'right'?

Having said that, it has to be admitted that some modern colouring applied by experts is exceedingly difficult to distinguish from 'old' colouring; indeed, it may well be more skilfully applied, for nobody can claim that all sixteenth- and seventeenth-century colourists were uniformly expert. In these circumstances it is tempting to suggest that where skill and expertise of a high order have been exercised the finished product should be accepted for what it is – a beautifully coloured map – but perhaps this faces us with an ethical dilemma too controversial to pursue here.

What to collect

As in other spheres of collecting the range of subsidiary themes to which a map collector may be drawn is sufficiently diverse to meet every possible interest. For a start the chapter headings in Part I of this work immediately give an idea of possible specialization: road maps, sea charts, town plans, early editions of Ordnance Survey maps and so on. In addition to these broad headings, collectors may be interested perhaps in one particular cartographer or the cartographers of one country or period as an adjunct to historical study; they may specialize in woodcut maps or, more commonly, there are those who hope to make as complete a collection as possible of one geographical area, whether it be an English county, early maps of the west coast of the United States, or Australia as a Continent. Obviously in this field the possibilities are endless, and, of course, there are those who think in investment terms.

Maps as an Investment

It would be naive to ignore the fact that collections are being assembled as investments and it is possible to argue both for and against this development. In 1979, £374,000 was paid at auction for an atlas containing the only known manuscript maps by Mercator: it was purchased by a pension fund and obviously the trustees felt that it was a safe resting place for such a substantial sum of money. It must be reassuring for collectors to know that, by implication, professional financial advisers feel that this is a safe field for investment.

Although it would be possible to quote actual percentage rises in the market value of individual maps over any given period it could be very misleading to do so. The condition, colouring, edition and many other factors, besides financial considerations (such as inflation) have a bearing on the value, which makes it difficult, if not impossible, to be precise. It is, however, possible to give some pointers based on the collecting fashions of the last twenty years. These are, of necessity, generalizations and must be read with that proviso in mind.

Experience has shown that the price of cheaper maps has not increased as rapidly as the more expensive ones. A possible explanation for this is that the cheaper maps are, in the main, more common and that the cost to a dealer – preparing for sale, framing, etc. – is a fixed amount regardless of the scarcity of the item. By definition, therefore, the percentage return will have to be proportionally larger on the cheaper items. To confuse issues even further it should be remembered that most dealers frame items in their own 'house-style' and will not usually make any allowance for frames when buying.

Certain areas of the world have been neglected by collectors for some time and it is possible to hazard a guess that maps of South America (especially Brazil), Africa, and China will increase in value more than other areas which have already shown spectacular price increases. Surprisingly, perhaps, maps of the British Isles have only recently become of interest and Americana was considerably underpriced for many years. Maps of France are virtually uncollected due to a total lack of interest in France itself and it would be possible to form a fine collection of French maps at a very moderate cost indeed.

Reproductions, fakes and forgeries

Reproductions of many early maps are readily obtainable and, indeed, it would often be impossible to purchase the original, e.g. the Hereford Map. These reproductions are invaluable for research and study and the potential student is recommended to obtain the catalogue of the fine reproduction atlases published by Theatrum Orbis Terrarum NV, Keizersgracht 526, Amsterdam, The Netherlands. The British Library also have a number of publications of interest including reproductions of Saxton's county maps, many others being obtainable from specialist map dealers.

Above all things the collector will not want to purchase a 'fake', but it is difficult, if not impossible, to give any hard and fast rules to prevent this occurrence. In recent years the writers have noticed reproduction maps which have been 'doctored' with the intention of deceiving potential purchasers – often included in auction sales these fakes would deceive all but the expert. Generally the line of the printing does not have the 'bite' of the original engraving and often areas of the map where lines are very close together have 'blocked' up and present a solid appearance rather than being composed of single fine lines in very close proximity. Old frames are readily obtainable and the authors have seen frames which have been cut down from larger sizes with back boards showing clean edges – showing the cutting down – which are then fastened into the frame with old nails.

If in any doubt at all the aspiring collector is well advised to ask expert advice. When purchasing a house, a boat, a car or even a horse, it is not usual to rush out and buy without an independent opinion and that is what should be done when buying maps. Established collectors and dealers have usually spent many years studying the subject and will generally give advice freely. The media seem to delight in exposing all the worst traits of dealers and rarely – if ever – suggest that purchasers should draw on the trade's expertise rather than constantly suspecting it of chicanery.

In the late 1970s two maps by Ortelius of North and South America and the 1587 World Map purporting to be original were drawn to the attention of the Public Archives of Canada, the National Map Collection. Upon examination they proved to be forgeries, specifically made to deceive, bearing the closest possible resemblance to the originals. Apart from scientific tests on the paper, ink and printed image, which showed that the maps were not old, the false platemark was 11 mm larger than the originals. It must be assumed, unfortunately, that forgeries of this type will continue and that their 'quality' will improve.

Displaying and caring for maps

Many antiques, including maps, are made from organic materials (which decay) and should ideally, therefore, be kept in an air conditioned environment. This is obviously impossible for the majority of collectors and a compromise must be sought.

Paper was initially made in the Orient from vegetable fibres and the first record of European papermaking is in the twelfth century by the Moors in Spain and, independently, in Southern Italy. White paper was first made in England in 1495, by which time it had already been manufactured on the European mainland for at least 100 years. Until about 1800 all fine European paper was made entirely of rags pulped in water by simple water-driven machinery. After manufacture the individual dried sheets of paper were 'sized' by immersion in vats of 'size' – or animal glue – and then left to dry. This process prevented the paper remaining absorbent – like blotting paper – and enabled the colourists to apply large areas of even colour comparatively easily. The size on many old maps has decayed and it is reassuring to know that during the last twenty or thirty years there has been a remarkable increase in the range of conservation techniques and it is now possible to treat virtually every type of blemish and deterioration found on paper.

Considerable differences of opinion exist concerning the roles of restorer and conservator and it may be of use to give a brief definition of their functions before expanding further. Conservation is essentially the use of various techniques (physical and chemical) both in storage and treatment to preserve a given item in its existing state, whilst restoration is the use of available methods to bring back a damaged article to its original condition. Difficulties can arise when owners of damaged material require work to be done which conflicts with the ethics of conservation or restoration.

When items of great historic interest are being treated it is obvious that nothing should be added to them – or taken away! It is, however, difficult to determine when missing material should be replaced – that is, of course, when the original state is known. It can be argued that it is acceptable to replace missing portions of a common map and it is also possible to contend, quite reasonably, that it is wrong to do so and that the spaces should be left blank. Curators, archivists, restorers, dealers and collectors have been discussing these problems for many years without reaching any firm conclusions and with so many conflicting requirements obviously a compromise must be reached; this has to be left to individual judgement.

Framing is a more easily solved problem although even here difficulties may be encountered by the unsuspecting. Traditionally, framers stuck down everything on paper or strawboard to ensure that when framed it would be completely flat; luckily a more enlightened attitude is prevalent today, although self-adhesive tape, acidic mounts and backing boards and even dry mounting are still to be found on framed maps; all these methods of handling can damage old paper. Most specialist map dealers can provide a skilled framing service and will willingly advise customers. Acid-free mounting boards may be obtained, although chemically neutralized boards should be avoided as they tend to revert to their original state by absorption from the atmosphere. At the first sign of decay the owner must take professional advice.

No one would deny for a moment that every care must be taken to preserve old maps but we should not be carried away by the urge to conserve; after all, great numbers of very early maps have survived without any special care at all. Amateur restoration or conservation can create more problems than they solve, very often presenting professionals with the task of trying to repair the irreparable.

Sources of information

We should not leave this chapter without a word on sources of information available to the new map collector. The bibliography at the end of this book (and in others of a similar nature) obviously provides the first step, but this is a specialized subject and unfortunately many of these works are not readily available although dealers will probably have copies of some of them. The larger public libraries can usually obtain copies even if they are not actually on the shelves. In addition there is the *Map Collector* magazine published quarterly by Map Collector Publications Limited, PO Box 53, Tring, Herts HP23 5BH, and the catalogues issued by most of the principal map dealers provide an absolutely invaluable, indeed indispensable, source of information on details of maps and cartographers and, of course, on selling prices. The catalogues issued by Robert Douma (Prints and Maps) Ltd (formerly Weinreb and Douma Ltd), serve as one of the best examples of this source of information.

Where old maps may be seen

Many collectors will probably be content to look at maps and catalogues in dealers' showrooms; those who wish to extend their interest will find that most of the older University libraries and the larger public reference libraries have collections of maps to display to the serious student. It will be understood that before asking to see valuable original maps, it is only reasonable to make an appointment with librarians and to declare one's interest. As a further very general guide, some of the major map collections, world-wide, are listed below but, it need scarcely be emphasized, the list is by no means complete and the serious researcher will soon be able to add his own sources of information.

London	British Library; Royal Geographical Society; Guildhall Library; National Maritime Museum
Oxford	Bodleian Library
Cambridge	University Library; Fitzwilliam Museum
Edinburgh	University Library
Aberystwyth	National Library of Wales
Alnwick Castle Collection	
Hereford Cathedral *Mappa Mundi*	
Paris	Bibliothèque Nationale
Strassburg	Universitätsbibliothek
The Hague	Rijksarchief
Amsterdam	Nederlandsh Historisch Sheepvaart Museum; Universiteits Bibliotheek

Rotterdam	Maritiem Museum	
Utrecht	Geografisch Instituut der Rijksuniversiteit	
Brussels	Archives Générales du Royaume; Bibliothèque Royale	
Antwerp	Museum Plantin-Moretus; National Sheepvaartmuseum	
Berlin (West)	Staatsbibliothek Preussischer Kulturbesitz	
(East)	Deutsche Staatsbibliothek	
Hamburg	Deutsche Hydrographische Institut	
Munich	Bayerische Staatsbibliothek	
Nuremberg	Germanische Nationalmuseum	
Württemberg	Schloss Wolfegg	
Vienna	Oesterreichische Nationalbibliothek	
Rome	Bibliotheca Nazionale	
	Bibliotheca Apostolica Vaticana	
Florence	Bibliotheca Medicea Laurenziana	
Venice	Bibliotheca Nazionale Marciana	
Basle	Universitätsbibliothek	
St Gallen	Stiftsbibliothek	
Zürich	Zentralbibliothek and Staatsarchiv	
Madrid	Biblioteca National	
Lisbon	Museum National de Arte Antiga	
Copenhagen	Det Kongelige Bibliothek	

Stockholm	Kungliga Biblioteket
Helsinki	University Library (Nordenskiöld Collection)
Warsaw	Bibliotheka Narodowa
Washington	Library of Congress
New York	American Geographical Society (now at University of Wisconsin, Milwaukee); Pierpoint Morgan Library; Public Library
Ann Arbor	University of Michigan, William L. Clements Library
Baltimore	Peabody Institute Library
	Johns Hopkins University Library
Chicago	Newberry Library
Harvard	University Library
Los Angeles	University of California, William Andrew Clark Memorial Library
Princeton	University Library
Providence, RI	John Carter Brown Library
San Marino, Cal.	Huntington Library
Yale	University Library
Montreal	La Société Historique du Lac Saint-Louis
Ottawa	National Map Collection

BIOGRAPHICAL SUPPLEMENT

ITALY (Chapter 11)

LIVIO SANUTO 1520–1576

Sanuto, a Venetian accomplished in the arts and music, turned his abilities to the study of mathematics and cosmography, becoming an avid collector of works on those subjects by earlier historians and seafarers. Apart from inventing instruments for use in astronomy, he planned a massive work to cover a description of the known world with maps which he believed would be more accurate than any previously published. In the event he died in 1576 having completed only the general part of his *Geografia* together with the description and mapping of Africa. The maps – the first Atlas of Africa – were finished and published 12 years after his death by his brother, Giulio Sanuto.

1588   *Geografia di M. Livio Sanuto*: 12 maps of Africa

PAOLO PETRINI *fl.* 1670–1722

Very little is known about Petrini except that for many years he was a publisher and map seller in Naples producing large and small maps often slavishly based on those by Guillaume Sanson and Nicholas de Fer (whose errors he usually copied). About 1718 he published a large-scale plan of Naples. All his work is very rare.

1700   *Atlante Partenopea*
        Included maps of the Continents and 26 other maps.
1700   *Mappa Mondo Vero Carta . . .* (fol.)
c. 1700 Maps of the World and the Continents (wall maps).
1722   Maps of the World and the Continents (fol.).

GERMANY & AUSTRIA (Chapter 12)

EHRHARD ETZLAUB *c.* 1462–1532

Etzlaub was one of the many remarkable figures who were prominent in mathematics, astronomy and map and globe making in Nuremberg at the end of the fifteenth century. As well as being a compass and instrument maker, he was a cartographer noted not only for large scale maps of Nuremberg and other cities and their surroundings but especially for his road map of Central Europe, the first printed road map of a wide area (see also Chapters 4 and 5). Etzlaub is also considered to be the originator of the form of map projection, later refined by Mercator and known to the world as Mercator's Projection. Etzlaub first used it in an engraving on the cover of a sundial *c.* 1511–13.

1492   Environs of Nuremberg
c. 1492– *Das ist der Rom-Weg* (The Rome Way)
1500
1501   Road map of Germany centred on Nuremberg

MARTIN WALDSEEMÜLLER (ILACOMYLUS) *c.* 1473–1519 (1520)

In the history of cartography Martin Waldseemüller has a unique place for his part in naming the new-found Continent of America. It has long been assumed that he came from Radolfzell am Boden See but recent research by German archivists reveals that he was born between the years 1470 and 1475 almost certainly in the village of Wolfenweiler near Freiburg im Breisgau (or possibly in Freiburg itself), but in any case he grew up in Freiburg and entered the university there in 1490. His fellow students included Johannes Schott (*fl. c.* 1500–1521), later a noted printer, and Matthias Ringman, a poet who wrote Waldseemüller's texts. The students' interest in cosmography was undoubtedly aroused by their tutor, Gregor Reisch, confessor to the Emperor Maximilian, noted for his philosophical work, *Margarita Philosophica* (1503), a widely read book, many editions of which included a World Map in Ptolemaic form. After learning the printing trade in Basle Waldseemüller moved to St. Didal (now St. Dié des Vosges) where he became professor of cosmography under the patronage of René II, Duke of Lorraine. It was at this time that Waltzemüller (as his name was probably spelled then) adopted as his nom-de-plume the name 'Ilacomylus', a Greek/Latin form of his name by which he became commonly known. It is believed that the Duke himself had acquired a copy of the *Mundus Novus* (1502), an account of the voyages of the Florentine seafarer Amerigo Vespucci which evidently so impressed Waldseemüller and Ringman that they not only disregarded the earlier discoveries of Columbus but set aside a planned new edition of Ptolemy to concentrate on their *Cosmographiae Introductio* with its World Map and set of globe gores (1507) in order to show the 'new' continent and 'those parts of the World unknown to Ptolemy'. The book was printed at St. Dié on the Duke's presses in three editions in 1507 and a later printing in 1509 at Strassburg. Of the 1000 copies of the map said to have been produced only one which came to light in 1901 (together with the only copy of the 1516 *Carta Marina*) has survived. Exhaustive analysis of the paper, printing blocks and types indicates that these surviving maps were printed about the same time, probably in Strassburg by Johannes Grüninger.

The text of the *Cosmographiae Introductio* in which the name 'America' is used was written by Ringman, and there are those who consider that Ringman's influence was dominant in the choice of the name. He died in 1511 and by then Waldseemüller was having doubts about the name they had coined, but already so many copies had been distributed that it was too late for second thoughts. After Ringman's death Waldseemüller concentrated on the new version of Ptolemy's *Geographia*, now regarded as the most important edition and which was the most authoritative work of its time until the issue of Münster's *Geographia* in 1540.

In 1513 Waldseemüller was honoured for his work by being appointed a 'life' Canon at St. Dié, and he died there at about the age of 45 in the 'Canon's House' on 16 March 1519 (1520 new style).

1507   *Universalis Cosmographia Secundum Ptholomaei Traditionem et Americi Vespucii Aliorumque Lustrationes*: World Map on 12 sheets

1511   Central Europe: road map
        1520 Re-issued (one copy known).

1513   Ptolemy's *Geographia*: published in Strassburg by Jacobus Eszler and Georgius Ubelin (large folio): 47 woodcut maps
        1520 Strassburg: Re-issued.

1516   *Carta Marina Navigatoria*. World chart on 12 sheets (one copy known) Later editions are noted under Laurent Fries (q.v.)

CHRISTIAN SGROOTEN (SCHROT, SCHROTENUS) *c.* 1532–1608

Sgrooten, a German cartographer who became 'Royal Geographer to Philip II of Spain' is best known for a beautiful large map on 9 sheets of the Holy Land. The map, which was divided into two portions, the larger covering most of Palestine, the smaller extending to Sinai and the Nile Delta, was compiled from notes prepared by Peter Laicksteen (*fl. c.* 1544–70) who had drawn a map of Jerusalem in 1544 and subsequently had travelled widely throughout the country. At the time, the map was highly regarded and was used by Ortelius, Speed, William Blaeu and many others.

1565   Germany: 9 sheets

1570   *Nova Descriptio Amplissimae Sanctae Terrae*: published in Antwerp at 'the Sign of the Four Winds' by Hieronymous Cock (Cocq)

JOHANN NATALIUS METELLUS (MATAL) 1520–1597

Metellus is an obscure figure about whom little is known except that he was born in Louvain, later being heard of in Cologne where he was probably a publisher as well as a cartographer. He compiled a set of maps of America (with a World Map) very similar to those of Cornelis van Wytfliet with which they are often confused. The maps by Metellus are much rarer than those of Wytfliet.

1598   *Geographische und Historische Beschreibung der überauss grossen Landschafft America* by José D'Acosta: published by Johann Christoffel, Cologne: 20 maps
        1600 Re-issued

ATHANASIUS KIRCHER 1602–1680

Athanasius Kircher, a German Jesuit educated at Fulda, was one of the most remarkable men of his time, seemingly interested in every aspect of life. He was an expert on China and its languages; Egypt and Ethiopia and the source of the Nile; he translated oriental scripts and hieroglyphics; made a scientific study of the evolution of the earth and its physical features; he wrote a treatise on the reasons for magnetic compass variations; and, in the midst of all that, found time to invent the magic lantern, for which he is probably best remembered! He travelled extensively and eventually settled in Rome (where he founded a museum named after him) and died there in 1680.

Maps in his book *Mundus Subterraneus* were the first to describe tides and ocean currents besides showing the sites of all the volcanoes known at that time. Also included was a map of 'Atlantis' as he perceived it.

1652	*Chorographia originis Nili*: Amsterdam 3 maps on one sheet showing different aspects of the source of the Nile – 'the fountains of the Nile'
1665	*Mundus Subterraneus*: Amsterdam (including World Map, *Tabula Geographica-Hydrographica motus oceani . . .*)
1675	*Arca Noë* (including World Map, *Geographia Conjecturalis De Orbis Terrestris Post Diluvium*) This map shows Kircher's ideas of how the Flood affected the ancient world

---

EBERHARD WERNER HAPPEL 1647–1690

1687	*Mundi Mirabilis Tripartus* (included world chart of ocean currents, dated 1675)

Homann Heirs (Homännische Erben)
JOHANN MATTHIAS HASE (HASIUS) 1684–*c.* 1742
JOHANN HÜBNER 1668–1731
JOHANN GEORG EBERSPERGER 1695–1760
JOHANN MICHAEL FRANZ 1700–1761
FRANZ LUDWIG GÜSEFELD 1744–1807

Over a very long period the firm published an immense number of maps in various forms – as standard atlases in many editions (the titles of which sometimes changed), composite atlases made up to order and individual maps. In consequence it is often very difficult to be precise in dating their work but the following is a useful guide to their publications.

c. 1724	*Atlas Novus* Re-issues to *c.* 1755
1732	*Atlas Minor* Re-issues to *c.* 1750
1735	*Atlas Germaniae (specialis)* Re-issues to *c.* 1777
1736	*Atlas Silesiae* Re-issues to *c.* 1750
1737	*Grosser Atlas* Re-issues to *c.* 1753
1740	*Atlas Historicus*

1747	*Homännischer Atlas* Re-issues to *c.* 1780
1747	*Atlas Novus Terrarum (Orbis)* Re-issues to 1753
c. 1752	*Atlas Compendiarus* Re-issues to *c.*1790
1753	*Atlas Geographicus Maior* Re-issues to *c.* 1784
1754	*Bequemer Hand-atlas*
1762	*Stadt Atlas*
c. 1762	*Atlas Homannianus* Collection of maps dated 1723 onwards
1769	*Atlas Novus Republicae Helveticae*: Nuremberg 1770 Re-issued in Zurich
c. 1770	*Atlas Mapparum geographicarum* Re-issues to *c.* 1793
1776	*Böhmische Atlas*
1777	*Atlas Methodicus*
1788	*Niederländische Atlas*
1797	*Weltatlas*
c. 1804	*Spanische Atlas*
c. 1804	*Atlas der Österreichische Monarchie*

ELIAS BAECK 1679–1747

1710	*Atlas geographicus*
1720–38	Various town plans

SAMUEL VON SCHMETTAUS 1684–1751

1749	*Nouvel Atlas de Marine*

HOLLAND & BELGIUM (Chapter 13)

PAULUS MERULA 1558–1607

Born at Dordrecht in Holland, Merula studied at a number of universities before settling at Leiden where he was appointed Professor of History. He also practised there as a solicitor and wrote numerous works on law and history, as well as a treatise on geography which included about 20 maps and views. The most important of these was a World Map engraved by Jan van Doetecum (Jr) based on the World Map by Petrus Plancius (1590): also included were a small World Map by Jodocus Hondius and other small maps taken from the *Tabularum Geographicarum* by Petrus Bertius.

1605	*Cosmographiae generalis libri tres.* *Item Geographiae particularis libri* IV . . . 1621 Re-issued without the large World

Map but including a smaller one and others corrected by Jodocus Hondius (Jr)
1636 Re-issued with fewer maps

FRANCISCO DE AFFERDEN (AEFFERDEN) 1653–1709
In spite of his Spanish sounding name, de Afferden was a Belgian cartographer who published in Antwerp in 1696 an atlas which appeared in several editions.
1696   *El Atlas Abbreviado*
            1697, 1709, 1711, 1721 Re-issued

FRANCE *(Chapter 14)*

LAURENT FRIES (LAURENTIUS FRISIUS) *c.* 1490–*c.* 1532
Laurent Fries, born in Mulhouse in Burgundy, travelled widely, studying as a physician and mathematician in Vienne, Padua, Montpellier and Colmar before settling in Strassburg. There he is first heard of working as a draughtsman on Peter Apian's highly decorative cordiform World Map, published in 1520. Apian's map was based on Waldseemüller's map of 1507 which no doubt inspired Fries's interest in the Ptolemy 'atlases' of 1513 and 1520 and brought him into contact with the publisher, Johannes Grüninger. It is thought that Grüninger had acquired the woodcuts of the 1520 edition with the intention of producing a new version to be edited by Fries. Under his direction the maps were redrawn and although many of them were unchanged, except for size, others were embellished with historical notes and figures, legends and the occasional sea monster. Three new maps were added. Of the two World Maps included, one, dated 1522 and initialled 'LF' in the title border, is of very special interest to collectors, being the earliest World Map bearing the name 'America' which is likely to come on the market.
1522   Ptolemy's *Geographia*: Strassburg: 50 wood-cut maps
            1525 Strassburg: Re-issued
            1535 Lyon: Re-issued, edited by Michael Servetus
            1541 Vienne (Dauphiné): Re-issue
1525   *Carta Marina*: reduced version on 12 sheets of Waldseemüller's map of 1516
            1527, 1530 Re-issued – only one copy of this map, dated 1530, is known

---

JEAN ROTZ (ROZE) *c.* 1505–*c.* 1560
Jean Rotz, born in Dieppe where his father, a Scotsman, had settled as a trader to the Far East, is regarded as one of the most important members of the Dieppe School of Cartography. He travelled widely throughout many parts of the known world and between the years 1542 and 1547 lived in London where he was 'Hydrographer' to Henry VIII, to whom his 'Boke' is dedicated with the resounding words 'This Boke of Idrography is made by me Johne Rotz sarvant to the King's Mooste Excellent Majeste. Gode save his Majeste'. With the approach of the King's death Rotz offered his services and, no doubt, knowledge of England's defences to Henry II of France who welcomed him back to Dieppe where he resettled as a merchant and shipbuilder for the French navy. Many authorities believe that the existence of Australia was probably known to Rotz and other members of the Dieppe School.
1542   *Boke of Idrography*: 1 World Map and 11 regional maps in portulan style on vellum

---

JEAN BAPTISTE POIRSON 1760–1831
Poirson was a talented geographer and engraver known for the production of magnificent, very large globes, claimed to be the best since those of Coronelli. He also compiled a large number of maps, examples of which are listed below, published in various geographical and historical works.
1799   Carolina
1803   Mississippi
1808   North America
1821   *Nouvelle géographie élémentaire*
1827   Mexique

EUSTACHE HÉRISSON *fl. c.* 1785–1823
Hérisson was an engraver, geographer and hydrographer active in Paris over many years. His work included a geographical dictionary and small maps of every kind.
1806–23   *Amérique*
1806   *Atlas ou Dictionnaire de Géographie Universelle*
1806–11   *Atlas Portatif*
1811   *Nouvel Atlas Portatif*
1818   World Atlas

ENGLAND & WALES *(Chapter 15)*

CAPTAIN JAMES HORSBURGH 1762–1836
During the first half of the nineteenth century British Admiralty charts became the accepted standard for use by seamen of practically all nations. No one made a

greater contribution to their reputation than James Horsburgh.

He was born in Fifeshire, went to sea at the age of 16, and after an adventurous ten years mainly in the Far East was shipwrecked in the Indian Ocean through the use of an inaccurate chart. From then onwards he turned to the study of navigation and allied subjects, determined to improve methods of charting the seas. He was soon producing new charts which came to the attention of Alexander Dalrymple, the Hydrographer to the East India Co., through whom they were published. Over the next 20 years spent in the Far East he kept meticulous notes and observations, producing new charts and compiling his greatest work, *The Directions for sailing to and from the East Indies, China* ... This has gone through a great many editions and is the basis of the present *East India Directory*.

In 1806 he was elected a Fellow of the Royal Society and in 1810 became Hydrographer to the East India Co.

c. 1794   Charts of the Straits of Macassar, Dampier's Strait and areas of the Philippine Islands.
1805–12   Charts of the East Indies.
1817   *East India Pilot.*

SCOTLAND (Chapter 16)

MAJOR GENERAL WILLIAM ROY 1726–1790
William Roy was born in Carluke in Lanarkshire and it is recorded that, by the time he was 21, he was serving as an assistant to Colonel David Watson, the Army's Deputy Quarter Master General during the 1745 Jacobite rising. In that campaign the need for adequate maps of Scotland became apparent and in 1747 it was decided to undertake a major survey of the country, starting in the Highlands. Although at that stage Roy held no military rank, he was responsible for the supervision of the Army survey teams and his hand can be seen in the final beautifully drawn maps of the Highlands. The mapping of southern Scotland, hurriedly finished in 1758, was less satisfactory. The experience gained in those years left Roy dedicated to the idea of a survey by triangulation of the whole of the British Isles on the lines of that being undertaken by the Cassini family in France. Unfortunately he was frustrated in that ambition until the very end of his life, but he spent the intervening years actively producing maps and plans of many different parts of

the country, including Roman military sites, and selecting suitable observation posts for the later National Survey. In Chapter 8 we have followed the events leading up to the foundation of the Ordnance Survey Office in 1791, the year after Roy died.

William Roy was commissioned in the Army in 1755 and served in Germany during the Seven Years War, later becoming Deputy Quarter Master General and Surveyor of Coastal Defences. He was elected a Fellow of the Royal Society in 1767 and of the Society of Antiquaries in 1776 in recognition of his archaeological work. Although details of his life are covered in specialist works on the Ordnance Survey, many general histories of cartography scarcely mention his name and yet, in view of his unremitting perseverance over a lifetime in preparing the way for large scale mapping of the country, he must surely be classed with the most distinguished British cartographers.

SPAIN (Chapter 19)

JOÃO TEIXEIRA c. 1602–1666
His 'chart' of Africa, published in Lisbon in 1649, was used for a century or more by other cartographers.

1649   *Cosmographo de sua Magestade* (East Indies Navigational Chart)
Map of Africa with inset plans of Mombasa and other ports – issued also in Thevenot's *Relations de Divers Voyages Curieux*

DENMARK (Chapter 19)

JOHANNES ISAKSEN PONTANUS 1571–1639
Pontanus came from Helsinki and settled for a time in Holland as a professor of mathematics, geography and history at Harderwyk where he compiled a two-volume work *Rerum et Urbis Amstelodensium Historia* which contained a decorative map of Europe, Africa and Asia with inset figures in national dress. The map appears in both volumes in different states.

In 1618 he was appointed by Christian IV of Denmark as 'royal historian' and in that capacity wrote a history of Denmark (*Rerum Danicarum Historia*) which included maps of Denmark and Holstein.

1611   *Tabula Geographica in qua Europa, Africa, Asia* ... Amsterdam

1631   *Daniae Regni Typus* (Denmark)
       Ducatus Holsatiae Nova Tabula (Holstein)
       published by Jodocus Hondius and Jan
       Jansson in Amsterdam

PROFESSOR CHRISTIAN CARL LOUS 1724–1894
ADMIRAL ANDREAS LOUS 1728–1797

1769–73   Chart of the Kattegat and the Baltic
1790   Chart of the North Sea

NORWAY *(Chapter 19)*

JOHANN HANSSON HEITMAN 1664–1740
Heitman, a sea captain and hydrographer, was one of
the first to survey the coasts of Norway in any detail.
Although his charts were not published separately, they
were used by Dutch publishers including the van
Keulen family.

1725   Charts of the North Sea and Oslofjord

ANDERS HOEG 1727–1796
Anders Hoeg, a lecturer in the art of navigation and a
sea captain, spent many years in company with the
Danes, A. and C. C. Lous (qq.v.), revising Dutch sea
charts of the North Sea and the Baltic.

1769   Chart of the North Sea

CARL FREDERIK GROVE 1758–1829
NIELS ANDREAS WIBE 1759–1814
BONONI D'AUBERT (Danish) 1768–1832

In 1786 the Danish hydrographer Paul de Lövenörn
initiated a survey by triangulation of the coasts of
Norway, a task which was undertaken and eventually
completed by the above team.

1793–1817 Charts of the Norwegian coast: published
          by the Dépot de la Marine, Paris

SWEDEN *(Chapter 19)*

PETTER GEDDA 1661–1697
Gedda was a pilot and hydrographer in Government
service who published the first Swedish chart book
which was based on earlier work of Admiral Werner
von Rosenfeldt (1639–1710). The charts were widely
copied by Hendrick Doncker, van Keulen and others.

1694–5   Chart Book of the Baltic and Kattegat: 10
          charts: Amsterdam: Swedish, Dutch and
          English versions

1699 Re-issued: 12 charts
1739 Revised and re-issued as Sea Atlas of
the Baltic by Gedda's successor Nils Ström-
crona (1664–1740)

ANDERS AKERMAN 1721–1778
Akerman, a cartographer, globe maker, and engraver
in Uppsala, compiled a series of new charts of the Baltic
which were soon replaced by the official surveys
undertaken by Admiral Nordenankar.

1768   Chart of the Gulf of Finland
1768   *Atlas Hydrografica*

ADMIRAL JOHAN NORDENANKAR 1722–1804
In 1772, in accordance with a Government decree,
Admiral Nordenankar was appointed to the task of
resurveying the coasts of Sweden. The new charts,
compiled in conjunction with Eric af Klint (1732–
1812), a hydrographer, and Fredrik Akrel (1748–1804),
an engineer, were first published in 1797 in Stockholm
and later were reproduced by Dutch publishers and by
William Faden in London.

1788–90   Maps of Sweden and Finland and Charts of
          the Baltic
1797   Sea Atlas
          c. 1832 Revised and re-issued in 2 volumes
          by Gustav af Klint (1771–1840)
          1849 Re-issued

SWITZERLAND *(Chapter 19)*

AEGIDIUS (GILG) TSCHUDI 1505–1572
Tschudi was a man of some distinction who represented
his country as ambassador at the Court of Augsburg.
Following his student days in Paris and Basle he
travelled widely throughout Switzerland preparing
detailed topographical notes and sketches evidently
with the mapping of the country much in mind. In due
course, in 1538 he produced a large woodcut map in
two versions, one with text in German, one in Latin.
The map, oriented to the south, was much acclaimed
and became the standard work until that of Hans
Konrad Gyger in the next century. Although no copies
have survived, it is known from later versions issued in
reduced form. Tschudi's later revised map printed in
Basle in 1560, of which one copy is known, was also
widely copied, by Mercator, among others.

1538   *Nova Rhaetiae-Helvetiae Descriptio*

1555 Re-issued in Rome (Antonio Salamanca)

1567 Re-issued in Venice (Paolo Forlani)

1570 Re-issued in Antwerp (Abraham
Ortelius and many others)

1560   *Helvetia et Rhaetia*

1585 Used by Gerard Mercator

JOS MURER 1530–1580

Little is known of Jos Murer except that he was a poet
and that he belonged to a notable circle of glass painters
in Zürich.

His fairly large woodcut map (84 × 102 cm) of
Canton Zürich is a handsome production combining
the elements of a picture map of the landscape of the
canton with bird's-eye views of the towns, evidently
much influenced by Italian and German maps of the
previous century.

His son, Christoph (1558–1614) engraved a map of
Switzerland in 1582.

1566   *Zürcher Staatsgebiet*: engraved on 6 sheets

1576   Map of the Black Sea used by Braun and
Hogenberg

THOMAS SCHOEPF *c.* 1527–1577

Thomas Schoepf came from the south of Germany but
studied in Basle, eventually practising as a doctor in
Bern where he remained until his death of the plague
in 1577.

His very large map of Canton Bern (128 × 187 cm) –
in his day the canton covered most of western
Switzerland – was the first map to be engraved on
copper in Switzerland where the long tradition of
woodblock printing, especially in Basle, was slow to
give way to new methods. The map, printed the year
after his death, was remarkably accurate and was used
by Mercator and other cartographers/publishers for
something like the next 200 years.

1578   *Bernishes Staatsgebiet*: engraved on 18 sheets

HANS KONRAD GYGER 1599–1674

Gyger was born into a gifted Zürich family noted for
their work as glass painters: other members were
doctors, astronomers, mathematicians, some of whom
were local map makers. After studying for a time with
Matthäus Merian he returned to Zürich to become a
military engineer and, even by 1620 at the age of 21, he
was working on the preparation of military maps which
led to the detailed mapping of Canton Zürich and other
cantons. He made full use of existing methods of
triangulation and devised new and very effective means

of showing land surface in relief but his methods,
perhaps not properly understood, were never generally
accepted.

For most of his life Gyger maintained contact with
his mentor, Matthäus Merian, for whose *Topographia* he
prepared a number of maps and town plans including a
splendid bird's-eye view of Baden (1638).

1634, 1635,
1637/8,
1657   Maps of Switzerland
1629–67   Maps of various cantons

HEINRICH LUDWIG MUOSS 1657–1721

Muoss, a printer of topographical books, compiled a
highly decorative and very popular map of Switzerland,
based on Gyger's map of 1657. The second edition of
1710 was issued as a wall map with a most elaborate
border showing views of all the principal towns with
historical notes.

1698   *Helvetia, Rhaetia, Vallesia*
1710 Re-issued

JOHANN JAKOB SCHEUCHZER 1672–1733

Johann Scheuchzer was one of the outstanding men of
his time. Distinguished as a doctor, mathematician,
astronomer, cartographer and artist, he was a member
of German, Prussian and Italian Academies and the
Royal Society in London; his services were sought after
by Peter the Great.

With such wide-ranging interests it is remarkable
that he was able to devote time and energy over 18
years to the physical task of re-mapping Switzerland.
His new survey was based on Gyger's last map of 1657
which was very much enlarged, revised and corrected,
Scheuchzer claiming that he had added 2,000 new place
names to it, but in spite of his artistry it lacked the
clarity of Gyger's map. Nevertheless, it was very popular
and was used in reduced form in various atlases by
Pieter Schenk, Gerard Valck and Covens and Mortier
in Amsterdam and by publishers in other centres.

1712–13   *Nova Helvetiae Tabula Geographica*: 4 sheets
1765 Re-issued in Zürich

GABRIEL WALSER 1695–1776

Walser was a churchman, turned historian and cartographer, who developed a special interest in drawing
and mapping the mountains and glaciers of Switzerland.
In the years 1763–68 the firm of Homann Heirs in
Nuremberg published 15 of his cantonal maps and then
used them as the basis for a Swiss atlas published in
1769. Surprisingly, this was only the second atlas of

Swiss maps printed in over 200 years, the first being by Johann Stumpf in 1548/52. The Nuremberg issue was popular and was reproduced in two editions in Zürich.

1769   *Atlas Novus Republicae Helveticae*
         1770 *Schweizerische Geographie*: two editions

JOHANN RUDOLF MEYER 1739–1813
JOHANN HEINRICH WEISS 1759–1826

In the last quarter of the eighteenth century when national surveys were being undertaken in most European countries, Johann Meyer, a wealthy merchant of Aarau, decided to organise – at his own expense – a new scientific survey of his country. In 1786, he enlisted the help of Johann Weiss, an engineer and topographer serving in the French army at Strassburg. Weiss was well versed in French methods of surveying and had already completed a map of Alsace (1781).

Working from two principal base lines Meyer and Weiss completed their survey in a comparatively short time, producing 16 maps which were published as an atlas in 1802. These were to remain the standard large-scale maps until the Dufour survey later in the century.

1802   *Schweizer-Atlas* (*Atlas Suisse*): 16 sheets
         The atlas included *Carte générale de la Suisse* compiled between *c.* 1788 and 1796 and first published in 1800.

GENERAL GUILLAUME HENRI DUFOUR 1787–1875

The trigonometrical survey supervised by General Dufour was designed primarily for military purposes but it also bridged the period of transition between the last of the privately financed surveys (the Meyer/Weiss maps of 1802) and the new official survey started by Hermann Siegfried in 1868.

1832–64   *Topographische Karte der Schweiz*: 25 sheets

HERMANN SIEGFRIED 1819–1879

The first sheets of the official 'Ordnance' survey map of Switzerland, commonly known as the Siegfried map, were issued in 1868 and, as in all European countries, are constantly revised and extended.

1868–1908 *Topographischer Atlas der Schweiz*: 593 sheets

RUSSIA (*Chapter 19*)

CAPTAIN ALEXEI NAGAJEV 1704–1781

1750   Chart of the Gulf of Finland
         1777 Re-issued
1757   Atlas of the Whole Baltic Sea
         1789, 1792, 1794 Re-issued

ADMIRAL ADAM FEDOROVIC (JOHAN) VON KRUSENSTERN 1770–1845

1813   *Atlas de l'Océan Pacifique*
         1824 (and later) Re-issued

LEONTI VASILEVICH SPAFEREN 1765–1845

1821–23   Atlas of the Gulf of Finland

ADMIRAL OTTO VON KOTZEBUE 1787–1846

1823   Atlas of the Three Voyages of Lieutenant Kotzebue round the World

AMERICA (*Chapter 20*)

JOHN SMITH 1580–1631

Experienced collectors will know that John Smith's maps of Virginia and New England, and the numerous derivatives, have been described and analysed at great length by many carto-bibliographers. To new collectors it must be said that any versions of the maps are now very rare and here we give only a brief descriptive note to set them in their historical context.

John Smith was one of the few survivors of that first small party of English settlers who sailed into Chesapeake Bay and the James River in April 1607. Their first years were dire in the extreme and eventual survival was due to the providential arrival of more colonists and to the efforts of their self-appointed leader, John Smith. It was all the more remarkable that Smith, in the short space of about two years (including some time in Indian captivity), was able to make accurate drawings of Chesapeake Bay and to explore, or at least to record, details of the immediate hinterland – always in the belief that a direct passage to the 'Indian Sea' lay within his grasp. He returned to England in 1609 and his map, engraved by William Hole and published in Oxford in 1612 by Joseph Barnes, remained the prototype for later maps of the region until the printing of Augustine Herrman's map in 1673.

Smith's later exploration of the coastline and mainland of New England and his description of the country with a map issued in 1616 were important influences in promoting colonisation from Europe.

1612   Virginia
         Numerous re-issues in Smith's *Generall Historie of Virginia* and in *Purchas his Pilgrimes* by Samuel Purchas (1624–6)

1616   New England: issued in Smith's *A Descrip-
            tion of New England* and later in his *Generall
            Historie*

CECIL CALVERT, 2nd BARON BALTIMORE

Soon after the foundation of the State of Maryland, the
first map of the region was published in London by
Lord Baltimore in *A Relation of Maryland* written to
attract settlers to the colony. Known as 'Lord Baltimore's Map' it became increasingly important in later
years for its delineations of the state boundaries which
were in constant dispute until the Mason/Dixon
settlement in 1768. Although Lord Baltimore evidently
engraved the map, it is not known who compiled it but
it has been attributed to the Dutch cartographer, Petrus
Montanus (Pieter van den Berg).

1635   *Noua Terrae-Mariae tabula*

JOHN FARRER (FERRER) *fl.* 1651

John Farrer's *Mapp of Virginia* is one of the more
intriguing examples of early map making. As Farrer
was in the service of the Virginia Company it must be
assumed that the map represented an official view of
the colony but it is hard to believe that even in 1651
credence could be given to Indian reports that over the
mountains 'there were great rivers that run into a great
sea' and that, in consequence 'The Sea of China and the
Indies' could be reached 'in 10 days march with 50
foote and 30 hors-men from the head of Jeames River'.
(One is tempted to ask why such a short journey hadn't
been made).

Although some features of the map are fanciful, it
does provide important geographical information and
shows the Swedish and Dutch plantations and, for the
first time, the name 'Carolana' appears. Sir Francis
Drake's portrait is set against the Pacific coast and his
claim to 'New Albion' (in 1577), is noted.

Copies of the map exist in several states, some of
which contained additions made by Farrer's daughter
Virginia and were issued under her name.

1651   *A Mapp of Virginia*: engraved by John
            Goddard and sold by John Stephenson in
            London
            *c.*1667–8 Re-issued by John Overton

AUGUSTINE HERRMAN (AUGUSTUS HEERMANS) 1621–1685

Herrman was a Bohemian immigrant whose map, the
finest of its time, was compiled with Thomas Within-
brook and published in London by John Seller. It
superseded John Smith's map of Virginia (1612),

replacing Indian names with English and was much
used by later surveyors and in the settlement of
boundary disputes: only four copies are known to have
survived.

1673   *Virginia and Maryland*

THOMAS HOLME 1624–1695

In 1682 William Penn and Thomas Holme, the
Surveyor General for Pennsylvania, laid out a plan for
the future city of Philadelphia which was printed in
London in the following year and is claimed to be the
first printed plan of a 'United States' city.

1683   *A Portraiture of the City of Philadelphia*
            1687 Re-issued in London by P. Lea
            c. 1715 Re-issued in London by G. Willdey
1687   *A Mapp of ye Improved part of Pensylvania in
            America, Divided into Counties, Townships and
            Lotts* (with an inset plan of Philadelphia):
            Published in London by P. Lea

CYPRIAN SOUTHACK 1662–1745

Southack, a Boston sea captain, pioneered the mapping
of the north-eastern seaboard, compiling numerous
charts made from his own observations during a
lifetime at sea. His *New England Coasting Pilot* was the
first marine 'atlas' published in America – only three
copies are known to have survived – and the 'chart' of
1717 was the earliest map printed in America showing
all the English colonies. Although later surveys show
the inadequacies of his work his charts were very
popular in their day.

1694   Chart of Boston Harbour (Boston)
1711   Chart of the St Lawrence River (Boston)
1717   *A New Chart of [the British Empire in] North
            America* (Boston)
c. 1729–34 *The New England Coasting Pilot*: 8 Maps
            (Boston)
            c. 1744, *c.* 1758, 1775 Re-issued in London
            on a single sheet by various publishers

EUSEBIO FRANCISCO KINO 1644–1711

Francisco Kino, a Spanish Jesuit priest, spent many
years in missionary work and exploration at the head
of the Gulf of California. His early journeys seemed to
confirm the belief that California was an island but
later exploration between 1698 and 1701 finally proved
that, in fact, it was a peninsula. Although Kino's
manuscript map (drawn in 1701) has disappeared,
copies of it were published twice in Paris in 1705.

1705   *Passage par terre à la Californie*

JOHN BONNER 1643–1726

John Bonner's plan of Boston was the earliest and most important one of the city. Although only one copy of the original printing is known, it was reproduced in Boston and London many times in various states until the end of the century.

1722   *The Town of Boston in New England* (Boston)

WILLIAM BRADFORD 1663–1752

The plan of New York 'made by James Lyne', which is believed to be the earliest published in the city, is commonly known as the 'Bradford' map, its dedication being signed by William Bradford, the first established printer there. It was re-engraved and reprinted many times in later years.

c. 1731   *A Plan of the City of New York from an actual Survey*

HENRY POPPLE *fl.* 1727–1743

Henry Popple is a shadowy figure about whom little is known except that he was a member of Queen Anne's household in 1713 and acted as 'Agent' for many years for British regiments serving in the American Colonies.

His map, the first on a large scale of North America, consisting of a key map and 20 individual sheets, not surprisingly contained many inaccuracies magnified by its scale. Some of its features ran counter to English claims in the frontier areas and, therefore, it was never officially recognised. But, in spite of its shortcomings, it was a splendid achievement for its time and showed an immense amount of detail in the interior. It was much used by later map makers. The maps were engraved in London by W. H. Toms and were sold by S. Harding 'on the Pavement in St Martin's Lane', price 2/- for the key map and £1.11.6 for the loose sheets.

1733   *A Map of the British Empire in America with the French and Spanish Settlements adjacent thereto*
1737 Re-issued by Covens and Mortier, Amsterdam
1742 Re-issued by G. L. Le Rouge, Paris
1747 Re-issued by Thomas Bowen, London

LEWIS EVANS *c.* 1700–1756

Lewis Evans's map of 1755 was the most ambitious and splendid map compiled by an American cartographer before Independence. Four years' travelling and surveying resulted in a work of great accuracy rivalling the map by John Mitchell (although covering a smaller area) issued in the same year. It was first printed in Philadelphia by Benjamin Franklin and David Hall but it was soon pirated in London by Thomas Kitchin and John Bowles and there were numerous copies by many other publishers up to about 1814. Evans's and Mitchell's maps were used over many years in the settlement of boundary disputes.

1749   *A Map of Pensilvania, New-Jersey, New York, And the Three Delaware Counties* (Philadelphia)
1752 Re-issued
1755   *A general Map of the Middle British Colonies in America*
1756–*c.* 1814 Numerous re-issues

COLONEL JOSHUA FRY *c.* 1700–1754
PETER JEFFERSON

In 1750 Colonel Fry, a surveyor and mathematician, and Peter Jefferson (father of Thomas Jefferson), also a surveyor, who had worked together on many mapping projects, were appointed by the Governor of Virginia to prepare a new survey of the region. Their map, published by Thomas Jefferys in London, made a notable contribution to knowledge of the interior and was later used by John Mitchell: in its 1755 revision it became very popular and was re-issued many times.

1751–54   *A Map of the [Most] Inhabited part of Virginia, containing the whole province of Maryland with Part of Pensilvania, New Jersey and North Carolina*
1755, 1768, 1775 Re-issued by Thomas Jefferys
1777 Re-issued by Wm. Faden
1755 (and later) Various French editions

GEORGE HEAP *fl.* 1752

The detailed plan of Philadelphia (with an inset showing the State House), drawn by George Heap, a surveyor working in conjunction with Nicholas Scull, the Surveyor General, was the first plan of the city published in America. It became extremely popular in its day and was reproduced many times by European publishers, but copies of the original print are exceedingly rare.

1752   *A Map of Philadelphia, and Parts Adjacent*
1768 Re-issued (without inset) by Thomas Jefferys
1777 Re-issued (without inset) by Wm. Faden
1777 Re-issued (without inset) by M. A. Lotter

NICHOLAS SCULL *fl.* 1748–1761

As Surveyor General of Pennsylvania, Nicholas Scull worked with George Heap on a plan of Philadelphia which became a very popular work: details are given above in the notes on George Heap. Scull's map of Pennsylvania was the first one of the province published in America and was subsequently republished in London and revised by his son, William Scull, in 1770.

1752   *A Map of Philadelphia, and Parts Adjacent*

1759   *Map of the improved Part of the Province of Pennsylvania*
       1768 Re-issued by Thomas Jefferys

JOSHUA FISHER 1707–1783

Many years' experience piloting shipping on the Delaware River enabled Fisher to compile the first reliable chart of the Bay and River, but for security reasons the engravings of certain channels of the river were suppressed on the first issue, of which only one copy has survived. Later re-issues of the complete chart are detailed below.

1756   *Delaware Bay*: chart on 3 sheets
       c. 1775 Re-issued in Philadelphia
       1776 Re-issued in London by a number of publishers
       1778 Re-issued in Paris by G. L. Le Rouge

WILLIAM GERARD DE BRAHM 1717–1799

De Brahm, a Dutch military engineer experienced in the latest European surveying techniques, emigrated to Georgia in 1751 and soon received the King's appointment as a state surveyor. His map of South Carolina and Georgia, completed by 1757 and published in London by Thomas Jefferys, was by far the most professional and accurate map of the region made up to that time and served as a model for other map makers for many years ahead. In the next 20 years he completed a detailed history and survey of the 'Southern District' which included many manuscript maps and town plans. In 1764 he was appointed 'Surveyor General of the Southern District of North America'.

1757   *A Map of South Carolina And a Part of Georgia* . . .
       1768, 1776 Re-issued by Thos. Jefferys
       1777, 1778 Re-issued by G. L. Le Rouge
       1777–1780 Re-issued by Wm. Faden

CAPTAIN THOMAS HUTCHINS 1730–1789

Captain Hutchins was a talented surveyor, engineer and guide whose reputation earned him the title 'Geographer to the United States of America', the only

time such an appointment was ever made. After Independence he carried out important surveys of West Florida and Carolina and he was associated with surveying the extension of the Mason/Dixon line and other inter-state boundaries.

1764/65   Map consisting of two parts: *A General Map of the Country on the Ohio and Muskingham [Rivers] shewing the Situation of the Indian Towns . . . and . . . the Indian Country through which the Army under the Command of Colonel Bouquet marched in the year 1764* (Philadelphia)
       1765 Redesigned and republished in *An Historical Account of the Expedition against the Ohio Indians* by Wm. Smith (Philadelphia)

CHARLES MASON (d. 1786)
JEREMIAH DIXON (d. 1779)

The famous map showing the new boundary lines between Maryland and Pennsylvania was the outcome of a survey carried out by the 'King's Surveyors' to resolve an eighty-year old dispute between the Baltimore and Penn families, arising originally from inaccuracies on earlier maps. Although the immediate aim of the survey in settling the inter-state claims was achieved – after much compromise – the longer term implications of their boundary line could scarcely have been foreseen by the surveyors. In the next century it became far more than a simple line on a map: it divided the Northern and Southern cultures over the abolition of slavery to the extent that the Southern States contemplated secession from the Union, whilst in the eyes of southern slaves it became the symbol of freedom.

Mason and Dixon, who were astronomers as well as surveyors, incorporated in their map the first accurate measurement of a degree of latitude made in America.

1768   *A Plan of the Boundary Lines between the Province of Maryland and the Three Lower Counties on Delaware with Part of the Parallel of Latitude which is the Boundary between the Provinces of Maryland and Pennsylvania*: published in Philadelphia

MAJOR JOHN MONTRESOR 1736–*c.* 1788

Born in Gibraltar, Major Montresor had a distinguished career as an engineer with the British forces in America: he served in the French and Indian wars and later at Bunker Hill and in the subsequent campaigns of the War of Independence. In 1775 he was appointed 'His Majesty's Chief Engineer in America'.

His official plan of New York (the 'Montresor Plan'), surveyed in 1766, was published in London in 1768 by Sayer and Jefferys. Copies are now very rare.

1768	*A Plan of the City of New-York and its Environs to Greenwich* 1775 Re-issued in London by A. Dury
1775	*A Map of the Province of New York, with Part of Pennsylvania, and New England*: 3 editions published in London by A. Dury 1777 Revised edition

BERNARD RATZER *fl.* 1756–1777
Ratzer was an army surveyor whose maps and plans were noted for their fine draughtsmanship as well as their accuracy. His collaborator in drawing the map of the Province of New York, Claude Joseph Sauthier, is best known for a series of manuscript plans of towns in North Carolina (1768–70).

1769–70	*Plan of the City of New York, in North America* (with an inset view of the city) 1776 Re-issued by Thos. Jefferys and Wm. Faden
1776	*A Map of the Province of New York which included New Jersey* (with C. J. Sauthier)
1777	*The Province of New Jersey, Divided into East and West commonly called The Jerseys*: published in London by Wm. Faden

CAPTAIN JOHN ABRAHAM COLLET *fl.* 1767–1776
John Collet, an engineer and surveyor of Swiss origin, compiled a number of manuscript maps and plans of high quality. His map of North Carolina was considered the best of its time and was used by Henry Mouzon and others until the end of the century.

1770	*A Compleat Map of North Carolina from an actual survey*: published in London by S. Hooper
1776	*Southern British Colonies in America* (with Henry Mouzon and others)

WILLIAM SCULL *fl.* 1770
William Scull, employed in his family mapping business, produced a much enlarged and improved version of a map of Pennsylvania originally drawn by his father, Nicholas Scull, in 1759. Apart from including new detail, his map also showed the newly surveyed Mason/Dixon line. The map itself indicates that it was printed 'for the author' in Philadelphia but it was soon re-issued in London and Paris.

1770	*Map of the Province of Pennsylvania* 1775 Re-issued in London by Sayer and Bennett 1778 Re-issued in Paris by G. L. Le Rouge

HENRY MOUZON 1741–1807
The map of North and South Carolina by 'Henry Mouzon and others' has an important place in the history of American cartography in being the earliest map to show the Carolinas as separate entities. It was largely based on earlier surveys by Gerard de Brahm (1757) and John Collett (1770) and was sufficiently detailed and accurate to be used by the opposing forces in the War of Independence.

1775	*An Accurate Map of North and South Carolina With Their Indian Frontiers* . . .: published in London by Sayer and Bennett 1778 Re-issued in Paris by G. L. Le Rouge 1794 Re-issued in London by Laurie and Whittle
1776	*Southern British Colonies in America* (with John Collett and others)

MAJOR SAMUEL HOLLAND 1728–1801
Major Holland, the first 'Surveyor General for British North America' was a cartographer of great experience whose work covered land surveys, town plans and sea charts. In 1760 he completed a new survey of an important stretch of the River St Lawrence in company with James Cook who was evidently much influenced by Holland's surveying methods. His best known work covering New York and New Jersey was printed several times in 1775–6.

1760	*A New Chart of the River St Lawrence* . . .: published in London by Thos. Jefferys 1775, 1777, 1779, 1799, 1806 Re-issued in *The North American Pilot*
1775	*The Provinces of New York and New Jersey*: published in London by Sayer and Jefferys 1776 Re-issued in revised form
1776	*A Map of the Northern Colonies* (with Thomas Pownall): published in London in *The American Military Atlas* (the 'Holster Atlas') by Sayer and Bennett
1802	*A New Map of the Province of Lower Canada* (London: Wm. Faden) 1813–43 Various re-issues by Wm. Faden and James Wyld

THOMAS POWNALL 1722–1805

Thomas Pownall, always known as Governor Pownall, was a controversial figure in political life in the years leading up to the War of Independence. He first went to America in 1753 and between 1757 and 1760 served a short term as Governor of Massachusetts and even shorter terms in New Jersey and South Carolina. Frequently at loggerheads with his Government over its policy towards the colonists of 'taxation without representation', he resigned his governorships and returned to England where he continued his efforts to avert the political upheavals he saw ahead. Apart from these interests, he was an antiquarian, mathematician, surveyor and an artist of some ability.

As a result of his travels in America, he published in 1776 *A Topographical Description of such parts of North America as are contained in the annexed Map of the Middle British Colonies in North America*. The map referred to was a re-issue of the Lewis Evans map of 1755 originally dedicated to Pownall. His other works included:

1776   *A Map of the Northern Colonies* (compiled with Samuel Holland): published in London by Sayer and Bennett in *The American Military Atlas* (the 'Holster Atlas')

1794   *A New Map of North America*: 4 sheets (London: Laurie and Whittle)

CLAUDE JOSEPH SAUTHIER *fl.* 1768–1779

Sauthier was a cartographer and surveyor who is probably best known for a series of plans (in manuscript) of towns in North Carolina compiled in the years 1768–70. Later, in 1776, in conjunction with Bernard Ratzer, he drew a map of the Province of New York and in 1779 a further one, in his own name, which was one of the finest large-scale, detailed maps of the period. On this map he used a prime meridian running through New York, the first occasion this had been done.

1776   *A Map of the Province of New York which included New Jersey* (with Bernard Ratzer)

1779   *A Chorographical Map of the Province of New York in North America*: published in London by Wm. Faden

JOHN NORMAN 1748–1817
WILLIAM NORMAN

According to an advertisement in the *Pennsylvania Journal* in 1777, John Norman, printer and map seller in Boston, published a map of *The Theatre of War in North America* which bore the words 'United States'. If this was so, it was the first use of the term on a printed map but unfortunately no copy has survived. It is

suggested that the map may have been based on one bearing the same title published in London in 1776 by Sayer and Bennett.

c. 1777   *The Theatre of War in North America*

1791   *The United States of America laid down from the best Authorities Agreeable to the Peace of 1783* (J. Norman)

1791   *The American Pilot* Re-issued 1794 (J. Norman), 1798, 1803 (with W. Norman)

J. B. ELIOT

Eliot, an engineer who served as an aide-de-camp to General Washington, compiled a war map which was published in Paris and was the first map to name the United States in its French translation 'États Unis'.

1778–81   *Carte du Théatre de la Guerre Actuel . . .*

JEDIDIAH MORSE 1761–1826

Jedidiah Morse was a Congregational minister born in Woodstock, Connecticut, who published his first geographical work at the age of 23. Although not a cartographer in his own right, his books on American geography were the first to meet the educational needs of the rising generations of Americans at the end of the eighteenth century and his reputation was such that, in his lifetime, he became known as 'the father of American geography'. One son, S. E. Morse, was also a map publisher and another, Samuel Morse, the inventor of the Morse code.

1784   *Geography Made Easy*: published in 25 editions

1789   *The American Geography; or, A View of the Present Situation of the United States of America*: published in Elizabeth Town, NJ: 2 maps
1792 Republished in London and Dublin by John Stockdale
1793 Republished in Boston as *The American Universal Geography*: 12 maps
1796 Republished: 28 maps

1797   *The American Gazeteer*

1802   *A New Gazeteer of the Eastern Continent; or, A Geographical Dictionary*

JOHN FILSON *c.* 1747–1788

In 1784, eight years before Kentucky became a full state of the Union, John Filson, a historian and surveyor from Pennsylvania, published a history of the state which included an important map, the accuracy of which was vouched for by Daniel Boone. The map, now very rare, was printed in Philadelphia but the book, *The Discovery, Settlement, and Present State of Kentucke*, was published in Wilmington.

1784   *A Map of Kentucke, Drawn from actual Observations*
       1785 Map re-engraved and published in *Histoire de Kentucke*, Chez Buisson, Paris
       1793 Re-issued in London by John Stockdale

JOSEPH SOUTHERN PURCELL *fl*. 1776–1788

Purcell was a British cartographer who became an American citizen after the War of Independence and completed a notable map of the Southern states.

1788   *A Map of the States of Virginia, North Carolina, South Carolina and Georgia*
       1789 Re-issued in *The American Geography* by Jedidiah Morse (Elizabeth Town, NJ)
       1792 Re-issued by John Stockdale (London and Dublin)

CHRISTOPHER COLLES 1738–1816

An engineer and cartographer of Irish descent, Colles carried out a number of surveys of which the most important was his *Survey of the Roads of the United States of America*, the first American road book (published in New York). He used the accepted method of the time in presenting his maps in strip form, 2 or 3 strips to a page with a wealth of accurate topographical information on all the main highways. Although at the time of issue there seems to have been little demand for such a guide, it now provides a mine of information for the historian but, unhappily for the ordinary collector, it is extremely rare.

1789   *A Survey of the Roads of the United States of America*

SAMUEL LEWIS *fl*. 1774–1816

In the years spanning the end of the eighteenth century and the beginning of the nineteenth, Samuel Lewis was one of the most prolific cartographers in the United States. Although he never published an atlas in his own name, he provided numerous maps for some of the best-known publishers of the time including the following:

1795–1809 Matthew Carey: *American Atlas*
1804   Aaron Arrowsmith: *A New and elegant general atlas* (Philadelphia)
1814   Fielding Lucas (Jr): *A New Elegant General Atlas*
1814   Matthew Carey: *American Pocket Atlas*

Other maps by Samuel Lewis included:

1814   *A Map of Lewis and Clark's Track Across the Western Portion of North America From the Mississippi to the Pacific Ocean* (Philadelphia)
1816   *Wall Map of the United States* – 6 ft square (Philadelphia)

ZADOK CRAMER 1773–1813

1806–24   *The Navigator*
          Charts of the Ohio and Mississippi Rivers: the first navigational charts of inland waterways in America

FIELDING LUCAS (JR) 1781–*c*. 1852

1824   *A new general atlas of the West India Islands*: Baltimore

WILLIAM DARBY 1775–1854

William Darby was a gifted surveyor who made a major contribution to the mapping of America at the beginning of the nineteenth century. Apart from town plans and a map of Florida (1821), his major work was a large map of Louisiana and also a book entitled *A General Description of the State of Louisiana* (1817), which also contained a map of the state. The large map was used by John Melish in compiling his notable wall map of the USA (1816).

1816   *A Map of the State of Louisiana, With Part Of The Mississippi Territory*: published by John Melish, Philadelphia
       1817 Re-issued by John Arrowsmith, London

SAMUEL CUMINGS *fl*. 1822

1822–54   *The Western Pilot*: charts of the Ohio and Mississippi Rivers issued in 10 editions supplanted the earlier charts published by Zadok Cramer

JOHN CHARLES FRÉMONT 1813–1890
JOSEPH N. NICOLLET d. 1843
CHARLES (GEORG CARL) PREUSS 1803–1854

Frémont was a member of the élite Corps of Topographical Engineers who in the mid-nineteenth century were responsible for mapping the Middle and Far West of the United States. He worked first under the instruction of Joseph Nicollet, an immigrant French scientist, and then with Charles Preuss whose maps incorporated the results of their joint exploration and surveys. These came to be recognised as the most important maps of the time and no less than 50,000 copies of the 1848 map were published.

1843	(Nicollet) *Hydrographical Basin of the Upper Mississippi*
1845	(Preuss/Frémont) *Map of an Exploratory Expedition to the Rocky Mountains in 1842 and to Oregon and North California in 1843–44*
1846	(Preuss) *Road from Missouri to Oregon*
1848	(Preuss/Frémont) *Map of Oregon and Upper California From the Surveys of John Charles Frémont And other Authorities*

AUSTRALIA (Chapter 20)

Looking back to that time it seems extraordinary that even by the year 1800 (a dozen years after the first settlers arrived) the 'new' continent still had no generally accepted name. Indeed, in 1780, on a map of the Pacific published in Stockholm by the Swedish cartographer Daniel Djurberg, yet another, the Maori word, 'Ulimuroa' was added to the list and was often copied at the time. Eventually it was the London map publisher, William Faden who, in 1803, issued *A Chart of the Indian Ocean . . . with the Addition of a Part of the Pacific Ocean* by L. S. de la Rochette which introduced a new version 'Australia Incognita' although, for good measure, all the fanciful names from the past, 'Beach', 'Lucach', 'Maletur' as well as 'New Holland' were included. Almost at the same time, Matthew Flinders, on his manuscript and printed charts dated from 1804 onwards, used 'Terra Australis or Australia' and thereafter the single name Australia came into common use.

Appendix A

EDITIONS OF PTOLEMY'S GEOGRAPHIA 1477–1730

Note: cp.pl. = copper plate engraving; w'cut = woodcut

DATE EDITION	RE-ISSUE	PLACE	COMPILER/EDITOR	PRINTER/PUBLISHER	TEXT	MAPS	NOTES
1477		Bologna	J. Angelus Ph. Beroaldus A. Vadius	Dominicus de Lapis	Latin	26 cp.pl. Folio	
1478		Rome	J. Angelus D. Calderinus	C. Schweynheym A. Buckinck	do	27 cp. pl. Folio	
	1490	Rome	do	Petrus de Turre	do	27 cp.pl. Folio	
	1507	Rome	M. Beneventanus J. Cota	B. Venetus de Vitalibus	do	33 cp.pl. Folio	Addition of 6 'modern' maps
	1508	Rome	do	do	do	34 cp.pl. Folio	Addition of World Map by Johann Ruysch: the first Ptolemy map to refer to discoveries in the New World
1480–82		Florence	Fr. Berlinghieri	N. Todescho	Italian	31 cp.pl. Folio	Contained 4 new maps: Italy, Spain, France, Palestine
1482		Ulm	Nicolaus Germanus	Leonard Holm	Latin	32 w'cut Folio	Contained 5 'modern' maps
	1486	Ulm	do	Johan Reger	do	32 w'cut Folio	do
1511		Venice	Bernardus Sylvanus	J. Pentius de Leucho	do	28 w'cut Folio	Including World Map on heart-shaped projection by Sylvanus: some maps printed in two colours – black and red
1513		Strassburg	Martin Waldseemüller J. Eszler & G. Ubelin	Johannes Schott	Latin	47 w'cut Folio	Including 20 'modern' maps
	1520	do	G. Ubelin	do	do	do	do
	1522	do	Laurentius Frisius (Fries)	Johannes Grüninger	do	50 w'cut Folio (size reduced)	Including 2 new maps and the 'Fries' Map of the World

| DATE | | | | | | | |
EDITION	RE-ISSUE	PLACE	COMPILER/ EDITOR	PRINTER/ PUBLISHER	TEXT	MAPS	NOTES
	1525	do	W. Pirckheimer Regiomontanus	J. Grüninger J. Koberger	do	do	do
	1535	Lyon	Michael Servetus	M. & G. Treschel	do	do	do
	1541	Vienne (Dauphiné)	do	G. Treschel	do	do	do
1540		Basle	Sebastian Münster	H. Petri	do	48 w'cut Folio	
	1541	do	do	do	do	do	
	1542	do	do	do	do	do	
	1545	do	do	do	do	54 w'cut Folio	Including 6 'modern' maps
	1552	do	do	do	do	do	Last woodcut edition
1548		Venice	Andrea Mattioli Giacomo Gastaldi	Nicolo Bascarini	Italian	60 cp.pl. 8vo	The first printed 'pocket' atlas
1561		Venice	G. Ruscelli	Vincenzo Valgrisi	Italian	64 cp.pl 4to	Based on 1548 edition
	1562	do	G. Ruscelli & G. Moleto	do	do	do	Based on 1561 edition
	1564	do	do	G. Ziletti	do	do	do
	1564	do	do	do	Latin	do	do
	1574	do	G. Ruscelli & G. Malombra	do	Italian	65 cp.pl. 4to	do, plus map of Rome
	1598–99	do	G. Ruscelli & G. Rosaccio	Heirs of Melchior Sessa	do	69 cp.pl. 4to	Maps revised and 5 added
1578		Duisburg	G. Mercator	G. Kempen	—	28 cp.pl. Folio	
	1584	Cologne	G. Mercator & A. Mylius	do	Latin	do	
	1605	Amsterdam– Frankfurt	Petrus Montanus	C. Nicolas J. Hondius	Latin & Greek	do	
	1618–19	Leyden	Petrus Bertius	J. Hondius	do	47 cp.pl. Folio	Addition of 19 maps by Ortelius
	1695	Utrecht	—	François Halma	—	28 cp.pl. Folio	No text
	1698	Franeker	—	do	—	do	do
	1704	Amsterdam & Utrecht	—	do	—	do	do
	1730	Amsterdam	—	R. & J. Westenios W. Smith	—	28 cp.pl. Folio	No text
1596		Venice	G. A. Magini G. Porro	Heirs of Simon Galignani	Latin	64 cp.pl. 4to	
	1597	Cologne	do	Petrus Keschedt	do	do	Maps from different plates
	1597–98	Venice	Leonardo Cernotti	G. B. & G. Galignani	Italian	64 cp.pl. Folio	Maps from 1596 plates
	1608	Cologne	do	P. Keschedt & A. Becker	Latin	64 cp.pl. 4to	Maps from 1597 plates
	1616	Venice	do	—	do	64 cp.pl. Folio	Maps from 1596 plates
	1617	Arnhem	Gaspar Ens	J. Jansson the Elder	do	64 cp.pl. 4to	Maps from 1597 plates
	1621	Padua	—	Paolo & Fr. Galignani	Italian	64 cp.pl. Folio	Maps from 1596 plates

BLAEU/JANSSON MAPS OF THE ENGLISH & WELSH COUNTIES

JOAN BLAEU 1596–1673
JAN JANSSON 1588–1664

Biographical details and publications of the above cartographers, including dates of their atlases of the English and Welsh counties, are given in Chapter 13, but in view of the importance of these maps to collectors more detailed information is provided in this Appendix.

JOAN BLAEU

Blaeu's county maps were included in two atlases, the *Atlas Novus* and the *Atlas Maior* issued between the years 1645 and 1672. There were 4 general maps and 55 of the counties, 53 based on various states of Speed's maps and 6 on Jansson's. With very minor alterations the maps remained unchanged throughout all issues and after the destruction by fire of Blaeu's printing business in 1672 no further atlases were produced but some individual maps, the plates of which survived the fire, were issued by other publishers.

Theatrum Orbis Terrarum sive Atlas Novus
  Vol. IV *England and Wales*
    Latin text 1645–46, 1648
    French text 1645–46, 1648
    German text 1645–46, 1647, 1648
    Dutch text 1646–47, 1648
    Spanish text 1659

Atlas Maior
  Vol. V *England and Wales*
    Latin text 1662
    French text 1663, 1667
    Dutch text 1664
    German text 1667
    Spanish text 1672
    No English text issues

JAN JANSSON

Although Joan Blaeu issued his atlas of the English and Welsh counties in 1645, a year before Jansson's *Atlas Novus*, Vol. IV, the latter had in fact published a number of newly engraved maps in a German text issue of the Mercator/Hondius atlas in 1636. Further, in an Appendix to an edition of the *Atlas Novus* in 1644, Jansson included 11 more county maps. All these maps are now rarely seen and were revised and re-engraved before publication in 1646.

Mercator/Hondius/Jansson Atlas
  1636   German text, including the following 14
             new engravings:
             British Isles (Ortelius's *Parergon*)
             England and Wales
             Cheshire, Essex, Lancashire, Norfolk,
             Somerset, Yorkshire
             Scotland
             Ireland and the four provinces
             1638 Re-issued only in the *Atlas Novus*
             with German and Dutch text

(Atlas Novus) Des Nieuwen Atlantis Aenhang
  1644   Dutch text, includes the following 11
             county maps:
             Cambridge, Derbyshire, Devon, Kent,
             Northumberland, Nottingham, Oxford,
             Suffolk, Cardigan, Pembroke/Carmarthen,
             Montgomery

Atlas Novus
  1646   Vol. IV *Great Britain*
             6 general maps of England, Wales, Scot-
             land, Ireland
             56 maps of the counties and provinces
             6 additional maps of Scotland in the 1659
             Dutch and German editions

Latin text 1646, 1659
French text 1646, 1647, 1652, 1656
German text 1647–49, 1652(58), 1659
Dutch text 1647–48, 1649, 1652, 1653, 1659

After Jansson's death further issues of these maps appeared in made-up atlases under various names of which the principal were:

1666	Jansson's Heirs: *Atlas Contractus*
c. 1683–94	Schenk and Valck: separate maps
1705	C. Allard: *Atlas Major*
1715–28	D. Mortier: *Atlas Anglois*

Collectors will know that in practice it is not always easy to distinguish between Blaeu and Jansson loose maps unless examples of the same area are available side by side for comparison. As this is rarely the case, the following points of difference (based on details in

R. A. Skelton's *County Atlases of the British Isles*) will serve as a useful guide.

Compass Roses Blaeu: rarely used; Jansson: used on nearly all 'sea' counties
Lettering Blaeu: bold, clear lettering without elaboration; Jansson: more discursive with elaborate flourishes
Coats of Arms Blaeu: plainer and more regularly arranged; Jansson: far more flamboyant, placed in irregular patterns with numerous cherubs attached to the shields by ribbons
Imprint Blaeu: 5 maps with imprint – British Isles, Wales, Oxford, Northumberland, Isle of Wight; Jansson: 38 maps with imprints, including Northumberland

The following 15 maps have no imprint and therefore other distinguishing features are noted:

	BLAEU	JANSSON
Britannia:		
Saxton Heptarchy	No rhumb lines	Rhumb lines
Surrey	(i) 7 coats of arms/3 blanks in 2 single columns	(i) 7 coats of arms/3 blank in 2 double columns
	(ii) royal coat of arms lacks supporters	(ii) royal coat of arms with supporters
Gloucestershire/ Monmouth	Gloucestershire only	Gloucestershire and Monmouth
Huntingdon	(i) right-hand figure in cartouche holding firearm	(i) left-hand figure in cartouche holding firearm
	(ii) scale imprint in two lines of type	(ii) scale imprint in single line of type
Northamptonshire	8 coats of arms/3 blanks	8 coats of arms/no blanks
Lincolnshire	10 coats of arms/2 blanks	10 coats of arms/1 blank
Nottinghamshire	(i) 6 coats of arms/2 blanks	(i) 6 coats of arms/1 blank
	(ii) cherubs in cartouche bottom right	(ii) 'rustic folk' in cartouche bottom right
	(iii) arms in single, broken line	(iii) arms in double line
Derbyshire	4 coats of arms/2 blanks	4 coats of arms/1 blank
Shropshire/ Staffordshire	Shropshire only	Shropshire and Staffordshire
Cheshire	(i) 7 coats of arms with names 4 coats of arms without names 1 blank	(i) 7 coats of arms
		(ii) compass rose
Merioneth/ Montgomery	(i) title: Montgomeria comitatus et comitatus Mervinia	(i) Mervinia et Montgomeria comitatus
	(ii) 1 coat of arms	(ii) no coats of arms
Yorkshire	(i) title bottom right	(i) title bottom left
	(ii) scale: miliar	(ii) scale: Militaria
	(iii) 2 coats of arms	(iii) no coats of arms
West Riding	(i) size: approx. 383 × 500 mm	(i) size: approx 416 × 500 mm
	No other appreciable differences	
East Riding	(i) 6 coats of arms/2 blank	(i) 6 coats of arms/1 blank
	(ii) title bottom left	(ii) title top right
North Riding	5 figures in title cartouche (fishing)	1 figure in title cartouche (huntsman)

Note: In quoting numbers of coats of arms, the Royal Arms have been excluded.

Blaeu/Jansson maps cont'd.

	BLAEU	JANSSON
Composition of maps:		
Isle of Man	One map	—
Isle of Man / Isle of Wight / Anglesey }	—	One map
Holy Island / Farne Island }	One map	—
Guernsey / Jersey }	One map	—
Holy Island / Farne Island / Guernsey / Jersey }	—	One map
Caernarvon / Anglesey }	One map	} North Wales
Denbigh / Flint }	One map	One map
Brecon	One map	} Title: *Principatus Walliae pars Australis: Vulgo*
Glamorgan	One map	*South Wales*

HISTORICAL CHART – MAP MAKING
600 BC–AD 1800

		HISTORICAL BACKGROUND	TIME SCALE	
			600 BC	610-546
				520
		The Spread of Hellenism		500
			400 BC	484-28
	335-23	The Conquests of Alexander the Great		384-22
	322	Library at Alexandria founded		
GRECO-ROMAN WORLD			200 BC	276-195
				180-25
				100
	27 BC-AD 14	Augustus Caesar	BC	20 BC-AD25
	43	Roman invasion of Britain	AD	20
				50
				100
				87-151
			AD 200	250
				250-350
		Decline of Rome		
	410-55	The Fall of Rome	AD 400	400
				550
				550
			AD 600	600
				731
				750
ASCENDANCY OF ISLAM	c. 800	Translations of Ptolemy available to the Arabs	AD 800	800
			AD 1000	1000
	1095-1291	The Crusades		1154
	1200-50	Invention of Compass	AD 1200	1250
	1271-95	Travels of Marco Polo		1300
				1300
				1350
				1375
	c. 1400	Greek Manuscripts of Ptolemy reach Italy	AD 1400	
	1395-1460	Henry the Navigator		1418
	1450	Invention of movable-type printing		
	1453	Fall of Constantinople		1427
	1486	Bart. Diaz to the Cape		1457-59
VOYAGES OF DISCOVERY	1492	Columbus to the New World		1464 (1491)
	1493-94	Treaty of Tordesillas: line of demarcation		1477
		between Spanish and Portuguese claims/possessions		1477
	1497	John Cabot to Labrador		
	1497	Amerigo Vespucci to the New World		1485
	1498	Vasco da Gama to India		1492
	1500	Cabral to Brazil	AD 1500	1493

LANDMARKS IN CARTOGRAPHIC HISTORY

Anaximander of Miletus	Reputed 'World' map: belief in 'flat' earth theory
Pythagoras	Mathematician: propounded theory of a spherical world
Hectaeus of Miletus	First known book on geography
Herodotus	Historian and traveller
Aristotle	Supported the ideas of Pythagoras
Eratosthenes of Alexandria	Calculation of circumference of the world
Hipparchus	First attempt to map the stars
Posidonius	Calculation of circumference of the world (inaccurate, but accepted by Ptolemy)
Strabo	Published *Geography of the World*
Vipsanius Agrippa	The 'Agrippa' map of the Roman world
Pomponius Mela	*Cosmographia*: return to flat earth theory
Marinus of Tyre	According to Ptolemy, drew sea charts of the Medterranean
Claudius Ptolemy of Alexandria	*c.* 150–60 Compilation of the *Geographia*
Gaius Julius Solinus	*Collection of Memorable Things (Polyhistor*
Peutinger Table	Road map of the Roman Empire, reputedly based on the Agrippa map: known from thirteenth century copy
Theodosius Macrobius	*Commentaries* included a world map: first printed edition in 1483
Madaba Mosaic	First Christian topographical work
Cosmas of Alexandria	*Christian Topography*, based on flat earth theory
Isidorus of Seville	World Map
The Venerable Bede	*Ecclesiastical History of the English People*
The Albi Map	
The Beatus Map	

Anglo-Saxon Map		
		c. 900 1300
El-Edrisi of Palermo	World Map	T-O maps in use
Matthew Paris of St Albans	Chronicler and map maker	
Hereford Mappa Mundi		
Sacrobosco (John of Hollywood)	*Treatise of the Sphere*: return to the theory of the	
Gough Map	Earth as a Globe	
Catalan Atlas		

Oldest surviving woodblock prints in Europe		*c.* 1200 1550
Claudius Clavus	Map of Scandinavia	Portulan Charts
Fra Mauro	World Map	
Nicolas Cusanus	Map of Germany	
First printed map	(Isidorus of Seville's map)	
First printed edition of Ptolemy maps – Bologna	Further editions of Ptolemy: 1487 (Rome), 1482 (Florence), 1482 86 (Ulm), 1490 (Rome)	
B. dalli Sonetti	First printed sea charts (Venice)	
Martin Behaim of Nuremberg	World Globe	
Nuremberg Chronicle		

1800 P. de Lövenörn

NOTABLE CARTOGRAPHERS

ITALY, PORTUGAL, SPAIN	GERMANY, AUSTRIA, SWITZERLAND	NETHERLANDS	FRANCE	GREAT BRITAIN	SCANDINAVIA
1757 T. López	1753 L. Euler		1748 G. de Vaugondy	1755 J. Mitchell	1761 L. C. Desnos
1762 G. A. Rizzi-Zannoni	1754 G. F. Müller		1751 J. de Beaurain	1760 Sayer and Bennett	
1771 M. Constansó	1786 J. H. Weiss		1751 R. (?J.) Janvier	1765 J. Ellis	
c. 1775 A. Zatta			1751 R. J. Julien	1766 J. Andrews	
c. 1776 P. Santini		1785 J. B. Elwe	1755 J. Palairet	c. 1767 A. Dalrymple	
			1756 L. Brion de la Tour	1773 Capt. J. Cook	1780 T. Bugge
			1762 R. Bonne	1775 W. Faden	1780 D. Djurberg
1786 V. Tofiño	1786 J. R. Meyer		1768 E. A. de Prétot	1779 J. Rennell	1781 C. J. Pontoppidan
	1786 F. A. Schrämbl		1773 G. T. F. Raynal	c. 1784 J. F. W. des Barres	1788 J. de Nordenankar
	1789 J. Jaeger		1788 E. Mentelle		1796 S. G. Hermelin
	1789 F. von Reilly		1792 C. F. Beautemps-Beaupré	1786 J. Cary	1800 P. de Lövenörn
				1789 Laurie and Whittle	1800 C. Malte Brun
1792 G. M. Cassini	(1805 Alex. von Humboldt)		1794 C. F. Delamarche		1800 V. Malte Brun
1800 J. de Espinosa			1797 Comte de la Pérouse	1796 A. Arrowsmith	

Dates in the 'Notable Cartographers' columns refer to a cartographer's first or principal work, and are only intended to set the names in historical context.

BIBLIOGRAPHY

Many of the works noted below are also quoted in the chapter or chapters to which they are especially applicable. They are in English unless otherwise stated.

ANDREWS, Dr. J. H., *Irish maps*. Eason and Son Ltd. Dublin 1978.

BAGROW, Leo, *History of Cartography* (edited by R. A. Skelton). London 1964, Watts.
Originally issued in German in 1951, this translation of 1960 is an essential work for those wishing to study early cartography and its history.

BAYNTON WILLIAMS, R., *Investing in Maps*. London 1969 (also in paperback), Barrie and Rockliff, The Cresset Press.
For those who wish to be given a general picture of the subject there is no better book – beautifully illustrated with more than 130 maps. The prices given are now rather out of date.

BOOTH, John, *Antique Maps of Wales*. Somerset 1966, Montacute Bookshop.
A brief but useful introduction to the subject.

— *Looking at Old Maps*. Westbury (Wilts) 1979. Cambridge House Books.

BRAMSEN, Bo, *Gamle Danmarkskort*. Copenhagen 1975, Rosenkilde og Bagger.
A history of Danish cartography (in Danish) with biographies of prominent map makers.

BRITISH LIBRARY, *Catalogue of Printed Maps, Charts and Plans*.

BROWN, Lloyd A., *The Story of Maps*. London 1951, Constable and Co. (New York 1979, Dover Publications Inc.)
A splendid wide-ranging account of the subject from the earliest times to the latest surveys. It contains 32 pages of bibliography.

Cartes et Figures de la Terre, Centre Georges Pompidou, Paris 1980.
Information on many early world and French maps.

CHUBB, Thomas, *The Printed Maps in the Atlases of Great Britain and Ireland*. London 1927, Burrow (Ed. J.) & Co. Ltd. (London 1966, reprinted, Dawson of Pall Mall).
Although now out-dated, for many years this was the standard work on County maps and is still a very useful reference book.

CRONE, G. R., *Maps and their Makers*. London 1953, 1962, Hutchinson University Library.
This comparatively short study remains an essential work for the student of cartography.

CUMMING, Wm. P., *The South East in Early Maps*. 1958–73, University of North Carolina Press.
An essential book for those wishing to make a detailed study of early American maps.

DARLINGTON, Ida and HOWGEGO, James, *Printed Maps of London Circa 1553–1850*. London 1964, Philip. (London 1978 (2nd edn), Dawson – James Howgego).
An exhaustive analysis of plans of London which it will be almost impossible to improve on.

EVANS, Ifor M. and LAWRENCE, Heather, *Christopher Saxton: Elizabethan Mapmaker*. London 1979, Holland Press.
The definitive work on the life of Christopher Saxton.

EVANS, O. Caradoc, *Maps of Wales and Welsh Cartographers*. Map Collectors' Circle No. 13, 1965–66.
Contains much useful information on Welsh County Maps.

FORDHAM, Sir George, *Studies in Carto-bibliography*. Oxford 1914, Clarendon Press. (Reprinted London 1969, Dawson of Pall Mall).
A book which is now 'getting on in years' but is still a valuable reference book, especially for maps of France.

GOLE, Susan, *Early Maps of India*. Edinburgh 1978, Charles Skilton Ltd.
A very useful summary of available information on maps of India.

HARVEY, P. D. A., *Topographical Maps*. London 1980, Dawson.

HARVEY, P. D. A. and THORPE, H., *The Printed Maps of Warwickshire 1576–1900*. Warwick County Council/University of Birmingham 1959.

HIND, Arthur M., *Engraving in England in the Sixteenth and Seventeenth Centuries: Vol. I The Tudor Period*. Cambridge 1952, Cambridge University Press.

HOWSE, Derek and SANDERSON, Michael, *The Sea Chart*. Newton Abbot 1973, David and Charles.
A short history of sea charts with a large number of illustrations of charts held in the National Maritime Museum.

IMAGO MUNDI, *The Journal of the International Society for the History of Cartography*, published annually.
Authoritative annual periodical devoted to articles on cartographical history by the most noted writers of the day.

KOEMAN, C., *Atlantes Neerlandici* (5 vols). Amsterdam 1967–71, Theatrum Orbis Terrarum NV.
Virtually complete analysis of the maps in all Dutch atlases and Pilot Books published in the Netherlands up to 1880.

LIBAULT, André, *Histoire de la Cartographie*. Paris, Chaix.
Concise history (in French) of cartography with special emphasis on French mapping.

LISTER, R., *How to Identify Old Maps and Globes*. London 1965, 1970, G. Bell and Sons. (Re-issued as *Old Maps and Globes*. London 1979, Bell and Hyman Ltd.)
Apart from interesting text, contains a splendid alphabetical list of cartographers, publishers, etc. which rarely fails to provide the information required even if only briefly.

LYNAM, Edward, *British Maps and Map Makers*. London 1947, Collins.
A short but extremely attractive account of mapping of the British Isles.
—*The Mapmaker's Art*. London 1953, The Batchworth Press.
A series of essays on the wider aspects of mapmaking.

MOIR, D. G. and others, *The Early Maps of Scotland to 1850 with a history of Scottish Maps*. 3rd edn, Edinburgh 1973, Royal Scottish Geographical Society.
Indispensable record of early maps of Scotland.

NATIONAL MARITIME MUSEUM, *Catalogue of the Library*: Volume 3, *Atlases and Cartography*. London 1971, HMSO.
A select listing of atlases and Pilot Books in the Museum library with collations of the maps in them. An invaluable primary reference book for the researcher.

NORDENSKIÖLD, A. E., *Facsimile Atlas to the Early History of Cartography*. Stockholm 1889 (paperback edn, New York 1973, Dover Publications Ltd.)
One of the first reference books about maps; new information has made it rather dated.

PHILLIPS, Philip Lee, *A list of Geographical Atlases in the Library of Congress*: Vols I–IV 1902–20 (reprinted 1971); Vol. V 1958; Vol. VI 1963.

SCHILDER, Günter, *Australia Unveiled*. Amsterdam, 1976, Theatrum Orbis Terrarum NV.
A most scholarly, detailed and exhaustive study of the early Dutch maps of Australia.

SCHWARTZ, Seymour I. and EHRENBERG, Ralph E., *The Mapping of America*. New York 1980, Harry N. Abrams Inc.
A magnificently produced and illustrated volume containing much information on maps of America from the sixteenth to the twentieth century.

SHIRLEY, Rodney W., *Early Printed Maps of the British Isles 1477–1650*. London 1980, Holland Press.
The definitive work on maps of the British Isles.
—*The Mapping of the World*. London 1983, Holland Press.
A monumental work, beautifully produced, on World Maps, which is likely to remain the standard reference book on the subject for many years to come.

SKELTON, R. A., *Decorative Printed Maps of the 15th to 18th Centuries*. London 1952 and 1965, Spring Books.
Based on an earlier work by A. L. Humphreys (1926), this is a widely used and quoted book showing by means of numerous illustrations the development of map design and decoration.
—*County Atlases of the British Isles 1579–1703*. London 1970, Carta Press.
The best work available on County Maps in the period covered.

THEATRUM ORBIS TERRARUM NV, Amsterdam.
·Reproductions of many rare atlases and Pilot Books with introductory essays by the best authorities. Atlas details are quoted in the appropriate chapters in Part II of this work.

TIBBETTS, G. R., *Arabia in Early Maps*. New York and London (Eng.) 1978, The Oleander Press.
A useful bibliography of early maps of Arabia.

TOOLEY, R. V., *Maps and Map-Makers*. London 1949–78 (6 editions), Batsford.
For thirty years *Maps and Map-Makers* has been the book to which those interested in cartography make their first approach; it remains a basic source of information.
—*Collector's Guide to Maps of the African Continent and Southern Africa*. London 1969, Carta Press.
The primary reference book for maps of Africa based on papers first published in the Map Collector's Circle series.
— *The Mapping of Australia*. London 1979, Holland Press.
Reprint of a specialized series of articles on maps of Australia which first appeared in the Map Collector's Circle series.
— *The Mapping of America*. London 1980, Holland Press.
A similar series of articles on maps of America from the Map Collector's Circle series (with additional information). Both are essential reading for a study of maps of Australia and America.
— *Maps in Italian Atlases of the 16th Century*, Imago Mundi, 1939.
Detailed analysis of early Italian maps.
— *Dictionary of Map Makers*. Tring 1979, Map Collector Publications Ltd.
A massive reference work, the result of a lifetime's study of the subject covering something like 20,000 entries.
— Map Collectors' Circle. 1963–73.
A series of specialized articles, edited by Tooley on every aspect of the subject, some of which have been reprinted in book form.

TOOLEY, R. V., BRICKER, C. and CRONE, G. R., *Landmarks of Map Making* (sometimes known as 'A History of Cartography'). Amsterdam, Brussels 1968, Elsevier Sequoia (London 1969, Thames & Hudson; New York 1976, Thomas Crowell; Oxford 1976, Phaidon Press).
A comprehensive survey of the development of cartography from the earliest times, splendidly illustrated with many maps in full size.

TRUSTEES OF THE WALTERS ART GALLERY, *World Encompassed, An Exhibition of the History of Maps*. Baltimore 1952.
Although many of the maps and atlases quoted are extremely rare, the accompanying text is always of the greatest interest to the researcher.

TYACKE, Sarah, *London Mapsellers 1660–1720* (a collection of advertisements for maps placed in the London Gazette 1668–1719 with biographical notes on the map-sellers).
Tring 1978, Map Collector Publications Ltd.
Invaluable biographical and mapping detail in the period covered.

WOODWARD, David, *Five Centuries of Map Printing*. Chicago 1975, University of Chicago Press.
A series of scholarly essays based on lectures given at the Newberry Library in 1972 covering the whole history of map printing

INDEX